CW00546034

Internet Banking: La   ractice

Internet Banking: Law and Practice

Abu Bakar Munir

Members of the LexisNexis Group worldwide

United Kingdom	LexisNexis UK, a Division of Reed Elsevier (UK) Ltd, Halsbury House, 35 Chancery Lane, LONDON WC2A 1EL, and 4 Hill Street, EDINBURGH EH2 3JZ
Argentina	LexisNexis Argentina, BUENOS AIRES
Australia	LexisNexis Butterworths, CHATSWOOD, New South Wales
Austria	LexisNexis Verlag ARD Orac GmbH & Co KG, VIENNA
Canada	LexisNexis Butterworths, MARKHAM, Ontario
Chile	LexisNexis Chile Ltda, SANTIAGO DE CHILE
Czech Republic	Nakladatelství Orac sro, PRAGUE
France	Editions du Juris-Classeur SA, PARIS
Germany	LexisNexis Deutschland GmbH, FRANKFURT and MUNSTER
Hong Kong	LexisNexis Butterworths, HONG KONG
Hungary	HVG-Orac, BUDAPEST
India	LexisNexis Butterworths, NEW DELHI
Ireland	LexisNexis, DUBLIN
Italy	Giuffrè Editore, MILAN
Malaysia	Malayan Law Journal Sdn Bhd, KUALA LUMPUR
New Zealand	LexisNexis Butterworths, WELLINGTON
Poland	Wydawnictwo Prawnicze LexisNexis, WARSAW
Singapore	LexisNexis Butterworths, SINGAPORE
South Africa	LexisNexis Butterworths, DURBAN
Switzerland	Stämpfli Verlag AG, BERNE
USA	LexisNexis, DAYTON, Ohio

© Reed Elsevier (UK) Ltd 2004

A CIP Catalogue record for this book is available from the British Library.

ISBN 0 406 97624 4

Project Management by The Partnership Publishing Solutions Ltd www.the-pps.co.uk

Typeset by Kerrypress Ltd, Luton www.kerrypress.co.uk

Printed and bound in Great Britain by Cromwell Press

Visit LexisNexis UK at www.lexisnexis.co.uk

Preface

Like other ICT inventions that promise both unprecedented benefits and scaring risks, Internet banking has been received with both excitement and worries. While it offers high levels of effectiveness such as online fund transfer, easily done from customers' desktops in the comfort of their home, it also haunts many as reflected in incidents involving theft of personal financial information (phishing), tracing of online footprints and intrusion of online activities of other customers.

Internet banking is in its infancy, though the number of service providers and customers is increasing. Some crucial areas are unclear for Internet banking consumers. These include the issues of distribution of liability amongst Internet banking stakeholders, particularly between the banks and customers in cases of fraud and systems failure, and issues relating to the use of personal data of customers by the banks.

This work is concerned with Internet banking and new banking products created by the Internet technology such as account aggregation and e-money. Focusing on Internet banking as a payment system, which allows the users to transfer money, the emphasis is on retail customers. It is an attempt to highlight the international initiatives and the positions in several countries such as the UK, Australia and Malaysia. The issues relating to cross-border Internet banking, however, are beyond its scope.

The thrust of this book is to examine the general conditions of Internet banking services, in the respective countries, from a legal perspective. It seeks to critically analyse the rules and regulations that, directly or indirectly, affect and impact on Internet banking. More importantly, it assesses the extent to which banks observe these rules and regulations, in practice. The message it carries is that if the Internet banking services can be safely delivered, with customers' information managed fairly and lawfully, and liability is apportioned justly, the whole process would be able to achieve better corporate governance. Trust plays an important role in e-commerce and trust has to be earned. Mutual trust will lead to co-operation and confidence. Good governance and consumer confidence, in turn, would deliver maximum business effectiveness and efficiency, which will benefit the banks and customers as well as the nation. As the Bank of England has noted:

'Payment systems are a vital part of the economic and financial infrastructure. Their efficient functioning, allowing transactions to be completed safely and on time, makes a key contribution to overall economic performance. But payment systems can also involve significant exposures and risks for members, and can be a channel for the transmission of disturbances from one part of the economy or financial system to another.'

This book is organised as follows. Chapters 1–6 give background information on Internet banking and its legal, regulatory and supervisory aspects. The legal and regulatory issues pertaining to account aggregation and e-money are also discussed. Chapter 7 discusses the European regulations effecting Internet banking. Chapters 8–12 analyse and examine these regulations and assess the practices of banks in the UK, Australia and Malaysia. The position stated is as at mid-2004.

Abu Bakar Munir

Contents

Table of Statutes

References at the right-hand side of the column are to paragraph number. Where a paragraph number is in **bold** this indicates that the Act is set out in part or in full.

Table of Statutory Instruments

References at the right-hand side of the column are to paragraph number. Where a paragraph number is in **bold** this indicates that the Statutory Instrument is set out in part or in full.

Table of European Legislation

References at the right-hand side of the column are to paragraph number. Where a paragraph number is in **bold** this indicates that the legislation is set out in part or in full.

Table of Cases

CHAPTER ONE

Internet Banking: Introduction and Background

Introduction

1.1   Bill Gates, in 1994, pronounced that the traditional banks are dinosaurs that the Internet will drive into extinction[1]. Some in the banking industry were offended by this perceived impertinent. Some took Gates' comments as a warning that software and technology developers should now be considered competitors rather than partners. Others viewed these comments as a timely wake-up call, challenging the banking industry to either take the lead in shaping and developing the technology that will be used to deliver financial services and electronic commerce in the twenty-first century, or be relegated to serving as a passive conduit for information travelling through technology developed and designed by others, which might not even utilise historic banking industry channels[2].

Though, as you will see later in this chapter, research shows that this prediction has failed, one thing remains very true is that technology is revamping the ways in which financial services are produced and delivered. Internet banking has finally reached the point at which it is being accepted by consumers and is financially successful for the offering institutions. In fact, Internet banking is now seen as a strategic necessity for most financial institutions. Perhaps Internet banking, as argued by some, will soon follow the same path as the Automatic Teller Machines (ATMs).

1   See Michael Meyer, 'Culture Club' *Newsweek* 11 July 1994. p 38.
2   Thomas P. Vartanian, Robert H. Ledig and Lynn Bruneau, *21st Century Money, Banking & Commerce* (1998) pp 3–4.

Internet banking: evolution or revolution?

1.2   Electronic banking has been around for some time in the form of ATMs and telephone transactions. More recently, the Internet, as a new delivery channel for banking services that benefits both customers and banks, has transformed electronic banking. Internet banking is seen as an evolution or as the latest development of electronic banking. Chris Reed outlined the six stages of development in consumer electronic banking[1]:

- The provision of facilities for account transactions through technology, which is owned and controlled by the banks – e.g. ATMs and magnetic stripe cards. This stage began nearly 30 years ago.

- Allowing limited dial-up access to consumer customers, using software supplied by the bank, from the early 1990s.

- Permitting access via open networks (primarily the Internet) and open software (e.g. Web browsers such as Netscape and Internet Explorer).

- Allowing accounts to be opened via the Internet.

- Providing facilities for non-account-transfer payment through electronic cash products.

- Selling other financial products via the Internet.

1 See Chris Reed, Ian Walden and Laura Edgar, *Cross-Border Electronic Banking, Challenges and Opportunities* (2000), p 143.

1.3 Internet banking is the use of the Internet as a delivery channel for the provision of financial services. Internet banking is simply banking, offered via a new delivery channel. It gives consumers another service, just like ATMs did. But unlike ATMs, Internet banking allows the interactive communication between banks and their customers, where an extensive amount of information can be exchanged electronically. Internet banking refers to the use of the Internet as a remote delivery channel for banking services, including traditional services, such as opening a deposit account or transferring funds among different accounts, as well as new banking services, such as electronic bill presentment and payment, which allow customers to receive and pay bills over a bank's website.

1.4 The US Office of Comptroller of Currency (OCC) refers to Internet banking as 'systems that enable bank customers to access accounts and general information on bank products and services through a personal computer or intelligent device'. In a similar vein, the *Minimum Guidelines on the Provision of Internet Banking Services by Licensed Banking Institution* issued by the Central Bank of Malaysia describes Internet banking as banking products and services offered by banking institutions on the Internet through access devices including personal computers and other intelligent devices.

1.5 So far, most Internet banking transactions are conducted through customers' personal computers that connect to a banking website via the Internet. For example, a customer at home accesses a financial institution's website via a modem and phone line or other telecommunications connection and an Internet Service Provider (ISP). Internet banking can also be conducted via wireless technology through both the Personal Digital Assistants (PDAs) or cellular phones.

1.6 Some banks use the phrase PC banking. There is a slight difference between PC banking and Internet banking. PC banking usually refers to 'dial-up' computer banking services. This is where the customers call a designated telephone number for access to their accounts. With PC banking the customer needs special software to act as an interface between the bank and their computer. The bank might provide its own proprietary software or require the customer to use a financial package. Internet banking requires no special dial-up or software: All the customer needs is their Internet browser. Once they're already on the Net, their bank's website is only a mouse-click away[1].

1   See Mark Grossman, 'Online Banking: The Future is Now' available at http://www.becker-poliakoff.com/publications/newsletters/cln/winter00/online_banking_fut.

1.7   Some analysts, however, argue that e-finance and Internet banking is a revolution that will sweep away the old order. Among others, the arguments are: that Internet banking is easy to set up, so lots of new entrants will arrive; old-world systems, cultures and structures will not encumber these new entrants; consumers will be less inclined to remain loyal; Internet banking will lead to an erosion of the 'endowment effect' currently enjoyed by the banks; and deposits will go elsewhere with the consequence that these banks will have to fight to regain and retain their customer base. Nobody really knows which of these versions will triumph[1]. William Witherell, Director of Finance, Fiscal and Enterprise Affairs at the OECD, who sees e-finance as a revolution, stated[2]:

> 'Some conclude from this limited experience that the Internet is merely another distribution channel that will have only an evolutionary effect, on financial markets. But it should be recognised that this channel is a profoundly different way of providing financial services that can lead to significant changes in business models, driving consolidation in some areas and fragmentation and increased competition in others.'

He further argued that while the contribution of e-finance to reshaping the financial industry to date has been smaller than expected, this might change rapidly. Wholesale activities are already well advanced and are growing fast. He noted, 'The trends already visible suggest to me that truly significant changes in the financial industry lie ahead'. He asserted that online brokerage is unbundling the traditional brokerage services, and account aggregation is opening the road towards a commoditisation of financial services and a further breakdown of the barriers between different parts of the financial sector[3].

1   See Carol Sergeant 'E-Banking: Risks and Responses', available at http://www.fsa.gov.uk/pubs/speeches/sp46.
2   William Witherell 'Realizing the Revolution in E-Finance', *I-Ways*, Second Quarter (2001) p 16.
3   *Ibid.*

Approaches to Internet banking

1.8   The Federal Reserve Bank of Chicago identified three Internet banking models. The 'hybrid model' – a traditional bank with an Internet delivery channel known as 'brick and click'; the 'spin-off e-bank model' – setting up a pure electronic or virtual spin-off bank with its own brand; and the 'alliances model' – developing strategic partnerships to create new products and broaden a partner's product offering[1]. Similarly, Sharpe identified four models that can be implemented by a traditional bank to establish its online presence, i.e., pure Internet only banking; online hybrids extending existing presence; online bank branded alliances with third parties; and online white labelling of financial services sold through third parties[2].

1 See Feng Li, 'Internet Banking in the U.K.: From New Distribution Channel to New Business Models', *Journal of Financial Transformation*, 58, available at http://www.capco.com/j06abs04.html.
2 *Ibid.*

1.9 Feng Li identified eight business models:

(1) new distribution channel – Internet as part of multi-channel strategy but no radical change in the basic strategy and business model of the bank;

(2) e-banking – use the Internet to underpin key processes and integrate different channels, transforming the main brand into an e-brand;

(3) baby e-bank – launched by incumbent banks and other financial companies with their own e-brand name and product range, often based on a new business model;

(4) pure play new entrants – pure virtual bank set up by non-financial companies;

(5) portals – aggregate financial product information from multiple sources acting as the access point for customers, often focusing on a particular product range or customer segments;

(6) online alliances – a bank outsources its Internet banking solution to a third party, but the services bear the bank's own brand name;

(7) white labelling – through partnership an incumbent bank enables a non-bank company to provide Internet banking services but not bearing the bank's brand name; and

(8) brand stretching – non-bank players with an established brand providing banking services through the Internet[1].

1 See Feng Li, 'Internet Banking in the U.K.: From New Distribution Channel to New Business Models', *Journal of Financial Transformation*, 58, available at http://www.capco.com/j06abs04.html.

1.10 Generally, in many parts of the world, banks offer Internet banking through two main business models: first, the 'brick and click' model – an existing bank with physical offices (bricks and mortar) offering Internet banking to its customers in addition to its traditional delivery channels. Second, a bank may be established as a 'virtual', 'branchless', or 'Internet-only' bank, with a computer server at its heart, housed in an office that serves as the bank's legal address or at some other location.

1.11 Virtual banks may offer customers the ability to make deposits and withdraw funds at Automated Teller Machines (ATMs) or other remote delivery channels owned by other institutions[1]. The US has about 30 virtual banks; Asia has two, launched in 2000 and 2001; and the European Union has several – either as separately licensed entities or as subsidiaries or branches of 'bricks and mortar' banks[2]. Internet-only, or the virtual model, has two basic variants: an independent venture, where Internet banking venture is created from scratch, or a subsidiary project (e-banking-in-the-bank). *Security First Network* bank in the US and *Enba* in Europe are two banks established under the independent venture. *Wingspan* launched by *Bank One Corporation* in the US and *Egg* launched by the *Prudential plc*, a leading UK insurance company, are two examples of e-bank-in-the-bank.

1   Karen Furst, William W. Lang and Daniel E. Nolle, *Internet Banking: Developments and Prospects*, Program on Information Resources Policy, Centre for Information Policy Research, Harvard University, (April 2002) p 5.
2   Saleh M. Nsouli and Andrea Schaechter 'Challenges of the E-Banking Revolution', *Finance and Development*, a quarterly magazine of the IMF, Sept 2002, Vol 39, No 3, available at http://www.imf.org/external/pubs/ft/fandd/2002/09/nsouli.htm.

1.12   The Bank of International Settlements (BIS) broadly categorises e-banking, both domestic and international, into three categories:

• Basic information websites, which only broadcast information on banking products and services offered to bank customers and the general public. It may receive and reply to customers' queries through e-mail.

• Simple transactional websites which allow bank customers to submit applications for different services, make enquiries about balances and submit instructions to the bank, but do not permit any account transfer.

• Advanced transactional websites that allow bank customers to electronically transfer funds to/from their account, pay bills and conduct other banking transactions online. These are fully transactional websites which allow customers to transfer funds, pay different bills, subscribe to other products of the bank and transact the purchase and sale of securities, etc.

1.13   Traditional banks offer the above forms of Internet banking services as an additional method of serving the customers. New banks deliver banking services primarily through Internet or other electronic delivery channels as the value added service. Some of these banks are known as 'virtual' banks or 'Internet-only' banks and may not have any physical presence in a country despite offering different banking services.

1.14   Feng Li classified the main functions of Internet banking into four broad categories: view-only functions; account control functions; new services application functions; and reconciliation functions. View-only functions are concerned with addressing details about balances and the last few transactions made by the customers. Account control functions are required to provide customers with a broad range of access and control over their accounts, such as transferring funds between accounts, the creation or amendment of standing orders, and paying bills to third parties. New banking service application functions (applying for new accounts – savings accounts, mortgages, loans, etc) are seen as crucial to banks, as they provide an opportunity to attract new customers, as well as retaining existing ones. Reconciliation functions enable customers to reconcile their accounts by downloading their own financial information from their bank accounts into their financial management software[1].

1 See Feng Li, 'Internet Banking in the U.K.: From New Distribution Channel to New Business Models',
   Journal of Financial Transformation, p 56, available at http://www.capco.com/j06abs04.html.

Bricks and mortar banks versus virtual banks

1.15 The current status of Internet banking shows that, contrary to what some
analysts' initially expected, pure Internet banks have gained only a limited share of
the market. In fact, the traditional banks have not been destroyed and, while a few
of the pure Net bank models may succeed, no newcomer has been able to
penetrate the banking sector on a large scale. The 'click and mortar' model – a
strategy combining physical and Internet presence – has thus become the dominant
model[1]. However, according to Feng Li, the threat is there: research involving 26
banks offering Internet banking in the UK found that the biggest threats to the
existing banks come from the Internet-only banks, especially baby e-banks[2].

1 United Nations Conference on Trade and Development, *E-Commerce and Development Report 2002*,
   p 134.
2 See Feng Li, 'Internet Banking in the U.K.: From New Distribution Channel to New Business Models',
   Journal of Financial Transformation, p 60, available at http://www.capco.com/j06abs04.html.

1.16 Virginia Philipp, who headed a TowerGroup study *Challenges for Virtual
Banking*, said:

'Beyond doubt, Internet-only banks are an endangered species. Six years ago, they
were toasted as a brave new breed that could transcend geography, operate without
the costly baggage of bricks, mortars, tellers, layers of vice-presidents, and obsolete
legacy systems and lead us all into a new world of paperless anytime anywhere
self-service banking. At the end of last year, only 40 out of an earlier 60 had survived.
Today, there are 20–25, and that number could eventually go down to 5–10.'[1]

1 Cited in Bill Orr, 'E-banking: What Next?' available at http://www.banking.com/aba/NextEbank.pdf.

1.17 Charles Goldfinger wrote:

'Since last year [2001], the pure Internet model appears to have further lost ground.
In the US, practically no pure Internet banking is left standing. In Europe, Zebank a
high-profile venture, backed by prestigious investors was sold to Egg ... Other "pure
Internet" banks such as Cahoot are being brought closer within the fold of their
parent. While Egg's success is impressive, its market capitalisation remains below its
IPO value and provides limited ammunition to credibly attack large banks, whose
market capitalisation is 25 to 40 times higher'[1]. According to Goldfinger, Internet
banking in Europe is increasingly dominated by the largest banks, which seek to lever
their leadership position in traditional services[2]. He argued, 'There is one significant
exception to the click and mortar model: the Egg bank in the UK ... It remains to be
seen whether Egg is a sole exception, a last specimen of the dying species or a
trailblazer of a new trend.'[3]

1 Charles Goldfinger, 'Internet Banking Update', September 2002, available at http://www.fininter.net/
   retail%20banking/internet_banking_update.htm.

2   *Ibid.*
3   *Ibid.*

1.18   What has gone wrong? Virginia Philipp suggested that everything went wrong. First, the high start-up costs – mainly due to the heavy marketing needed to acquire new accounts; second, new technology, though most of it out-sourced, cost even more millions; third, operating on the leading edge required high-salaried managers and marketers; and fourth, e-banks had two other built-in disadvantages for their customers: how to withdraw cash and how to deposit paper cheques.

1.19   In its recent report on Internet banking, the OCC offers another theory of what happened. The business strategy seems to have been predicated on a belief that demand for e-banking would grow rapidly in the near term, allowing the new venture to cover its high capital costs. Like so many dot.com start-ups, e-banks simply couldn't hold their breath long enough[1].

1   Bill Orr, 'E-banking: What Next?' available at http://www.banking.com/aba/NextEbank.pdf.

1.20   The Economic Advisor and Senior Economist of the Federal Reserve Bank of Chicago, Robert De Young conducted a study on the performance of Internet-only banking. He found that[1]:

> 'Most banks that use the Internet-only business model are struggling for profitability, and emerging conventional wisdom states that Internet-only banking is a failed business model. But this may be premature. As Internet-only banks age, they accumulate experience which may allow them to operate more efficiently in the future, and as they grow larger they may generate scale-based savings not available to traditional banks that use less capital-intensive production and distribution technologies.'

The study finds that if the experience-based technology effects and/or the scale-based technology effects are large enough, the performance gap between Internet-only banks and traditional banks could narrow in the future[2].

1   Robert De Young, 'The Financial Progress of Pure-play Internet Banks', Bank for International Settlements (BIS) Papers No 7, *Electronic Finance: A New Perspective and Challenges*, (Nov. 2001) available at http://www.bis.org/publ/bispap07a.pdf.
2   *Ibid.*

1.21   The study also, on the one hand, finds results that are largely consistent with conventional wisdom. On average, Internet-only banks have substantially less profit than traditional banks. They have generated lower business volumes than traditional bank start-ups and any savings generated by lower physical overheads appear to be offset by other types of non-interest expenditure. The study, on the other hand, finds that profitability ratios and non-interest expenses ratios improve more quickly over time in the Internet-only start-ups than in the traditional start-ups[1].

1   Robert De Young, 'The Financial Progress of Pure-play Internet Banks', Bank for International Settlements (BIS) Papers No 7, *Electronic Finance: A New Perspective and Challenges*, (Nov. 2001) available at http://www.bis.org/publ/bispap07a.pdf.

1.22 According to De Young, if these trends continue into the future, the Internet-only banking model could eventually prove to be a viable business model, despite its generally poor financial performance to date[1]. To succeed, as Virginia Philipp argues, e-banks must stay away from mass marketing with massive costs. Her advice is to not build the bank around depository accounts, but around a mix of standard financial services plus wealth management, financial planning, and online lending, thereby aiming to own a big share of a targeted niche market.

[1] *Ibid.*

1.23 Setsuya Sato and John Hawkins wrote, 'The opinion that traditional banks were dinosaurs that the Internet would drive into extinction is no longer widely held. They are of the view that the current conventional wisdom is that the 'click and mortar' model will prevail, at least in the medium term. According to them there is now increased recognition that, as public trust is so crucial to banking, an established brand name is important and many customers wish to be able to do some banking physically[1].

[1] Setsuya Sato and John Hawkins, 'Electronic Finance: An Overview of the Issues', Bank For International Settlements (BIS) Papers No 7, available at http://www.bis.org/publ/bispap07a.pdf.

1.24 The most important pro-competition feature of the Internet is the reduction of fixed costs and transaction costs – this allows new competitors into the banking system. However, the two major entry barriers for virtual banks are reputation and large funds to pool risks. At first glance there is no way for an entrant to overcome these barriers and be able to compete with those long-established and well-trusted traditional banks. But researchers have noticed that large firms with a high reputation among customers and an existing large customer base may be potential entrants[1].

[1] See Lihui Lin, Xianjun Geng and Andrew Whinston, 'A New Perspective to Finance and Competition and Challenges for Financial Institutions in the Internet Era', BIS Papers No7, available at http://www.bis.org/publ/bispap07b.pdf.

1.25 Professor Feng Li stated, 'The threat from Internet-only banks is certainly not over. So far, Internet-only banks have failed to eat into the market share of established banks in a significant manner for several reasons, but this situation may change in the medium-to long-term'[1]. He articulated the reasons. First, the established banks and building societies have invested very heavily in the last few years in their own Internet channels and offered their customer multi-channel banking, as well as a range of benefits that Internet-only banks have offered. This has played a key role for these established players in retaining their customers and maintaining their market shares[2]. Second, banking on the Internet involves radical changes in customer behaviour, which will take time to establish. When people gradually get used to doing more and more things online, the psychological barriers in banking online will reduce. Third, the recent dot.com crash made it very difficult for Internet-only banks to compete aggressively with established players[3]. However, this does not change the fundamentals of Internet banking and the advantages of Internet-only banks. Finally, there has been a lot of talk about customer loyalty and trust with established banks, which is true to some extent. However, in many cases, it is the difficulties and hassles involved in switching banks that have prevented people from leaving their existing banks, even when they are unhappy with the services. Some new services will make switching banks much easier[4].

1   See Feng Li, 'Internet Banking in the U.K.: From New Distribution Channel to New Business Models', *Journal of Financial Transformation*, p 64, available at http://www.capco.com/j06abs04.html.
2   *Ibid.*
3   *Ibid.*
4   *Ibid.*

Facts and figures

1.26   Evolution or revolution, it matters not. The reality is what matters; Internet banking is a global phenomenon and is becoming a driving force shaping the future of the banking industry. All banks, including those that were cautious in the past, intend to offer access to their products and services via the Internet, which is seen as a major distribution and communication channel[1]. It is widespread, particularly in Austria, Korea, the Scandinavian countries, Singapore, Malaysia, Spain and Switzerland where more than 75% of all banks offer such services. While relatively new, Internet banking promises to be the way consumers will bank in the 21st century. According to the data by Cybercitizen Finance, out of 58 million Internet user populations in July 1998, some 35 million (60%) were conducting some form of financial service activity via the Internet. The United Nations Conference on Trade and Development (UNCTAD) in its E-Commerce and Development Report 2001 stated that 'the banking industry in developed countries will grow at the rate of 3% till 2003, while the Internet banking segment will grow at a rate of 25% annually'[2].

1   See Feng Li, 'Internet Banking in the U.K.: From New Distribution Channel to New Business Models', *Journal of Financial Transformation*, p 60, available at http://www.capco.com/j06abs04.html.
2   United Nations Conference on Trade and Development, *E-Commerce and Development Report* (2001) p 143.

1.27   In the US, as of June 1997, based on information from 185 banks surveyed, the US General Accounting Office (GAO) projected rapid growth in online banking over the next year and a half as the number of US banks implementing online systems is expected to increase about fivefold nationwide[1]. More recent data suggest that:

> 'At least 3,610 federally insured depository institutions – about 17 per cent of all U.S. banks, saving associations and credit unions – offered some form of Internet banking services as of February 1999. About 20 per cent of these depository institutions offered fully transactional websites ... According to FDIC and NCUA statistics, in the 11 months ending February 1999, the number of banks, thrifts and credit unions with transactional websites almost tripled.'[2]

In mid-2001, 44% of national banks maintained transactional websites, almost double the number in the third quarter of 1999[3]. In terms of the number of customers, Internet banking is growing faster than most financial services institutions had ever expected. It is estimated that the share of US households using

Internet banking will increase from 20% in 2001 to 33% in 2005, and that by 2010, there might be 55 million users[4]. Today, roughly 4.5 million households use Internet banking and or bill payment at least once a month, and that number is expected to increase to 33.5 million – nearly 31% of all US households – by 2005[5].

1   Cheryl R. Lee, 'Cyberbanking: A New Frontier for Discrimination?' *Rutgers Computer and Technology Law Journal,* (2000) p 283.
2   *Ibid.*
3   Karen Furst, William W. Lang and Daniel E. Nolle, *Internet Banking: Developments and Prospects*, Program on Information Resources Policy, Centre for Information Policy Research, Harvard University, (April 2002) p 5.
4   See www.onlinebankingreport.com/resources/sr7.html.
5   DNI, 'Transforming Consumer Banking Through Internet Technology' available at http://www.dynamicnet.net/news/white_papers/internetbanking.htm.

1.28 In Canada, the percentage of Canadians who bank primarily through the Internet has doubled in the past two years. According to a survey conducted in 2002, 16% of respondents said that the Internet is the primary means through which they conduct the majority of their financial transactions, compared to 8% in a similar poll two years before. The survey also shows approximately one third (34%) of respondents now do at least some of their banking online. According to the survey, the trend towards the use of online banking will continue to rise. Of those surveyed, 56% expect to be conducting banking transactions through the Internet within the next two to three years, compared to 46% in 2000[1].

1   See Canadian Banker Association, 'Technology and Banking: A survey of Consumer Attitudes' available at http://www.cba.ca/en/viewdocument.asp?fl=3&sl=142&docid=408&pg=1.

1.29 In Europe, as of 2002 according to Qualisteam, which maintains a directory of European banks on the net, there were over 800 European Union banks offering Internet-based services[1]. Datamonitor forecasts that the number of European customers using PC-based Internet banking services over the next five years will treble, from 23 million at the end of 2000 to over 75 million in 2005[2]. Although the PC will remain the most popular access method for online banking services, Datamonitor also foresees a bright future for banking services via mobile phones and other wireless devices, especially with the growth in 2.5G and 3G networks that will allow for richer services to be delivered via wireless networks. The report forecasts that some 35 million customers will be banking via WAP by 2005. The greatest number of Internet banking customers in Europe is predicted to be found in Germany, the UK and the Nordic markets of Denmark, Finland, Norway and Sweden. Datamonitor also predicts that Italy will be the fastest-growing market[3].

1   See Charles Goldfinger,'Internet Banking Issues Paper' available at http://www.fininter.net/retai .../ Internet%20Banking%20%20Issues%20paper%20draft.ht.
2   Telecomworldwire, 3 August 2001, available at http://www.findarticles.com/cf_bzwr/m0ECZ/2001_ August_3/76960831/print.jhtml
3   *Ibid.*

1.30 According to the Market Intelligence Strategy Centre, Australians are among the top users of Internet banking with 18% of Australians having access to the Internet and being registered users of e-banking. The figure puts Australia ahead of the US and the UK, where around 14% of the people with Internet access use e-banking services. In the Asian economies of South Korea, Hong Kong, Singapore,

China and Taiwan, according to research released by ACNielsen Online on 29 May 2002, online banking is expanding. It states that the total active online banking population for the five countries has grown 63% from a regional total of 6.5 million in 2000 to 10.6 million Internet bankers in 2001. The ACNielsen research found that South Korea has been the largest number of active Internet bankers (5.3 million), followed by China (2.6 million) and Taiwan (1.7 million). Being much smaller in population size, Hong Kong and Singapore have smaller online banking population (600,000) and (400,000) respectively.

1.31   In terms of customer size, South Korean and Chinese Internet banks are the largest in the region. Of the top 20 Internet banks, Republic of Korea has twelve, China has five, and Taiwan, Hong Kong and Singapore each have one Internet bank. In the Republic of Korea, Internet banking has increased at a rapid pace, the number of online users having risen from 2 million in 2000 to 5.3 million in December 2001. The country is a leader in the region with 54% of users having multiple online banking relationships. The biggest Internet bank in Asia Pacific is South Korea's Kookmin (H&CB), which has 2.4 million Internet banking customers. Next is China's China Merchant Bank, with 1.4 million customers. The largest Internet bank in Taiwan, China Trust Commercial Bank, has close to 900,000 Internet banking customers. In Hong Kong, HSBC is market leader with around 360,000 online banking customers, while in Singapore the market leader is DBS/POSB with some 320,000.

1.32   According to a World Bank survey, the average online banking penetration for developing countries by the end of 1999 was close to 5%. For some countries, the penetration was considerably higher and growing rapidly. In Brazil, the number of e-banking users reached 8 million in 2001 and is constantly increasing. In India, over 50 banks offer online services. For example, the largest private bank, ICICI, has impressive figures: It now has four times as many online banking users, who represent over 15% of the total[1].

1   United Nations Conference on Trade and Development, *E-Commerce and Development Report 2002*, p 134.

Internet banking: advantages and challenges

1.33   Internet banking allows customers to access banking services 24 hours a day, seven days a week. Access is fast, convenient and available around the clock wherever the customer is. Like ATMs, Internet banking empowers customers to choose when and where they conduct their banking. An American Banking Association and Gallup Poll survey revealed that the primary reason customers maintain an account with a particular financial institution is convenience. This implies that in order to maintain customers today, banks need to offer their services through multiple distribution channels: physical branches, telephones, ATMs, kiosks, screen phones, PCs and the Internet[1]. Customers could save money and time when banking online. It is very convenient; customers do not have to wait in line at a bank – the click of a mouse can do what needs to be done.

1 See www.onlinebankingreport.com/resources/sr7.html.

1.34 Internet banking allows financial service institutions to capture a larger percentage of their customer's asset base. The Internet allows banks to offer new services – brokerage, mutual funds, insurance, mortgages, car loans and credit cards – either directly or indirectly from their websites. Banks or branch offices that do not offer these services have the opportunity to co-brand offerings with specialty companies[1].

1 See www.onlinebankingreport.com/resources/sr7.html.

1.35 The potential cost savings for Internet banking are dramatic. An American Bankers Association study placed the cost of handling a paper cheque transaction at between $0.42 and $2.00. Although Internet banking is so new that the recovery of development and start-up investments skew transaction costs, the cost could ultimately rival the reported $0.15 to $0.50 cost of an ATM transaction[1]. A 1996, Booz Allen & Hamilton study showed that the Internet banking transaction cost is the lowest, at $0.01, compared to the full service branch at $1.07, telephone at $0.54, ATM at $0.27 and PC banking at $0.02[2]. Online banking cuts costs for banks. Starting-up an online banking service is estimated to cost between $50,000–$200,000, with yearly maintenance costs of $1–$4 per account. But if customers use the online services this investment will pay off. The more customers that use Internet banking the further the fixed costs will be stretched, until the Internet banking services that are being offered become profitable. A study in 2000 reported that 30% of banks' websites and related Internet operations are unprofitable, reinforcing the point that banks need as many online customers as they can get[3].

1 Karen Furst, William W. Lang and Daniel E. Nolle, *Internet Banking: Developments and Prospects*, Program on Information Resources Policy, Centre for Information Policy Research, Harvard University, (April 2002) p 5.
2 Booz, Allen & Hamilton, *Banking Survey*, (July 1996) cited in DNI, 'Transforming Consumer Banking Through Internet Technology' available at http://www.dynamicnet.net/news/white_papers/internetbanking.htm.
3 Chong Soo Pyun, 'Internet banking in the U.S., Japan and Europe', *Multinational Business Review*, (fall 2002) pp 73–81.

1.36 Internet banking helps reduce the loss of customers due to relocation. One of the primary reasons people change banking institutions is that they have relocated from one area to another and, as a matter of convenience, desire a bank that provides access and services in their new location. Although many banks offer ATM, bank-by-mail and telephone banking services, customers often find that these services do not meet all of their needs. With Internet banking comes the ability to conduct most, if not all, of a typical customer's banking online, either via web access or through personal finance software. A comprehensive online banking system gives customers the perception of actually visiting the bank, interacting with employees and conducting business[1].

1 See www.onlinebankingreport.com/resources/sr7.html.

1.37 Internet banking removes the traditional geographical barriers and could reach out to customers in different countries. Anybody with Internet access is a potential customer irrespective of his location. Since the Internet has provided an ever-growing market, so has Internet banking. Another reason why Internet banking is beneficial for banks is the high retention ratio shown after customers use online services. A survey by Bank of America concluded that customers are 80% less likely to switch banks once they have set up their online banking[1].

1 Michelle Higgins, 'Honest, the Check IS in the E-mail', *Wall Street Journal*, 4 Sept. 2002.

1.38 Given the advantages of Internet banking, most banks regard Internet banking as a business priority and a strategic necessity. Some opined that Internet banking would soon follow the same path of ATMs, migrating from a strong competitive differentiator to a basic and expected service. Consumers will expect to be able to check balances, pay bills, transfer funds and review transactions from anywhere, much as they now expect to retrieve cash wherever they go in the world. While ATMs took approximately 15 years to be widely accepted, Internet banking will take a fraction of the time[1].

1 See www.onlinebankingreport.com/resources/sr7.html.

1.39 The traditional banks with a strong customer base have a competitive advantage over newcomers. However, to maintain this advantage is not easy. The key success is to keep abreast of technological change and sophistication; this allows a bank to understand the potential of Internet technologies and to integrate them into a coherent business strategy. For 'click and mortar' banks, transforming bank branches into multipurpose advisory centres would also encourage clients to move to Internet banking, since the majority of Internet users also make use of bank branches and ATMs. The idea is to transform bank branches into 'one-stop shops', i.e. well-networked financial advisory centres for clients[1].

1 United Nations Conference on Trade and Development, *E-Commerce and Development Report 2002*, p 134.

1.40 To further develop e-finance and e-banking, the United Nations Conference on Trade and Development, suggests[1]:

'Banks need to show customers that they provide the same security standards on the Internet as in traditional banking. Moreover, like credit cards associations and companies, banks should assume, at least in the initial stages, full responsibility for covering the costs incurred by clients as a result of a security breach and unauthorised transaction. To encourage migration to Internet banking, the banks should also offer better interest rates and cheaper accounts. The ability to gain customers' trust thanks to security, willingness to take responsibility and the offer of financial incentives has been an important feature of the most successful pure Net banks.'

1 United Nations Conference on Trade and Development, *E-Commerce and Development Report 2002*, p 134.

Internet banking: lessons for banks and the future

1.41   Some argue that Internet banking is a killer application of electronic commerce. A few sceptics, however, differ. The *Economist,* in November 2000 stated, 'Promises of the Internet banking proved largely hollow.' According to Andrew Hilton, Director of the Centre for Study of Financial Innovations, Internet banking is a 'fragile flower' or to put it more colloquially, 'Internet banking ain't a killer application'[1]. The market will determine whether Internet banking is a killer application of e-commerce. The indication so far is that Internet banking is moving towards that direction.

1   See Charles Goldfinger, 'Internet Banking Issues Paper' available at http://www.fininter.net/retai …/ Internet%20Banking%20%20Issues%20paper%20draft.ht.

1.42   By 2005 the share of Internet banking could rise from 8.5 to 50% in industrial countries and from 1 to 10% in emerging markets. With better connectivity, Internet banking transactions in the emerging market could rise even further, to 20% by 2005[1]. Despite situational disadvantages (such as weaker telecommunications infrastructure), and more adverse demand and supply factors, Internet-based services are sometimes as popular in emerging markets as in industrial countries – or even more popular. For example, Internet banking is nearly as widespread in Brazil as in the US. This suggests that around the globe, e-finance is fairly easy to introduce and for customers to assimilate. It may also suggest that in countries with weak financial services, customers have a strong incentive to move to e-finance providers. Banking services may still be limited in these countries, but e-finance offers an opportunity to expand access[2].

1   Stijn Claessens, Thomas Glaessner, and Daniela Klingebiel, 'E-Finance in Emerging Markets: Is Leapfrogging Possible?' Financial Sector Discussion Paper No 7, The World Bank, (June 2001).
2   *Ibid.*

1.43   The difference between countries depends on whether they have reached critical mass. In Nordic countries, online banking shot from some 20% in 2000 to nearly 80% in 2001. And in Sweden online trading jumped from 55% to 94%. But in Italy growth in banking rose from just 1% to 22%, because the country has not yet reached critical mass in e-finance. But by 2010 it might, and e-banking growth in Italy could exceed 70%[1].

1   Stijn Claessens, Thomas Glaessner, and Daniela Klingebiel, 'E-Finance in Emerging Markets: Is Leapfrogging Possible?' Financial Sector Discussion Paper No 7, The World Bank, (June 2001).

1.44   According to new research from Forrester, over 60 million Europeans now bank online. The company's latest study reveals that one in five Europeans currently bank online. This is equivalent to 37% of all Internet users in the continent. Datamonitor forecast that there will be 84 million Internet banking customers in Europe by 2007. The latest study by the research company states that the number of online banking customers had reached 60 million in 2003, up from 23 million in 2000[1].

1   Cited in NUA Internet Surveys available at http://www.nua.ie/surveys/index.cgi?f=VS&art_id= 905358746&rel=true.

1.45 Yet another research study by Jupiter forecasts that the number of online banking users in Europe will increase from 54 million in 2002 to 103 million in 2007. The company expects the number of online banking users to grow at a Compound Annual Rate (CAR) of 14%. In America, another research company Gartner forecast that consumer use of online banking will grow at a CAR of 14% up to year-end 2007. By that time, some 30% of Americans (67 million individuals) will be using online banking services. In Canada, a new study from NFO CF group reveals that online banking is now more popular than telephone banking[1]. The analysts from the Office of the Comptroller of the Currency of the US noted:

> 'While Internet banking is the subject of a large amount of discussion, it remains the case that only a small percentage of banking transactions are done online, and only a third of all banks currently offer Internet banking. Nevertheless, the adoption of Internet banking by banks has grown at a very rapid pace.'[2]

In the US, use of Internet banking, while forecast to grow significantly, is still relatively modest. On the customer side, the so-far modest take-up of Internet banking may be due to a lack of compelling value-added proposition, a problem that may not be applicable for potential business Internet banking customers. Nevertheless, most consumers bank at banks that offer an Internet banking service, and so usage patterns could change suddenly[3].

1   Cited in NUA Internet Surveys available at http://www.nua.ie/surveys/index.cgi?f=VS&art_id= 905358746&rel=true.
2   John Carlson, Karen Furst, William W. Lang, and Daniel E. Nolle, 'Internet Banking: Market Developments and Regulatory Issues' (May 2001) presented to Society of Government Economists Conference 2000, Washington, D.C.
3   *Ibid.*

1.46 It is interesting to see whether there is any relationship between Internet banking and profitability. Some analysts find that except for the smallest size banks, Internet banks are more profitable than non-Internet banks. They also speculate that it is probably too soon to see a systematic impact of Internet banking on banks' profitability[1]. Research shows that there is no simple correlation between Internet banking and profitability. Another finding is that the difference in profitability of old Internet and new Internet small banks is not due to the existence of Internet banking, but rather due to the different conditions at those banks offering Internet banking before and after the second quarter of 1998[2].

1   See Karen Furst, William W. Lang, and Daniel E. Nolle, 'Internet Banking: Development and Prospects', Economic and Policy Analysis Working Paper 2000–9, Office of the Comptroller of the Currency.
2   Stijn Claessens, Thomas Glaessner, and Daniela Klingebiel, 'E-Finance in Emerging Markets: Is Leapfrogging Possible?' Financial Sector Discussion Paper No 7, The World Bank, (June 2001).

1.47 The report by the Policy Analysis Division of the Office of the Comptroller of the Currency of the United States, among others, lists the following findings[1]:

● Banks of all sizes that offer Internet Banking tend to rely less on interest-yielding activities and core deposits than non-Internet banks do.

- Among institutions offering Internet banking, large banks are far more likely than small banks to offer a broad range of services over the Internet.

- Bank profitability is strongly co-related with Internet banking, but offering Internet banking does not have a statistically significant impact on profitability. Rather, the aggressive business posture of early adopters of Internet banking probably explains both their relatively higher profitability and their decision to offer Internet banking.

- Among banks that offer Internet banking, larger banks and banks that have offered this service for a longer time were significantly more likely to offer a wider range of services over the Internet.

- Customer use of Internet banking is disproportionately concentrated among a few large banks.

1   Karen Furst, William W. Lang and Daniel E. Nolle, *Internet Banking: Developments and Prospects*, Program on Information Resources Policy, Centre for Information Policy Research, Harvard University, (April 2002) p 5.

1.48 At the micro level, as far as Asia is concerned, the International Data Corporation Asia/Pacific research found that 'Asian Internet users are banking online in record numbers, but many banks are ignoring their best Internet banking customers'. The IDC, who conducted a study in Australia, China, Hong Kong, Singapore and Taiwan, has identified a number of interesting trends that warrant further study. These include[1]:

- Internet channels will increase transaction volumes in the short term: growth in transactions through the Internet channel is increasing at a faster rate than the decrease in transactions through the branch. This inverse relationship has led to a situation where a sizable portion of Internet banking customers still rely heavily on the branch, while concurrently using the Internet channel. This is an expensive, but short-term phenomenon. Transaction volumes via the branch will decrease as customers get more comfortable online.

- Customers with fewest branch visits are most active online: Customers who visit the branch one or fewer times per month have the highest Internet banking usage. This indicates that there are a growing segment of customers who interact almost exclusively through self-directed channels. Banks have so far done a poor job addressing the concerns and needs of this group.

- Age and income assumptions are no longer valid: Internet banking usage is not the province of the young and young people are not the most active Internet banking users. A bank's best Internet customer (high Internet activity, low branch activity) falls within the 22–55 age group and is at the highest income levels.

- Education and incentives are the key to success: In all surveyed countries, respondents indicated a strong desire for more education and said they would increase online activity as a result. They feel banks have done a poor job on education, convincing them that Internet banking is safe, and making sites easy to use. Incentives are also lacking, which is a serious problem because many bankers have already tapped their supply of early adopters. The next wave of customers will not be as easy to pull online, and incentives must play a part.

- More going on than just transactions: Respondents utilise Internet banking far more than transaction volumes indicate. Even customers who do not log in to a site, derive significant value from the site itself. Banks can develop a large, loyal web-using customer base by offering a good quality, informative site. Online origination of offline purchases can also be achieved by using the web to educate customers before they appear at a branch.

1 IDC Asia Pacific Press Release, 25 March 2002, available at http://www.idc.com.sg/Press/2002/AP_PR_internet_banking.htm.

1.49 There are several reasons contributing to the slow Internet banking growth in some parts of the world. Firstly, there is no good coordination between the banks and their customers. Banks may have various channels of their online banking services but they are so out of whack, even employees are not sure what products are available online. If banks are struggling to figure out what they plan to offer online and how much they will charge for it, they are going to have an extremely difficult time advertising it. If the customers recognise that banks are struggling with their own online issues, how can banks expect customers to have confidence in their services?[1]

Secondly, many customers are afraid of using online banking because they are not sure how to use it. They also fear that online banking will not have proper security. Only 49% of bank customers feel online services are secure. This means that banks will have to do a better job in educating their customers about how to use the services as well as about the security of their online banking systems. Perhaps if banks were to set up some sort of training class explaining these issues, more people would be willing to give Internet banking a try[2].

Thirdly, many banks do not have very user-friendly websites, making them difficult for customers to use. And if a company has a good website, users easily get annoyed if they cannot find what they need. People are also bothered by lack of face-to-face contact, especially when they run into a problem and need some sort of help, or customer service[3].

Fourthly, it relates to the initial time that must be invested to set up an online account. It takes a decent amount of time to sign up for Internet banking services and to set them up to the customers' preference. Many people will not use Internet banking services if they are not sure that it is worth the risk and trouble. Banks need to make the set up process more convenient.

Lastly, Internet banking will never be able to offer the personal feeling that traditional bricks and mortar banks offer. Some people just enjoy going into the bank, which gives them a sense of security when they hand over their money[4].

1   Jeff Bracker, Krista Hunemuller, Jim Nygren, Derrick Huffey and James Rothmeyer, 'History to Future of Banking' available at http://www.cba.uni.edu/slides/160150_student_papers/History%20to%20 Future%20of%20Banking.pdf.
2   Karen Epper Hoffman, cited in Jeff Bracker, Krista Hunemuller, Jim Nygren, Derrick Huffey and James Rothmeyer, *ibid.*
3   *Ibid.*
4   *Ibid.*

1.50   Internet banking offers advantages and benefits to the banks as well as customers. The advantages and benefits are too great to overlook. As more and more people use the Internet, Internet banking is becoming more widespread. However, there are barriers to widespread consumer adoption. These barriers will have to be removed for Internet banking to flourish.

Generally, consumers worldwide are enthusiastic about Internet banking. The Angus Reid Group and Royal Bank of Canada study found that, 'of those Americans surveyed who have tried banking online, three in four say they're "very likely" to continue'. About 10% of American Internet users say they are 'very likely' to trade and/or make other investments online in the near future. In Canada, the study found that nearly one in five Canadian Internet users has already tried Internet banking. Nearly one in three says they will soon, and nearly everyone who has already tried it says they'll do it again. Perhaps, the following statement from Gus Schattenberg, Angus Reid Global Vice-President, provides a good indication of the present and future of Internet banking[1]:

> 'We're finding across the world that as people go online, banking is one of the commercial applications that have an immediate appeal. Online banking has a following among users in the most developed Internet markets but there are even some emergent markets where online banking is carving a niche among the leading edge of users.'

1   Cited in Michael Pastore, 'Canadians Lead American in Online Banking Interest' CyberAtlas, available at http://www.clickz.com/stats/markets/finance/print.php/%205961_399961

1.51   Let us share the words of the UNCTAD on the impact of e-finance. It noted that until 2000 it was commonly thought that e-business would revolutionise the financial industry and destroy the existing 'dinosaurs'. However, the evolution of e-finance clearly demonstrates the advantages of suppliers of established financial services, be they banking, transaction processing, credit information or insurance, as long as they have the capacity to evolve and to embrace the new approaches and technologies[1].

As far as Internet banking is concerned, once again, the dominant business model today is 'click and mortar' and an innovation is most likely to succeed if the leading players adopt it. This does not mean that financial services will not change, as they have been doing for the past decades. Rather, the change will be more gradual and will probably take place mainly inside the established systems and structures. While the dynamics of e-finance do not entail a sudden upheaval, it will probably lead to a profound and lasting transformation of financial services[2]. E-finance will enhance the information and technology content of financial services and thus further blur the boundaries between finance and technology, information and transaction, and financial institutions and technology providers.

As Professor Feng Li has put it, 'the banking industry has changed significantly, but more radical shake-ups are still to come – and they may come much sooner than many have expected'[3]. These changes raise a number of substantive supervisory, legal and regulatory issues, some of which are discussed in the subsequent chapters.

1 United Nations Conference on Trade and Development, *E-Commerce and Development Report 2002*, p 147.
2 *Ibid.*
3 See Feng Li, 'Internet Banking in the U.K.: From New Distribution Channel to New Business Models', *Journal of Financial Transformation*, p 64, available at http://www.capco.com/j06abs04.html.

CHAPTER TWO

Prudential Regulation and Supervision of Internet Banking

Introduction

2.1 Regulation can best be divided into structural regulation, prudential regula-tion and investor protection, although there are significant links between the three. Structural regulation refers to the type of activities that different categories of financial institution are permitted to carry out, and prudential regulation refers to supervision in terms of, *inter alia,* liquidity, capital adequacy and solvency of financial institutions. The term 'supervision' is used here to mean the monitoring of financial institutions for investor protection, prudential regulation, and structural regulation purposes combined. Investor protection legislation overlaps with both prudential and structural regulation in that the investor is in theory protected from financial institutions becoming insolvent through excessive risk-taking, and is protected from conflicts of interest by separation of types of business, but it also extends much further into the manner in which investment business is carried out. These three types of regulation can all be carried out through formal legal rules, through self-imposed rules or self-regulation, or some combination of all three[1].

1 Michael Pawley, David Winstone and Patrick Bentley, *UK Financial Institutions and Market* (1993) pp 235–236.

2.2 Prudential regulation is necessary to protect customers and to provide stability to the financial system, and one of its major functions is to deter financial institutions from taking on excessive levels of risks. Prudential regulations have the objective of improving financial stability, consumer protection and allocating efficiency. It has to be noted that regulations do not intend to stop financial institutions taking on risk, as this is a fundamental part of their activities. Risk-taking is fundamental to the efficient operation of financial markets and the economy as a whole. It is necessary, however, for regulators to deter exceptional risk-taking or to minimise the risk. The difficulty here, of course, is to determine what is excessive and what is not, or how to minimise the risk[1].

1 Michael Pawley, David Winstone and Patrick Bentley, *UK Financial Institutions and Market* (1993) pp 235–236.

2.3 Prudential regulation dictates internal management practices and is especially relevant in the context of corporate governance. Investor protection regulation may overlap with prudential regulation since it focuses on the prevention and detection of fraudulent activities, malpractices and unsound investments[1]. Prudential supervision relates to preventive measures undertaken by the regulatory authorities in respect of maintaining the safety and soundness of the banks[2]. Prudential supervision, at the bank regulatory level, arguably ensures a sound banking system, and thus protection for customers.

1 I.L. Van Jaarsveld 'Domestic and International Banking Regulation and Supervision – Defying the Challenges', *The South African Journal* (2002) Vol 119, Part 1, 72–73.
2 *Ibid.*

Internet banking: risks and new challenges for regulators

2.4 Banking, by its nature, is a high-risk business. The major risks associated with banking activities are: strategic, reputational, operational (including security – sometimes called transactional and legal risks), credit, price, foreign exchange, interest rate and liquidity. Internet banking increases some of these traditional risks and also creates new ones. Thus, inherent in Internet banking are risks[1]. The core business and the information technology are tightly coupled, thereby influencing the overall risk profile of Internet banking[2].

1 A Working Group, *Internet Banking*, available at http://www.isaca.org/standard/guide27.htm.
2 *Ibid.*

2.5 Regulators and supervisors all over the world are concerned that while banks should remain efficient and cost effective, they must be conscious of the different types of risks that Internet banking entails and have systems in place to manage the same. Because of rapid changes in information technology, there is no finality either in types of risks or their control measures; both evolve continuously[1]. However, it is possible to identify the risks in broad terms: operational risks, legal and regulatory risks, reputational risks, strategic risks and security risks.

1 Reserve Bank of India Working Group, Report on Internet Banking, available at http://www.securities.com/Public/Public98/RBI/Publicn/pub010622–1.html, p 24.

2.6 Operational risk, also referred to as transactional risk, is the most common form of risk associated with Internet banking. It takes the form of inaccurate processing of transactions, non-enforceability of contracts, compromises in data integrity, data privacy and confidentiality, intrusion into the bank's systems and transactions etc[1]. This is because Internet banking relies very much on new technology. Security threats can come from inside and outside the system. The risk can also arise out of weaknesses in design, implementation and monitoring of banks' information system. Besides inadequacies in technology, human factors such as negligence by customers and employees, fraudulent activity of employees and hackers can become sources of operational risk[2].

1 Reserve Bank of India Working Group, Report on Internet Banking, available at http://www.securities.com/Public/Public98/RBI/Publicn/pub010622–1.html, p 24.
2 *Ibid.*

2.7 Internet banking is based on technology that, by its nature, is designed to extend the geographic reach of banks and customers. Such market expansion can extend beyond national borders. The Internet also allows services to be provided from anywhere in the world. Thus, there is a danger that banks will try to avoid regulation and supervision. The other legal and regulatory risks include the uncertainty about legal requirements in some countries and jurisdiction ambiguities with respect to the responsibilities of different national authorities[1]. Banks might not be fully versed in a jurisdiction's local laws and regulations. Banks may be exposed to legal risks associated with non-compliance with different national laws and regulations including consumer protection laws, record keeping and reporting requirements, privacy rules and money laundering laws.

1 Reserve Bank of India Working Group, Report on Internet Banking, available at http://www.securities.com/Public/Public98/RBI/Publicn/pub010622–1.html, p 27.

2.8 Reputational risk, according to Carol Sergeant of the UK Financial Services Authority (FSA), is considerably heightened for banks using the Internet. Breaches of security and disruptions to the system's availability can damage a bank's reputation. Most observers agree that as Internet banking becomes more wide-spread and complex, the necessity for banks to assess and manage operational and reputational risks will become more crucial. Security failure at a particular institution could not only cause large losses for that institution, but could spawn a general lack of confidence in Internet banking innovations, thereby retarding development. In addition, unlike other remote banking methods such as telephone banking, security risks surrounding the Internet may be especially challenging to address because the Internet is a network designed to promote open access. There is a risk that one rogue Internet bank could cause significant problems for all banks providing services via the Internet. This is a new type of systematic risk and is causing concern to Internet banking providers.

2.9 Strategic risk is risk associated with the introduction of a new product or service. The degree of this risk depends upon how well the bank has addressed the various issues related to development of a business plan, availability of sufficient resources to support the plan, credibility of the vendor and level of technology used in comparison to the available technology. Carol Sergeant stated:

> 'On strategic risk e-banking is relatively new and, as a result, there can be a lack of understanding among senior management about its potential and implications. E-initiatives can spring up in a coherent and piecemeal manner in firms. They can be expensive and can fail to recoup their cost. Furthermore, they are often positioned as loss leaders, but may not attract the types of customers that banks want or expect and may have unexpected implications on existing business lines.'

2.10 Security risks arise from unauthorised access to a bank's critical system. A breach of security could result in direct financial loss to the bank. It could also result in loss of data, theft of or tampering with customer information, or the disabling of a bank's computer system thus denying service. This would lead to reputational risk, loss of reputation, and infringing consumers' privacy. This will also lead to operational risk, inability to provide services to the customers. Security risk, operational risk and reputational risk are inter-related. Thus, managing each and all of them is of paramount importance. The issue of security is often cited as a major obstacle to widespread consumer adoption of Internet banking.

International regulations on Internet banking

Risk management principles for electronic banking

2.11 International banking supervision takes place under the guidance of the Basel Committee on Banking Supervision. The Basel Committee is a committee of banking supervisory advisors established in 1975 by the governors of the central banks of the Group of Ten countries[1]. It was set up under the auspices of the Bank for International Settlements (BIS) in Basel, Switzerland as a consequence of huge worldwide bank failures. In May 2001, the Electronic Banking Group of the Basel Committee published a consolidated, coherent, comprehensive and updated document entitled *Risk Management Principles for Electronic Banking*.

1   It was first called the Committee on Banking Regulations and Supervisory Practices, and consists of representatives of bank supervisory authorities and central banks from Belgium, Canada, Germany, Italy, Japan, Luxembourg, the Netherlands, Spain, Sweden, Switzerland, the UK and the US.

2.12 The principles, which are identified in this report, are not set forth as legal provisions, absolute requirements or even 'best practice' but rather as guidance to promote safe and sound e-banking activities. The Committee believes that setting detailed risk management requirements in the area of e-banking might be counter-productive because these would be likely to become rapidly outdated by the speed of change related to technological and product innovation. The Report noted:

'The Committee has therefore preferred to express supervisory expectations and guidance in the form of Risk Management Principles in order to promote safety and soundness for e-banking activities, while preserving the necessary flexibility in implementation that derives in part from the speed of change in this area. Further, the Committee recognises that each bank's risk profile is different and requires a tailored risk mitigation approach appropriate for the scale of the e-banking operations, the materiality of the risk present, and the willingness and ability of the institution to manage these risks. This implies that a "one size fits all" approach to e-banking risk management issues may not be appropriate.'

According to the Committee, the *Risk Management Principles* and sound practices identified in the Report are expected to be used as tools by national supervisors and implemented with adaptations to reflect specific national requirements and individual risk profiles where necessary.

2.13 The Basel Committee has identified 14 risk management principles for electronic banking to help banking institutions expand their existing risk oversight policies and processes covering their e-banking activities. The principles fall into three broad, and often overlapping, categories of issues, namely: board and management oversight, security controls and legal and reputational risk management.

Board and management oversight (principles 1–3)

2.14 The first principle is that the board of directors and senior management should establish effective management oversight over the risks associated with e-banking activities, including the establishment of specific accountability, policies, and controls to manage these risks. Second, the board of directors and senior management should review and approve the key aspects of the bank's security control process. Third, the board of directors and senior management should establish a comprehensive and ongoing due diligence and oversight process for managing the bank's outsourcing relationships and other third-party dependencies supporting e-banking.

2.15 According to the Committee, under the first principle, vigilant management oversight is essential for the provision of effective internal controls of e-banking activities. The following aspects of e-banking may pose considerable challenges to traditional risk management processes:

- Major elements of the delivery channel (the Internet and related technologies) are outside the direct control of the bank.

- The Internet facilitates delivery of services across multiple national jurisdictions, including those currently not served by the institution through physical locations.

- The complexity of issues that are associated with e-banking and that involve highly technical language and concepts are in many cases outside the traditional experience of the board and senior management.

2.16 Under the second principle, the Committee lists the following key elements of an effective e-banking security process:

- Assignment of explicit management/staff responsibility for overseeing the establishment and maintenance of corporate security policies.

- Sufficient physical controls to prevent unauthorised physical access to the computing environment.

- Sufficient logical controls and monitoring processes to prevent unauthorised internal and external access to e-banking applications and databases.

- Regular review and testing of security measures and controls, including the continuous tracking of current industry security developments and installation of appropriate software upgrades, service packs and other required measures.

2.17 The third principle requires the board of directors and senior management to establish a comprehensive process for managing the risks associated with outsourcing and other third-party dependencies. Board and senior management should specifically focus on ensuring that:

- The bank fully understands the risk associated with entering into an outsourcing or partnership arrangement for its e-banking systems or applications.

- An appropriate due diligence review of the competency and financial viability of any third-party service provider or partner is conducted prior to entering into any contract for e-banking services.

- The contractual accountability of all parties to the outstanding or partnership relationship is clearly defined. For instance, responsibilities for providing information to and receiving information from the service provider should be clearly defined.

- All outsourced e-banking systems and operations are subject to risk management, security and privacy policies that meet the bank's own standards.

- Periodic independent internal and/or external audits are conducted for outsourced operations to at least the same scope required if such operations were conducted in-house.

- Appropriate contingency plans for outsourced e-banking activities exist.

Security controls (principles 4–10)

2.18 The Basel Committee noted that while the board of directors has the responsibility for ensuring that appropriate security control processes are in place for e-banking, the substance of these processes needs special attention because of the enhanced security challenges posed by e-banking. The following issues are particularly pertinent:

- Authenticity.

- Non-repudiation.

- Data and transaction integrity.

- Segregation of duties.

- Authorisation controls.

- Maintenance of audit trails.

- Confidentiality of key bank information.

2.19 The principles established by the Committee as guidance to promote safe and sound e-banking practices are:

- Banks should take appropriate measures to authenticate the identity and authorisation of customers with whom they conduct business over the Internet.

- Banks should use transaction authentication methods that promote non-repudiation and establish accountability for e-banking transactions.

- Banks should ensure that appropriate measures are in place to promote adequate segregation of duties within e-banking systems, databases and applications.

- Banks should ensure that proper authorisation controls and access privileges are in place for e-banking systems, databases and applications.

- Banks should ensure that appropriate measures are in place to protect the data integrity of e-banking transactions, records and information.

- Banks should ensure that a clear audit trail exists for all e-banking transactions.

- Banks should take appropriate measures to preserve the confidentiality of key e-banking information. Measures taken to preserve confidentiality should be commensurate with the sensitivity of the information being transmitted and/or stored in databases.

Legal and reputational risk management (principles 11–14)

2.20 Principle 11 states that banks should ensure that adequate information is provided on their websites to allow potential customers to make an informed conclusion about the bank's identity and its regulatory status prior to entering into e-banking transactions. Examples of information that a bank could provide on its website include:

- The name of the bank and the location of its head office (and local offices if applicable).

- The identity of the primary bank supervisory authority(ies) responsible for the supervision of the bank's head office.

- How customers can contact the bank's customer service centre regarding service problems, complaints, suspected misuse of accounts etc.

- How customers can access and use applicable Ombudsman or consumer complaint schemes.

- How customers can obtain access to information on applicable national compensation or deposit insurance coverage and the level of protection that they afford (or links to websites that provide such information).

- Other information that may be appropriate or required by specific jurisdictions.

2.21 In principle 12 the Committee stresses the importance of protecting the privacy of customers. This principle provides that banks should take appropriate measures to ensure adherence to customer privacy requirements applicable to the jurisdictions to which the bank is providing e-banking products and services. According to the Committee, banks should make reasonable endeavours to ensure that:

- The bank's customer privacy policies and standards take account of and comply with all privacy regulations and laws applicable to the jurisdictions to which it is providing e-banking products and services.

- Customers are made aware of the bank's privacy policies and relevant privacy issues concerning use of e-banking products and services.

- Customers may decline ('opt out') from permitting the bank to share, with a third party for cross-marketing purposes, any information about the customer's personal needs, interests, financial position or banking activity.

- Customer data are not used for the purposes beyond which they are specifically allowed or for purposes beyond which customers have authorised.

2.22 Principle 13 states that banks should have effective capacity, business continuity and contingency planning processes to help ensure the availability of e-banking systems and services. Banks need to ensure that:

- Current e-banking system capacity and future scalability are analysed in light of the overall market dynamics for e-commerce and the projected rate of customer acceptance of e-banking products and services.

- E-banking transaction processing capacity estimates are established, stress tested and periodically reviewed.

- Appropriate business continuity and contingency plans for critical e-banking processing and delivery systems are in place and regularly tested.

2.23 Principle 14 states that banks should develop appropriate incident response plans to manage, contain and minimise problems arising from unexpected events, including internal and external attacks that may hamper the provision of e-banking systems and services.

The Committee lists out the following matters to be developed by the banks to ensure effective response to unforeseen incidents:

- Incident response plans to address recovery of e-banking systems and services under various scenarios, businesses and geographic locations. Scenario analysis should include consideration of the likelihood of the risk occurring and its impact on the bank. E-banking systems that are outsourced to third-party service providers should be an integral part of these plans.

- Mechanisms to identify an incident or crisis as soon as it occurs, assess its materiality, and control the reputation risk associated with any disruption in service.

- A communication strategy to adequately address external market and media concerns that may arise in the event of security breaches, online attacks and/or failures of e-banking systems.

- A clear process for alerting the appropriate authorities in the event of material security breaches or disruptive incidents.

- Incident response teams, with the authority to act in an emergency and sufficiently trained in analysing incident detection/response systems and interpreting the significance of related output.

- A clear chain of command, encompassing both internal as well as outsourced operations, to ensure that prompt action is taken that is appropriate to the significance of the incident. In addition, escalation and internal communication procedures should be developed and include notification of the board where appropriate.

- A process to ensure all relevant external parties, including bank customers, counterparts and the media, are informed in a timely and appropriate manner of material e-banking disruptions and business resumption developments.

- A process for collecting and preserving forensic evidence to facilitate appropriate post-mortem reviews of any e-banking incidents as well as to assist in the prosecution of attackers.

Initiatives of the Organisation for Economic Co-operation and Development

2.24 The Organisation for Economic Co-operation and Development (OECD) has been very active in the area of e-commerce. Several guidelines have been issued that would have significant implications for Internet banking. On 9 December 1999, the organisation published the *Guidelines for Consumer Protection in the Context of Electronic Commerce,* which is designed to offer effective consumer protection for online business-to-consumer transactions. The aim of the Guidelines is to encourage: fair business, advertising and marketing practices; clear information about an online business's identity, the goods or services it offers and the terms and conditions of any transaction; a transparent process for the confirmation of transactions; secure payment mechanisms; fair, timely and affordable dispute resolution and redress; privacy protection; and consumer and business education. This section will only outline the principles that have an impact on Internet banking.

2.25 The Guidelines in the preamble recognise that certain special characteristics of electronic commerce may create commercial situations which are unfamiliar to consumers and which put their interests at risk. It is increasingly important for consumers and businesses to be informed and aware of their rights and obligations in the electronic market place. It is also recognised that consumer confidence in electronic commerce is enhanced by the continued development of transparent and effective consumer protection mechanisms that limit the presence of fraudulent, misleading or unfair commercial conduct on-line.

2.26 In the Guidelines, the OECD has developed some general principles concerning electronic commerce. The Guidelines provide that consumers who participate in electronic commerce should be afforded transparent and effective consumer protection that is not less than the level of protection afforded in other forms of commerce. Governments, businesses, consumers and their representatives should work together to achieve such protection and determine what changes may be necessary to address the special circumstances of electronic commerce.

2.27 A long list of general principles have been developed relating to fair business, advertising and marketing practices:

- Business should not make any representation, or omission, or engage in any practice that is likely to be deceptive, misleading, fraudulent or unfair.

- Businesses selling, promoting or marketing goods or services to consumers should not engage in practices that are likely to cause unreasonable risk of harm to consumers.

- Whenever businesses make information available about themselves or the goods or service they provide, they should present such information in a clear, conspicuous, accurate and easily accessible manner.

- Businesses should comply with any representations they make regarding policies or practices relating to their transactions with consumers.

- Businesses should take into account the global nature of electronic commerce and, whenever possible, should consider the various regulatory characteristics of the markets they target.

- Businesses should not exploit the special characteristics of electronic commerce to hide their true identity or location, or avoid compliance with consumer protection standards and/or enforcement mechanisms.

- Businesses should not use unfair contract terms.

- Advertising and marketing should be clearly identifiable as such.

- Advertising and marketing should identify the business on whose behalf the marketing or advertising is being conducted; failure to do so would be deceptive.

- Businesses should be able to substantiate any express or implied representations as long as the representations are maintained for a reasonable time thereafter.

- Businesses should develop and implement effective and easy-to-use procedures that allow consumers to choose whether or not they wish to receive unsolicited commercial e-mail messages.

- Where consumers have indicated that they do not want to receive unsolicited commercial e-mail messages, such choice should be respected.

- In a number of countries, unsolicited commercial e-mail is subject to specific legal or self-regulatory requirements.

- Businesses should take special care in advertising or marketing that is targeted at children, the elderly, the seriously ill, and others who may not have the capacity to fully understand the information with which they are presented.

2.28   The online disclosures are divided into information about the business, information about the goods or services, and information about the transaction. Under the information about the business, the Guidelines state that businesses engaged in electronic commerce with consumers should provide accurate, clear and easily accessible information about themselves sufficient to allow, at a minimum: identification of the business; prompt, easy and effective consumer communication with the business; appropriate and effective resolution of disputes; a service offering legal processes; and location of the business and its principals by law enforcement and regulatory officials.

2.29   With respect to the information on goods or services, it is stated that businesses engaged in electronic commerce with consumers should provide accurate and easily accessible information describing the goods or services offered; sufficient to enable consumers to make an informed decision about whether to enter into the transaction and in a manner that makes it possible for consumers to maintain an adequate record of such information.

2.30   On the information about the transaction, businesses engaged in electronic commerce should provide sufficient information about the terms, conditions and costs associated with a transaction to enable consumers to make an informed decision about whether to enter into the transaction. Such information should be clear, accurate, easily accessible, and provided in a manner that gives consumers an adequate opportunity for review before entering into the transaction. Businesses should provide consumers with a clear and full text of the relevant terms and conditions of the transaction in a manner that makes it possible for consumers to access and maintain an adequate record of such information.

2.31   With regard to dispute resolution and redress, the Guidelines recognise that consideration should be given to whether the existing framework for applicable law and jurisdiction should be modified, or applied differently, to ensure effective and transparent consumer protection in the context of the continued growth of electronic commerce. The consumers, according to the Guidelines, should be provided with meaningful access to fair and timely alternative dispute resolution and redress without undue cost or burden. On privacy, business-to-consumer electronic commerce should be conducted in accordance with the privacy principles set out in the *OECD Guidelines Governing the Protection of Privacy and Transborder Flows of Personal Data* (1980). Lastly, concerning education and awareness, the OECD urges governments, businesses and consumer representatives to work together to educate consumers about electronic commerce, to foster informed decision-making by consumers participating in electronic commerce, and to increase business and consumer awareness of the consumer protection framework that applies to their online activities.

2.32 On 25 July 2002, the OECD issued the *Guidelines for the Security of Information Systems and Networks: Towards a Culture of Security*. The Guidelines states that security issues should be topics of concern and responsibility at all levels of government and business. The Guidelines constitute a foundation for work towards a culture of security throughout society. The OECD considers finance as a critical infrastructure that depends on the Internet. The Guidelines are not meant to suggest that any solution exists for security or what policies, practices, measures and procedures are appropriate to any particular situation. The Guidelines rather provide a framework of principles to promote better understanding of how participants[1] may benefit from, and contribute to, the development of a culture of security. The Guidelines aim to:

- Promote a culture of security among all participants as a means of protecting information systems and networks.

- Raise awareness about the risk to information systems and networks; the policies, practices, measures and procedures available to address those risks; and the need for their adoption and implementation.

- Foster greater confidence among all participants in information systems and networks and the way in which they are provided and used.

- Create a general frame of reference that will help participants understand security issues and respect ethical values in the development and implementation of coherent policies, practices, measures and procedures for the security of information systems and networks.

- Promote co-operation and information sharing, as appropriate, among all participants in the development and implementation of security policies, practices, measures and procedures.

- Promote the consideration of security as an important objective among all participants involved in the development or implementation of standards.

1 Participants refer to governments, businesses, other organisations and individual users who develop, own, provide, manage and use information systems and networks.

2.33 The OECD adopted nine principles to enable participants to consider security in the design and use of all information systems and networks. The principles are complimentary and should be read as a whole. They concern participants at all levels, including policy and operational levels.

Principle 1 – awareness: Participants should be aware of the need for security of information systems and networks and what they can do to enhance security. Awareness of the risks and available safeguards is the first line of defence for the security of information systems and networks.

Principle 2 – responsibility: This principle states that all participants are responsible for the security of information systems and networks. Participants should be accountable in a manner appropriate to their individual roles.

Principle 3 – response: Participants should act in a timely and co-operative manner to prevent, detect and respond to security incidents. Participants should share information about threats and vulnerabilities, as appropriate, and implement procedures for rapid and effective co-operation to prevent, detect and respond to security incidents.

Principle 4 – ethics: This principle provides that participants should respect the legitimate interests of others. Participants need to recognise that their action or inaction may harm others.

Principle 5 – democracy: The security of information systems and networks should be compatible with the essential values of a democratic society.

Principle 6 – risk assessment: This principle requires the participants to conduct risk assessment.

Principle 7 – security design and implementation: Participants should incorporate security as an essential element of information systems and networks. Both technical and non-technical safeguards and solutions are required and should be proportionate to the value of the information on the organisation's systems and networks. Security should be a fundamental element of all products, services, systems and networks, and an integral part of system design and architecture.

Principle 8 – security management: Participants should adopt a comprehensive approach to security management. Security management should be based on risk assessment and should be dynamic, encompassing all levels of participants' activities and all aspects of their operations.

Principle 9 – reassessment: This principle requires the participants to review and reassess the security of information systems and networks and make appropriate modifications to security policies, practices, measures and procedures.

Industry initiatives

2.34 In the US, the Banking Industry Technology Secretariat (BITS), the Technology Group for the Financial Services Roundtable, was created in 1996 to foster the growth of electronic commerce for the benefit of financial institutions and their customers. Members of this non-profit industry consortium include the 100 largest integrated financial institutions in the US. Throughout its work, BITS seeks to sustain consumer confidence and trust by ensuring security, privacy and integrity of financial transactions. In April 2003, BITS published a paper *Fraud Prevention Strategies for Internet Banking*, which seeks to minimise the risks and make the Internet a safer, sounder, and more trusted environment for everyone. The paper focuses on the most frequent methods by which Internet banking fraud is perpetrated: identity theft; friendly fraud; and internal fraud.

2.35 According to this document, in order to mitigate the risks associated with online banking, financial institution policies and systematic controls should create an environment in which fraud can be prevented, detected, monitored and benchmarked against industry standards. These policies and controls should: require 'reasonable efforts' be made to ascertain the true identity of individual customers; have a 'know your customer' policy; and have adequate ongoing monitoring systems in place to identify suspicious transactions, and unusual wire activities. There are also various operational controls available to mitigate fraud risk. Combining technology and sound banking practices can help maintain the security and integrity of financial transactions. Because most online transactions occur in real time, validation and monitoring should, whenever possible, be conducted in real time, rather than overnight or through batch processing.

2.36 The paper recommended several suggestions for use in tandem or individually as part of a comprehensive Internet fraud-prevention strategy that includes a deterrent to identity theft. In the application process, the banks can take the following steps. Firstly, limit timeframes during which applications must be completed in order to deter fraud operators from keeping an application open while researching customer data. Secondly, provide a secure channel for receipt of the customer's data to assure that the information is not intercepted. Thirdly, create an audit trail or request, which may include capture of IP address and/or date/time information, to assist in authenticating the customer at a later date. The paper lists out what the banks should do to authenticate the applicant as well as after-applicant approval. Here, the goal is to strike an acceptable balance between convenience to the *bona fide* customer in opening a new account online and deterring the identity thief. The paper states that by using many, if not all, of the suggestions, financial institutions can better prevent fraud and detect identity thieves. Assuming that the customer has been properly verified and accepted at the opening of an account, enrolment for online banking consists of validating that the person attempting to enrol is in fact the same one who opened the original account. The BITS paper provides the details of the verifying process, which involved identification and authentication, post-authentication setup, operational controls after enrolment, and additional fraud prevention and detection.

2.37 According to the BITS, a financial institution's overall structure will determine how it addresses online banking risks. However, certain methods of addressing these risks can be applied to all institutions. Many risks associated with online banking can be found in multiple business units within the institution (call centres, consumer lending, etc). Therefore, in order to avoid duplication and identify gaps in risk coverage, responsibilities should be clearly defined. A policy should be developed that clearly establishes the rights, roles, responsibilities and authority of the group to manage the risks. At a minimum the policy should: establish the scope of the risks to be managed by the group, establish the authority for the group to develop the standards and guidelines necessary to execute the policy, determine reporting responsibilities and management authority for the group, and address interactions with other business units.

2.38 The BITS believes that losses associated with online banking should be tracked in accordance with the American Bankers' Association's standard reporting categories. Perhaps because of confusion over how to track Internet-related losses, many institutions find tracking the losses difficult. Some may also be hesitant to report Internet-related losses due to reputation risk concerns. The paper states[1]:

> 'However, organizations should understand that customers are generally aware that losses will occur, and that they should be accurately tracked and reported. Accurate tracking is critical to accurately assess the level of exposure an institution faces, and to determine whether losses are increasing or decreasing.'

It is recognised that consumer education is critical to preventing Internet fraud. Most individuals, according to the paper, will take action if they believe it will decrease their chances of being victimised by fraud, as long as the action does not significantly inconvenience them. By educating customers, financial institutions can decrease their fraud losses. The document provides some consumer tips to prevent fraud.

1   BITS Financial Services Roundtable, *Fraud Prevention Strategies for Internet Banking*, (April 2003) p 25.

Prudential regulation of Internet banking in selected jurisdictions

United States of America

2.39 According to William J. McDonough, President of the Federal Reserve Bank of New York, 'there are three elements of a modern supervision framework – effective bank level management, market discipline and official supervision'[1]. The OCC believes that the 'government must refrain from unnecessarily interfering with market forces propelling innovation forward'. As a result, the OCC has tried to focus the attention of bank regulators on areas where markets 'may fail to address the concerns raised by emerging retail banking and payment technologies'[2].

1   Cited in PricewaterhouseCoopers, *Protect and Survive – Regulation of E-Commerce in the Financial Services Industry*, p 33, available at http://www.pwcglobal.com/images/fs/bank/revolutionwhitepaper. pdf.
2   *Ibid.*

2.40 In October 1999, the OCC published a specialised booklet as part of its Comptroller's Handbook that deals solely with Internet banking. The *Comptroller*

Handbook on Internet Banking classifies banks' Internet service offerings as informational, communicative or transactional, based on their levels of functionality and interactivity. As the level of interactivity increases so does the risk of security breaches and the need for internal control systems. The Handbook discusses the risks facing banks offering Internet services. It generally defines risk as the potential that events, either expected or unexpected, may have an adverse impact on the earnings or capital of a bank. The OCC advises that the nine categories associated with Internet banking activities are: credit, compliance, foreign exchange, interest rate, liquidity, price, reputation, transaction, and strategic. To minimise these risks, the OCC refers banks to the three-step risk management process mentioned in Bulletin 98–3, Technology Risk Management.

2.41 The OCC stresses the importance of internal controls in risk management processes. Internal control systems related to Internet banking services should be commensurate with the level of risk presented by the services. The required internal controls will depend on the objectives of the bank and the types of Internet services offered. The duty is on the bank management to determine the bank's goals and objectives with respect to its Internet banking offerings and then to establish a system of internal controls sufficient to ensure that the goals and objectives are met.

2.42 The Handbook also addresses the decision of whether banks should offer in-house or outsourced Internet banking services. The decision is for the bank to decide depending upon several factors. If an outside vendor handles the service, the bank is still responsible for monitoring the security, reliability and general performance of the service vendor. The bank should enter into a formal service agreement with the vendor that clearly establishes all of the rights and responsibilities of the parties.

2.43 The OCC discusses several issues relating to consumer and business confidence in Internet banking. It emphasises that public confidence is essential to the success of Internet banking. Therefore banks must employ policies, procedures and technology directed at easing consumer apprehension. Specifically, banks need to address consumer concerns including: security, authentication, trust, non-repudiation, privacy, and availability.

2.44 As mentioned earlier, the OCC has also issued Bulletin 98–3, *Technology Risk Management Guidance for Bankers and Examiners*, intended to provide guidance to national banks concerning how they should identify, measure, monitor and control the risks associated with the use of technology. This Bulletin addresses two main issues. First, it outlines the primary risks related to the use of technology by banks. Second, it describes a risk management process designed to minimise these risks.

2.45 According to the OCC, a bank that is implementing new technology should, 'engage in a rigorous analytic process' to identify and quantify technology-related risks. To the extent possible, a bank should establish controls to manage risk exposure. With this goal in mind, the OCC proposes a technology-related risk management process. The three-step process requires a bank to: (1) plan for its use of technology; (2) decide how it will implement the technology; and (3) measure and monitor its risk-taking.

2.46   The first element of the risk management process is planning. According to the OCC, effective planning includes: (1) involving the board of directors and senior management in decision-making throughout the planning process; (2) gathering and analysing relevant information regarding new and existing technologies; and (3) assessing needs and reviewing relevant options.

2.47   The second step concerns the implementation of new technology. Proper implementation includes bank use of appropriate internal controls such as clear and measurable goals, and the allocation of specific responsibilities to specific personnel. Other proper implementation principles include having policies and procedures to manage risk related to the bank's use of technology, to ensure that key employees and vendors have the expertise and training to handle new technology, to thoroughly test new technology systems and products; and having contingency plans designed to reduce bank vulnerability to system failures, unauthorised intrusions, and other problems.

2.48   The third step in the risk management process requires the bank to ensure that its measurement and monitoring efforts effectively identify ways to manage risk exposure. The OCC stated that it would review a bank's technology-related risks together with other risks in order to determine the bank's overall risk profile within the context of the OCC's 'supervisory by risk' framework. The OCC would also evaluate the bank's auditing and quality assurance programmes to determine whether the institution's measurement and monitoring policies are sufficient.

2.49   In the area of privacy, the OCC has issued Advisory Letter 99–6, *Guidance to National Banks on Web Site Privacy Statements*, which provides national banks and examining personnel with examples of effective practices for informing consumers about bank privacy policies. The three components of these practices are: clear disclosure about the handling of customer information; consistent policies concerning private customer information; and mechanisms to enhance compliance with bank privacy policies. Effective disclosure consists of two elements, disclosing the proper information and choosing an effective mechanism to make the disclosure. Banks also need internal guidelines for implementing those policies.

2.50   The Federal Deposit Insurance Corporation (FDIC) in August 1998 issued a notice to encourage banks to develop voluntary privacy guidelines. The FDIC identified three primary concerns by consumers: (1) how personal information is collected; (2) how the entity collecting the information uses it, particularly for purposes not specified in the original transaction; and (3) whether personal information is transferred to third parties and how they will use it. The FDIC articulates several fundamental elements of a successful privacy policy. Foremost on this list is the need for banks to provide their customers with notice of the banks' information collection practices. This notice should include the identity of the party collecting the consumer data, how the information will be collected, why the information is being collected, how the information will be used, and how the consumer may limit disclosure of the information.

Singapore

2.51 On 19 July 2000, the Monetary Authority of Singapore (MAS) issued its *Policy Statement on Internet Banking* wherein it disclosed its approach to the licensing, regulation and supervision of Internet banking in Singapore. The MAS's Managing Director is of the view that prudent regulation should include protecting the interests of market participants in the presence of information asymmetry between providers and consumers, safeguarding the integrity and credibility of the financial market, and protecting the economy from the ramification of financial systematic failures.

2.52 Two broad business models have emerged in Internet banking: first, Internet banking within existing banks, either as an additional channel for their traditional core services or in the form of a specialised division. Second, stand-alone entities, such as Internet-only banks (IOBs), owned either by existing banks or by new players entering the banking industry.

2.53 The existing policy of the MAS allows all banks licensed in Singapore to use the Internet to provide their banking services. MAS in its Policy Statement stated that it would maintain a broad and flexible prudential framework to allow for continued innovation in technology and new business models, as well as the licensing of new players.

2.54 The MAS stated that the types of risk inherent in Internet banking, whether offered within existing banks or in standalone entities such as IOBs, do not fundamentally differ from those in traditional banking. As the current framework for prudential regulation and supervision already provides flexibility for innovation in new business models, the MAS will require a new framework to facilitate innovations in Internet banking or to mitigate its risks. However, as certain types of risks will be accentuated in Internet banking, banks will have to stress the different aspects of risk management, and the focus of MAS's supervision will match this.

2.55 In this respect, the MAS will take a risk-focused supervisory approach, tailored to individual banks' circumstances and strategies rather than a 'one-size-fits-all' regulation. Depending on the overall risk profile of the individual bank, the MAS may in specific cases require the bank to take additional prudential measures to mitigate these risks.

2.56 It is the responsibility of the bank management to have in place, on an ongoing basis, clear strategies and processes to manage the risks of Internet banking operations. The MAS will require public disclosure of such undertaking, as part of its requirements for all the banks to enhance disclosure of their risk management systems.

2.57 The MAS requires the management of the banks to pay special attention to the security, technology-related, liquidity and operational risks which may be accentuated in their Internet banking operations. With regard to security and technology-related risks, banks are required to:

- implement appropriate workflow, authentication, and processes and control procedures surrounding physical and system access;

- develop, test, implement and maintain disaster recovery and business contingency plans;

- appoint an independent third party specialist to access its security and operations; and

- communicate clearly to customers their policies with regard to the rights and responsibilities of the bank and customer on all matters to do with online transactions, in particular issues arising from beaches and errors in security, systems and related procedures.

2.58 In the MAS's view, banks, especially IOBs, should establish robust liquidity contingency plans, and appropriate asset-liability management systems due to the potential for more volatile transactions as international experience suggests that Internet banking customers tend to be more price sensitive, and hence more likely to move their deposits from one bank to another. This tendency is accentuated by the convenience of conducting Internet transactions. Technology failures that disrupt or impair services may also trigger abnormal transactions by customers.

2.59 Banks may also face greater operational risks if they extensively outsource processing operations in Internet banking. Banks would, therefore, be well advised to manage such outsourcing carefully. In particular, they should maintain comprehensive audit trails of such operations, and provide the MAS with unrestricted access to such information, as in traditional banking.

2.60 The MAS also noted that IBOs may face higher business risks arising from the new business model. Accordingly, IOBs must be conscious of maintaining and continually updating a detailed system of performance measurement to manage the higher risks. For example, efforts to build market share through pricing strategies and advertising must be tested against robust market assumptions.

2.61 If Singapore-incorporated banks choose to engage in Internet banking within the bank, no additional license will be required. The MAS will take into account the following factors in assessing an application for a new banking license by a Singapore-incorporated banking subsidiary or a branch of a foreign bank:

- track record, reputation and financial soundness of the applicant and its parent institution/major shareholders;

- strength of home country supervision, and the willingness and ability of the home supervisor to co-operate with the MAS;

- whether the applicant has a well-developed strategy in banking or financial services, supported by business plans which include a detailed assessment of the continued economic viability of the business; and

- whether the applicant has sound risk management systems and processes, including the management of security, technology-related and liquidity risks, and adequate procedures to meet 'know-your-customer' requirements.

2.62 Should a Singapore-incorporated bank choose to establish a banking subsidiary to pursue new business models such as IOBs in alliances with joint-venture partners, the MAS will require the Singapore-incorporated bank to have control over the venture as follows:

- The Singapore-incorporated parent must maintain more than 50% shareholding in the subsidiary bank. Subsequently, after the subsidiary has become well established and demonstrated its viability, the MAS is prepared to consider allowing the Singapore-incorporated parent's shareholding to fall to 50% or below. However, in such cases, the Singapore-incorporated parent bank must retain the largest shareholding and effective management control of the venture.

- The Chairman of the subsidiary bank must be appointed by the Singapore-incorporated parent. This is in addition to the requirements under the MAS Notice 622 to banks regarding the nomination of committees and the appointment of directors and chief executives of Singapore-incorporated banks.

- The Singapore-incorporated parent bank, and any alliance partners involved, must furnish Letters of Undertaking ('LUs') pledging their support of the new subsidiary bank. For the joint-venture partner, the LU must be provided by a party acceptable to the MAS. This strong party could be the partner itself, or one or more of its parents or associated companies.

2.63 The MAS will also assess the suitability of the joint-venture partners, taking into account, among other things, their reputation, track record and financial soundness. The MAS's current admission framework for branches of foreign banks allows the admission of new or non-traditional players. Such banks may be owned by existing banks or by non-bank players who have ventured into the banking business. New or non-traditional foreign banks will have to meet the same entry requirements as traditional banks.

2.64 New banking players who lack a long enough track record will still be considered provided they have strong compensating factors in respect of the other criteria set out. However, in all cases, the MAS will require new players to be incorporated in jurisdictions with a strong regulatory environment, and to have a home supervisor able and willing to co-operate in the MAS's supervision of the bank. The MAS's Deputy Managing Director stated, 'we want to maintain prudent regulatory oversight so as to preserve public confidence in the financial system, while encouraging financial institutions to take full advantage of new technologies to improve efficiency and competitiveness'. The MAS will also require further disclosure by banks of their risk management systems, and expect them to inform customers of both the benefits and risks of new products and services.

2.65 In June 2003, the MAS published the *Internet Banking Technology Risks Management Guidelines* – statements of the best industry practices that institutions are encouraged to adopt. The objective of the Guidelines is to promote the adoption of sound processes in managing technology risks and the implementation of security practices. In terms of the status of the Guidelines, it is stated that[1]:

> 'MAS intends to incorporate these guidelines into supervisory expectations for the purpose of assessing the adequacy of technology risk controls and security measures adopted by financial institutions. Each institution can expect that MAS will take a keen interest as to how and what extent it has achieved compliance with these guidelines.'

[1] Monetary Authority of Singapore, *Internet Banking Technology Risk Management Guidelines* (June 2003) p 28.

2.66 According to the MAS, all banks providing Internet banking must establish a sound and robust risk management process that will enable them to identify, assess, measure and respond to technology risks in a proactive and effective manner. Therefore, the aim of the guideline is to require banks to adopt risk management principles and security practices which will assist them in: establishing a sound and robust technology risk management process; strengthening system availability, security and recovery capability; and deploying strong cryptography and key management practices to protect customer data[1]. A sound and robust risk management framework requires the board and management to be responsible and accountable for managing and controlling technology risks. This responsibility calls for banks to perform risk identification and assessment.

[1] Monetary Authority of Singapore, *Internet Banking Technology Risk Management Guidelines* (June 2003) p 2.

2.67 Risk issues relating to Internet banking should be assessed and resolved during the conceptualisation and developmental stages. Risk control procedures and security measures should be put in place prior to or at the implementation phase. A risk management framework, according to the Guidelines, would require the following actions to be taken: identify, classify and assess risks that are relevant to the bank's operation; develop a documented plan containing policies, practices and procedures that address and control these risks; implement and regularly test the plan; monitor risks and the effectiveness of the plan on an ongoing basis; and update the plan periodically to take account of changes in technology, legal development and business environment including external and internal threats to information security.

2.68 On security and control objectives, the MAS observed that the Internet is a global network that is intrinsically insecure. It is imperative that banks implement strong security measures that can adequately address and control the risks and security threats. Banks must provide the assurance that transactions performed over the Internet are adequately protected and authenticated. This would require a security policy to be established to enable the following objectives to be met: data confidentiality; system and data integrity; authentication and non-repudiation; system availability; and customer protection.

2.69 The Guidelines state that security principles and practices can limit the risk of external and internal threats against the security and integrity of Internet-based systems. Security practices usually involve combinations of hardware and software tools, administrative procedures and personnel management functions that contribute to building secure systems and operations. These security principles, practices and procedures are collectively known as the security policy and processes of an organisation. Relating to human resource management, the Guidelines insist that personnel involved in developing, maintaining and operating websites and systems should be adequately trained in security principles and practices. Three of the most basic internal security principles for protecting systems are: the never alone principle; the segregation of duties principle; and the access control principle. The MAS requires banks to conform to a long list of security practices (a to z) outlined in the Guidelines.

2.70 According to the Guidelines, it is vital that banks include in their incident response procedures a predetermined action plan to address public relations issues. Being able to maintain customer confidence throughout a crisis period or an emergency situation is of great importance to the reputation and soundness of the bank. Incident response, disaster recovery and business continuity preparations need to be regularly reviewed, updated and tested to ensure their effectiveness. On outsourcing management, it is incumbent upon the banks to ensure that their service providers are capable of delivering the level of performance and service reliability, capability and security needed in their Internet banking businesses. Importantly, the Guidelines made it clear that a bank's responsibilities and accountabilities are not diminished or relieved by outsourcing its operations to third parties or joint venture partners[1]. The Guidelines set out the rules regarding the management of outsourcing risks, monitoring outsourcing arrangements, and contingency and business continuity planning in case the current service providers are not able to continue operations or render the services required.

1 Monetary Authority of Singapore, *Internet Banking Technology Risk Management Guidelines* (June 2003) p 21.

2.71 The MAS requires the banks: to provide clear information to their customers about the risks and benefits of using Internet banking before they subscribe to the services; to inform customers of the rights, obligations and responsibilities of customers and the bank in a clear and precise manner; to make the terms and conditions of the Internet banking services available within the Internet banking application; to require a positive acknowledgement of the terms and conditions from the customers upon log-on or subscription to a particular service or product; to publish their customer privacy and security policy; to post on their websites information concerning customer dispute handling, reporting and resolution procedures; and to advise and explain to customers the security measures and reasonable precautions they should take when accessing their online accounts. Instead of insisting that the information be written in a simple language, the Guidelines states that information written in prolix legalese and technical terminology would cause legibility and comprehension difficulties for customers.

2.72 To raise security awareness, the MAS requires the banks to educate customers on the need to protect their personal identification numbers, passwords, personal details and other confidential data. PIN security instructions should be displayed prominently in the user log-on or PIN entry web page. The Guidelines outline a series of advice to be adopted by the banks to help customers construct robust PINs as well as adopt better security measures.

Hong Kong

2.73 The Hong Kong Monetary Authority (HKMA) has issued a number of general circulars on e-banking, focusing in particular on the need for security. Authorised institutions wishing to move into e-banking would need to:

- Demonstrate how they would restrict access to the system and its databases to sanctioned users.

- Authenticate the identity and authority of the parties concerned to ensure the enforceability of transactions.

- Maintain the confidentiality of information while it is in transit through the network.

- Ensure that the data has not been modified either accidentally or fraudulently.

The HKMA insists that such Internet security arrangements should provide an adequate audit trail. Authorised institutions must also draw up contingency plans to maintain the availability of services, particularly in the provision of time-sensitive information and processing value-bearing transactions. The HKMA requires that risk management systems and internal controls should be regularly reviewed and evaluated.

2.74 While banks do not need to seek formal approval from the HKMA to offer Internet banking services, they should discuss their plans with the HKMA in advance. This is to enable the HKMA to assess whether the institution's proposed Internet banking system is sound and the service provided through the Internet will have adequate security. The HKMA expects that the security aspects of the system will have been reviewed by qualified independent experts and that the risk management systems and internal controls will be reviewed and evaluated on a regular basis. The HKMA would also discuss with the bank on how the risks are shared between the bank and its customers. What is expected from the bank in terms of security? David Carse, the Deputy Chief Executive of the HKMA said[1]:

> 'Note that we are not looking for absolute security. This does not exist in either the electronic or physical world of banking. However, the level of security should be "fit for purpose", i.e. appropriate to the type of transactions to be conducted. The important thing is for the banks to undertake a rigorous analysis of what their security needs are in the context of the particular service that they are planning to offer.'

1 David Carse, 'The Regulatory Framework of E-Banking' a keynote speech at the Symposium on Applied R&D: Enhancing Global Competitiveness in the Next Millennium, 8 October 1999.

2.75 On 5 May 2000, the HKMA issued the *Guideline on Authorisation of Virtual Banks*. It sets out the principles which the Monetary Authority (MA) will take into account in deciding whether to authorise 'virtual banks' applying to conduct banking business in Hong Kong. The HKMA defined 'virtual banks' as a company, which delivers banking services primarily, if not entirely, through the Internet or other electronic delivery channels. It does not refer to existing licensed banks, which make use of the Internet or other electronic means as an alternative channel to deliver their products and services to customers. Nevertheless, HKMA stresses that some of the principles set out in the Guidelines, particularly those relating to the risk management of electronic banking activities, will also be relevant to such banks. Under the General principles, the HKMA outlines the following:

- The MA will not object to the establishment of virtual banks in Hong Kong provided that they can satisfy the same prudential criteria that apply to conventional banks.

- A virtual bank wishing to carry out banking business in Hong Kong must maintain a physical presence in that country.

- A virtual bank must maintain a level of security appropriate to the type of business it intends to carry out.

- A virtual bank must analyse the nature of the particular types of risk which it is exposed to and put in place appropriate policies, procedures and controls to deal with these risks.

- A virtual bank must be able to present a business plan, which strikes an appropriate balance between the desire to build market share and the need to earn a reasonable return on assets and equity.

- Virtual banks may outsource their computer operations to a third party service provider provided that the principles in the MA's guidelines on outsourcing are complied with.

The Guideline states that the terms and conditions should be *fair* and *balanced* to both the bank and its customers. Customers must be made aware of their responsibilities to maintain security in the use of virtual banking services and their potential liability if they do not. In particular, the terms and conditions should highlight how any losses from security breaches, systems failure or human error will be apportioned between the bank and its customers. In this regard, the MA's view is that unless a customer acts fraudulently or with gross negligence, such as failing to properly safeguard his password, he should not be responsible for any direct loss suffered by him as a result of unauthorised transactions conducted through his account.

2.76 Virtual banks should discuss their plans for outsourcing with the HKMA in advance. They should demonstrate that the principles in the HKMA's guidelines on outsourcing would be complied with. In particular, the HKMA must be satisfied that the computer operation outsourced remains subject to adequate security controls, that confidentiality of customer's information will not be compromised and that the requirements under the Personal Data (Privacy) Ordinance are complied with. The MA must have the right to carry out inspections of the security arrangements and other controls in place of the service provider or to obtain reports from a supervisory authority, external auditors and other experts. The HKMA must also be satisfied that his powers and duties under the Ordinance (in particular, s 52 relating to the power to take control of an institution) will not be hindered by the outsourcing arrangements.

2.77 The HKMA, in the principles applicable to locally incorporated virtual banks states that a locally incorporated virtual bank cannot be newly established other than through the conversion of an existing locally incorporated authorised institution. A locally incorporated virtual bank can only be established by one of the following two routes:

1   Upgrading an existing locally incorporated restricted licensed bank or deposit-taking company into a virtual bank.

2   Converting an existing locally incorporated bank into a virtual bank.

The Guideline requires that a locally incorporated virtual bank should be at least 50% owned by a well-established bank or other supervised financial institution of good standing in the financial community and with appropriate experience.

2.78 According to the HKMA, ownership of virtual banks is particularly important because they are usually new ventures which could be subject to higher risks in the initial years of operation and it is essential that there should be a strong parent to provide guidance and financial support. In this regard, the parent bank (or equivalent institution) should aim to provide additional capital and/or liquidity support when such a need arises. The HKMA would also expect the parent bank (or equivalent institution) to play an active role in overseeing the business and affairs of the virtual bank through its participation in the board of directors.

2.79 An overseas, incorporated, virtual bank, which wishes to establish itself in Hong Kong in branch form, must come from a country where there is an established regulatory framework for electronic banking. It must have total assets of more than US$16 billion. It will be subject to the 'three-building' condition in respect of its physical but not in respect of its cyber network. This means that the bank is not allowed to maintain offices in more than three buildings to which customers have access.

2.80   In this context, 'office' is defined to include any Automated Teller Machine or similar terminal device, which provides facilities to customers or others. The MA's view is that personal computers, mobile telephones or similar electronic devices 'maintained' by the customers themselves would not fall within the definition of office. Therefore, the three-building condition would not prevent an overseas-incorporated virtual bank from developing a cyber network in Hong Kong.

2.81   In 2001, the HKMA issued the *Supervisory Policy Manual Concerning the Regulation of Advertising Material for Deposits Issued over the Internet*, which seeks to regulate the Internet deposit-taking advertising materials originated from non-authorised institutions (AIs) and targeted at members of the public in Hong Kong.

India

2.82   On 14 June 2001, the Reserve Bank of India (RBI) issued the Guidelines on Internet Banking to implement the recommendation of the Working Group on Internet Banking that had examined different aspects of Internet Banking. This group has focused on three major areas of Internet banking: (i) technology and security issues, (ii) legal issues and (iii) regulatory and supervisory issues.

2.83   The RBI, under the technology and security standards, lists, among other things, the following guidelines:

- Banks should designate a network and database administrator with clearly defined roles.

- Banks should have a security policy duly approved by the board of directors.

- At the minimum, banks should use the proxy server type of firewall so that there is no direct connection between the Internet and the bank's system.

- PKI (Public Key Infrastructure) is the most favoured technology for secure Internet banking services. However, as it is not yet commonly available, so banks should use the following alternative systems during the transition, until PKI is put in place:
  - (i) Usage of SSL (Secured Socket Layer), which ensures server authentication and use of client side certificates issued by the banks themselves using a Certificate Server.
  - (ii) The use of at least 128-bit SSL for securing browser to web server communications and, in addition, encryption of sensitive data likes passwords in transit within the enterprise itself.

- All applications of banks should have proper record-keeping facilities for legal purposes. It may be necessary to keep all received and sent messages both in encrypted and decrypted form.

- Security infrastructure should be properly tested before using the systems and applications for normal operations. Banks should upgrade the systems by installing patches released by developers to remove bugs and loopholes, and upgrade to newer versions, which give better security and control.

The Guidelines state that there is an obligation on the part of the banks not only to establish the identity but also to make enquiries about the integrity and reputation of the prospective customer. Therefore, even though requests for opening an account can be accepted over the Internet, accounts should be opened only after proper introduction and physical verification of the identity of the customer.

2.84 The Guidelines recognise that in Internet banking, the risk of banks not meeting the obligation to maintain secrecy and confidentiality of a customer's data is high. Therefore, banks should institute adequate risk control measures to manage such risks.

Banks should clearly notify customers of the timeframe and the circumstances in which any stop-payment instructions could be accepted. The Consumer Protection Act 1986 defines the rights of consumers in India and is applicable to banking services as well. Currently, the rights and liabilities of customers availing of Internet banking services are being determined by bilateral agreements between banks and customers. Considering the banking practice and rights enjoyed by customers in traditional banking, banks' liability to the customers on account of unauthorised transfer through hacking, and denial of service on account of technological failure etc, needs to be assessed and banks providing Internet banking should insure themselves against such risks.

2.85 With regard to regulatory and supervisory issues, the RBI's advice is:

- Only such banks which are licensed and supervised in India and have a physical presence in India will be permitted to offer Internet banking products to residents of India.

- The products should be restricted to account holders only and should not be offered in other jurisdictions.

- The services should only include local currency products.

- The 'in-out' scenario where customers in cross border jurisdictions are offered banking services by Indian banks (or branches of foreign banks in India) and the 'out-in' scenario where Indian residents are offered banking services by banks operating in cross-border jurisdictions are generally not permitted and this approach will apply to Internet banking also.

- Overseas branches of Indian banks will be permitted to offer Internet banking services to their overseas customers subject to their satisfying the home supervisor, in addition to the host supervisor.

2.86 The RBI also issued the following instructions:

- All banks, which propose to offer transactional services on the Internet, should obtain prior approval from RBI. A bank's application for such permission should indicate its business plan, analysis of costs and benefits, operational arrangements like technology adopted, business partners, third party service providers and systems, and control procedures the bank proposes to adopt for managing risks. The bank should also submit a security policy covering recommendations and a certificate from an independent auditor that the minimum requirements prescribed have been met.

- Banks will report to RBI every breach or failure of security systems and procedure and the latter, at its discretion, may decide to commission special audit/inspection of such banks.

- Banks should develop outsourcing guidelines to manage risks arising out of third party service providers, such as, disruption in service, defective services and personnel of service providers gaining intimate knowledge of banks' systems and misutilising the same, etc, effectively.

- Bilateral contracts between the payee and payee's bank, the participating banks and service provider, and the banks themselves will form the legal basis for such transactions. The rights and obligations of each party must be clearly defined and should be valid in a court of law.

- Banks must make mandatory disclosure of risks, responsibilities and liabilities of the customers in doing business through the Internet through a disclosure template. The banks should also provide their latest published financial results over the net.

- Hyperlinks from banks' websites often raise the issue of reputational risk. Such links should not mislead the customer into believing that banks sponsor any particular product or any business unrelated to banking. Hyperlinks from a banks' websites should be confined to only those portals which they have payment arrangements or sites of their subsidiaries or principals.

2.87 The board of directors should review, approve and monitor Internet banking technology related projects. The board of directors should ensure that appropriate policies and procedures are in place to manage Internet banking-related risks. Senior management is required to conduct periodic security risk assessments to identify internal and external threats. The security measures instituted should be current and properly implemented. Banks are required to establish specific reporting requirements for security breaches.

2.88 Concerning outsourcing, banks are allowed to outsource their Internet banking systems to *resident* service providers and software vendors. However, the following conditions must be satisfied: the processes to be outsourced must not take away the decision-making function of the bank and must not threaten strategic flexibility and process control of banks; the outsourcing arrangement should not impair the image, integrity and credibility of the bank; and there should be cost savings in outsourcing such functions.

CHAPTER THREE

Account Aggregation: Legal and Regulatory Issues

Introduction

3.1   The Internet is facilitating the introduction and creation of new financial products. Today, it is possible for people to easily access all their updated financial information in one single place at the click of a button. This service is called account aggregation, web aggregation or data aggregation. It is becoming increasingly prevalent in the US, emerging in Europe and Asia, although there are different views on the size of the consumers' uptake. Using a single password, a customer could link data from all his financial accounts at a single website, along with e-mail accounts, calendars, and news headlines.

3.2   Some are of the view that account aggregation is the next 'big thing' in Internet retail banking. At the moment, Internet banking is fragmented – customers have to access different websites for each of the various banking or other financial services they subscribe to. Each site has a separate password and provides a view of only one account at a time. Account aggregation, on the other hand, allows customers to view all their financial information, including bank balances and transaction data, on one website. Account aggregation therefore eliminates the 'hassle factor' in having to remember different passwords for different websites, together with time wasted in logging on and off each site[1].

1   See John Worthy and Nick Graham, 'Account Aggregation – Avoiding the Pitfalls in Internet Banking' in Denton Wilde Sapte Banking Briefings (January 2002) p 12.

3.3   Account aggregation services, however, generate a range of legal and regulatory issues. The Australian Securities & Investments Commission (ASIC) lists out a series of issues that need to be addressed which include: disclosure, liability for unauthorised transactions, liability for losses, privacy, security, consumer education, complaints and dispute resolution, cost of aggregation services, cross-jurisdiction issues and regulation of aggregators[1].

1   ASIC, *Account Aggregation in the Financial Services Sector*, Issues Paper (May 2001).

3.4   In the UK, the current debate is very much focused on the need to protect consumers not only from financial loss, but also from being caught in a tangle of legal complications[1]. Across the Atlantic, in the US, the concern has shifted from issues on unregulated non-financial institution aggregation providers and the problems that they might create for the issues of profitability of aggregation to how to obtain more robust data that can be used as a basis for transactions and analysis, and the risks of outsourcing and privacy[2]. As one analyst commented, 'account aggregation has established itself as one of the fastest growing and most controversial segments of the financial services market'[3].

1   See Jason Chuah, 'Internet Banking Services – Questioning the Current Response to Account Aggregation,' *Journal of International Banking Law*, (2002).
2   See Ann H. Spiotto, 'Financial Account Aggregation: The Liability Perspective,' Federal Reserve Bank of Chicago, Occasional Paper Series (April 2002) available at http://www.chcagofed.org/publications/publipolicystudies.
3   Zachary Tumin, 'Account Aggregation in Financial Services,' Vertical Innovation (May 2002) available at http://www.verticalinnovation.com/news/05–04-02.php.

What is account aggregation?

3.5   Aggregation is the process of collecting a consumer's information, reformatting it and presenting it to the customer. The information is usually collected from banks, credit card issuers, brokers, utility companies and insurance companies, but can also be collected from other websites, like airlines' frequent flyer sites, news and weather sources[1]. The Financial Services Authority (FSA) of the UK defined aggregation as a service that allows customers to view their online accounts and other information held with different institutions at a single location on the Internet. This means that customers can create a single page updated regularly, which contains all their financial account statements[2].

1   Andrea Lee Negroni and Patricia S. Mugavero, 'Opportunities in Account Aggregation,' *Mortgage Banking Magazine* (December 2000) p 1.
2   Financial Services Authority, *The FSA's Approach to the Regulation of E-commerce* (June 2001) p 69.

3.6   The current sixth edition of the Banking Code, which came into effect on 1 March 2003, refers to account aggregation as 'services that allow the customer to have details of some or all of the online accounts he or she holds with financial institutions, and other information, presented on one web page. These services may be operated by a financial institution (with whom the customer may already hold an account) or they may be provided by a website not owned by a financial institution'.

3.7   A Morgan Stanley Report indicates the essence of aggregation[1]:

'Web aggregation services are provided by companies – either financial institutions or third party Internet companies – [that consumers] can authorise to collect [their] account information so [they] can view it at a single place on the Internet. [The consumer gives] the web aggregator [his/her] account information (which may include checking, savings, insurance, mortgage, credit card, investment and brokerage accounts), [his/her] ID codes and passwords. In turn, the web aggregator collects [his/her] account information online and allows [him/her] to access it, with a password, on its website for "one stop" viewing.'

1 Cited in Ann H. Spiotto, 'Financial Account Aggregation: The Liability Perspective,' Federal Reserve Bank of Chicago, Occasional Paper Series (April 2002) available at http://www.chcagofed.org/publications/publipolicystudies.

3.8 Account aggregators use a type of software that retrieves specified information from accessible web pages. They collate and display that information onto a single page. Aggregators can be financial institutions, extensions of existing portals, or third-party Internet companies. In theory, there is no limit to the type of information that can be collated by account aggregation services. However, the information accessed generally falls into two types; information that can only be viewed by entering a user name and password and information that is publicly available[1]. To register with and use an aggregation service, a consumer needs to: nominate a username and password to access the services; nominate websites and the information to be collected from those websites, and enter the consumer's username and password for each website where the consumer must be identified before the personal information can be retrieved[2]. Once registered with an aggregation service, the consumer can access all of their nominated financial information, as well as other information, simply by logging onto the aggregation service. Thus, the consumer needs to remember only one username and password[3].

1 ASIC, *Account Aggregation in the Financial Services Sector*, Issues Paper (May 2001).
2 *Ibid.*
3 *Ibid.*

3.9 There are three varieties of account aggregation. First, direct feed or permissive aggregation, where the party offering the aggregation service may offer it directly from its own website on the Internet. The financial institutions develop a direct data feed that can be used to aggregate customers' data. It involves a contractual agreement between the institutions where the information originates and the aggregator. It requires the implementation of specific software. After confirming, via account numbers, passwords, and other identifiers, that an aggregator is authorised to collect information on behalf of an account holder, an institution transmits to the aggregator specific account information using a communication protocol that is standard to both parties. The aggregator then makes the information available to the account holder on the aggregator's own website[1]. The advantage is that the gathered data is likely to be more accurate than that collected by screen scraping. The disadvantage is that the service provider has to invest money and man hours in creating and maintaining the feed[2].

1 See Star Systems, Inc, *Web Aggregation: A Snapshot* (August 2000).
2 See David Emery, 'All About Account Aggregation', money.telegraph, 04/09/2001, available at http://portal.telegraph.co.uk/money/main.jhtml?xml=/money/2001/2001/09/03/cmagg.xml.

3.10 One of the main features of the direct feed aggregation route is that it is a co-operative process between financial institutions where data is voluntarily shared – similar to the model used for Automatic Teller Machines[1]. Unisys argues that this is generally agreed by most experts to be the ideal. It overcomes the shortfalls of the second method, and provides a robust platform for extended functionality and level of service[2].

1 Unisys, 'Account Aggregation: Consolidate or be Consolidated?' available at http:www.unisys.com/
   financial/insights/white_papers/papers.htm? insights ID=9385.
2 *Ibid.*

3.11 The second method is described as 'third party screen-scraping', 'web harvesting' or 'secured data mining'. Upon contracting with an aggregator for services, the customer reveals all the names and identifying information of all the accounts he/she wishes to have consolidated by the aggregator. This information, which includes user passwords, is then used by the aggregator, who 'scrapes' or 'harvests' the relevant data from the multiple database operated by the financial institution in which such data is held. Unlike direct feed, screen-scraping requires no agreement between the aggregator and the institutions whose information is being lifted: in fact, screen-scraping generally takes place without the 'scraped' institution's knowledge or permission[1]. Armed with all the necessary account numbers, ID.numbers and passwords, a screen-scraping aggregator becomes electronically indistinguishable from the actual account holder, and thereby is able to gain access to the same screen of data that would be displayed for the true account holder. The aggregator then copies and transmits the data back to its site for access by the account holder[2]. Simply put, the aggregator retrieves data at set times from the customer's bank's computers and maps the information directly into its own server. Customers who log on to the service get a total view of their accounts captured at the time of the last scraping, and real-time snapshots by hitting a 'refresh' button[3].

1 See Star Systems, Inc, *Web Aggregation: A Snapshot* (August 2000).
2 *Ibid.*
3 See David Emery, 'All About Account Aggregation', money.telegraph, 04/09/2001, available at
   http://portal.telegraph.co.uk/money/main.jhtml?xml=/money/2001/2001/09/03/cmagg.xml.

3.12 Screen-scraping is unauthorised, but the aggregator usually notifies the service provider before starting. The advantage of screen-scraping is that it costs the service provider nothing. A disadvantage is that an unco-operative service provider can try to disrupt the data gathering by, say, changing the data format, although this rarely occurs[1].

1 See David Emery, 'All About Account Aggregation', money.telegraph, 04/09/2001, available at
   http://portal.telegraph.co.uk/money/main.jhtml?xml=/money/2001/2001/09/03/cmagg.xml.

3.13 Thirdly, user-driven aggregation. The customer uses software supplied by a third party to screen-scrape, download and consolidate account data on a dedicated PC. The customer effectively becomes the aggregator and stores usernames, PINs and data in a Triple DES encrypted 'digital safe'[1]. The third party holds the encryption key and supplies the software but plays no active role in the data-gathering process. The advantage of user-driven aggregation is that it overcomes the legal pitfalls of screen-scraping. The system may also be more secure than screen-scraping and data feeding because aggregation is initiated from a dedicated computer. US-driven aggregation may also prove to be the only form of screen-scraping compatible with digital certificates if their use becomes widespread or mandatory[2].

Account aggregation: present and future

3.14   Alex Grinberg, the CEO of eWise was reported as saying that the year 2003 was going to be a significant year for a number of financial institutions in Australia rolling out aggregation services. He said that the market in Australia for Internet banking is robust and the company would expect, over the next 12–18 months, for all the main Australian banks to be offering account aggregation[1]. Just two years ago, ASIC reported that there has not been a large take-up of account aggregation services by Australian consumers. ASIC quoted one source who suggested that there were about 5,000 account aggregations in Australia[2].

1   Cited in Darryl Nelson, 'Account Aggregation Arrives,' Jan 2003, available at http://wirelessauthority.com.au/r/article/jsp/sid/12748
2   See ASIC, *Account Aggregation in the Financial Services Sector*, Issues Paper (May 2001).

3.15   The FSA's 2001 report considered account aggregation as a new service. A MORI Poll conducted for Egg in September 2002, found that 83% of online banking consumers in the UK want account aggregation. Alex Grinberg claims that the Egg account aggregation service, 'Egg Money Manager' introduced in April 2002 has reached more than 100,000 users in less than six months, and the user base is growing by 15–20,000 each month. Morgan Stanley Dean Witters estimated that there would be over 22 million users of account aggregation services in the US by the year 2003. Citibank reported that within three months of launching their aggregation site, myciticom in 2001, they had reached their one-year target of 50,000 users and currently register 2,000 new users daily in the US.

3.16   Some analysts agree that account aggregation is growing fast. Steve Mott, CEO of BetterBuyDesign, a well-known Internet consulting firm, states that account aggregation has the fastest financial institution and consumer adoption rate in the online financial services industry's 22-year history[1]. Many are optimistic that the future looks good. Anil Arora, the CEO of Yodlee, the leading account aggregation service provider, asserts that account aggregation – once perceived as a threat to financial institutions – will simplify the financial landscape. He was quoted as saying[2]: 'these days, a customer goes to a private banker or financial adviser with all his data. This becomes a "shoebox exercise" – with aggregation, this process can be automated'.

1   Cited Zachary Tumin, 'Account Aggregation in Financial Services,' Vertical Innovation (May 2002) available at http://www.verticalinnovation.com/news/05–04-02.php.
2   See *The Asian Banker*, 19 February 2003.

3.17   Forrester Research, Morgan Stanley, and Celent Communications all predict that the number of account aggregation users will grow to at least 80 million Americans by the end of 2005. A new report from Datamonitor predicts that 35 million European consumers will be using account aggregation services by 2005.

The report also found that 49% of online banking customers will be managing their affairs using an account aggregation service by 2005, when there will be 121 million online banking customers in Western Europe and the US.

3.18 In Australia, the ASIC reported that 'there are predictions that use will rapidly increase over the next few years'. In Asia, several banks have offered account aggregation services. Twelve banks out of 17 major banks in South Korea have already provided the service. Japan's largest bank, Bank of Tokyo-Mitsubishi, introduced an account aggregation service in 2003. The service called WealthPalette, allows selected customers of the bank to aggregate financial accounts located within the bank as well as those of its US affiliate, Union Bank of California. The service also collects information from three other major banks, nine brokerage companies, three credit card companies and two life insurance companies in Japan. WealthPalette has been introduced in a pilot programme with about 5,000 of the bank's best customers.

3.19 The remark of Richard Franchella and William Chettle of the Prudential Securities Inc., perhaps, provides a good description of the present and future of account aggregation worldwide:

> 'account aggregation may not seem like a big deal right now, but every year it will be used by more and more clients. And as it grows, it has the potential to completely transform the way the financial services industry does business'[1].

It is predicted that account aggregation in the future will become one of the basic financial services. Some, who are very optimistic, have said[2]:

> 'We believe that in the future financial aggregators will become one of the basic financial services. It is also likely to become as natural as having bank ATMs on every street corner. Aggregation services will become as versatile as a basic information service.'

1 Richard Franchella and William Chettle, 'Account Aggregation – The Ultimate' *Market Share* (September 2001).
2 Hiroshi Fujii, Taeko Okano, Stuart Madnick and Michael Siegel, 'E-Aggregation: The Present and Future of Online Financial Services in Asia-Pacific' MIT Sloan School of Management Working Paper (July 2002).

3.20 The sceptics of account aggregation are, perhaps, in the minority. For example, Geoffrey Smith in Business Week Online wrote, 'Account aggregation is turning out to be another web dream gone bust. Account aggregation is just online clutter whose disappearance would not be missed.' He argued that as a stand-alone product, account aggregation has little hope. The technology has a fatal flaw: even though you can access data, you cannot do anything with it, except look at it. He further stated that account aggregation is unreliable and often useless[1]. Like other new products, it can be argued that these are the teething pains and problems that account aggregation has to overcome. The reality is that account aggregation offers enormous potential for client service. It is suggested that for the potential to be fully realised, account aggregation must be robust, accurate, timely (real time or near real time) and provide a high degree of portfolio analysis while at the same time be easy to use for the do-it-yourself customer[2].

1 Geoffrey Smith, ' Account Aggregation Falls Apart,' *Business Week Online* (2 July 2002) available at http://www.businessweek.com/technology/content/jul2002/tc2002072_3404.htm
2 Richard Franchella and William Chettle, 'Account Aggregation – The Ultimate' *Market Share* (September 2001).

3.21 According to Unisys, nearly one-third of the current users of aggregation services obtain their services from Internet portals – Yahoo! Finance, America Online, MSN's Money Central and OnMoney.com. This may have serious implications for financial institutions. The Booz-Allen Hamilton survey in 2001, undertaken in the US, estimates that 34% of portal customers have significantly reduced, or stopped altogether, accessing the financial institution's website. Another finding of the survey is that account aggregation is a powerful strategic weapon, and financial institutions risk losing customer relations and sales opportunities when their customers aggregate elsewhere. A study conducted in October 2002 by Oliver Wyman & Co. found that aggregation resulted in a 6% rise in customer retention. The study also found that account aggregation could generate an extra $150 per-customer through cross-selling.

3.22 Considering these factors and given the attractiveness of account aggregation to customers, financial institutions must turn the potential threats into an opportunity, or face further disintermediation. There are three major threats to financial institutions that aggregators pose. First, the financial institution's presence to the consumer is significantly reduced. This represents an erosion of a financial institution's online brand name. Second, the financial institution no longer has control over the user's experience on their websites and losses the potential benefits of cross-selling other financial products and services to the customer. Finally, the possibility for security breaches increases[1].

1 Speer & Associates, Inc., 'Strategic Commentary' S&A (December 2000) Vol 12, No 9.

3.23 In this environment, according to Booz-Allen & Hamilton, financial institutions need to be the aggregation site. As an officer from the US Office of the Comptroller of the Currency has noted[1]:

'... Banks could lose important opportunities and face the risk of being relegated to mere data providers if they do not make account aggregation available to customers who are in the market for such services. Put starkly, the choice for banking organizations may be to aggregate, or be aggregated.'

1 Julie L Williams, 1st Senior Deputy Comptroller and Chief Counsel, Office of the Comptroller of the Currency, 'The Impact of Account Aggregation on the Financial Services Industry' Speech to the American Banker's 2nd Account Aggregation conference (23 April 2001).

3.24 Financial institutions initially viewed aggregators as a threat to their operations and tried to block data aggregation activity, even suing aggregators to prevent screen-scraping, citing concerns about security and liability. In less than a year, the antagonism has mellowed to competition and in some cases, co-operation.

Citigroup's MyCiti aggregation site uses Yodlee technology, for example[1]. As of late 2001, there were over 100 financial institutions and a few web portals offering account aggregation services in the US.

1   Andrea Lee Negroni and Patricia S. Mugavero, 'Opportunities in Account Aggregation,' *Mortgage Banking Magazine* (December 2000) p 1.

3.25   Some argue that the future trend will be the existence of more Universal Financial Aggregators (UFA)[1] and Global Financial Aggregators (GFA)[2]. They argue that UFA and GFA would play an important role for the success of online banking[3]. The UFA and GFA hold the key to future success in online universal and global banking. The prediction is that the need for financial aggregation services will increase as Internet-based applications simplify financial transactions[4].

1   UFA is defined as a financial aggregator that collects information on multiple financial products and services.
2   GFA is an aggregator that collects data from sites in multiple countries.
3   Hiroshi Fujii, Taeko Okano, Stuart Madnick and Michael Siegel, 'E-Aggregation: The Present and Future of Online Financial Services in Asia-Pacific' MIT Sloan School of Management Working Paper (July 2002).
4   *Ibid.*

3.26   On the same issue of the future trend of account aggregation, Star Systems, Inc. sees three important developments. First, more and more types of accounts are being aggregated. Second, web aggregation products and technology are evolving rapidly towards enabling consumers to conduct a full range of financial transactions online, in real time, which include money transfer among accounts and to third parties. A third trend involves the software currently under development that will, with customers' permission, continually evaluate their aggregated account information and – based on their financial goals and risk tolerance – automatically reallocate assets as needed to maximise value and return-optimisation[1].

1   See Star Systems, Inc., *Web Aggregation: A Snapshot* (August 2000).

The legal and regulatory issues

3.27   Comparing screen-scraping and data feed approaches, Unisys states:

> 'at present, screen-scraping is very much viewed as a necessary evil until permissive aggregation (direct feed) becomes a standard. Permissive aggregation is generally agreed by most experts to be the ideal. It overcomes the shortfall of the screen-scraping process.'[1]

The direct-feed model is 'contractually controlled' and establishes a relationship of agency between the financial institution and the aggregator. Thus, it is able to overcome the problem of lack of authorisation, which is prevalent in the screen-scraping model. In this connection, it might be said that the direct-feed model is an excellent example of how technology has very adequately accommodated the law's demands[2]. The FSA states that although the direct-feed model is likely to become increasingly common over the course of this year and next, currently it is screen-scraping which is mainly used within the industry.

1 Unisys, 'Account Aggregation: Consolidate or be Consolidated?' available at http:www.unisys.com/ financial/insights/white_papers/papers.htm? insights ID=9385.
2 Jason Chuah, 'Internet Banking Services – Questioning the Current Response to Account Aggregation' (2002) JIBL.

3.28 It is rare for an online activity to raise as many and as varied legal questions as those raised by the new phenomenon of account aggregation. The rapid growth of the aggregation industry has left the industry, law-makers, regulators and customers wondering what laws apply. Because it is based on relatively new technology, account aggregation does not fit comfortably within some of the existing regulatory schemes. A number of issues are not specifically addressed in the current legal, regulatory and policy regimes.

Breach of contract

3.29 The first issue is whether the aggregators, by asking consumers to disclose their passwords, are guilty of wrongfully inducing a breach of contract between the consumers and their financial institutions. On the part of the consumers, giving their passwords and providing other information and signing up to an aggregation service, may amount to breaching the terms and conditions of their online accounts. The FSA states:

'The terms and conditions of many online service providers, including banks, explicitly specify that customers should not divulge their password, or other private security information, to third parties. By signing up to an aggregator service and breaching the terms and conditions of their other online accounts, customers may be left liable for any future errors or fraud on those accounts, no matter how they occurred.'

3.30 The ASIC is firmly of the view that financial institutions should be clearly informing their customers, and in particular their online customers, what their views are on the use of account aggregation services generally and, more specifically, their views about disclosure of PINs to aggregators. When providing such disclosure to customers, the financial institutions should also make clear whether their views vary at all depending upon whom the provider is or the technology used. Where financial institutions believe that disclosure of PIN to an aggregator is a breach of the EFT Code's security requirements they should not only inform consumers of this fact but also of the potential consequences of undertaking such a breach[1].

1 See a presentation by Delia Rickard, Deputy Executive Director, Consumer Protection, ASIC, 'Protecting Account Aggregation Consumers' to the 11 September 2001 Conference on Account Aggregation.

3.31 According to the ASIC, its website survey shows that there are three different approaches by the financial institutions. First, they say nothing about their attitudes on account aggregation; second, they advise, in effect, that consumers use aggregation services at their own risk; and third, they tell their customers that disclosure of PINs to approved aggregators is permitted.

Computer crime

3.32 When an aggregator scrapes the site of a financial institution to obtain details of a customer's account, the aggregator accesses both software and data on the scraped site's computer system. In many countries, the computer crime legislations do call the unlawful access to programmes or data an offence. In the UK, knowingly accessing any programme or data on another person's computer without his/her permission is a criminal offence under s 1 of the Computer Misuse Act 1990. The elements of the offence are, first, 'knowingly accessing a programme or data', and second, that this is done 'without authorisation'. This is intended to catch hackers or others who try to gain unauthorised access to computer systems. However, it could, inadvertently, catch screen-scraping which operates without the 'authorisation' of the target website. An aggregator could argue that access was undertaken as agent for the customer, and was therefore authorised. However, given that the online account provider's terms are likely to prohibit this, there is a risk that account aggregation could fall within this section.

3.33 The computer crime legislations of other jurisdictions have similar offences. In Australia, s 309 of the Crimes Act creates offences of intentionally obtaining access to data stored in a computer 'without authority or lawful excuse'. Under the US Computer Fraud and Abuse Act (CFAA), it is an offence 'to knowingly access a computer without authorization or in excess of authorization in order to obtain information contained in a financial record of a financial institution or in a consumer file'.

3.34 Consequently, an aggregator who extracts information from an account provider's website without the express consent of the customer could be liable under these provisions. To avoid committing a criminal offence, an aggregator may obtain the permission of the financial institution to provide an aggregation service. Alternatively, for the aggregator to escape liability, it may rely upon the consumer's permission. The FSA argues that where the customer's authority to access the data is personal to the customer and he/she is required not to divulge his password to anyone else, the question arises how anyone other than the operator of the computer, which is being scraped, can provide authorisation for a programme to be accessed on their computer system. The FSA's view is that any financial institution contemplating the provision of an aggregation service must seek expert legal advice as to whether their business model would breach criminal law.

3.35 Under the US CFAA, the elements of the offence are, first, intentionally accessing a computer without authorisation, or exceeding authorised access, and second, obtaining information either derived from any record held by a financial institution pertaining to a customer's relationship with the financial institution, or from any protected computer (a computer exclusively for the use of a financial institution or any computer used in interstate or foreign commerce or communication), or intentionally accessing a protected computer without authorisation, and causing damage as a result.

3.36 Interestingly, the CFAA also provides for a civil cause of action by any person suffering loss by reason of a violation of the Act, arising from impairment to the integrity or availability of data, a system or information, injunctive relief or other equitable remedies. Consumers are provided with PINs to access online services with the intent that they will use those PINs to use the online services. As indicated above, one question that arises is whether the PIN, once issued, is a blanket authority for the consumer to access (and authorise others to access) their account information, or whether the provider may prescribe terms and conditions limiting the purposes for which it may be used and the parties who may use it[1]. In that regard, the recent case of *America Online Inc. v LCGM Inc*[2]. suggests that a breach of the terms of use for an online service is sufficient basis for a finding of unauthorised access for the purposes of the CFAA.

1   Available at http://www.dentonwildesapte.com/PDF/TransMIT_EBusiness_Feb2002.pdf
2   46 F Supp 2d 244 (ED Va 1998).

Allocation of liability

3.37 One of the most important issues associated with the use of account aggregation services is the allocation of liability for losses caused by unauthorised transactions. Unauthorised transactions can occur in a number of different ways: system malfunction, employee or agent fraud, disclosure of password to a third party, and hacker attack. There is currently no regulation or other document that governs liability and other relationships between financial institutions, aggregators and consumers. In allocating liability between a consumer and aggregator, the normal laws of contract will apply, as there are no regulatory or self-regulatory rules that apply. In practice, this means that aggregators are generally free to set the terms and conditions for liability. At present, in Australia, according to the ASIC[1]:

> 'Of the services available in Australia today we run the gamut from those attempting to deny all liability on the aggregator's part for anything other than undisclosed statutory warranties, to those who accept a capped liability in certain circumstances to those who accept unlimited liability in limited circumstances.'

1   Delia Rickard, Deputy Executive Director, Consumer Protection, ASIC, 'Protecting Account Aggregation Consumers' to the 11 September 2001 Conference on Account Aggregation.

3.38 In Australia, with respect to the relationship between consumers and financial institutions, the rules on the apportionment of liability are provided for in the EFT Code, which are generally incorporated into the financial institution's terms and conditions. Clause 5.6 of the EFT Code provides that an account holder may be liable for an unauthorised transaction where the user's password has been disclosed. Clause 5.7 clarifies this provision, to specifically exclude circumstances where the disclosure by the user was either expressly authorised by the relevant financial institution, or where the institution 'expressly or impliedly promotes, endorses or authorises the use' of the aggregation service. The ASIC states that an examination of the current rules between aggregators and consumers, and between financial institutions and consumers shows that, where there is disclosure to a third party, and unless the circumstances in clause 5.7 of the EFT Code apply, consumers will be most likely to bear liability for losses caused by any unauthorised transactions.

3.39 The ASIC believes that there is a need for a debate on the appropriate allocation of liability in the range of circumstances where things can go wrong. According to the ASIC, disclaiming all liability in circumstances where employee fraud results in unauthorised transactions or attempting to cap liability for such employee fraud is not a fair allocation of liability. The ASIC argues that the following principles, based on a situation where fault is not clear, would provide a useful starting point for any debate:

- liability should be allocated to the party or parties that can reduce the incidence of losses at the lowest cost;

- liability should be allocated to the party or parties best able to spread the losses, and

- liability allocation rules should be simple, clear and decisive, so as to minimise the costs of administering them (and consumer confusion).

3.40 In the UK, the latest edition of the Banking Code contains a provision on liability. Section 12.11 states 'if you use an account aggregation service you may be liable for any fraud or mistakes that happen on your accounts as a result'. The *Guidance for Subscribers* issued by the Code sponsors does not offer any guidance on how to interpret this new provision of the new version of the Code. The preface of the Code states that subscribers remain free to interpret the Code. The Guidance represents a general interpretation of the Code to be used in determining the industry standard. Since there is no guidance, perhaps, as mentioned in the preface, 'common sense should be used in interpreting the Code'.

3.41 In the US, there have been some debates over whether the Electronic Fund Transfer Act (EFTA) and Regulation E, enacted in 1978, specifically designed to protect consumers during the emergence of ATM transactions, can be applied to account aggregators. The OCC states, 'Currently Regulation E, which implements the EFTA, does not specifically address the responsibilities of aggregators. In the absence of guidance, bank management should be conservative when interpreting possible Regulation E compliance obligations in connection with aggregation services'.

3.42 The underlying problem relates to the definition of financial institution. Regulation E defined a financial institution to include a bank, savings association, credit union, or any other person that directly or indirectly holds an account belonging to a customer, or that *issues an access device* and agrees with a consumer to provide electronic fund transfer services. An access device means a card, code or other means of access to a consumer's account.

3.43 Aggregators that also provide electronic fund transfer services could come within the current coverage of Regulation E in two ways. If the aggregator is a bank, and holds consumer accounts in the bank, the aggregator is covered by Regulation E when it agrees with the consumer to provide electronic fund transfer services to or from the account[1]. Aggregator banks that do not hold the consumer's account could also fall within the coverage of Regulation E. An aggregator bank may be covered if it issues a card, PIN, or other access device to the consumer and agrees to provide electronic fund transfer services with respect to accounts at other institutions. If the aggregator bank does not have an agreement with these other institutions concerning the electronic fund transfer services, a special set of rules under Regulation E for service providers will apply[2].

1   OCC Bulletin, *Bank-Provided Account Aggregation Services* (28 February 2001).
2   *Ibid.*

3.44 Banks and aggregation service providers should consider the possibility that providing customers with an automatic log-in feature to conduct electronic fund transfers on other entities' websites could trigger the application of Regulation E. The automatic log-in feature allows customers to click a hyperlink and thereby cause the usernames and passwords stored at the aggregator to be used to log onto other websites. Banks that provide this feature might be considered to offer, in essence, an access device for electronic fund transfer services[1]. The OCC has this to say on the allocation of liability[2]:

'Banks that provide their customers with usernames and passwords for electronic banking should be aware of possible exposure to liability under Regulation E. The potential exposure arises when their customer shares those usernames and passwords with an aggregator. If an attacker then steals the usernames and passwords from the aggregator and performs unauthorized transactions, *it is unclear* under the current regulation which party would bear responsibility for an authorized transfer.'

1   OCC Bulletin, *Bank-Provided Account Aggregation Services* (28 February 2001).
2   *Ibid.*

3.45 Banking industry associations had apparently urged the Federal Reserve Bank (FRB) to consider aggregators as 'financial institutions' and subject them to Regulation E. The associations raised concerns that, if aggregators were not subject to Regulation E, banks would be liable if unauthorised transactions took place using the aggregation service. They also argued that consumers should be entitled to the same protection when they initiated a transaction through an aggregator site, as when they initiated a transaction directly through their financial institution[1].

1   ASIC, *Account Aggregation in the Financial Services Sector,* Issues Paper (May 2001).

3.46 Under Regulation E, consumers are not liable at all for carelessness with their PIN or password. Instead they are liable for losses caused by delays in reporting lost or stolen cards, or failing to report unauthorised transactions appearing on a periodic statement. This means that regulatory choice as to who should be liable for unauthorised transactions is between the aggregator and the financial institution. In contrast, in Australia, as mentioned before, the choice will be between the aggregator, the financial institution and the customer. The customer can be held liable if he has contributed to the loss by disclosing his password[1].

1 ASIC, *Account Aggregation in the Financial Services Sector*, Issues Paper (May 2001).

3.47 Regulation E limits consumer liability for unauthorised transactions to the lesser of $50 or the actual amount transferred prior to the time the customer notifies the financial institution within two days of learning of theft or loss of the device. If the customer fails to notify the institution in a timely manner the consumer's liability may not exceed $500.

3.48 Financial aggregation activity occurs in a grey area, and while protecting consumers is a prime consideration of regulators, there are concerns with the ramifications of over-regulating and interference too early. Following the request for comments, in August 2001, the FRB received comments in connection with a more general review of banking regulation governing the online delivery of financial services. A number of respondents indicated that, generally, they did not want the FRB to take action in anticipation of a need but rather that the FRB should wait until a real need for change is shown. Significantly, some argued that premature regulation might unintentionally deter private sector providers from pioneering more creative and efficient solutions potentially beneficial to consumers. In the US, an analyst argues[1]:

> 'It seems too early in the development of aggregation services for any regulatory or legislative action to be appropriate or necessary. It appears prudent to let the business develop before considering action to allocate liability given (1) the absence of any significant dollar losses clearly tied to aggregation services and (2) the current relatively small number of consumers using aggregation. While theoretical problem areas have been identified, reports of actual financial losses as a result of aggregation have not risen to the public consciousness or to the problem level – in fact, it is possible that so far they are virtually non-existent.'

1 Ann H. Spiotto, 'Financial Account Aggregation: The Liability Perspective,' Federal Reserve Bank of Chicago, Occasional Paper Series (April 2002) available at http://www.chcagofed.org/publications/publipolicystudies.

Protection of customers' data

3.49 Another important area concerns the protection of customers' data. The successful resolution of issues surrounding security and privacy of customer information will be essential to widespread customer acceptance of account aggregation. Yet, the essence of aggregation – a concentration of non-public customer financial information from various sources at one source – increases the magnitude of privacy issues that may arise, and the consequences if something goes wrong. Given the extent of the information held, lapses in security, or breaches in privacy of customers' aggregated financial information, could be devastating[1]. The ASIC outlines a series of the key privacy issues for consumers using account aggregation services:

- Is there a clear and obvious privacy statement?

- What personal and account information is collected and/or stored by the aggregator?

- Who has access to personal and account information (including passwords, usernames, balances and type of account)?

- How will personal and account information be used by the aggregator?

- Will personal and account information be used for cross-selling by the aggregator or a third party?

- If so, will an opt-in or an opt-out system be used for consumers who do not want their information used in this way?

- Will the aggregator sell or otherwise disclose personal and account information to a related business or a third party, with or without consumer consent?

- Does the privacy statement address the security risks of transmitting personal information over the Internet?

- What happens to personal and account information if a consumer chooses to discontinue using the service?

- Will the privacy statement continue to have effect if the aggregation service goes into liquidation?

1   Julie L Williams, 1st Senior Deputy Comptroller and Chief Counsel, Office of the Comptroller of the Currency, 'The Impact of Aggregation on the Financial Industry' before the American Banker's 2nd Account Aggregation Conference (23 April 2001).

3.50   In Australia and the UK, the Privacy (Private Sector) Amendment Act 2000 and the Data Protection Act 1998, respectively, will be applied to account aggregators and the services provided. The Office of the Federal Privacy Commissioner of Australia has advised that, in its view, aggregators will be subject to the provisions of that Act, and will have to comply with the National Privacy Principles. Similarly, under the UK Data Protection Act, the aggregators will be considered as data controllers, will be subject to the Act and are required to observe the data protection principles.

3.51   In the US, the Gramm-Leach-Bliley Act 1999 (GLBA) sets out the procedures that financial institutions must follow to protect consumer privacy. Under the GLBA, there is certainty that aggregators are included within the definition of a financial institution. The FTC in its explanation on 24 May 2000, rules that the definition of a financial institution includes an Internet company that compiles, or aggregates, an individual's online accounts, at that company's website, as a service to the individual, who then may access all of their account information through that

Internet site. The GLBA requires disclosure of policies and practices regarding disclosure of financial information, prohibits disclosure to an unaffiliated third party unless consumers are provided with an option to opt-out, and requires the establishment of safeguards to protect the security and integrity of financial information.

3.52 Before a financial institution can share information with non-affiliated parties, the institution must disclose the practice to the consumer and give him/her an opportunity to opt-out. The opt-out option must be well explained. The OCC states that beyond legal requirements, banks are strongly encouraged to proceed carefully before disclosing consumer information acquired in connection with aggregation services for any purposes other than providing the aggregation services sought by the customer.

3.53 The OCC does provide some guidance. A bank that provides aggregation services should ensure that its privacy policy accurately reflects the categories of information that it collects and discloses in its aggregator role. These may differ from the type of information provided on its own banking products or services that the bank collects and discloses with respect to customers. Given that a bank which offers aggregation services may have access to a customer's entire financial portfolio; the bank may need separate notices for its aggregation customers in order to permit these customers to make an informed decision about the bank's privacy policies and practices[1]. The OCC states, 'Given that a bank's success in providing aggregation services depends in large part on maintaining a high level of trust by its customers, any disclosure of information to third parties that undermines that trust would not be consistent with safe and sound banking practices'[2].

1　OCC Bulletin, *Bank-Provided Account Aggregation Services* (28 February 2001).
2　*Ibid.*

Database protection

3.54 An aggregator obtains its data from hundreds of thousands of information sources, each containing factual data such as product prices or daily balances. In legal terms these sources have been called collections of information and databases interchangeably. These databases often take substantial efforts to be created and maintained. Therefore database owners have great incentives to protect their investment[1].

1　Hongwei Zhu, Stuart E Madnick and Michael D Siegel, 'The Interplay of Web Aggregation and Regulation,' Massachusetts Institute of Technology, Working Paper Series, November 2002.

3.55 The EU Database Directive 1996 (Directive) created new rights protecting commercial databases. This Directive recognises the need for protecting the investment of database owners by granting them a *sui generis* (of its own kind) right. Article 7(1) of the Directive provides that member states shall provide for a right for the maker of a database. It must be shown that there has been qualitatively and/or quantitatively a substantial investment in either the obtaining, verification or presentation of the contents. Database is defined as a collection of independent works, data or other materials arranged in a systematic or methodical way and individually accessible by electronic or other means. Also, this Directive, in art 3, gives copyright protection to the selection and arrangement of the content of the database.

3.56 The Directive has been implemented in the UK by the Copyright and Rights in Databases Regulations 1997 (Regulations). The maker of a database is defined in reg 14 as the person who takes the initiative in obtaining, verifying or presenting the contents of a database and assumes the risk of investing in the obtaining, verification or presentation. This definition introduces the possibility of more than one maker, as one person may initiate the obtaining, verifying or presenting whereas another may assume the risk of the investment. The Regulations created a *sui generis* right using different terminology – database right. Regulation 13 provides that *sui generis* protection, described as 'database right', is conferred if a substantial investment has been made in obtaining, verifying or presenting the contents of the database. Thus, there are two conditions to be satisfied for database right to subsist, first, the matter involves database, and second, 'substantial investment' has been made in obtaining, verifying or presenting the contents of the database.

3.57 How do you determine whether the investment put in has been substantial? Some clues are there in the Directive and the Regulation. Recital 40 of the Directive provides that the object of the *sui generis* is to ensure protection of *any* investment in obtaining, verifying or presenting the contents of a database. Article 7 of the Directive goes on to make it clear that the investment must be substantial, and this is to be measured either on a quantitative or a qualitative basis, or by a combination of both qualitative and quantitative measures. This approach is repeated in the definition of 'substantial' in the Regulations. In addition, the Regulations provide that the investment includes any investment, whether of financial, human or technical resources.

3.58 Under reg 16, infringements of database right can occur if a person, without the consent of the owner of the right, extracts or re-utilises *all* or a *substantial* part of the contents of the database. The restricted acts are the extraction or re-utilisation of all or a substantial part of the contents of the database. 'Extraction' is defined in reg 12(1) as the permanent temporary transfer of the contents of a database to another medium by any means or in any form. 'Re-utilisation' means making the contents of a database available to the public by any means. The repeated and systematic extraction or re-utilisation of *insubstantial* parts of the contents of a database may amount to the extraction or re-utilisation of a substantial part of those contents.

3.59 It can be argued that the removal of information from a website by an account aggregator might breach the database right of the database creator. There is no conclusive authority to suggest that the database right will protect a database that stores customers' details and account transactions. The question is whether there is enough effort in the creation of the database and in keeping the database up-to-date[1]. It can also be argued that the withdrawal of the information from a database relating to one customer is not substantial because the details of one customer are extremely minor compared to the number of customers held on the database in question. The database creators, however, could rely on the argument that repeated extraction of a number of different customers' details on a regular basis would amount to a substantial extraction from the database.

1   See Emily Wiewiorka, 'Account Aggregation' (2001–02) Comps & Law 12(5) 27.

3.60   Article 11(3) of the EU Directive provides that 'foreign' databases are eligible for protection afforded by the *sui generis* right only if the Council concludes an agreement extending this form of protection for specified countries outside the EU. In other words, the basis for the protection of foreign databases is reciprocity rather than the normal rule governing copyright of 'national treatment'.

3.61   Under the US Copyright Act 1976, it is the 'originality', not the effort, that is protected. In the landmark case of *Rural Telephone Service Co. v Fiest Publications Inc*[1], the Supreme Court refused to extend copyright protection to white pages of a telephone directory on the ground that such factual compilations lack the requisite medium of originality to qualify for copyright protection. The Court held that a minimum level of originality or creativity used in the selection and arrangements of facts was necessary to obtain database copyright protection; mere 'sweat of the brow' was insufficient.

1   499 US 340, (1991), see also *Montgomery County Association of Realtors Inc v Realty Photo Master* DMD, 1995 and *Warren Publishing Inc. v Microdos Data Corp* 11th Cir 1995.

3.62   Following *Feist*, Levenue noted the paradoxical impact of the effect of the judgment, '… The US stands at the forefront in the development of computer technology, representing the world leader in the database market. Nevertheless, the US currently recognises no intellectual property protection for the content of databases such as a database right'. He believed that the chances were good that such a change would be forthcoming[1].

1   Lavenue, LM, 'Database Rights and Technical Data Rights: The Expansion of Intellectual Property for the Protection of Databases' (1997) 38 Santa Clara L. Rev 1.

3.63   There were attempts in the US to adopt the EU approach of granting the *sui generis* right based on the effort of obtaining and creating the database, sweat of the brow doctrine. Four bills have been introduced since 1996 and all failed to pass. The Committee on the Judiciary's Report 1999 (Collections of Information Antipiracy Bill) explained the reasons for the legislative initiative in the US:

'In Europe, a six-year legislative process culminated in the issuance of a European Union Directive on Legal Protection of Databases in 1996. Among other things, the Directive creates a new *sui generis* form of protection of database to supplement copyright. However, it denies this new protection to collections of information originating in the United States or other countries unless the other country offers 'comparable' protection to collections originating in the European Union. When fully implemented, the European Directive could place US firms at an enormous competitive disadvantage throughout the entire European market.'

3.64 According to Mark Davison, the history of the proposals for American legislation concerning *sui generis* protection for databases or collection of information is a complicated one. He wrote, '... the history of the American legislative proposals, the starting point for proposals in the US was the finishing point for the EU and the finishing point, at least at the time of writing, is very similar to the EU's starting point'[1]. The US is still to pass any *sui generis* legislation and protection of databases is derived from principally copyright, misappropriation and contract. Nevertheless, the various bills that have been proposed demonstrate the considerable range of possible models of protection[2]. He argues that from the perspective of database owners, there are three significant problems posed by the American copyright law. First, many databases derive their value to users from their comprehensiveness. Often, it is lack of selection that makes a database most useful, as selection implies excluding some material from a large field of information. Second, the information within many databases does not lend itself to any innovative means of arranging it. Third, is the defence of fair use. The emphasis upon not protecting factual material within copyright works (and discounting the impact on a potential market of taking that factual material) dilutes the protection provided, even if the database does meet the necessary standard of originality[3].

1 Mark J. Davison, *The Legal Protection of Databases* (2003) p 213.
2 *Ibid.*
3 *Ibid*, at p 171.

3.65 Some argue that the 'sweat of the brow' doctrine does not and should not apply to the data extracted by aggregators. They argue that product databases compiled by online vendors are to inform buyers and facilitate sales of products, not the data. The compilation effort should be counted as part of product-selling activities. The re-use of this data by aggregators is also to inform buyers and facilitates sales of products, which would enhance rather than corrode the initial investment of data compilation. For financial account aggregation, some of the data is the result of user-initiated transactions (e.g. deposit, withdrawal, and fund transfer), which is effectively entered by the user, not the financial institution. In addition, aggregation is performed with authorisation from the user who arguably owns the information about him/herself[1]. They are of the opinion that the function of the database is very much like a security box in a bank (i.e., users put their personal information in a secure system), accessible by an authorised entity on the user's behalf. In both cases the effort of compiling databases does not constitute the core business of aggregatees[2].

1 Hongwei Zhu, Stuart E. Madnick and Michael D. Siegel, 'The Interplay of Web Aggregation and Regulation,' Massachusetts Institute of Technology, Working Paper Series, November 2002.
2 *Ibid.*

3.66 They also argue that even if some of the aggregated data falls under the 'sweat of the brow' doctrine, the impact of legislation on information aggregation will be limited for the following reasons. First, the EU Database Directive has been regarded as the strictest regulation for database protection. Even so, aggregators have been successfully operating in most EU countries. Second, it is hard to identify from where factual information originally comes, once aggregated. Given the large quantity of factual information and the huge number of sources involved in aggregation, enforcement is a big problem. Third, database creators often gain incredible reach to potential customers through aggregators. The interweaving interests in sharing and re-using information reduce, if not completely eliminate, the need for litigation. Fourth, even database creators need to rely on other sources to compile their database. In this sense, there are few 'pure' database creators. Finally, consumers and providers want and need web aggregation; the compelling benefits should not be overlooked. Regulations should be structured to exploit the new opportunities of web aggregation[1].

1 Hongwei Zhu, Stuart E. Madnick and Michael D. Siegel, 'The Interplay of Web Aggregation and Regulation,' Massachusetts Institute of Technology, Working Paper Series, November 2002.

Trespass to chattels

3.67 Database owners have used the theory of trespass to chattels, the common law action in tort, as the cause of action against the aggregators. It may be possible to characterise the scraping or harvesting utilised by an account aggregation service as a trespass. There are two determining factors for the cause of action in this area of law. First, the exact means by which the aggregation software accesses the scraped database and second, whether the court will consider the concept of trespass relevant and applicable to cyberspace and activity in an online environment[1].

1 See Adrian Lawrence, 'Account Aggregation: A New Technological Challenge to the Law' Cyberspace Law Resources, available at http://www.austlii.edu.au/au/other/CyberLRes/2001/19/.

3.68 The scraped institution must prove an intentional and direct interference with its exclusive possessive rights, and a deprivation of those rights by the aggregator. The factors to be considered include: whether the scraped data can be considered 'goods'; whether the accessing of information by the aggregation constitutes a direct interference; and whether it is necessary to establish damage or physical contact with the good before tort is actionable[1]. There have been some decided cases in the US on this issue. In *eBay Inc v Bidder's Edge, Inc*[2], the court granted eBay a preliminary injunction based on the trespass claim. The Court held that the claim of trespass required eBay to show that Bidder's Edge had intentionally interfered with its possessory interest in the computer system, causing loss to eBay. The Court found that eBay could show that it was deprived of the ability to use the portion of its own property for its own purposes. It was held that a company's bandwidth and server capacity can constitute 'property'. It was also held that the Internet scraper's activities amounted to an 'appropriation of the company's personal property'.

1 See Adrian Lawrence, 'Account Aggregation: A New Technological Challenge to the Law' Cyberspace Law Resources, available at http://www.austlii.edu.au/au/other/CyberLRes/2001/19/.
2 100 F Supp 2d 1058 (2000).

3.69 The Court issued a preliminary injunction to stop Bidder's Edge from aggregating information from eBay based on the reasoning that significant harm could be caused if such activities are allowed. The judge ruled that the software robots 'consume the processing and storage resources of a system, making that portion of the system's capacity unavailable to the system owner or other users. Consumption of sufficient system resources can overload the system such that it will malfunction or crash'. However, in a similar case the court rejected Ticketmaster's trespass claim against Tickets.com because 'it is hard to see how entering a publicly available website could be called a trespass, since all are invited to enter'.

3.70 Generally, legal experts have strongly opposed the application of trespass theory to the Internet[1]. With regard to account aggregation, it can be argued that the theory of trespass to chattels is unlikely to apply because very little interference with a financial institution or information provider's system is necessary to obtain the information. The specificity of the searches by the financial web aggregators and the terms of agreement under which the searches are often now being conducted would make the trespass to chattels claim untenable[2].

1   In a friend-of-the-court brief regarding the *eBay v Bidder's Edge* case, 28 law professors pointed out that it is inappropriate to substitute possible future harm for the actual harm required by the law of trespass to chattels. They concluded that the ruling threatens efficient information exchange on the Internet and the public interests demand a reversal in this case. The case was settled outside of court in early 2001.
2   Julia Alpert Gladstone, 'Data Mines and Battlefields: Looking at Financial Aggregators to Understand the Legal Boundaries and Ownership Rights in the Use of Personal Data' Journal of Computer & Information Law [2001], Vol xix, p 328, see also Hongwei Zhu, Stuart E. Madnick and Michael D. Siegel, 'The Interplay of Web Aggregation and Regulation,' Massachusetts Institute of Technology, Working Paper Series, November 2002.

Account aggregation: to regulate or not to regulate

3.71 The FSA does not regulate account aggregation, which is neither an 'authorisable activity' nor a financial promotion. The FSA states:

'The act of providing aggregation services is not an authorisable authority. Nor does it constitute communicating a financial promotion. Therefore, any firm (authorised or not) is free to provide aggregation services. If the FSA were to develop any standards or requirements for authorised firms relating to the aggregation services, non-authorised firms that offered this service, such as portal or infomediaries, would be free to ignore them'.

It admits that it has no powers to regulate account aggregation and states 'FSA is conscious that, as with any new and dynamic service, *the legal certainty may not always be possible*'. Philip Thorpe, FSA Managing Director, speaking at a conference in London on 15 May 2001, said[1]:

'We have been examining the issues raised by the development of aggregation services as part of a wider review of the risks presented by e-commerce in financial services. These services enable consumers to view any number of online accounts –

from bank accounts to reward schemes such as airmiles – in a single location on the web. Many types of firm, such as banks and Internet portals, could potentially provide an aggregation service and it is known that several firms are planning to launch services in the UK. We therefore feel it is important to set out the regulatory position now. The key message for consumers is that the FSA will have no powers to regulate the provision of account aggregation. This activity will fall outside the jurisdiction of the FSA and, as a result, we cannot guarantee you the protection of the regulatory system if something should go wrong. While we can see the attraction in using the services of an aggregator, it is important that you weigh up the risks involved too.'

1   See FSA Press Release – FSA/PN/057/2001, 'New Online Account Aggregation Service Will Not Be Regulated, Warns the FSA', available at http://www.fsa.gov.uk/pubs/press/2001/057.html

3.72   As already mentioned, the FSA has taken the view that the provision of account aggregation services is not a regulated activity as such – instead, it will be treated as an unregulated infomediary service. Of course, if the services are provided by the financial services institutions, they remain obliged to exercise 'appropriate levels of diligence' in introducing account aggregation, particularly in relation to untested legal issues. The FSA clarifies its approach to account aggregation in a number of important areas:

● that accessing data from a variety of sources and consolidating the information onto a single web page is not regulated under financial services legislation, although services an aggregator may choose to add to its site, for example providing investment advice, or arranging deals, may trigger an authorisation requirement;

● as with any new business activity, authorised firms planning to undertake account aggregation are expected to undertake appropriate levels of due diligence, in particular on the legal issues relating to certain methods of aggregation where the law has not been tested. Authorised firms should seek legal advice from an expert and reputable source and should not provide aggregation services if the advice received is that an aspect of their business model is more likely than not to be illegal, even if prosecution is believed to be unlikely; and

● a consumer who decides to use an aggregation service which asks the consumer to disclose his or her password, should check very carefully that he or she is not breaching an account provider's terms and conditions, and whether the level of security provided by his or her online bank or investment firm will be diminished by that use.

3.73   Unlike the FSA, the ASIC believes that it has an interest and the role to play in this area of account aggregation. The interest arises from the ASIC involvement in the EFT Code and its general consumer protection responsibilities in the financial sector. The ASIC states[1]:

'Although we may not have jurisdictional responsibility for aggregation services provided by organizations that are not financial institutions, the key driver for account aggregation services is the ability to aggregate information from financial institutions. In those circumstances, ASIC has a key role to play in facilitating discussion and encouraging the development of appropriate solutions.'

1   ASIC, *Account Aggregation in the Financial Services Sector*, Issues Paper (May 2001), p 49.

3.74   The ASIC asserts that appropriate rules of practice need to be developed, published and implemented by aggregators and financial institutions. These could be through an aggregators' module in the EFT Code, a separate aggregators' code or an ASIC guide on good practice. The ASIC even suggests that it is worth considering whether there is a need for regulation or legislation. In the meantime, the ASIC encourages aggregators to provide information to consumers on matters concerning privacy terms and conditions, liability and risks, security, charges, currency of information, applicable consumer protection regulations, availability of complaints and dispute resolution processes, identity of the aggregator and relationship between the aggregator and financial institutions. The financial institutions should also advise their customers of their attitudes to customer use of aggregation services.

3.75   As mentioned earlier, the US OCC has released the Bulletin on 28 February 2001, outlining risks for national banks in offering account aggregation services and the management controls needed to minimise the risks. The guidance is directed towards banks, and focuses specifically on minimising the risks for financial institutions, rather than the risks for consumers. However, it can be argued that compliance with the guidelines is likely to create a safer environment for consumers wishing to use account aggregation services.

3.76   The Bulletin discusses the risks related to bank-provided account aggregation services and suggests control mechanisms that banks should consider using if they offer aggregation services. The Bulletin states that the providers of account aggregation services are exposed to significant, strategic, reputation, transaction and compliance risks. It states that banks that provide account aggregation services should implement risk management control to: safeguard customer information; select and monitor vendors; comply with legal and regulatory requirements; and educate and disclose information to customers. The Bulletin also describes the need for appropriate security controls that involve, among other things, authentication and certification of bank customers, record-keeping that may need to be co-ordinated with other websites, and maintaining the security of usernames and passwords used to access websites of entities other than the bank. Some other key points are:

- Aggregation services may provide banks with an opportunity to expand and deepen their customer relationships by levering their position as trusted financial intermediaries.

- Aggregation business models and services are evolving, as are the underlying legal and operational structures. This evolution accentuates strategic, reputation, transaction, and compliance-related risks.

- Key controls involve security, compliance, vendor management, data-gathering and use, contracting, and customer education, disclosures, and service.

- Banks should implement risk management controls to safeguard customer information, to select and monitor vendors, to comply with legal and regulatory requirements, and to educate and disclose information to customers.

- Banks that provide aggregation services should establish procedures to monitor market and regulatory developments to keep pace with changing requirements.

3.77 The OCC has also issued a Bulletin to provide guidance to banks providing aggregation services and relying on third parties to provide the technology that supports the service. The Bulletin published on 26 February 2001, requires the banks to address the risks relating to outsourcing. Four essential elements are expected from the banks: (1) understanding the risks associated with an outsourcing arrangement, (2) exercising due diligence in selecting the service provider, (3) ensuring that written contracts address key risk factors associated with the activity, and (4) overseeing performance by the service provider. The US seems to adopt a hands-off approach on the regulation of account aggregation. Ann H. Spiotto argues[1]:

'Laws and regulations should not be added or revised until it has been demonstrated that the existing ones are not adequate to handle a new service. To the extent that theoretical problems are "solved" by new legislation/regulations before problems actually develop, the solutions may be irrelevant, unnecessary or produce unanticipated negative consequences.'

At this time, Spiotto argues that it appears sensible for banking regulators to: (1) allow the financial services industry to exercise its judgment in developing aggregation under the existing regulatory framework; (2) continue monitoring business practices and developments in connection with aggregation; and (3) take regulatory action only if the need is demonstrated.

1   See Ann H. Spiotto, 'Financial Account Aggregation: The Liability Perspective,' Federal Reserve Bank of Chicago, Occasional Paper Series (April 2002) available at http://www.chcagofed.org/publications/publipolicystudies.

Industry initiatives

3.78 The Banking Industry Technology Secretariat (BITS) is formed by the CEOs of the largest bank-holding institutions in the US. In April 2001, BITS published the *Voluntary Guidelines for Aggregation Services*. The Guidelines focus on the risks and liabilities attributed to the screen-scraping process, aimed at educating business and consumers about the risks and possible ways to mitigate against them. The

Guidelines address five specific issues of concern: security, privacy, business practices, customer education, and legal and regulatory implications.

3.79 On security, the Guidelines include suggestions for security requirements for aggregators in their collection and storage of customer information. Much of the value of the Voluntary Guidelines rests in the ability of financial institutions to use the guidelines to identify relevant issues for contract discussion. The BITS developed three sets of guidelines; first, security guidelines for 'trusted' aggregation services, second, guidelines for aggregation authentication and data-feed, and third, account aggregation data-feed standards. These guidelines provide a detailed set of security practices focusing on the collection and storage of customer information. They relate to technical aspects and are beyond the scope of this book. The BITS recognises that:

'The nature of the services, if not properly implemented and trusted, can pose security risks to the customers of the services, the institutions whose customer information is being aggregated (institutional account holders – IAHs), and the companies providing aggregation services (aggregation service providers -ASPs).'

3.80 With regard to privacy, the BITS has developed the *Aggregation Privacy and Information Use Guidelines* (APIUG). The goal of the APIUG is to provide voluntary principles that recognise the impact of new information functionality and a more complex supplier environment compared to traditional consumer financial services products. The APIUG are intended to be relevant to the aggregation services environment in the US. Two core concepts to incorporate in the protection of privacy require giving notice to participants of the information needed to make successful choices in interacting with the power of choice among a variety of options. The APIUG elaborate the ways to include the concepts of 'notice' and 'choice' and they provide the detail guidelines for the ASP and IAH.

3.81 The business practices guidelines focus on the key information that should be shared between ASPs and IAHs. The BITS will serve as the central point of contact for the effective collection and dissemination of information. The BITS undertake some responsibilities which include; maintaining the most current versions of the BITS Voluntary Guidelines for aggregators' services and distributing to companies; facilitating the distribution of information between aggregation companies and information providers; and creating a facility to provide web access to the Voluntary Guidelines and to share information about implementation of the guidelines.

3.82 The section on customer education of the Voluntary Guidelines provides guidance to financial institutions and financial aggregators on the appropriate disclosure to be provided to consumers. The BITS identified several issues and developed recommendations for educating end-users about the use of aggregation services. The recommendations apply to IAH, financial institutions and the ASP. The topics include aggregation relationship disclosure, PIN-sharing policies, end-user protection, customer service, data accuracy, disclosure distribution, privacy, marketing messages, security, service discontinuation, and the use of user data for development/test purposes. The guidelines are intended to enhance customer relationships and serve educational purposes. Participants are strongly encouraged to abide by the guidelines. The BITS, in the legal and regulatory issues section, identify and develop a list of applicable laws and regulations related to financial aggregation.

3.83 In the UK, on 19 December 2001, the Association for Payment Clearing Services (APACS) issued the *Best Practice Aggregation Guidelines* (to be referred to as 'the Guidelines'). The APACS states the aim of the Guidelines in this manner:

> 'As aggregation services are not subject to the protection of regulation by the FSA, a key aim in developing guidelines has been to protect consumers from irresponsible aggregators, and to maintain confidence in aggregation and e-banking systems generally.'

3.84 The Guidelines set out best practice to be followed by those providing aggregation services to customers and the providers of the customers' data. The APACS believes that the underlying principle behind the Guidelines is that aggregation should take place with the consent of all parties involved. Specifically, data providers need to provide their consent for data to be collected from their sites. The APACS recommends the adoption of the Guidelines by all parties involved in aggregation. However, the Guidelines are voluntary, and there is no obligation on APACS members or any other parties to adopt their use.

3.85 The Guidelines set out elements of best practice, which include matters concerning security, password practice, privacy, customer education and responsibilities, dealing with customer queries and the impact on data providers' systems. It states that there is a need to ensure that security is not compromised as a result of aggregation. The security practices of an aggregator and any associated destination sites should provide a level of security that is acceptable to each data provider whose customers use the service. The APACS in the Guidelines recommends that the parties involved in an aggregation service conform to the BITS Security Guidelines. It states that the BITS Security Guidelines are just as applicable to aggregation services in the UK as they are in the US. The APACS identified some areas where the BITS Guidelines are not consistent with best practice in the UK. In those areas, it is recommended that the more stringent UK practices be adopted.

3.86 According to the Guidelines, there is a responsibility to ensure the adoption of good password practices. If data providers amend terms and conditions to allow password disclosure to certain 'approved' destination sites, it must be made clear to the customer at which sites password disclosure is permissible and at which it is not. The staff of a destination site (or the staff of its agent) should never ask users to provide them with any part of their authentication material for their data providers' services. Nor should any staff be able to access such authentication material.

3.87 With respect to privacy, the Guidelines state that all parties have an obligation to abide by the relevant provisions of the Data Protection Act 1998. In particular, destination sites should provide their users with a clear and unambiguous statement on their privacy policy. It must be made clear to consumers what use will be made, by destination sites or a aggregator, of any personal data held. The user of the destination site must separately agree to such use of the data, rather than consent just being included in the overall terms and conditions for the service.

3.88 With regard to customer education and responsibilities, the Guidelines state that destination sites and data providers need to educate their customers about aggregation, pointing out the potential risks as well as the benefits. In particular, destination sites need to provide information about how up-to-date the presented information is (i.e. when it was collected or received from the data provider and to which time period it relates). If there are specific qualifications that apply to data from one source compared with another (for example, whether funds are cleared or not) these, where available, should be made clear at the destination site. Data providers and destination sites must ensure that their terms and conditions are consistent with the advice they give their customers. In particular, if a data provider permits their customers to use an aggregation service, the terms and conditions relating to password disclosure should allow such use. The destination sites need to provide a clear statement to consumers of their liability should things go wrong.

3.89 In dealing with customer queries, customers using an aggregation site need to be clear on who they should approach in the case of queries or problems. A contact telephone number should be displayed prominently on the destination site. To overcome any areas of possible consumer confusion, aggregators and destination sites must respond speedily to any requests from data providers to amend the way the data is presented.

3.90 Finally, the Guidelines require the destination sites and aggregators to be sensitive to the impact that aggregation will have on data providers' systems and must work with data providers to minimise the adverse effects. The destination sites and aggregators will need to agree with data providers the requirement for an audit trail which is important in handling customer queries.

CHAPTER FOUR

Legal and Regulatory Aspects of E-Money

The basic structure of e-money systems

4.1 Electronic money or e-money has been described as 'an electronic surrogate for coins and bank notes'[1]. Generally, the term e-money or e-cash refers to a variety of mechanisms that will facilitate payments at stores and on the Internet through computer-based communication technologies[2]. Currently, there is no formally adopted international terminology with respect to electronic money systems. Article 1(b) of the *Directive on the Taking up, the Pursuit and the Prudential Supervision of the Business of Electronic Money Institutions* (hereafter Electronic Money Institutions Directive) defines electronic money in the following terms: monetary value as represented by a claim on the issuer, which is:

(i)   stored on an electronic device;

(ii)   issued on receipt of funds of an amount not less in value than the monetary value issued;

(iii)   accepted as a means of payment by undertakings other than the issuer.

These criteria make it quite clear that electronic money is to be a substitute for physical cash or money. It is intended in this definition for the electronic money to bear all the characteristics of physical cash. It is significant for example to note that it must not be in an amount which is more in value than the funds actually received by the issuer. It should essentially be of the same value to physical cash, possibly minus any charges and fee payable. Additionally, there is to be general usage, that is to say, as cash it must be acceptable to undertakings or persons other than the issuer – electronic money circulated in a closed group controlled by the issuer (for example, electronic money issued by a theme park for use within the park itself) does not qualify as electronic cash for the purposes of the Directive[3]. Also, it must be stored on an electronic device.

1   The recitals to the Directive of the European Parliament and of the Council on the taking up, pursuit of and prudential supervision of the business of electronic money institutions.
2   Catherine Lee Wilson, 'Banking on the Net: Extending Bank Regulation to Electronic Money and Beyond' (1997) 30 Creighton L Rev 671, at 683–84.
3   See Jason Chuah, 'The New E.U. Directive to Regulate Electronic Money Institutions – A Critique of the E.U's Approach to Electronic Money', [2000] JIBL 181.

4.2   Many experts agree that due to the rapid rate of development and change currently occurring in these technologies, an efficient way to distinguish among the emerging systems is to focus on the issuing entity and whether the systems operate in an open or closed environment. In 1997, the Financial Action Task Force (FATF), an intergovernmental research body, in its report categorised e-money systems into four models:

- The merchant issuer model, in which the card issuer and seller of goods and services are the same.

- The bank issuer model for closed and open systems, in which the merchant and the card issuer are different parties, while transactions are cleared through traditional banking mechanisms.

- The non-bank issuer model, where users buy e-money from issuers using real money, spend the e-money at participating merchants, and the issuers subsequently redeem the cash from merchant.

- The peer-to-peer model, in which the bank or non-bank issues e-money, which is then transferable between users, with no interference by a financial institution except at the initial point of issuance and then the redemption, if ever, of the money by individuals or merchants.

4.3   In terms of form or technology, this new payment device can generally be divided into two classes: (1) electronic value stored on a card, or stored-value card, and (2) electronic value stored on a computer, which is normally referred to as electronic coins.

4.4   There are several different classifications of stored-value cards. First, a stored-value card may utilise either a magnetic stripe technology or an imbedded microchip to record value. A stored-value card using microchip technology may be referred to as a 'smart card' – not simply because it has the capacity to store significantly more information than a magnetic stripe but because it can perform calculations on this data as well. Second, a stored-value card may be reloadable or disposable. Third, a stored-value card may be part of a closed or an open system. In a closed system, the value on the card is designed to be used only for goods or services provided by the card issuer or within a limited institutional or geographic area such as a university campus. By contrast, in an open system, the geographic range of the product is broader and the issuer is not necessarily the provider of goods and services. Rather, the issuer may act solely as a third party provider of financial services – as an intermediary that facilitates the transaction between consumer and merchant by providing payment clearance through a stored-value system. Open systems may be further subdivided into single-issuer models versus multiple-issuer models[1].

1   See Jeffery A Abrahamson, 'The Digital Future of Money: A US Perspective,' [1997] JIBFL 417.

4.5   Mondex is an example of an open system, single-issuer model (whereby the card is issued and redeemed by the Mondex franchise) whereas Visa cash is an example of an open system, multiple-issuer model (whereby the card may be issued and redeemed by several institutions). Mondex is an electronic cash system based on a smart card that is able to accept, store and distribute money. In general, the Mondex model is a hybrid of the non-bank issuers and peer-to-peer models as designated by the FATF.

4.6 Based on a multi-step distribution process, the model starts with an entity called the 'originator', which issues and redeems Mondex value in the local currency to distributing member institutions ('members'). These members, in turn, will pay the originator for the issued 'value' and the originator will earn investment income and float on the amount paid by the member during the time period between receipt of payment and future settlement of the value. Members then sell the Mondex value to, and collect it from, users[1].

1   See Timothy H. Ehrlich, 'To Regulate or Not? Managing the Risks of E-Money and its Potential Application in Money Laundering Schemes', *Harvard Journal of Law & Technology*, Vol 11, No 3 (Summer 1998) p 843.

4.7 Mondex value can both be stored on a smart card and used in several different ways. For example, value can be loaded and reloaded from an Automatic Teller Machine ('ATM'), over the telephone or personal computer, or through a special floppy-based device called a 'wallet'. Regarding the use of Mondex value, the smart card allows holders to make purchases over the web; download cash from a bank, an ATM, or a network; and pay for merchandise in stores or vending machines. In sharp contrast to e-cash and CyberCash, however, the Mondex system also enables users to make card-to-card transfers using electronic wallets without any interaction or knowledge of a third party (e.g. banks, merchants). This is due to the fact that there is no centralised system for transactions in the Mondex model[1].

1   See Timothy H. Ehrlich, 'To Regulate or Not? Managing the Risks of E-Money and its Potential Application in Money Laundering Schemes', *Harvard Journal of Law & Technology*, Vol 11, No 3 (Summer 1998) p 843.

4.8 E-cash, developed by the Netherlands Company Digicash, is an example of a bank issuer model e-money and of a system of electronic value stored on a computer. In other words it is issued by the banks and utilises PCs to store value. In this system, instead of purchasing a stored-value card, the user purchases digital coins from a participating bank. A digital coin is a unique serial number that is associated with a specific amount or denomination of monetary value. These coins are encrypted, communicated electronically and stored on the user's computer until the user is ready to spend them.

4.9 When a user requests e-cash value, the participating bank will debit an account of the user on the bank's books and credit an e-cash liability account on the bank's book. To spend a coin, the user will transfer it via the Internet to a merchant, the user simply commands its computer to transfer the coins to the merchant's web page or bank account. The coin will then be sent to the issuer who performs online validation of the coin to assure that it is authentic and that it has not been previously spent. Importantly, this validation may be performed blindly – without the bank knowing who is verifying the coin. Likewise, when the coin is returned to the bank from the merchant, the consumer's identity is not revealed to the bank. This procedure is designed to assure the privacy of the spender[1].

1   Olivier Hance and Suzan Dionne Balz, *The New Virtual Money: Law & Practice* (1999).

4.10   Cybercash, developed by Cybercash Inc., is another example of a system of electronic value stored on a computer but one that operates on the non-bank issuer model. Under this system, a user can load coins either from a bank account or a credit card onto a CyberCash 'wallet' stored on a user's computer. When a user loads the wallet, funds are transferred from the user's bank account to an account in a federally insured bank maintained by CyberCash. CyberCash accounts for all of the user's funds in his/her wallet. Then when the Cybercash holder finds something he/she wants to buy over the computer network, they only need to click on the item on the screen to complete the transaction. With the click of the mouse, an almost instantaneous process occurs: the user's electronic wallet on the computer is activated; coins are collected from the wallet to update the user's balance; the coins are delivered by CyberCash to the merchant as payment; an the product is sent to the user, either electronically over the Internet (e.g. news services) or through the mail. Finally, all transaction information is passed through a central database maintained by CyberCash, but the files are not accessible to CyberCash unless the user unloads the files with the user's own private key[1].

1   Jane Kaufman Winn, 'Clash of the Titans: Regulating the Competition between Established and Emerging Electronic Payment Systems', Berkeley Technology Law Journal [1999], vol 14: 675.

4.11   Visa Cash was introduced in the US by three Visa member financial institutions – First Union, Nations Bank and Wachovia – in July 1996 at the Olympic games in Atlanta. Visa Cash is available in either disposable or reloadable form. The value collected by the merchants is cleared between participating banks using Visa's existing clearing system (Visanet) and the settlement arrangements currently in use for Visa credit card transactions. As of February 1997, approximately 15,000 terminals worldwide (comprising about 50 merchants) accepted Visa Cash, and approximately 3.7 million Visa Cash cards had been issued.

4.12   Electronic value can also be stored on personal computers and used for transactions on computer networks (or other communications networks). Whereas stored-value cards are intended to be used at the point of sale (typically where consumer and merchant meet face-to-face), value stored on personal computers may be transmitted over networks (i.e. used for transactions where the buyer is at a location remote from the seller and actual place of sale)[1].

1   Olivier Hance and Suzan Dionne Balz, at 421.

4.13   Visa and Mondex Systems are similar. However, a difference emerges in what consumers can do with the electronic value they have bought. In the case of the Visa cash, the consumer can use the electronic value to make payments for goods to participating merchants by inserting his or her card in the merchant's terminal. The terminal then deducts the relevant amount of value from the card and 'sends' the value to Visa for settlement. The consumer cannot transfer value to a person other than a participating merchant, unless he or she does so by handing over a pre-loaded smart card in its entirety to that person[1]. The Visa value that is collected by the merchants is cleared between participating banks using Visa's existing clearing system and through the settlement arrangements currently in use for Visa credit transactions. Consequently, unmonitored and unregulated peer-to-peer transfers are not allowed.

1   See Trystan C.G. Tether, 'Electronic Cash – The Regulatory Issues' [1997] JIBFL 203.

4.14 By contrast, Mondex card technology enables a consumer to transfer electronic value on his or her card to any other person with a Mondex card, whether that person is a merchant or another consumer. The transfer is effected simply by linking the two cards together, either physically or via the telephone system and, most importantly, without any need to involve the bank of either cardholder or the Mondex system generally[1].

1   See Trystan C.G. Tether, 'Electronic Cash – The Regulatory Issues'[1997] JIBFL 203.

The future of e-money

4.15 The magnitude of the benefits that these e-money products offer to consumers remains unclear due to their current lack of widespread adoption. In general, however, industry analysts agree that e-money systems, at their most basic level, stand ready to present users with all of the advantages of traditional currencies and much more. For example, all e-money products developed now and in the future will most likely offer consumers a 'store of value, a medium of exchange, a numeraire ... and convenience, just like traditional currencies and paper monies'[1]. Similarly, they create the potential for complete anonymity of the user, as wire transfers currently do to a certain extent. They also allow currency to be transferred almost instantaneously from point to point, and for bulky paper currencies to be replaced with intangible, easily manipulated electrons[2].

1   *Money Laundering via Smart Cards,* Report on Smart Cards (17 March 1997) cited in Timothy H. Ehrlich, 'To Regulate or Not? Managing the Risks of E-Money and its Potential Application in Money Laundering Schemes', *Harvard Journal of Law & Technology,* Vol 11, No 3 (Summer 1998) p 422.
2   *Ibid.*

4.16 In a recent study[1], the Group of Ten[2] suggested that e-money systems might also provide users with the additional benefits of a less expensive payment method, a faster and more convenient means of payment, and an increase in the variety of payment options[3]. Similarly, e-money might also present fewer risks for consumers than many extant forms of payment. The prepaid nature of e-money could result in a lower risk of refusal than in traditional exchanges, such as when a credit card is expired or deactivated or when a merchant is unable to make change for currency or refuses to accept a personal cheque. This feature might reduce the risk of a consumer being unable to complete a payment in the amount or at the time and location they desire despite having enough money in an account to cover the transaction[4].

1   Group of Ten Electronic Money: Consumer Protection, Law Enforcement, Supervisory and Cross Border Issues; Rep. of the Working Party on Electronic Money (15 April 1997).

2   The Group of Ten Working Party on electronic Money is comprised of representatives from finance Ministries, central banks and international organisations brought together under the auspices of the Group of Seven Heads of State and Government. They are Belgium, Canada, France, Germany, Italy, Japan, the Netherlands, Sweden, Switzerland, the UK and US.
3   *Money Laundering via Smart Cards,* Report on Smart Cards (17 March 1997) cited in Timothy H. Ehrlich, 'To Regulate or Not? Managing the Risks of E-Money and its Potential Application in Money Laundering Schemes', *Harvard Journal of Law & Technology,* Vol 11, No 3 (Summer 1998) p 422.
4   *Ibid;* see also Saul Miller, 'Payment in an On-line World', in Lillian Edwards and Charlotte Waelde (eds) *Law & the Internet: A Framework for Electronic Commerce* (2000) p 55, at pp 75–76.

4.17   One commentator states that the market for electronic payment services remains crowded with competing vendors and putative standard-setters, none of which have yet gained a commanding lead over the pack of aspirants[1]. Other commentators state that virtual money may seem like a step towards the creation of a global village, but consumers' spending habits vary greatly among different countries. Consumers in some countries prefer to use cash rather than electronic payments. In other countries, consumers may prefer the use of fiduciary money to the use of cash[2]. Jane Kaufman Winn further argues that new entrants in the market for electronic payment services may enjoy greater success outside mature markets such as the US than inside them. In Europe, for instance, consumers are less accustomed to using payment devices that include an element of float for consumers. As a result, acceptance of smart cards as a payment device has been much greater. The dismal failure to date in the US market of smart cards as a payment device demonstrates that US consumers are showing a greater degree of sophistication with regard to product features and a greater resistance to change, especially in light of the success of innovative new offerings in other areas of Internet electronic commerce. The greatest success for such new payment devices may ultimately come in markets in developing countries such as China, where there are virtually no alternative electronic payment technologies. In such markets, there may be no business case for rolling out older models of electronic payment systems where the basic infrastructure is still lacking and consumers may accept the most up-to-date technology available quite happily[3].

1   Jane Kaufman Winn, at p 700.
2   Olivier Hance and Suzan Dionne Balz, at p 60.
3   Jane Kaufman Winn, at p 700.

4.18   Emerging payment technologies that gain substantial market share in Europe, Japan or developing countries may be able to lever that market share to re-enter the US market on more favourable terms in the future. As US financial services markets become more integrated into global markets, it is unlikely that the flow of standards and products will always be from the US outward. In the near term, however, established services such as credit cards, debit cards and ATM machines that were perfected in the US and other developed countries, may continue to crowd out more technologically-sophisticated alternatives[1].

1   Jane Kaufman Winn, at p702.

The legal status of e-money and its effect on the money supply

4.19 In most countries the right to create legal tender is a right reserved by the law to the government of that country. In the US, the federal government's exclusive power to coin money was established constitutionally. The Stamp Payments Act of 1862 prohibits the issuance of certain kinds of obligations intended to circulate as money, by either banks or non-banks. In Canada, only the Bank of Canada is empowered to issue money intended for circulation in Canada. According to the Federal Currency and Exchange Act, only bills and coins thus issued can legally discharge a debt. In the UK legal tender is defined by statute and is essentially limited to UK coins and Bank of England notes[1].

1   Coinage Act 1971 as amended by s 1(3) of the Currency Act 1983 and s 1(2) of the Currency and Bank Notes Act 1954.

4.20 Electronic money does not constitute 'legal tender' because it is not a medium of exchange that is authorised, adopted or backed by the government. E-money is only backed by the issuer's promise to pay. E-money may, however, constitute 'money' because parties are free to make contracts based on a medium of exchange of their choosing[1].

1   The Oxford Dictionary definition of 'money' is 'current coin as medium of exchange, measure of value ... hence, anything serving the same purpose as a coin'; and 'money in reference to its purchasing power ... hence, possessions or property viewed as convertible into money.' The Dictionary of Finance defines 'money' as 'a means of facilitating exchange of goods and accumulation financial wealth, commonly recognisable as banknotes, coins, bank deposits; and a medium of exchange; a unit of value; a store of wealth.'

     The legal definition of 'money' contained in *Halsbury's Words & Phrases* is, 'the term "money" is commonly regarded as one which does not bear precise meaning in the eyes of the law. It depends on the *context* in which it is used (*Perrin v Morgan* [1943] AC 399). It can be a testator's personal property, and /or real property.'

4.21 In many electronic cash systems, electronic cash 'tokens' are issued in exchange for money. These tokens may then be sent to someone, who then becomes the owner of the sum of money represented by the tokens. The float account of the issuer, against which the tokens are issued, is a commercial liability, as opposed to a Central Bank liability, and thus the tokens do not constitute legal tender. These tokens are like any negotiable instrument drawn on a commercial bank. They represent a value exchanged, and the exchange is not final until the settlement at the Central Bank. They do not create value, this being the exclusive power of the Central Bank[1].

1   Olivier Hance and Suzan Dionne Balz, at p 344.

4.22 In the US, William J. McDonough, the President of the Federal Reserve Bank of New York, has stated:

'[G]overnment-issued money is often viewed as being very special, and creating an electronic analogue in the private sector raises a number of public policy issues largely because historically paper-based currency has been issued by central banks and deposit-based money either by central banks, in the form of bank reserve accounts, or by supervised depository institutions in the form of demand deposits or NOW accounts. This arrangement developed for basic reasons: (1) to address the need for a safe medium of exchange, and (2) to provide a mechanism for the central bank to implement monetary policy ...'[1]

1   Address before the BAI Conference on The National Conference Payments System of 8 October 1996, available at http://www.ny.frb.org/pihome/news/speeches/sp 961008.html.

4.23   These questions of control over monetary policy form part of the debate as to whether or not issuance of electronic cash should be restricted to banks. Representatives of the Federal Reserve, however, have suggested that electronic cash, whether issued by banks or non-banks, will not have a serious impact on its ability to control the money supply and monetary policy. For example, in a 1996 address, Governor Edward W. Kelly Jr. of the FRB said that if:

'... every resident of the United States held $150.00 US on a stored value card or electronic cash account, which I view as highly optimistic over a near-to-medium-term horizon, the total value outstanding would amount to less than $50 billion US, or only about 10% of the currency stock.' The Federal Reserve board has also stated that the policy issues raised by the potential impact of retail electronic payment and banking on monetary policy banking supervision, and the payment system, as well as on consumer privacy and industry competition, '... are the same as those in the 1970s by national EFT Commission ... Then as now, the potential impact on monetary policy of new electronic payment products has been greatly exaggerated. As with the use of the ACH, we would not expect that the expansion of electronic delivery of existing banking services will have appreciable effects on the money supply or the money markets ... [C]oncerns about loss of 'control' of the money supply are misdirected. In the last twenty years, major shifts caused by other financial innovations have led to some changes over time in the ways in which monetary policy is formulated, with the monetary aggregates now playing a lesser role. Moreover, financial innovation has not seriously undermined central banks' ability to implement policy, although adaptations have sometimes been called for'[1].

1   Address before the CyberPayments '96 Conference of 18 June 1996, Dallas Texas, available at http://www.bog.frb.fed.us/BOARDDOCS/SPEECHES/199606618.htm.

4.24   In Canada, where electronic cash really is in its very early stages (Mondex, Proton and VISA Cash are running pilot projects in several Canadian jurisdictions), the Bank of Canada has restrained itself to remarking that electronic money has the potential, over time, to affect the monetary aggregates by reducing the number of bank notes in circulation[1]. In Europe, the European Central Bank (ECB) published a report on electronic money in August 1998. The ECB is primarily concerned with issues of monetary policy, notably the need to preserve both price stability and the unit-of-account function of money. The report accentuates the risks of over issue stating that:

'... [I]f electronic money is issued through the conversion of the banknotes or sight deposits, it does not change the money supply and price stability is not endangered. If electronic money is issued on the basis of a credit mechanism, however, it could have an effect on money supply and price stability.'[2]

According to the report, '... the question of over issue of electronic money is also related to the question of whether electronic money could endanger the unit of account role as incorporated in central bank money.'[3]

1   Bank of Canada, Annual Report 1997.
2   European Central Bank, Report on Electronic Money 47 (Frankfurt an Main) August 1998.
3   Olivier Hance and Suzan Dionne Balz, at p 14.

Differing approaches: United States v European Union

4.25   In general, the US government has consistently refused to take a definitive stand on how e-money should be treated under American law. The federal government has chosen to follow a 'wait and see' approach regarding e-money. This inaction can be attributed to the federal government's general view that it is too early for the creation of regulation and to the widespread opinion that the technologies and Internet payment systems are 'still in their infancy'. Many experts and government officials, consequently, have concluded that e-money products should be allowed to develop in a competitive marketplace free of legal restrictions before any systematic attempt is made to regulate them.

4.26   The former US President, Bill Clinton, noted that the commercial and technological development of electronic payment systems is changing rapidly, making it hard to develop timely and appropriate policy. Reasoning that inflexible rules and regulations could harm the nascent industry, he advocated that electronic payment experiments be monitored on a case-by-case basis[1].

1   Kerry Lynn Macintosh, 'How to Encourage Global Electronic Commerce: The Case for Private Currencies on the Internet,' *Harvard Journal of Law & Technology*, Vol II, No 3 (Summer 1998) pp 733–735–736.

4.27   Statements of the Federal Reserve Board (FRB) officials accurately reflected the US government's position, then and now. In 1995, Alan Blinder, former Vice-Chairman of the FRB said, 'The uncertainties regarding the future of "e-money" are so overwhelming that we mainly suggest patience and study rather than regulatory restrictions'[1]. In 1996, Governor Edward W. Kelly Jr. of the FRB stated:

'Heavy-handed, pre-emptive efforts at regulating these products and the competitive process before significant social risks have been demonstrated would likely handicap innovation for no compelling reason ... While we do not see the need for substantive regulations at this time, there is an ongoing need to review existing regulations and supervisory practices in order to adapt to technological as well as financial innovations ...'[2]

1 FATF Paper.
2 Address before the Cyberpayments Conference on 18 June 1996.

4.28 Simultaneously, law enforcement officials and regulators have made efforts to co-operate with the e-money industry in order to understand emerging issues and to share with them potential enforcement concerns generated by their products. As of yet, however, no official suggestions or proposals from any of these groups have been universally adopted and applied by the federal government. Consequently, the laws that govern digital money remain unclear[1].

1 Jane Kaufman Winn, at p 850–851.

4.29 In contrast, in Europe several institutions have published several reports on various aspects of e-money. The European Monetary Institute (EMI) report of 1994 specifically noted: '... money embedded in electronic purses does not have legal tender'. As matter of policy, the EMI considered that the central banks should retain a certain degree of control with respect to prepaid card issuers, since it is the central banks, which are responsible for overseeing the payment systems of their respective countries. The EMI did nonetheless mention that the development of prepaid cards could have an impact on monetary policy and on the role of the central banks as issuers of banknotes.

4.30 The report is of the opinion that the issuance of electronic money be reserved to the central banks. In this regard, the report states:

> '[C]urrent legal opinion in most European countries holds the view that, under existing legislation, the banknote monopoly does not extend to electronic purses. This implies that: 1) the issuance of electronic purses by parties other than central banks is possible; and 2) that the central banks' statutory obligations do not create any legal obligation for them to issue electronic purses themselves ...'[1]

1 Olivier Hance and Suzan Dionne Balz, at p 421.

4.31 The EMI 1998 Opinion stated that regardless of the nature of issue of the electronic money, minimum requirements should be met, since funds collected for against the issuance of electronic money are by nature redeemable. These minimum requirements include prudential supervision of the issuers, solid and transparent legal arrangements, technical security, protection from criminal abuse and statistics regarding issuance, redeemability at par of the electronic money issued, and the possibility for central banks to impose reserve requirements on all issuers of electronic money. Finally, the Opinion noted that an insurance scheme for electronic money issuers could be envisaged as a way to protect the public. The EMI nevertheless stated that '... [T]he most straightforward solution would be to limit the issuance of electronic money to credit institutions, as this would avoid changing the existing institutional setting for monetary policy and banking business'[1].

1 *Ibid, at* 422.

4.32 The European Central Bank (ECB) Report of 1998 highlights the kinds of measures, which should be taken as regards electronic money so as '... to maintain the integrity and stability of financial markets' and '... encourage the efficiency and soundness of payment systems in such a way as ... not to hinder the conduct of monetary policy'. The Report addresses: (i) central banks, which should set up an appropriate oversight regimem, (ii) authorities in charge of establishing and implementing a prudential supervisory network; and (iii) market participating, who should all take appropriate action to deal with the specific features of the electronic money. The ECB is of the opinion that it is time to define minimum requirements for electronic money systems. The Report follows the 1998 EMI Report, and states that the most straightforward solution would be to limit electronic money issuance to credit institutions. The European Parliament report on *Electronic Money and Economic and Monetary Union* 1997 states that:

> '... [T]he development of sound electronic money and secure electronic proof of identity are two essential foundations of the electronic market place. Care must be taken, however, to ensure that electronic money evolves within a secure regulatory framework, notably as regards civil liberties, the supervision of databases, the protection of consumers and the establishment of a sound and competitive level playing field amongst electronic money issuers.'[1]

1 *Ibid.* at 428.

4.33 The Report recommended that the European Union Commission develop a proposal concerning the establishment of a regulatory framework for the issuance of money, which allows all institutions which meet the requirements of public confidence, interoperability and stability of the financial system, to issue electronic money under a single European passport and the supervision of the competent authorities.

The Electronic Money Institutions Directive

4.34 In September 1998, the European Commission adopted the Electronic Money Institutions Directive. The purpose of the Directive is to establish a harmonised regulatory framework that would be tailored to the specific nature of e-money services. It would also allow for the entrance into the field of new market players, which are not necessarily credit institutions. The Directive is intended to complement the current Commission Recommendation on Electronic Instruments, which provides guidance on how electronic payment should be regulated. The Recommendation has no legal effect and focuses on the standards to be applied to preserve consumer protection in relation to the use of electronic payment instruments. As mentioned earlier, art 1(b) of the Directive defines electronic money as 'monetary value as represented by a claim on the issuer which is stored on an electronic device, issued on receipt of funds of an amount not less than the monetary value issued, and accepted as means of payment by undertakings other than the issuer'. No reference is made to the technology in the provisions in an effort to create a technology-neutral framework and to refrain from stifling technological innovation. The recitals do, however, make reference to an electronic device such as a chip card or computer memory.

4.35   Article 1(a) sets out the scope of the Directive. It states; 'electronic money institutions' shall mean an undertaking or any legal other person, other than a credit institution as defined in art 1 first indent, paragraph (a) of Directive 77/780/EEC, which issues means of payment in the form of electronic money. The Directive limits the business activities of electronic money institutions, other than issuing of electronic money, to:

(a)   the provision of closely related financial and non-financial services such as the administering of electronic money by the performance of operational and other ancillary functions related to its issuance, and the issuing and adminis-tering of other means of payment *but excluding the granting of any form of credit;* and

(b)   the storing of data on the electronic device on behalf of other undertakings or public institutions [emphasis added].

4.36   These provisions clearly reiterate the position that non-bank electronic money issuers should not be allowed to grant credit[1]. The Electronic Money Institutions Directive applies specifically to non-bank issuers of electronic money. An issuer of electronic money must be either a traditional credit institution or one which falls within the definition of the new law. Article 1(4) prohibits carrying the business of issuing electronic money by persons or undertakings falling outside these two groups[2].

1   Jason Chuah, 'The New E.U. Directive to Regulate Electronic Money Institutions – A Critique of the E.U's Approach to Electronic Money' (2000) JIBL 181.
2   *Ibid.*

4.37   The recitals to the Directive emphasise the goal of ensuring fair competi-tion between electronic money issuers and other credit institutions through the regime implemented. The Directive outlines a certain number of rules. It requires electronic money institutions to have an initial capital requirement of at least 1 million euros. They are at all times required to own funds which are equal to or above 2% of the higher of the current amount or the average of the preceding six months' total amount of their financial liabilities related to outstanding electronic money. Investments are restricted only to zero credit risk investment and/or highly liquid instruments. The strict limitations on investment of funds aim to ensure that the e-money institution's financial liabilities, related to outstanding electronic money, are backed by sufficiently liquid low risk assets at all times thus ensuring that there are funds available to redeem value without posing a risk to the financial stability of the issuer. E-money institutions must have sound and prudent manage-ment, administrative and accounting procedures and adequate internal control mechanisms.

4.38   Member states may, however, waive the application of certain of the Directive requirements as regards relatively small economy institutions or those whose activity is purely national. The price for exemption is set out in art 8(2). E-money institutions under a waiver may not benefit from the single passport[1] within the single market.

1 Under the Banking Directive, the single passport allows credit institutions, recognised in one member state, full access to offer services in another member state without needing to seek further approval and recognition (see Directive 89/646).

CHAPTER FIVE

Online Privacy and E-Commerce

Introduction

5.1 Bill Gates admitted that loss of privacy is a major worry where the network is concerned. He wrote that a great deal of information is already being gathered about each of us, by private companies as well as by government agencies, and we often have no idea how it is used or whether it is accurate[1]. David Fieldman says:

> 'Personal information is important. In the electronic age, those who control information about my health, wealth, ambitions and weaknesses can manipulate, if not control my life. More information about more people is more readily accessible than ever before, and the growth will not abate.'[2]

1 Bill Gates, *The Road Ahead* (1996) p 302.
2 David Fieldman, 'Information and Privacy' in Jack Beatson and Yvonne Cripps, *Freedom of Expression and Freedom of Information, Essays in Honour of Sir David Williams* (2000) p 299.

5.2 The efficiency of the computer network has caused more and more personal information to be stored in computer-readable form. Gigabytes of private personal communications are transferred on a daily basis. A May 1999 survey on privacy in *The Economist* notes:

> 'The trade in consumer information has hugely expanded in the past ten years. One single company, Axicom Corporation in Conway, Arkansas, has a data base combining public and consumer information that covers 95% of American households.'[1]

The potential for privacy invasions of a magnitude never before seen exists in today's computerised world. It has received judicial recognition. Lord Hoffmann in *R v Brown*[2] stated:

> 'Vast amounts of information about everyone are stored in computers, capable of instant transmission anywhere in the world and accessible at the touch of a keyboard. The right to keep oneself to oneself, to tell other people that certain things are none of their business, is under technological threat.'

The banking industry is a data-intensive sector. The data relates to large numbers of contracts maintained with large numbers of customers. Clients and customers range from private individuals to large corporate bodies such as public companies and public authorities. Other clients include partnerships and sole traders. In addition, the orders received from the customers generate new flows of information. These data-flows run within individual banks, within banking groups and between different banks.

1 'The End of Privacy', *The Economist* (1 May 1999) p 21.
2 [1996] 1 All ER 545, 556.

The right to privacy

5.3 Lawyers, judges, philosophers and scholars have attempted to define the scope and meaning of privacy. The legal origins of privacy can be traced back to the US and to the end of last century, more particularly to the famous article of Charles Warren and Louis D. Brandeis, 'The Right to Privacy', which today stands as a classical piece of legal literature. It was in Warren and Brandeis' article that privacy was for the first time clearly asserted as a valuable social interest that ought to be explicitly protected by judges. In order to support their claim, Warren and Brandeis argued that privacy had already been considered as an implicit value worthy of protection in the common law. Common law rights to intellectual and artistic property already existed and their judicial protection were reinterpreted as indicative of a broader interest in privacy. Thus more specific rights brought to light broader principles. This interest in privacy implicit in the common law led Warren and Brandeis to conclude that privacy itself was to be considered as a common law right. Being a common law right, privacy ought to be entitled to independent recognition and receive general and consistent application[1]. Warren and Brandeis' article introduced the issue of the protection of privacy but left the question of the definition of privacy far from settled[2]. In 1995 Alan Westin, a long-time privacy scholar said at a conference that no definition of privacy is possible, because privacy issues are fundamentally matters of values, interests and power[3]. He, however, had attempted to define privacy earlier. According to him, privacy is the desire of people to choose freely under what circumstances and to what extent they will expose themselves, their attitudes and their behaviour to others[4].

1 See Blanca R. Ruiz, *Privacy in Telecommunications: A European and an American Approach* (1997) pp 23–24.
2 *Ibid.*
3 See Robert Gellman; 'Does Privacy Law Work?' in Philip E Agre and Mac Rotenberg (eds) *Technology and Privacy: The New Landscape* (1997) pp 193–194.
4 Alan F Westin, *Privacy and Freedom* (1967).

5.4 Privacy protection is frequently seen as a way of drawing the line at how far society can intrude into a person's affairs. It can be divided into the following facets:

● *Information privacy*, involving the establishment of rules governing the collection and handling of personal data such as credit information and medical records;

● *Bodily* privacy, concerning the protection of people's physical beings against invasive procedures such as drug testing and cavity searches;

- *Privacy of communications,* covering the security and privacy of mail, telephones, email and other forms of communication; and

- *Territorial privacy,* concerning the setting of limits on intrusion into the domestic and other environment such as the workplace or public space.

5.5 The Preamble to the Australian Privacy Charter provides, 'A free and democratic society requires respect for the autonomy of individuals, and limits on the power of both state and private organizations to intrude on that autonomy ...' It also states, 'Privacy is a key value which underpins human dignity and other key values such as freedom of association and freedom of speech ...' and '[P]privacy is a basic human right and the reasonable expectation of every person.'[1]

1   Australian Privacy Charter Group, *The Australian Charter* (University of New South Wales Law School) (1994).

5.6   Privacy is at the very soul of being human. Professor Lasswell, in his *Conflict of Loyalties,* argued that internationally, there is a 'presumption in favour of privacy and that it naturally follows from our respect for freedom of choice, for autonomy, for self-direction on the part of everyone'. Lasswell summed it up in these terms:

> 'Privacy is not just one possible means among others to insure some other value, but ... it is necessarily related to ends and relations of the most fundamental sort: respect, love, friendship and trust. Privacy is not merely a good technique for furthering these fundamental relations; rather without privacy they are simply inconceivable.'

5.7   It may be considered trite that privacy is intimately associated with the basic values of human dignity and personal autonomy: it has been termed 'the fundamental right from which all others are derived'. Thus, the right to privacy has been expressed as a fundamental human right. Article 12 of the UN Universal Declaration of Human Rights adopted in 1948, proclaims that:

> 'No one should be subjected to arbitrary interface with his privacy, family, home or correspondence, or to attacks on his honour or reputation. Everyone has the right to the protection of the law against such interferences or attacks.'

5.8   Numerous other international human rights covenants give specific reference to privacy as a right. The International Covenant on Civil and Political Rights (ICCPR), the UN Convention on Migrant Workers and the UN Convention on the Rights of the Child adopt the same language.

5.9   On the regional level, various treaties can make these rights legally enforceable. Article 8 of the 1950 European Convention for the Protection of Human Rights and Fundamental Freedoms states:

> '(1) Everyone has the right to respect for his private and family life, his home and his correspondence.

(2) There shall be no interference by a public authority with the exercise of this right except in accordance with the law and as necessary in a democratic society in the interests of national security, public safety or the economic well-being of the country, for the prevention of disorder or crime, for the protection of health or morals, or for the protection of the rights and freedoms of others.

5.10 The Convention created the European Commission of Human Rights and the European Court of Human Rights to oversee enforcement. Both have been particularly active in the enforcement of privacy rights and have consistently viewed art 8's protections expansively and the restrictions narrowly. The Commission found in its first decision on privacy:

'For numerous Anglo-Saxon and French authors, the right to respect "private life" is the right to privacy, the right to live, as far as one wish, protected from publicity … In the opinion of the Commission, however, the right to respect for private life does not end there. It comprises also, to a certain degree, the right to establish and develop relationships with other human beings, especially in the emotional field for the development and fulfilment of one's own personality.'[1]

1 *X v Iceland,* 5 Eur Comm'n H.R. Dec. & Rep. (1976) pp 86–87.

5.11 Other regional treaties also provide for the right to privacy. Article 11 of the American Convention on Human Rights sets out the right to privacy in terms similar to the Universal Declaration. In 1965, the Organization for American States proclaimed the American Declaration of the Rights and Duties of Man, which called for the protection of numerous human rights including privacy. The Inter-American Court of Human Rights began to address privacy issues in its cases. Similarly, identical wordings as provided for in art 12 of the UN Universal Declaration of Human Rights are used in many constitutions of the governments of the world.

5.12 A distinction must be drawn between privacy in all its manifold aspects, and information privacy as one particular aspect of it. As indicated earlier, the general claim to privacy includes such things as not to have our territory invaded by strangers, not to have our books read, or our records played, or our clothes worn by others without our permission, even if this causes us no loss and tells those others nothing about us. But, the area of 'information privacy' is narrower; here, what we claim is that others should not obtain knowledge about us without our consent. In Professor Westin's words, this is 'the claim of individuals to determine for themselves when, how and to what extent information about them is communicated to others'.

5.13 Professor Arthur Miller puts it even more briefly, defining it as 'the individual's ability to control the circulation of information relating to him'[1]. This is the aspect of the right of privacy with which the present work is principally concerned, since it is the one which has been the most profoundly affected – and some would say most dangerously threatened – by recent developments in information technology[2].

1   See James Michael, *Privacy and Human Rights: An International and Comparative Study, with Special Reference to Developments in Information Technology* (1994) p 3.
2   *Ibid.*

Value of personal data

5.14   Personal information is important and has become a commodity. It is as a commodity that personal information has commercial interest and for this reason it becomes tempting to use it extensively[1]. There are several examples that can illustrate this development. In particular, there are many sites that in exchange for personal data sell their products at a lower price and there are, likewise, services which actually pay the user to surf the net when he/she provides personal data to be used for marketing purposes. There is no such thing as a free lunch and this phenomenon demonstrates the economic value of information[2].

1   Peter Blume, 'Data Protection Issues With Respect to E-Commerce', *CRi* 1/2001, 11, 14.
2   *Ibid.*

5.15   For an increasing number of people connecting to the Internet has become a daily routine, whether it be to send e-mails, visit websites, participate in a discussion forum or chat room or, increasingly, to purchase goods and services online. These routine sessions on the Internet imply the disclosure by millions of users of marketable details concerning their private life. Technically, each visit to the Internet can be traced and data collected[1]. Electronic recording of 'click-stream data' may take place at various levels including in the proxy servers, or in the servers of the access or content providers. The same is true when visiting any website, where collection of data is also possible even in the absence of registration. Indeed, the mere connection to a website enables the website owner to collect information on the user, such as their IP address, the configuration of some elements of their computer, the connection data, the type of transaction carried out, files transferred to the user's browser and the browser type and version[2].

1   Tanguy Van Overstraeten and Emmanuel Szafran, 'Data Protection and Privacy on the Internet: Technical Considerations and European Legal Framework' (2001) CTLR 7(3) 56.
2   *Ibid.*

5.16   The US Federal Trade Commission (FTC) 2000 Report states:

'Websites collect a vast amount of personal information from and about consumers. This information is routinely collected from consumers through registration forms, order forms, surveys, contests and other means, and includes personal identifying information which can be used to locate or identify an individual, and non-identifying information. The Commission's Survey findings demonstrate that nearly all websites collect personal identifying information from consumers ... Most of the sites surveyed, therefore, are capable of creating personal profiles of online consumers by tying any demographic, interest, purchasing behaviour, or surfing behaviour informa-tion they collect to personal identifying information[1].

1   Federal Trade Commission, ' Privacy On-line: Fair Information Practices in the Electronic Market-
place', A Report to Congress (May 2000) pp 9–10.

5.17   According to *The Economist* privacy has become one of the most fought-
over battlegrounds of the information economy. At the heart of the struggle is a
basic dilemma: most people want to retain some controls over who knows what
about them, and yet information about individuals is the life-blood of most of the
burgeoning new service businesses. Without their growing databases, firms would
not be able to tailor their products to individual tastes, handle secure electronic
transactions, offer streamlined payment and delivery, or target their advertising and
promotion[1].

1   *The Economist,* (18 December 1999) p 55.

5.18   *The Economist* also stated that, in America, the sale of personal data in
government and commercial databases is far more widespread. It is the Internet,
which has brought America's 'reference industry', as the sellers of personal data like
to call themselves to the attention of the public. It further stated that the leading
firms now offer online searches of hundreds of public databases as if those records
were neatly indexed in one giant database. For instance one company, Database
Technologies (DBT), says it can simultaneously access over one thousand data
sources, containing billions of records. DBT makes its products available only to
traditional customers such as law enforcement agencies, licensed private detectives
and companies with more than US$1 billion revenue[1]. Internet Profiles Corp in San
Francisco, uses its software to track who visits a particular website, what is looked
at and for how long. This company sells this information to the relevant website
operator for $5,000 per report.

1   *Ibid* at 56.

5.19   In 1990, Lotus Corporation offered *Marketplace: Households*, a CD-ROM
containing transaction generated information (TGI) on the buying patterns and
incomes of 120 million Americans. A firestorm of protest forced Lotus to withdraw
the product. AOL confirmed that it was compiling the names and addresses of its
subscribers and packaging lists with demographic information to sell to marketing
companies and manufacturers. (Subscribers who do not want their names released
may specify by sending a message to AOL.) Mark Rotenberg, director of the
Electronic Privacy Information Centre (EPIC), says that subscribers go from 'being
in the AOL chat room to the AOL fishbowl.'[1]

1   See David Brin, *The Transparent Society: Will Technology Force Us to Choose Between Privacy and Freedom?*
(1998) p 57.

5.20   The European Union Working Party, in its document *Privacy on the Internet –
An Integrated EU Approach to Online Data Protection*[1], perhaps provides the best
illustration of how valuable personal data is. It states that the capture of user
information in online environments is considered to have economic and strategic
importance. Recent cases confirm the increasing value attached by businesses to

consumer profiles. Lists of customers are being sold or shared, most often, through mergers of IT companies, which thus increase the detail and number of profiles they can use. The document states:

> 'There will eventually be acquisitions that are based on consumer data, where the primary asset that's being bought is the customer data ... Consumer data right now is the currency of e-commerce in a lot of ways. Those are valuable customers because they've shown that they're buyers, and they've bought from a competing store ... Names in a database save a company from spending marketing dollars to acquire a customer – usually about US$100 per customer.'

1 Accessed on 21 November 2000, available at www.europa.eu.int/cmm/dg15/en/media.dataprot/ index/htm.

5.21 According to the Working Party, consumer data have also been offered for sale when Internet companies go bankrupt. A company selling toys recently included the sale of its customer profiles as part of the company's liquidation. These customer profiles were collected from users under the privacy policy that no information would ever be shared with a third party without the express consent of the user. The profiles include names, addresses, billing information, shopping behavioural information and family profiles with the names and birth dates of children. The Working Party recommends that a comprehensive data protection policy must take account of a balanced choice between economic interest and human rights. Two big issues remain unresolved[1]:

- Nowadays a large volume of individual data on many Internet users has been collected on the Internet without the prior knowledge and/or consent of the data subject, mainly due to the invisible side effects of Internet technology. It is foreseeable that, in the next few years, more and more personal data will be exchanged for material gain, but how far can the Internet user go in doing this? What kind of personal data can be shared by the data subject itself, for how long and under what circumstances?

- If the funding of particular websites (e.g. search engines) comes mainly from the cyber marketing industry, there may be a temptation to use personalised profiling to ensure that services which were previously free exclude people who do not have sufficient income, have not responded to hundreds of advertising banners or wish to preserve their privacy.

1 Accessed on 21 November 2000, available at www.europa.eu.int/cmm/dg15/en/media.dataprot/ index/htm.

Consumer expectations and business attitudes – what do studies say?

5.22 In October 2000, PriceWaterhouse Coopers commissioned an independent survey of consumers in Europe and South Africa to explore their attitudes towards privacy on the Internet[1]. The survey also explored differences in attitudes among experienced users (players), non-experienced users (newcomers), online shoppers and non-shoppers. The research found that consumers consistently expressed *high* levels of concern about their privacy when using the Internet. Nearly one in three European Internet users rated their level of concern as 'high'. The consumers' concerns about their privacy centred on two main areas: first, intrusion, or the fear of being monitored or spied on, and second, the risk of misuse of information or fraud when buying goods or services on the Internet. The research also found that over half (55%) of consumers suffer from unwanted e-mails; and around one fifth (20%) suffer from the experience of having their personal details passed to others without their knowledge. The research stated that:

> 'Paradoxically, the more consumers used the Internet, the more likely they were to worry about privacy: "players" were more likely to express concerns about spying and intrusion than "newcomers" (32% to 27%). Elsewhere, the research found that players and newcomers expressed similar (low) levels of confidence in feeling that their privacy is protected on the Internet. Interestingly, Internet Service Providers (ISPs) are among the least trusted of institutions. Only 21% of respondents said they would trust them with their details.'

1   The report of the survey is available at www.pwcglobal.com/ebusinessinsights.

5.23   In the US, surveys conducted by Louis Harris and Associates have shown a progressive increase in the public's concern for privacy, up, from 67% in 1978, to 84% in 1994. A review of this trend noted, 'People seem to believe that the loss of privacy will become an even greater problem in the future than it was in the 1980s'.

5.24   A 1992 survey by Louis Harris and Equifax, a leading consumer credit information service, found that the American public's concern with threats to their privacy remained consistently high – 78% in 1992 versus 79% in 1991 and 1990. Much of the concern revolved around the security of personal information in computers, with 89% believing that computers had made it easier for someone to improperly access confidential information. 76% of respondents felt that consumers had lost all control of the way their personal information was being used and exchanged by companies. The 1995 Equifax-Harris Mid-Decade Consumer Privacy Survey found consistently high levels of concern for privacy (82%), with 80% of Americans believing they had lost all control over their personal information[1].

1   See Ann Cavoukian and Don Tapscott, *Who Knows: Safeguarding Your Privacy in a Networked World* (1997) pp 88–89.

5.25   Another 1995 privacy survey by Yankelovich Partners, found that 90% of Americans were in favour of legislation to protect them from businesses invading their privacy. This finding was surprisingly similar to an earlier survey conducted by Time/CNN in 1991, which found that Americans' concern for their privacy was rising and they wanted strict controls over others' use of their personal information. In response to the question, 'Should companies that sell information to others be required by law to ask permission from individuals before making the information available?' a resounding 93% said, 'yes'. Further, 88% felt that companies who intended to sell their information should be subject to legislation to make that information available to data subjects so they would have the opportunity to correct any errors[1].

1   See Ann Cavoukian and Don Tapscott, *Who Knows: Safeguarding Your Privacy in a Networked World* (1997) pp 88–89.

5.26   In 1993, Ekos Research released its report, *Privacy Revealed,* which showed consumer concern for privacy to be very high: 92% expressed concern about their personal privacy (52% reporting 'extreme concern'); 81% felt they should be informed in advance when their personal information was being collected; 83% felt strongly that their permission should be obtained before an organisation shared information with others; and 87% strongly believed that they should be told how information obtained from them would be used[1].

1   See Ann Cavoukian and Don Tapscott, *Who Knows: Safeguarding Your Privacy in a Networked World* (1997) pp 88–89.

5.27   A 1998 survey of the American public conducted by Louis Harris and Associates, Inc and Alan Westin found that[1]:

- Very strong majorities of net users and net purchasers want business websites to post notices explaining how they will use the personal information customers provide when buying products or services on the web. Net users (91%) and net purchasers (96%) say this is important to them, with 69% of net users and 72% of net purchasers saying it is 'very important' to have such assurance.

- Of net purchasers, 73% of net users, and 65% of computer users are confident that most businesses will follow the policies they publish.

- Similar majorities of those not yet online say this would be important to them if they were online. 94% of computer users and 79% of non-computer users say it would be important – with 81% of computer users and 63% of non-computer users saying it is 'very important' for business websites to post privacy policies online.

- Of those who say they are not likely to access the Internet in the next year, greater privacy protection is the factor that would most likely convince them to do so. Of five factors presented, these non-users rated their positive likely effect on using the Net as follows:

    - Privacy of personal information and communications would be protected – 44%.
    - Security of financial transactions on the Internet was assured – 40%.
    - Use became less complicated – 40%.
    - More control over businesses sending unwanted marketing messages – 36%.
    - Cost was reduced – 35%.

1   See PriceWaterhouseCoopers, 'Privacy … A Weak Link in the Cyber-Chain' (1999) p 12.

5.28 In 1999 the Louis Harris/Alan Westin survey of consumer attitudes toward privacy reveals that more than 80% of US adults believe they have lost control over how companies collect and use consumers' personal information. More than 75% of consumers want, among other rights, to be informed of what kind of personal information companies are collecting, how it will be used, and the chance to see the information and verify its accuracy.

5.29 The Federal Trade Commission in its document[1] stated that 92% of consumers are concerned (67% are 'very concerned') about the misuse of their information online. Concerns about privacy online reach even those not troubled by threats to privacy in the offline world. Thus, 76% of consumers who are not generally concerned about the misuse of their personal information fear privacy intrusions on the Internet. As mentioned earlier, the FTC Report stated:

> 'Indeed, surveys show that those consumers most concerned about threats to their privacy online are the least likely to engage in online commerce, and many consumers who have never made an online purchase identify privacy concerns as a key reason for their inaction ... The level of consumer unease is reflected in the results of a recent study in which 92% of respondents from online households stated that they do not trust online companies to keep their personal information confidential, and 82% agreed that the government should regulate how online companies use personal information.'

1 Federal Trade Commission, ' Privacy On-line: Fair Information Practices in the Electronic Market-place', A Report to Congress (May 2000) pp 9–10.

5.30 In Australia, a survey carried out early in 2000, indicated that up to 92% of Australian companies were collecting personal information through websites. A 1999 national poll revealed that 56% of Australians were particularly worried about the invasion of privacy created by new information technologies[1].

1 Roy Morgan Research Centre, 'Big Brother Bothers Most Australians', *The Bulletin* (30 August 1999), cited in Paul Kelly, 'Recent Developments in Private-Sector Personal data Protection in Australia: Will There be an Upside Down Under?' [2000] *Journal of Computer and Information Law* Vol XIX 91.

5.31 It is not surprising that privacy concerns affect the commercial behaviour of consumers. The IBM research shows that 50% of consumers in Germany, the UK and the US had refused to give information on websites because of privacy concerns, and between 39% and 47% of people stated that privacy issues had stopped them from making online purchases. In addition, around one-third of Internet users demonstrate 'privacy assertive behaviour', such as giving false information when asked to register online.

5.32 Businesses can no longer take their customers for granted. The customer of today has great expectations, and if a company fails to meet them, the customer will move on to companies that can. Thus, the business community needs to take privacy protection seriously. Let us take a look at the businesses' attitudes towards consumer online privacy so far.

5.33 In June 1997, the EPIC released a study of 100 top sites on the World Wide Web. Although many of these sites captured personal information from visitors and users, the study reported that virtually none had privacy policies that complied with globally accepted privacy standards. Those that did have privacy policies rarely made them easy to find. In the US, the FTC in its 1998 Report, *Privacy Online: A Report to Congress* stated:

> 'The Commission's survey of over 1,400 websites reveals that the industry's efforts to encourage voluntary adoption of the most basic fair information practice principle – notice – have fallen far short of what is needed to protect consumers. The Commission's survey shows that the vast majority of websites – upward of 85% – collect personal information from consumers. Few of the sites – only 14% – provide any notice with respect to their information practices, and fewer still – approximately 2% – provide notice by means of a comprehensive privacy policy. The results with respect to the collection of information from children are also troubling.'

5.34 The Commission in its 1998 Report, described the widely-accepted fair information practice principles of *Notice, Choice, Access,* and *Security.* In 1999, Georgetown University Professor, Mary Culnan, conducted a survey of a random sample drawn from the most-heavily trafficked sites on the World Wide Web and a survey of the busiest 100 sites. The former, known as the Georgetown Internet Privacy Policy Survey, found significant improvement in the frequency of privacy disclosures, but also that only 10% of the sites posted disclosures that even touched on all four fair information practice principles.

5.35 In July 1999, the FTC issued a new report, entitled *Self-Regulation and Privacy Online: A Report to Congress.* This report concluded that the online businesses had made considerable strides in the ensuing year and recommended that no additional privacy protection legislation be passed. The basis for this conclusion was a new survey, which studied 364 of the Web's popular commercial sites, which draw 99% of the Web's traffic. Of those sites, 93% collected some type of personal information about their users. Of that 93%, 65.7 displayed some form of a privacy policy. However, only 10% of those sites had a comprehensive policy which: notifies consumers; contains opt out provisions; allows individuals to review the collected information; commits to keeping the information secure; and explains how to contact the website regarding the privacy policy. Despite the low number of websites with comprehensive privacy policies, the FTC decided that additional legislation to protect online privacy is not necessary at present. Strident criticism has emerged of the FTC's report. Critics have argued that the number of websites studied was too small, and that the survey did not measure whether and how websites enforce their privacy policies.

5.36 In February and March 2000, the FTC conducted another survey of commercial sites' information practices, using a list of the busiest US commercial sites on the World Wide Web. Two groups of sites were studied: (1) a random sample of 335 websites (the 'Random Sample') and (2) 91 of the 100 busiest sites (the 'Most Popular Group'). As was true in 1998, the 2000 Survey results show that websites collect a vast amount of personal information from and about consumers. Almost all sites (97% in the Random Sample and 99% in the Most Popular Group) collect an e-mail address or some other type of personal identifying information.

5.37 The 2000 survey results show that there has been continued improvement in the percentage of websites that post at least one privacy disclosure (88% in the Random Sample and 100% in the Most Popular Group). The Commission's 2000 Survey went beyond the mere counting of disclosures, however, and analysed the nature and substance of these privacy disclosures in light of the fair information practice principles of Notice, Choice, Access, and Security. It found that only 20% of websites in the Random Sample that collect personal identifying information implement, at least in part, all four fair information practice principles (42% in the Most Popular Group).

5.38 The survey shows that only 41% of sites in the Random Sample and 60% of sites in the Most Popular Group meet the basic Notice and Choice standards. The survey found that less than one-tenth, or approximately 8%, of sites in the Random Sample, and 45% of sites in the Most Popular Group, display a privacy seal. These privacy seal programmes that have been adopted, and which require companies to implement certain fair information practices and monitor their compliance, promise an efficient way to implement privacy protection.

5.39 The Organisation for Economic Co-Operation and Development (OECD) Secretariat commissioned a survey during the month of April 1998 on some 50 websites, mainly commercial sites open to the general public. The aim of the study was to analyse the extent to which, and how, the OECD Guidelines on data protection were put into practice on these different websites. The sample includes three sites in Australia, five in Canada, one in Denmark, two in Finland, six in France, one in Germany, two in Italy, two in Japan, one in Mexico, two in Spain, two in the UK and 23 in the US. The survey reported:

> 'The most striking conclusion that can be drawn from this study is that there is a marked discrepancy between the world of the various institutions and organisations that develop ideas and instruments for data protection on the one hand, and the world of websites on the other. The latter, or the great majority of them, whatever their sincerity or their good intentions with regard to their visitors, actually give the impression today that they pay too little attention to the issues involved in the protection of privacy and transborder data flows, and, most importantly, that they lack precise and consistent direction for privacy protection applicable to online networks.'[1]

1 See the Group of Experts on Information Security and Privacy, *Practices to Implement the OECD Privacy Guidelines on Global Networks*, DSTI/ICCP/REG(98) 6/FINAL.22.

5.40 Basically, the three main objectionable intrusions into privacy on the Internet are: first, when information is collected about someone without his/her knowledge or consent. Second, when companies on the Internet maintain websites, but do not have a privacy policy or do not follow their own privacy policies. Third, when websites collect, store or transmit sensitive information about a person's finances, medical records or engage in the collection of information from children.

Cookies and privacy

What's a cookie?

5.41   The word "cookie" comes from "magic cookie", a term in programming languages for a piece of information shared between co-operating pieces of software. The choice of the word cookie appears to come from the American tradition of giving and sharing edible cookies[1]. According to a scholar[2]:

> Cookies are pieces of information generated by a web server and stored in the user's computer, ready for future access. Cookies are embedded in the HTML information flowing back and forth between the user's computer and the servers … Essentially, cookies make use of user-specific information transmitted by the web server onto the user's computer so that the information might be available for later access by itself or other servers.

It is a piece of information in the form of a very small text file that is placed on an Internet user's hard drive. They are generated by a web page server, which is basically the computer that operates a website. Cookies usually contain a name, a value, expiration date, and the site that it came from. The information the cookie contains is set by the server and it can be used by that server whenever the user visits the site. A cookie can be thought of as an Internet user's identification card, which tell a web site when the user returned.

The first batch of cookies were originally cooked up as simple mechanism to help make it easier for users to access their favourite web sites without having to go through a lengthy process of identifying themselves every time they visit. According to the noble purposes of the original Netscape Web browser standard, cookies exist by default only for the duration of the actual web browsing session[3]. Once the user exits the browser, cookies acquired during the session are deleted. In addition cookies, by default, can only be accessed by the web server and the web page that stored the cookie in the first place[4]. Unfortunately, the original intent of the cookie has been subverted by some unscrupulous entities who have found a way to use this process to actually track the visitors' movement across the web[5].

Cookies make the interaction between users and website faster and easier. Websites use cookies mainly because they save time and make the browsing experience more efficient and enjoyable[6]. The common uses of cookies include the ability of the web servers to determine how many and how often individuals visit their site, store user preferences (customisation), and implement shopping carts and "quick check out" option for consumers. Cookies are also extremely beneficial to many web sites that depend on advertising, since these small files allow the sites to determine what advertisements are being clicked on and seen by users. Finally, according to Doubleclick, cookies also prevent users from repeatedly seeing the same advertisement over and over by keeping track of how many times a user has been shown a banner at any website on which Doubleclick customers advertise.

1   See a guide to deleting and controlling cookies by Mason, OUT-LAW.COM, available at http://aboutcookies.org/cookiefaq.html.
2   Viktor Mayer-Schonberger, 'The Cookie Concept', available at http://www.cookiecentral.com/content.phtml?area=2&id=1.
3   See Viktor Mayer-Schonberger, 'The Internet and Privacy Legislation: Cookies for a Treat? 1 W. Va. JL. & Tech. 1.1 (1997) available at http://www.wvu.edu/~wvjolt/Arch?Mayer/Mayer.htm.
4   Ibid.
5   See cookiecentral.com, 'What Went Wrong', available at http://www.cookiecentral.com/content.phtml?area=2&id=14. The Netscape described in its earlier privacy policy, a cookie as a harmless piece of information temporarily stored in the computer after being sent to user browser.
6   Supra n. 2.

Cookies and online profiling

5.42   Netscape created cookies in 1994 as a special browser feature to simplify the lives of its users by allowing them to bypass all the preliminary steps they had already undertaken previously. In essence, cookies were supposed to be akin to preference files, keeping track of how a user wants a site to look or function so that he is not required to input routine information each time he visits. Of course, this also provided retailers with the perfect window to observe every movement their customer made on their sites through their clickstreams. Netscape consumers were not initially informed about these cookies on their browsers and Netscape clearly did not anticipate the public outcry that has occurred as a result.

Two years after the birth of its first cookies and the resulting negative publicity, Netscape added a disabling tool for the next browser version. However, this was merely an opt-out scheme, which required the user to affirmatively reject the cookies, a process which itself required navigation through a number of different screens. Hence, only the most technologically savvy of users have been able to detect and disable cookies.

As already mentioned, cookies were developed as a way for simplifying and personalising a website visit. But they have now evolved, amid much controversy, to also being used as a tracking tool for marketing purposes. Advertisers see cookies as a way to enhance personally targeted or "one-to-one" marketing. Cookies can be used to build up a profile of where one goes and which banner advertisements he/she clicks on. This information is then used to target advertisements specifically at him/her.

The most hyped use of cookies is to personalise website, but their real purpose for many website operators is to target advertising/marketing. Targeted advertising attempts to match the product or service being sold with the audience most likely to buy it. The UK's Direct Marketing Association describes cookies as "an integral information gathering tool for web traders and states that "[cookies] are used to determine the most visited areas of site and the borrowing habits of users. This information in turn enables web traders to effectively plan their advertising and marketing strategy"[1].

Anytime someone interacts with a website by clicking on a link, this can be recorded and inferences can be made about him/her interests. The Infoseek and Lycos search engines even set cookies which record what terms a user searched for. By means of "psychographic analysis' of the sites the users visit, the products they buy, and the articles they read, an observer can deduce all sorts of information about their political leanings, religion, sexual orientation, habits, associations, and beliefs. And all this is being stored without the knowledge of the users. A legal scholar, Professor Ann Bartow quotes the following analogy[2]:

> Imagine walking through a mall where every store, unbeknownst to you, placed a sign on your back. The sign tells every other store you visit exactly where you have been, what you looked at, and what you purchased. Something very close to this is possible on the Internet.

The U.S Federal Trade Commission (FTC), a government body responsible for enforcing consumer protection laws, considers online profiling a serious concern, and on November 8, 1999 it held a one day workshop which brought together representatives from some of the major online businesses as well as consumer right and privacy advocacy groups. In 2000, the FTC stated[3]:

> In general, these network advertising companies do not merely supply banner ads; they also gather data about the consumers who view their ads. This is accomplished primarily by the use of "cookies" which track individual's action on the Web. The information gathered by network advertisers is often, but not always, anonymous, that is, the profiles are frequently linked to the identification number of the advertising network's cookies on the consumer's computer rather than the name of a specific person. In some circumstances, however, the profiles derived from tracking consumers' activities on the Web are linked or merged with personally identifiable information.

According to the FTC, the profiles created by the advertising networks can be extremely detailed. A cookie placed by a network advertising company can track a consumer on any web site served by that company, thereby allowing data collection across disparate and unrelated sites on the web. Also, because the cookies used by ad networks are generally persistent, their tracking occurs over an extended period of time, resuming each time the individual logs on to the Internet. When this "clickstream" information is combined with third-party data, these profiles can include hundreds of distinct data fields[4].

1 Quoted in Herbert Smith, 'Privacy and Cookies' available at http://www.herbertsmith.com/
   publications/publications.asp?id=203, last visited 08/03/2004.
2 Quoted in Gordon Coleman, 'Online Tracking: How Anonymous is the Internet? Part 4: Online
   Profiling' available at http://www.slais.ubc.ca/courses/libr500/fall1999/www-_presentations/g-
   _coleman/profiling.htm, last visited 06/04/2004.

3 See the Prepared Statement of the Federal Trade Commission, 'Online Profiling: Benefits and Concerns' Before the Committee on Commerce, Science, and Transportation United States Senate, June 13, 2000, available at http://www.ftc.gov/os/2000/06/onlineprofile.htm.
4 *Ibid.*

Cases on Cookies

5.43 One commentator noted, 'The WWW offers a wide variety of communication, information and interaction. Cookies provide for necessary customisation. But the Internet is not outside the law. Existing regulations, targeted at protecting personal information, limit the use and application of cookies. Current cookie usage violates such norms. Content providers continuing to use cookies that violate these regulations and browser producers unwilling or incapable of bringing their products into accordance with these laws both risk legal liability. It should be their concern to avoid legal action; and it should be our concern to safeguard our privacy'.[1]

There have been a number of cases concerning cookies in the United States. In January 2000, in *Judnick v DoubleClick Inc,* (unreported), another challenge to the use of Internet user information was filed in the California State Court. This is a putative class action proceeding against DoubleClick, Inc., an online advertising firm that operates a network of thousands of advertising sites on the World Wide Web. The lawsuit accuses DoubleClick of improperly obtaining information regarding Internet users through the use of web-based technology, including cookies, and using the information to, (1) identify and track users and (2) obtain user's confidential information without their consent. The lawsuit requests the court to bar DoubleClick from collecting information from users without their written consent, but does not seek damages.

The suit alleges that DoubleClick uses cookies to collect information from Internet users who access sites within its advertising network. DoubleClick then allegedly cross-references this information with a direct marketing database compiled by Abacus Direct, a company DoubleClick acquired in November 1999. The Abacus database includes personal consumer information on areas including retail purchasing patterns, home addresses, and credit card usage. The *Judnick* lawsuit claims that these actions violate California State unfair and deceptive trade practices laws. This suit was consolidated with other lawsuits from Texas and New York in 2001. The suits charged that DuobleClick violated state and federal laws by surreptitiously tracking and collecting consumers' personally identifiable data and combining it with information on their web surfing habits.

The Court granted DoubleClick the approval to settle all class-action lawsuits. The settlement agreement requires DoubleClick to provide consumers with a privacy policy that will clearly describe in "easy-to-read sentences" its online ad-serving service, use of cookies, as well other services and technologies. The settlement also requires the company to purge certain data files of personally identifiable information, including names, addresses, telephone numbers and e-mail addresses.

Among other provisions, the settlement requires DoubleClick to obtain permission, or so-called opt-in agreements, from Internet surfers before it can tie personally identifiable information with web surfing history. In addition, Double-Click must conduct a public information campaign consisting of 300 million banner ads that educate consumers on Internet privacy.

In re *DoubleClick, Inc. Privacy Litigation*[2] the plaintiffs challenged DoubleClick's practice of building detailed profiles of Internet users by placing cookies on the hard drives of persons who visit websites affiliated with DoubleClick. DoubleClick uses cookies to store information about the user so it can be collected by the company as a way of identifying computer users who will be likely candidates to respond to banner advertisements on websites. The plaintiffs filed suit alleging that cookie placement amounted to an invasion of privacy and the unjust enrichment of DoubleClick, and also violated federal laws.

The plaintiffs contended that DuobleClick placement of cookies on plaintiffs' hard drives constituted unauthorised access and, as a result DoubleClick's collection of information from the cookies violated Title II of the Electronic Communications Privacy Act (ECPA).

The Court agreed with DoubleClick argument and held that all of the communications DuobleClick accessed through its cookies had been authorised or had fallen outside of Title II's scope. According to the Court, because plaintiffs only alleged that DoubleClick accessed communications from plaintiffs to DoubleClick-affiliated websites, the issue became whether the websites gave DoubleClick adequate authorisation under Title II to access those communications.

Plaintiffs' second claim was that DoubleClick violated the Federal Wiretap Act which provides for criminal punishment and a private right of action against any person who intentionally intercepts wire, oral, or electronic communications. DoubleClick argued that its actions fell under an explicit statutory exception. The exception provides that "it shall not be unlawful ...for a person ... to intercept a wire, oral, or electronic communication ...where one of the parties to the communication has given prior consent to such interception unless such communication is intercepted for the purpose of committing any criminal or tortuous act".

DoubleClick argued that the DoubleClick-affiliated websites consented to its interceptions, and, as a result, its conduct was exempted from the Wiretap Act's general prohibition. The Court agreed and held that DoubleClick-affiliated websites are 'parties to the communication[s]' from plaintiffs and have given sufficient consent to DoubleClick to intercept them.

In re *Pharmatrak, Inc. Privacy Litigation*[3], a group of Internet users sued Pharmatrak, along with several of its pharmaceutical company clients, for violating the ECPA. As already mentioned, under the ECPA, it is unlawful to intercept communications between two parties intentionally if neither consents to the interception. Pharmatrak's data monitoring service, NETcompare, collected information about web users as they accessed its clients' sites, to perform intra-industry comparisons of web site traffic and usage in the pharmaceutical industry.

The issues before the Court of Appeals were whether Pharmatrak's service had constituted an impermissible "interception" and, if so, whether its pharmaceutical clients had "consented' to such interception. Taking the latter question first, the Court of Appeals held that the burden of proving consent, at least in a civil case, fell upon Pharmatrak. The Court ruled that the party claiming consent must prove either actual consent or, in its absence, show 'convincingly' that implied consent was given. On the facts, the Court held that consent was not present. The Court distinguished this case from *DoubleClick Inc. Privacy Litigation* on the grounds that, in that case, the host websites had enlisted the service of DoubleClick for the purpose of creating user profiles. The Court also found that no consumer consent could e implied, because the pharmaceutical companies' websites "gave no indication that use meant consent to collection of personal information by a third party."

The Court of Appeals held that Pharmatrak's collection of personal data constituted an "interception" under the ECPA. The Court ruled that Pharmatrak was engaged in an interception under even the narrowest interception standard. Specifically, the Court concluded that Pharmatrak's obtaining the data in real-time was sufficient to constitute an "interception" under the ECPA.

5.44 Until recently, many users were unaware of cookies and the fact that information was being extracted from browsers. As publicity about cookies has increased, sophisticated Internet travellers have retaliated by disabling cookies on their browsers. In many instances, websites have responded with software that denies entry to browsers' whose cookies are disabled. Lately, some firms have been able to link information gathered by cookies with real people and not just with their computers. It appears that to most Internet users the most objectionable aspect of cookies is the involuntary nature of the information extraction. If Internet travellers were informed about the presence of cookies, the fact that information is being extracted, the uses for that information, and had an opportunity to refuse to give the information without being excluded from a lot of the sites on the Internet, fewer objections would be heard[1].

1   David Baumer and JC Poindexter, *Cyberlaw and E-Commerce* (2002) pp 164–165.

5.45 Some scholars argue that the use or sale of personal information in some contexts goes beyond just profit-making opportunities. It may involve a kind of profiling designed to influence the political process and voting behaviour. Alfred C. Amar Jr quoted with agreement the statement of Oscar H. Gandy[1]:

'In fact, the fundamental concern about privacy in cyberspace is about the ways in which the collection, processing and use of personal information in the computer network environment contribute to a loss of individual power and autonomy.'

1   Alfred C. Aman JR, 'Information, Privacy, and Technology: Citizens, Clients, or Consumers?' in Jack Beatson and Yvonne Cripps (eds.) *Freedom of Expression and Freedom of Information, Essays in Honour of Sir David Williams* (2000) p 327.

International data protection

5.46   The relationship between privacy on the one hand and data protection on the other has not always been easy to reconcile. Data protection is often viewed as a technical term relating to specific information management practices. In contrast, privacy in general is more likely to be considered as a fundamental human right and accorded specific protection under human rights conventions or constitutions.

5.47   It is, however, possible to discuss privacy issues in the terminology of risk and risk assessment, concepts which are, perhaps, more familiar in a business environment. Three risk factors can be identified which could be considered to be elements of privacy. The first of these is the risk of injustice due to significant inaccuracy in personal data, unjust interference, 'function creep' (the gradual use of data for purposes other than those for which it was collected) or reversal of the presumption of innocence, as seen in data-matching when correlation of information from disparate sources may produce an impression which is greater than the sum of the parts. The second risk is to one's personal control over the collection of personal information as a result of excessive and unjustified surveillance (which would presumably include monitoring the use of particular websites), collection of data without the data subject's consent and also the prohibition or active discouragement of the means to remedy these risks, such as the use of encryption and anonymising software. Finally there is a risk to dignity as a result of exposure or embarrassment due to an absence of transparency in information procedures, physical intrusion into private spaces, unnecessary identification or absence of anonymity, or unnecessary or unjustified disclosure of personal information without consent. Many of these have echoes of data protection issues and, in the technical sense, data protection measures may be considered as risk management devices, which need to balance the risk to the individual from unnecessary invasion of privacy with the measures necessary to control that risk. It may be that such differences in terminology are not as disparate as they might appear at first sight[1].

1   Diane Rowland and Elizabeth Macdonald, *Information Technology Law,* (2000) p 342.

5.48   Francis Aldhouse, the UK Data Protection Deputy Registrar, says that 'data protection is a form of privacy protection ... so it has come to be accepted that the code of good information handling practice found in the usual Data Protection Principles is best regarded as a development of the right to private life'.

5.49   In international circles, concern about the potential effect of automatic data processing upon the right to privacy began to grow during the late 1960s and early 1970s. But the eventual drafting of international measures specifically for the purpose of protecting privacy interests against the possible misuse of information by automatic means was carried out entirely by regional institutions, mostly

European ones. Although the rapid growth of this activity in data protection was deliberately directed at protecting one aspect of personal privacy, it is very unlikely that it would have grown so rapidly had it not been for a quite unexpected economic aspect. Some countries, especially those committed by treaty to reducing tariff barriers, began to fear that others might use their national data protection laws as non-tariff trade barriers. The development of international standards would not only establish minimum requirements for national legislation, but it could also be used to create a community of countries which met those requirements and which agreed on a free market of information among themselves, to the potential exclusion of others.

5.50 There are three main international instruments governing data protection:

• The Council of Europe Convention for the Protection of Individuals with regards to the Processing of Personal Data 1981.

• The Organisation for Economic Co-operation and Development (OECD) Guidelines governing the Protection of Privacy and Transborder Flows of Personal Data 1980.

• The European Community Directive on the Protection of Individuals with regard to the Processing of Personal Data and on the Free Movement of Such Data 1995.

The Council of Europe Convention for the Protection of Individuals with regard to Automatic Processing of Personal Data

5.51 The Council of Europe Convention for the Protection of Individuals with regard to Automatic Processing of Personal Data 1981 was promulgated because data protection has been seen as a question of human rights. The fundamental idea of the Convention is to protect privacy. The Convention was adopted and published in 1980, opened for signature in 1981 and came into effect in 1985. It is now legally binding on its adhering parties. The Convention has three major functions; it establishes basic rules for data protection measures to be adopted by adhering states; it sets out special rules about transborder data flows; and it establishes mechanisms for consultation, if not enforcement.

5.52 The Convention is not a 'European' Convention; the absence of 'European' from its formal title emphasises that it is open for adherence and ratification by non-European countries. The core of principles gives considerable scope of variation to suit different constitutional and legal systems in their domestic implementation. Article 4 obligates each party to take the necessary measures in its domestic law to give effect to the basic principles of data protection.

5.53 Article 5 sets out the basic principles of data protection, as to both the contents of the data and their processing. It provides that personal data undergoing automatic processing shall be:

- obtained fairly and lawfully;

- stored for specified and legitimate purposes and not used in a way incompatible with those purposes;

- adequate, relevant and not excessive in relation to the purpose for which they are stored;

- accurate and, where necessary, kept up to date;

- preserved in a form which permits identification of the data subjects for no longer than is required for the purpose for which those data are stored.

5.54 The 'special categories' of personal data in art 6 are not to be processed automatically 'unless domestic law provides appropriate safeguards'. The list represents a broad consensus on the sort of personal information regarded as particularly sensitive by representatives of the European countries in the late twentieth century. They are 'personal data revealing racial origin, political opinions or religious or other beliefs, as well as data concerning health or sexual life', and 'the same shall apply to personal data relating to criminal convictions'. This is a minimum list, and it is open to Parties under art 11 to give effect to cultural values by giving similar special protection to other kinds of personal data.

5.55 Article 8 is about 'additional safeguards for the data subjects', but might be better called 'rights of data subjects', except that the Convention does not necessarily require the creation of rights. The article requires domestic legislation to give data subjects the right to know whether there are automated data files on them; to find out the contents of such files; to have errors corrected or deleted; and to have a remedy if these rights are violated. Although the right to know of the existence of files does not require a public register of their controllers, other measures, such as notification to a data subject when the file is opened, would be required to provide equivalent protection. It is not clear from the text whether the right to rectification includes retrospective notification to everyone who has received the erroneous information, but it would seem at least arguable that it does[1].

1 See James Michael, *Privacy and Human Rights: An International and Comparative Study, with Special Reference to Developments in Information Technology* (1994) p 3.

5.56 Article 9 attempts to define the circumstances in which states are justified in departing from the principles. The resemblance of the qualifying second paragraph to several of the rights under the European Convention on Human Rights is deliberate. The easiest exception is for personal data files 'used for statistics or for scientific research where there is obviously no risk of an infringement of the privacy of the data subjects'. Less easy is the allowance of derogation from arts 5, 6 and 8 when such derogation is provided for by the law of the Party and constitutes a necessary measure in a democratic society in the interest of:

- protecting state security, public safety, the monetary interests of the state or the suppression of criminal offences;

- protecting the data subject or the rights and freedoms of others.

5.57 Article 10 states that the domestic methods of implementing the principles must include remedies, while art 11 makes it clear that the Convention sets basic standards and that, parties can give greater protection to data subjects, such as rights of access to manual files. The rest of the Convention is concerned with transborder data flows and machinery for implementation.

The Organisation for Economic Co-operation and Development (OECD) Guidelines Governing the Protection of Privacy and Transborder Flows of Personal Data

5.58 The OECD saw the national protection laws as protectionist regulations and non-tariff trade barriers. The Guidelines are in the language of recommendation rather than obligation. The basic principles are similar to those of the Convention, but written in less specific terms.

5.59 It is clearly stated that the Guidelines should be regarded as minimum standards, which are capable of being supplemented by additional measures for the protection of privacy and individual liberties. The Guidelines establish eight information privacy principles:

- The collection limitation principle requires that information must only be obtained via lawful means and with the knowledge or consent of the data subject.

- The data quality principle provides that only information relevant for the purpose of the collection be required by the collector of the data and such data must be up-to-date, accurate and complete.

- The purpose specification principle states that the purpose or purposes for which the data is gathered must be disclosed to the data subject at the time it is collected and that such data shall only be used for that purpose or purposes.

- The use limitation principle requires that information not be disclosed to a third party by the person who has collected it without the consent of the data subject, unless, it is demanded by law.

- The security safeguards principle sets out that information must be protected by the collector, who, must take reasonable security precautions to guard against loss, destruction, and unauthorised use, access, modification or disclosure of it.

- The openness principle advocates that the data subjects ought to be able to readily determine the whereabouts, use and purpose of personal data relating to them.

- The individual participation principle requires that a data subject can obtain a confirmation from the data collector that information is held by it, obtain details of this information within a reasonable time, for a reasonable charge, if any, in a reasonable manner and in an intelligible form. Data subjects should also be given reasons where access to data is denied and given the right to challenge this decision. Finally, data subjects ought to have the ability to rectify inaccurate information and, where necessary, have it erased.

- The accountability principle sets out that the data collector ought to be accountable for complying with the above principles.

5.60 Part Three of the Guidelines is concerned with ensuring the free flow of information and indicating permissible barriers. Guideline 15 suggests that countries consider the implications of domestic processing of personal data to circumvent the data protection laws of other countries. This is a diplomatic way of saying that member countries should not be data havens or assist them. Guidelines 16 and 17 urge uninterrupted flows of personal data between member countries, except for any member which does not 'substantially observe' the Guidelines. Meanwhile Guideline 18 urges members to refrain from developing laws, policies and practices in the name of the protection of privacy and individual liberties, which, by exceeding requirements for the protection of privacy and to individual liberties, are inconsistent with the free transborder flow of personal data.

5.61 Part Four is on national implementation. It recommends that member countries should establish legal, administrative or other procedures or institutions for the protection of privacy and individual liberties in respect of personal data. Member countries should in particular endeavour to:

- adopt appropriate domestic legislation;

- encourage and support self-regulation, whether in the form of codes of conduct or otherwise;

- provide for reasonable means for individuals to exercise their rights;

- provide for adequate sanctions and remedies in case of failures to comply with measures which implement the principles; and

- ensure that there is no unfair discrimination against data subjects.

The European Community Directive on the Protection of Individuals with regards to the Processing of Personal Data and on the Free Movement of Such Data 1995

5.62 The Directive has two objectives, which are stated in art 1, as being:

- the protection of the fundamental rights and freedoms of natural persons and in particular their right to privacy with respect to the processing of personal data; and

- the prevention of barriers to the free flow of personal data across the community by virtue of reasons connected with the above protection.

5.63 In other words, by harmonising data law across the Community, member states are not allowed to restrict or prohibit the freedom of movement of personal data within the community by arguing, for example, that another member state does not provide an adequate level of protection for personal data. The recitals to the Directive stress and emphasise the twin objectives and the desirability of harmonising data protection law so as to afford a high level of protection in terms of fundamental rights and freedoms, in particular the right to privacy[1].

1   See David Bainbridge, *EC Data Protection Directive* (1996) p 42.

5.64 Recital 11 states that the protection of individuals' rights and freedoms contained in the Directive give substance to and amplify those contained in the Council of Europe Convention. The second recital to the Directive expresses some of the anxieties, which are left with regard to modern technologies of data processing and the need to ensure that they are only used to ensure the public good:

> '... data-processing systems are designed to serve man; whereas they must, whatever the nationality or residence of natural persons, respect their fundamental rights and freedoms, notably the right to privacy, and to contribute to economic and social progress, trade expansion and the well being of individuals.'

5.65 The Directive was introduced in view of the reality that increasingly frequent recourse was being made to the processing of personal data in the various spheres of economic and social activity. At the same time the development of information technology is making the processing and exchange of such data considerably easier.

5.66 The Directive applies to '... [T]he processing of personal data wholly or partly by automatic means, and to the processing otherwise than by automatic means of personal data which form part of a filing system or are intended to form part of a filing system'. It requires EU member states to ensure that individuals have certain rights[1] and that standards are set for data quality. The Directive only permits data to be held relating to individuals with their consent, and such consent must be expressed, informed and freely given. The Directive regulates structured collections of manual data as well as data held in computerised form. It also restricts the export of personal data outside the EU to countries, which do not have 'adequate' levels of data protection.

1   For example: the right to information, the right to access, the right to rectification and the right of opposition.

5.67 The Directive contains data quality principles in art 6. It requires that personal data must be:

- processed fairly and lawfully;

- collected for specified, explicit and legitimate purposes and not further processed in a way incompatible with those purposes;

- adequate, relevant and not excessive in relation to the purposes for which the data was collected and/or further processed;

- accurate and, where necessary, kept up-to-date, every reasonable step must be taken to ensure that data which is inaccurate or incomplete, having regard to the purposes for which it was collected or for which it is further processed, is erased or rectified; and

- kept in a form, which permits identification of data subjects for no longer than necessary for the purposes for which the data was collected or for which it is further processed. member states shall lay down appropriate safeguards for personal data stored for longer periods for historical, statistical or scientific use.

5.68 The controller is charged with the responsibility of ensuring the data quality principles are complied with. Article 7 provides that personal data may be processed only if:

(a) the data subject has given his consent unambiguously; or

(b) processing is necessary for the performance of a contract to which the data subject is a party or in order to take steps at the request of the data subject prior to entering into a contract; or

(c) processing is necessary for compliance with a legal obligation to which the controller is subject; or

(d) processing is necessary in order to protect the vital interest of the data subject; or

(e) processing is necessary for the performance of a task carried out in the public interest or in the exercise of the official authority vested in the controller or in a third party to whom the data are disclosed; or

(f) processing is necessary for the purpose of the legitimate interests pursued by the controller or by the third party or parties to whom the data is disclosed, except where such interests are overridden by the interests or fundamental rights and freedoms of the data subject, which require protection.

5.69 Article 17 of the Directive requires the implementation of appropriate technical and organisational measures to protect personal data from accidental or unlawful destruction or accidental loss, alteration, unauthorised disclosure or access and all other forms of unlawful processing. The transmission of data over networks is highlighted as a particular area of concern.

5.70 Article 8 of the Directive covers the processing of specific categories of information called 'sensitive data'. It prohibits the processing of the sensitive data as data revealing racial or ethnic origin, political affiliates/opinions, religious or philosophical beliefs, trade union membership and/or where the processing concerns health or sex life. However, the exceptions are provided for in art 8(2):

(a)   the data subject has given his explicit consent;

(b)   processing is necessary for employment law obligations and rights of the data controller;

(c)   processing is necessary to protect the vital interests of the data subject or where the data subject is physically or legally incapable of giving consent;

(d)   processing is carried out in the course of its legitimate activities with appropriate guarantees by a foundation, association or any other non-profit-seeking body;

(e)   the processing relates to data which is manifestly made public by the data subject or is necessary for the establishment, exercise or defence of legal claims.

5.71   The data subject must be informed of certain details such as the identity of the controller, the purpose or purposes of the processing, the recipient of the data, his/her right of access to the data etc. The data subject is guaranteed the right to object to the processing of his/her personal data and the right of access to the data.

Applicability of the data protection legislation to online environments

5.72   With data protection, as with other aspects of IT law, there is continual discussion as to whether the law is sufficiently flexible to keep pace with technological change. Ann Cavoukian, Ontario's Privacy Commissioner, argues that the challenge is to transport the basic privacy principles that currently exist in the physical world – laws, customs and practices – into the virtual world. She states:

'fair information practices provide a framework by which to access technology-based solutions and to serve as a benchmark in creating those solutions. Reidenberg and Schwartz believe that the implementation of fair information practices is exceedingly complex in the fluid context of the Internet and technology may itself offer new opportunities for the protection of personal data. They argue that the key questions ... revolve around the extent to which infrastructure arrangements create data protection problems and the extent to which data protection can be built within the architecture of online services.'[1]

One commentator, specifically, argues that:

'None of the international privacy treaties directly recognises current computer network technology. The OECD Guidelines and the Council of Europe Convention were adopted long before computer networks were commonplace. The EU data protection Directive is more recent, but it too fails to address network issues. Technology has simply overwhelmed some traditional approaches to privacy protection and some legal assumptions upon which the approaches rely.'[2]

1   See Alan McKenna, 'Playing Fair with Consumer Privacy in the Global Online Environment', *Information & Communications Technology Law*, Vol 10, No 3 (2001) pp 339, 340–341.
2   Robert Gellman, 'Conflict and Overlap in Privacy Regulation: National, International, and Private' in Brian Kahin and Charles Nesson (eds) *Borders in Cyberspace: Information Policy and the Global Information Infrastructure* (1997) p 274.

5.73   It is not acceptable that the international privacy treaties do not recognise current computer network technology and therefore do not apply to the online world. The OECD Guidelines provide for general principles that can be applied offline and/or online. They are technologically neutral principles.

5.74   As for the Council of Europe Convention the title itself, 'Convention for the Protection of Individuals with Regard to Automatic Processing of Personal Data', reflects that the focus is on network technology. Furthermore the purpose of the convention was to protect the fundamental freedom of every individual 'with regard to *automatic processing* of personal data relating to him'.

5.75   The drafters of the EU Data Protection Directive were fully aware of the need to keep abreast of developments. Recital 14 of the preamble to the Directive stated:

'Whereas, given the importance of the developments under way, in the framework of the information society, of the techniques used to capture, transmit, manipulate, record, store or communicate sound and image data relating to natural persons, this Directive should be applicable to processing involving such data.'

5.76   In one of the replies to Frequently Asked Questions on the Commission's website, the Commission states that, 'it would be illogical and without legal justification to exempt such means of transfers (through the Internet) of data from the scope of the Directive.' Recital 14 of the preamble to the EU E-Commerce Directive 2000 recognises the Data Protection Directive. It states:

'The protection of individuals with regard to the processing of personal data is solely governed by the Directive on the protection of individuals with regard to the processing of personal data and on the free movement of such data ... which are fully applicable to information society services ... the implementation and application of this Directive should be made in full compliance with the principles relating to the protection of personal data.'

5.77   In short, it means that the implementation of the E-Commerce Directive must be in line with data protection law and principles provided for in the Data Protection Directive. The Working Party stated, '... [T]he general data protection directive applies to any processing of personal data falling within its scope, irrespective of the technical means used'.

5.78 The UK's Registrar attached Appendix 6 to the Eleventh Report, entitled, *Data Protection and the Internet.* The Registrar opined:

'It is sometimes said that the Internet is unregulated. That is not the case. It is true that it is not a monolithic entity that it is not a legal person, that there is no authority, which controls the whole, that it is not regulated under a single jurisdiction. But that does not mean that its use escapes regulation altogether. In using the Internet you cannot ignore the law on, for example, copyright, defamation, obscenity and data protection. Use of the Internet by a user in the UK does, as regards any processing of personal data, fall under the Data Protection Act 1984 and the jurisdiction of the Data Protection Registrar.'

5.79 In the first Report of the Data Protection Commissioner on the 16th year of operation of the Data Protection 1984 issued in June 2000, the Commissioner stated that the Data Protection Act 1998 applies to the processing of personal data over the Internet in the same way as it applies to the processing of data by more traditional automatic means. The Commissioner, however, recognises that organisations and individuals may find it difficult to envisage what steps they should take to ensure that they comply with their data protection obligations in the online environment.

Recent initiatives on online privacy

5.80 The OECD Ministers adopted the Declaration on the Protection of Privacy on Global Networks on 7–9 October 1998. The Ministers declared that they will reaffirm their commitment to the protection of privacy on global networks in order to ensure the respect of important rights, build confidence in global networks and to prevent unnecessary restrictions on transborder flows of personal data. They agreed to work to build bridges between the different approaches adopted by member countries to ensure privacy protection on global networks based on the OECD Guidelines[1].

1 See the Group of Experts on Information Security and Privacy, *Practices to Implement the OECD Privacy Guidelines on Global Networks*, DSTI/ICCP/REG (98) 6/FINAL.22.

5.81 More importantly the Ministers declare that they will take the necessary steps, within the framework of their respective laws and practices, to ensure that the OECD Privacy Guidelines are effectively implemented. Specific actions will be taken to achieve the following objectives:

• encourage the adoption of privacy policies, whether implemented by legal, self-regulatory, administrative or technological means;

• encourage the online notification of privacy policies to users;

• ensure that effective enforcement mechanisms are available both to address non-compliance with privacy principles and policies and to ensure access to redress;

- promote user education and awareness about online privacy issues and the means at their disposal for protecting privacy on global networks;

- encourage the use of privacy-enhancing technologies; and

- encourage the use of contractual solutions and the development of model contractual solutions for online transborder data flows.

5.82   The promises are to review progress made in furtherance of the objectives of the Declaration within a period of two years, and to assess the need for further action to ensure the protection of personal data on global networks in pursuit of these objectives. The OECD Secretariat has drawn up the ten series suggestion for a privacy-friendly website design.

5.83   On 21 January 2003, OECD issued a document *Privacy Online: Policy and Practical Guidance*. At the national level, member countries should take further steps to help ensure the adoption of privacy policies through encouraging organisations with a presence online to, among others, systematically, conduct an extensive review of their privacy practices and to develop a privacy policy that would give effect to the OECD privacy principles. Member countries are encouraged to review their laws and self-regulatory schemes and amend them if necessary and to reassess the privacy practices and policy on a regular basis. Member countries are also encouraged to ensure the online notification of privacy policies to users, the availability of enforcement and redress mechanisms in cases of non-compliance with privacy principles and policies, the promotion of user education and awareness about online privacy and the means of protecting the privacy, the use of privacy enhancing technologies and the development of privacy functions in other technologies. At the global level they should reaffirm their intention to co-operate among themselves and with the other participants to implement the OECD Privacy Guidelines online in the public and private sectors. Member countries should also consider reassessing periodically the need for any other action to ensure the protection of personal data at the global level.

5.84   The document contains practical guidance for businesses and other organi-sations as well as for individual users and consumers. Businesses can develop privacy policies based on the OECD Guidelines and post them on their home page. They can also evaluate whether the self-regulatory tools are appropriate and if so implement them and work with the government to develop innovative and flexible implementation models. Individual users and consumers can act directly or through a representative group to advocate the use of effective privacy practices by businesses, to seek more general transparency and education and enforce their legal rights at national law.

5.85   The EU Working Party on the Protection of Individuals with regard to the Processing of Personal Data, authorised by the Directive to advise and provide guidance about the Directive, issued a paper in 1999, about Internet issues and the Directive. The paper *Invisible and Automatic Processing of Personal Data on the Internet Performed by Software and Hardware* discusses issues pertaining to automatic and invisible data processing on the Internet. The paper focused on one of the most important data protection principles of the Directive – that data subjects (Internet users) should be informed about the collection, storage or transmission of data about themselves, with regards to the use of the data and the purpose for that use.

5.86   To comply with the Directive, the Working Party makes recommendations for Internet products, although all of the examples in the paper focus on web browsers:

- For web browsers, users should be informed about what information the browser will transfer to a web server and also the purpose for the transfer;

- Internet users should be informed when a cookie is to be received, stored or sent by Internet software. The message informing the user should indicate which information will be stored in the cookie, how long the cookie will be valid and what its purpose is;

- Web browsers should be configured by default to send minimum information through the Internet. For example, cookies should not be automatically sent or stored, by default;

- During installation, a web browser should not automatically collect information about the installer, such as the installer's name, computer type, location, or other information about the user's identity or communication profile;

- Internet users should be able to configure web browsers to control what information the browser can collect or transmit; and

- Internet users should be able to accept or reject cookies as a whole, as well as specifically edit a cookie file's contents.

5.87   In November 2000, the Working Party issued a report on online privacy. The report contains a number of recommendations with respect to online privacy policy. First, the Working Party stresses, 'adequate means are [to be] put into place in order to ensure that the user gets all the information he/she needs to make an informed choice'. Further, it opines that:

> 'although having a privacy policy posted on the website is a good way of providing general information to the public, it is necessary to provide information to the data subject from which the data are being collected in a simple and accessible way each time that data are collected, e.g. in the same screen where he/she has to fill in his/her data or through a box prompt'.

5.88   Second, the report observes that compliance with the data protection legislation can be guaranteed only if 'data controllers can rely on a coherent and co-ordinated interpretation and application of the European data protection rules'.

5.89   Third, the Working Party recommends that use be made of privacy compliant, privacy friendly and privacy enhancing technologies. The report states that those involved in the design and development of technical tools are encouraged to consult the National Data Protection Authorities about the existing data protection legal requirement. The Working Party recommends that a system of certification marks be set up for compliance-products by the EU.

5.90   Fourth, the Working Party suggests that effective means of enforcement of legal and technical requirements be guaranteed. It also suggests that national authorities set up self-monitoring schemes to encourage self-regulation. The national authorities are advised to promote privacy labelling schemes. In this respect, the Working Party announces that it intends to take action in this field in order to ensure in particular that privacy labels are granted to websites which are in line with European data protection legislation.

5.91   The Working Party adopted the *Recommendation on Certain Minimum Requirements for Collecting Personal Data Online in the European Union* on 17 May 2001[1]. The main objective of the Recommendation is to give practical added value for the implementation of the general principles of the EU Data Protection Directive. The Working Party considers the Recommendation as a first initiative to spell out on the European level a 'minimum' set of obligations in a way that can easily be followed by controller operating websites. The Recommendation is addressed in particular to:

● the controllers collecting data online;

● individual Internet users;

● the bodies wishing to award a label certifying conformity of the processing procedures used with the European Data Protection Directive; and

● the European data protection authorities.

1   Document 5020/01/EN/Final, available at http://europa.eu.int/comm/internal_market/en/media/dataprot/wpdocs/index.htm.

5.92   In addition, the Working Party is of the opinion that the Recommendation should also serve as reference for developing standards for software and hardware intended for the collection and processing of personal data on the Internet.

5.93   The Working Party also considers that complete information on the privacy policy should be directly accessible on the home page of the site and anywhere where personal data are collected online. The title of the heading to click on should be sufficiently highlighted, explicit and specific to allow the Internet user to have a clear idea of which content he/she is sending is being collected.

5.94   The third section of the document is entitled Recommendations for implementing other rights and obligations. The Working Party is of the view that the Recommendations in this section are of immediate practical value for both controllers and Internet users. They are:

● Collect only data as far as necessary to achieve the purpose specified.

- Ensure that data is processed only in so far as it is legitimate on the basis of one of the criteria enumerated in art 7 of the directive 95/46/EC.

- Ensure effective exercise of the right to access and to rectify, rights which it should be possible to exercise both at the physical address of the controller and online. Security measures should exist to guarantee that only the data subject has online access to the information which concerns him/her.

- Implement the 'finality' or 'purpose' principle, which requires that personal data only be used where necessary for a specific purpose. In other words, without a legitimate reason, personal data cannot be used and the individual remains anonymous.

- Provide for and promote anonymous consultation of a commercial site without requests for identification of the user by name, first name, e-mail address or other identifying data.

- Fix a storage period for the data collected. Data can only be kept for as long as this is justified by the purpose of the processing specified and pursued (art 6 of Directive 95/46/EC and art 6 of Directive 97/66/EC).

- Take the steps necessary to ensure data security during processing including transmission (for example restrict and define the persons authorised to have access to the data, use strong encryption etc. Article 17 of the Directive 95/46/EC).

- Where a processor is involved, for example, to host a website, conclude a contract requiring the processor to put in place appropriate security measures in accordance also with the law of the member state where the processor is located and only process personal data on the data controller's instructions.

- As appropriate under national law, notify the supervisory authority (when the site controller is established in the European Union or when he has a representative in the European Union). The registration number of the notification can appear on the site, to great advantage, under the heading dedicated to data protection.

- When transferring information to a third country where adequate protection is not guaranteed, ensure that the transfer of data only takes place if it is in line with one of the derogations provided for in art 26 of Directive 95/46/EC. In such cases, inform the individual about the adequate guarantees provided in order to make the transfer lawful.

National initiatives

5.95 The EU member states were bound to implement the EU Directive into their national legislation by 25 October 1998. So far, countries that have adopted the corresponding new laws are Austria, Belgium, Denmark (partially), Finland, Greece, Italy, Portugal, Spain, Sweden and the UK. In January 2000, the European

Commission decided to take Denmark, France, Germany, Ireland, Luxembourg and the Netherlands to the European Court of Justice for failure to notify all the measures necessary to implement the Directive[1]. The UK government has replaced its 1984 Act with the one of 1998. Germany adopted federal legislation in 2000. In total there are some forty countries that have adopted the comprehensive legislation.

1 See http://europa.eu.int/comm/internal_market/en/media/dataprot/news/2k-10.htm.

5.96 Outside Europe, some countries have adopted regulation while others prefer the self-regulatory approach. Canada enacted federal legislation, The Personal Information Protection and Electronic Documents Act, in 2000, which takes effect in January 2001. In Asia, Hong Kong enacted a Personal Data (Privacy) Ordinance in 1995. Japan's 1988 Act for the Protection of Computer Processed Personal Data Held by Administrative Organs was based on the OECD Guidelines. The Japanese parliament, Diet, in May 2002, began debate on new legislation entitled 'Act for Protection of Personal Data', which was approved by the Japanese cabinet in March 2001. The Prime Minister stated, 'While taking into consideration the usefulness of personal information, this bill protects the rights of individuals against invasion of privacy and is an indispensable foundation for safeguarding the way we live'. South Korea enacted the Communications Privacy Act in 1993 and revised it in 1997. Taiwan has had a Computer Processed Data Personal Data Protection Act since August 1995, governing both public and private bodies. New Zealand's Privacy Act 1993 has been amended several times since it was enacted. Australia recently amended its Privacy Act to extend it to the private sector. Thailand has enacted an Official Information Act, which sets out the code of information practices on personal information system run by state agencies. Singapore adopted the industry-based self-regulatory 'E-Commerce Code for the Protection of Personal Information and Communications of Consumers of Internet Commerce'. Recently, Singapore has prepared the Private Sector Model Data Protection Code, a comprehensive data protection regime for the private sector. According to the National Internet Advisory Committee Legal Subcommittee, which prepared it, the code, as an interim measure, should be given official recognition and adherence is invited on a voluntary basis. In the longer term, it remains to be seen whether a reliance on voluntary controls in the public sector would be completely effective or whether an appropriate degree of legislative intervention may be required.

5.97 While data protection laws enjoy common ground in terms of most of the above principles, they presently differ in terms of their ambit. Some countries' laws only apply to data processing by public sector bodies, while most other countries' laws and all of the international data protection laws apply also to data processing by private sector bodies. Some countries' laws only apply to computerised/ automated processing of data, while most other countries' laws apply also to non-automated processing. Some countries' laws give express protection for data relating to legal/juridical persons (i.e. corporations and the like), in addition to data relating to individual natural/physical persons, while most other countries' laws expressly protect only the latter data.

5.98 Differences occur also with respect to the regulatory regimes established pursuant to each law. For instance, while most countries' laws provide for the establishment of a special independent agency (the 'data protection authority') to oversee the laws' implementation, this is not the case with respect to the laws of the US and Japan. To take another example, while most countries' laws contain express restrictions on the flow of personal data to other countries that lack adequate data protection safeguards, some countries' laws do not. To take a third example, while some countries laws do not allow certain data-processing operations to commence without the operations first being checked and licensed by the relevant data protection authority, other countries' laws permit all or most operations to commence simply on the data protection authority first being notified of the operations.

United States self-regulatory approach

5.99 The US approach to protecting consumer privacy relies significantly on industry self-regulation. This policy was made clear in Clinton's Administration Framework for Global Electronic Commerce. The Framework is the equivalent of a Clinton administration Mission Statement regarding electronic commerce. It is based upon these five principles:

- The private sector should lead.

- Governments should avoid undue restrictions on electronic commerce.

- Where governmental involvement is needed, its aim should be to support and enforce predictable, minimalist, consistent and simple legal environments for commerce.

- Governments should recognise the unique qualities of the Internet.

- Electronic Commerce over the Internet should be facilitated on a global basis.

5.100 Regarding privacy issues, the Framework endorses self-regulatory regimes. The US also has taken a sectoral approach to privacy, enacting laws that apply to specific industries and practices. Some examples are: Fair Credit Reporting Act 1970, Privacy Act 1974, Cable Communications Policy Act 1984, Electronic Communication Privacy Act 1986, Video Privacy Protection Act 1988, Telephone Consumer Protection Act 1991, Drivers Privacy Protection Act 1994 and Children's Online Privacy Protection Act 1998.

5.101 One commentator stated:

'It would perhaps be more accurate to say that the USA lacks *meaningful* personal data privacy laws. One of the main problems cited about US data privacy laws is that there are simply too many of them. A scan through *The Privacy Law Sourcebook 1999* provides the reader with a list of 14 federal laws with some personal data privacy element, and the addition of state laws and regulations would create a list running into the hundreds. Yet as Rotenberg notes, the US federal privacy statutes have tended to arise less out of a concerted attempt to provide US citizens with a coherent personal data privacy regime, than out of a series of attempts either to fill legal lacuna that the courts had specifically refused to address, or to assuage public concern arising from the use and abuse of new technologies[1].

1   Andrew Charlesworth, 'Data Privacy in Cyberspace; Not national vs. International but Commercial vs. Individual', in Lilian Edwards & Charlotte Waelde (eds) *Law and the Internet* (2000) p 79.

5.102   The pressures on America stem principally from the stipulation in art 25 of the EU Directive that data transfers to a third country may take place only if that country ensures an adequate level of protection. This provision threatens the flow of trade between the US and EU.

5.103   After a series of difficult negotiations and several drafts, an announcement was made in early March 2000, that European and US negotiators had in fact finalised a data privacy agreement based on the safe harbour principles. On July 21, 2000 the US Department of Commerce issued the final draft of the Safe Harbour Principles:

- *NOTICE:* An organization must inform individuals about the purposes for which it collects and uses information about them, how to contact the organization with any inquiries or complaints, the types of third parties to which it discloses the information, and the choices and means the organization offers individuals for limiting its use and disclosure. This notice must be provided in clear and conspicuous language when individuals are first asked to provide personal information to the organization or as soon thereafter as is practicable, but in any event the organization uses or discloses such information for a purpose other than that for which it was originally collected or processed by the transferring organization or discloses it for the first time to a third party.

- *CHOICE:* An organization must offer individuals the opportunity to choose (opt out) whether and how their personal information is:

  (a)   to be disclosed to third parties, where disclosure is for a purpose other than the purpose for which it was originally collected or subsequently authorized by the individual; or

  (b)   to be used where such use is for a purpose that is incompatible with the purpose(s) for which it was originally collected, or subsequently authorized by the individual. Individuals must be provided with clear and conspicuous, readily available, and affordable mechanisms to exercise choice.

For sensitive information, (i.e. personal information specifying medical or health conditions, racial or ethnic origin, political opinions, religious or philosophical beliefs, trade union membership or information specifying the sex life of the individual) they must be given affirmative or explicit (opt in) choice if the information is to be disclosed to a third party or used for a purpose other than those for which it was originally collected or subsequently authorized by the individual through the exercise of opt in choice. In any case, an organization should treat as sensitive any information received from a third party where the third party identifies it as sensitive.

- *ONWARD TRANSFER:* An Organization may only disclose personal information to third parties consistent with the principles of notice and choice. Where an organization has not provided choice and the organization wishes to transfer the data to a third party, it may do so if it first either ascertains that the third party subscribes to the principles or is subject to the Directive or another adequacy finding or enters into a written agreement with such third party requiring that the third party provide at least the same level of privacy protection as is required by the relevant principles. If the organization complies with these requirements, it shall not be held responsible (unless the organization agrees otherwise) when a third party to which it transfers such information processes it in a way contrary to any restrictions or representations, unless the organization knew or should have known the third party would process it in such a contrary way and the organization has not taken reasonable steps to prevent or stop such processing.
- *SECURITY:* Organization creating, maintaining, using or disseminating personal information must take reasonable precautions to protect it from loss, misuse and unauthorized access, disclosure, alteration and destruction.
- *DATA INTERGRITY:* Consistent with the principles, personal information must be relevant for the purpose for which it is to the used. An organization may not process personal information in a way that is incompatible with the purposes for which it has been collected or subsequently authorized by the individual. To the extent necessary for those purposes, an organization should take reasonable steps to ensure that data is reliable for its intended use, accurate, complete, and current.
- *ACCESS:* Individuals must have access to personal information about them that an organization holds and be able to correct, amend, or delete that information where it is inaccurate, except where the burden or expense of providing access would be disproportionate to the risks to the individual's privacy in the case in question, or where the rights of persons other than the individual would be violated.
- *ENFORCEMENT:* Effective privacy protection must include mechanisms for assuring compliance with the principles, recourse for individuals to whom the data relate affected by non-compliance with the principles, and consequences for the organization when the principles are not followed. At a minimum, such mechanisms must include (a) readily available and affordable independent recourse mechanisms by which each individual's complaints and disputes are investigated and resolved by reference to the principles and damages awarded where the applicable law or private sector initiatives so provide; (b) follow up procedures for verifying that the attestations and assertions businesses make about their privacy practices are true and that privacy practices have been implemented as presented; and (c) obligations to remedy problems arising out of failure to comply with the principles by organizations announcing their adherence to them and consequences for such organizations. Sanctions must be sufficiently rigorous to ensure compliance by organizations.

5.104 The Safe Harbour Principles are to be used 'solely by US organisations receiving personal data from the European Union for the purpose of qualifying for the safe harbour and the presumption of "adequacy" it creates.'[1] US organisations qualify for the so-called safe harbour on a purely voluntary basis by complying with the Principles and publicly declaring that they intend to do so. Organisations can do this by joining a self-regulatory privacy programme that adheres to the Principles or they may develop their own self-regulatory privacy policies provided that they conform to the Principles. Safe Harbour benefits are assured from the date that an organisation self-certifies, to the US Department of Commerce, its adherence to the Principles. As at 4 June 2001, just 48 US companies had registered as adhering to the Safe Harbour Principles[2].

1 United States Department of Commerce Safe Harbour Privacy Principles (21 July 2000) http://www.ita.doc.gov/td/ecom/SHPRINCIPLESFINAL.htm.
2 See Alan McKenna, 'Playing Fair with Consumer Privacy in the Global Online Environment' (2001) *Information & Communications Technology Law* Vol 10, No 3, 342.

5.105   The FTC in its 2000 Report recommended that Congress enact legislation to protect privacy online. According to the FTC:

> 'Based on the past years of work addressing Internet privacy issues, including examination of prior surveys and workshops with consumers and industry, it is evident that online privacy continues to present an enormous public policy challenge. The Commission applauds the significant efforts of the private sector and commends industry leaders in developing self-regulatory initiatives. The 2000 Survey, however, demonstrates that industry efforts alone have not been sufficient. Because self-regulatory initiatives to date fall far short of broad-based implementation of effective self-regulatory programmes, the Commission has concluded that such efforts alone cannot ensure that the online marketplace as a whole will emulate the standards adopted by industry leaders. While there will continue to be a major role for industry self-regulation in the future, the Commission recommends that Congress enact legislation that, in conjunction with continuing self-regulatory programmes, will ensure adequate protection of consumer privacy online.'

5.106   The legislation recommended by the Commission would set forth a basic level of privacy protection for consumer-oriented commercial websites. It would establish basic standards of practice for the collection of information online, and provide an implementing agency with the authority to promulgate more detailed standards pursuant to the Administrative Procedure Act.

5.107   Ironically, the FTC, just two months after recommending that legislation be passed to protect consumer privacy online, issued an equally controversial report, *Online Profiling: A Report to Congress*[1], in which, they endorsed an industry self-regulatory plan put forward by the Network Advertising Initiative (NAI). Under the NAI self-regulatory principles agreed by the FTC, previously collected non-personally identifiable (Non-PII) data cannot be linked to personally identifiable information (PII) without the affirmative (opt-in) consent of the consumer, however, 'network advertisers will not merge PII with Non-PII collected on a going forward basis ... [U]nless the customer has been afforded robust notice and choice about such merger before it occurs.' Thus, a network advertiser can, before it collects Non-PII, give robust notice of its intentions to collect Non-PII and subsequently merge this with PII, and as long as it gives consumers the chance to opt-out of this action, then this will be allowable[2]. In respect of PII, 'robust notice' of collection and an 'opt-out' choice is required before such information is used for profiling. Privacy advocacy groups, Electronic Privacy information centre (EPIC) and Junkbusters, in a critical report on NAI plan state:

> 'As most Internet users do not realise that online profiling is occurring at all, opt-out places an unreasonable burden on consumers to indicate their preference to *not* be tracked. Any company that tracks users, anonymously or otherwise, should not do so until the user opts-in, affirmatively agreeing to allow it to occur.'[3]

1 Federal Trade Commission, 'On-line Profiling: A Report to Congress', Part 2, Recommendations (July 2000).
2 *Ibid.*
3 EPIC/Junkbusters, 'Network Advertising Initiative: Principles Not Privacy' (July 2000) p 7, cited in Alan McKenna, 'Playing Fair with Consumer Privacy in the Global Online Environment' (2001) *Information & Communications Technology Law*, Vol 10, No 3, 344.

5.108 The Head of the Commerce Department of National Telecommunications and Information Administration (NTIA), Nancy Victor, recently hinted that the Bush Administration would probably favour a light touch, encouraging the high-tech industry to develop voluntary guidelines rather than imposing regulations or pushing for new law. She said, 'Up until now, and I think this will probably continue, we have been supportive of industry self-regulation. I think that industry has made great strides, but I think there's still more work to do.'[1] This has received an endorsement from the newly appointed Chairman of the FTC. At the privacy conference on 4 October 2001, the Chairman stated that there are clearly good arguments for such legislation: online privacy legislation could increase consumer confidence in the Internet by establishing a clear set of rules about how personal information is collected and used. Moreover, federal legislation could help ensure consistent regulation of collection practices across the 50 states. Nevertheless, it is too soon to conclude that we can fashion workable legislation to accomplish these goals[2].

1 Reuters (5 September 2001) available at http://www.zdnet.com/zdnn.
2 FTC Chairman, Timothy J. Muris, 'Protecting Consumers' Privacy: 2002 and Beyond' available at http://www.ftc.gov/speeches/muris/privisp1002.htm.

CHAPTER SIX

Data Protection and Internet Banking

Introduction

6.1 Walter Wriston, the former chair and CEO of Citicorp, once wrote, 'Information about money has become as important as money itself.' One of the biggest concerns about Internet banking has always been the protection of consumers' data. John D. Wright, Assistant General Counsel, Regulation and Technology, Wells Fargo, one of the leading American banks in the area of Internet and electronic banking, noted[1]:

> 'Privacy and its many dimensions is one of the most significant challenges facing the financial services today. It is a, particular, challenge to organisations that are especially advanced in electronic banking, since technology permits the ready gathering and analysis of vast quantities of information about individuals and their financial transactions. Indeed, it seems obvious that the advent of Internet banking and the fears about the misuse of personal data gathered by businesses online has strongly fuelled the present privacy debate.'

1 John D. Wright, 'Electronic Banking: New Developments and Regulatory Risks' available at http://www.imf.org/external/np/leg/sem2002/cdmfl/eng/wright.pdf, p 3.

6.2 According to a recent study by the American Institute of Certified Public Accountants nearly 80% of the people planning to do business over the Internet would go to a different website if they could not gain assurance over the security of their information, its integrity or what the company's privacy policy was with respect to the use of that information[1]. While technology clearly is the lead performer on the e-commerce stage, more and more companies are recognising that privacy plays a more than just supporting role. It is becoming a major issue that banks have to tackle. It is all about building consumer trust in Internet banking.

1 John D. Wright, 'Electronic Banking: New Developments and Regulatory Risks' available at http://www.imf.org/external/np/leg/sem2002/cdmfl/eng/wright.pdf, p 3.

Protection of financial information in the United States

6.3 The Safe Harbour only applies to companies under the jurisdiction of the Federal Trade Commission and the Department of Transportation. It means that those companies that fall under the jurisdiction of these organisations are eligible to participate in the Safe Harbour. The banking and financial sector is excluded. This does not mean that the banking sector is not subject to the adequacy requirement of the EU Directive. In fact, the European Union will have to make a decision in the future as to whether the US law for protecting the privacy of financial information complies with the EU's Directive requirement. This section describes some of the current Federal statutes that protect financial information with special attention on the most recent statute of the Financial Services Modernization Act or Gramm-Leach-Bliley Act (GLB) 1999. Some industry efforts are also highlighted.

The Fair Credit Reporting Act 1970

6.4 The Fair Credit Reporting Act (FCRA) generally governs the collection, evaluation, maintenance and dissemination of reports on consumers collected for the purpose of evaluating their qualification for credit, insurance, employment, and certain other transactions. It only applies, however, to 'consumer credit reports' issued by 'consumer credit agencies'. FCRA restricts the dissemination of consumer reports to 'permissible purposes', but does not generally grant consumers the right to prevent the disclosure of personal information. It does, however, prohibit the maintenance or disclosure of obsolete or inaccurate information about consumers.

6.5 In 1996, the US Congress passed the Consumer Credit Reporting Reform Act, which contains amendments to the FCRA effectively as of 30 September 1997. These amendments have several implications for banks and online banking. They clarify that affiliated companies may share 'experience information' concerning consumers. Experience information is information relating solely to transactions or experiences between the consumer and the person making the report. A bank may also share *any information* (such as application information, demographic information, and credit reports) concerning a consumer, if it is 'clearly and conspicuously', disclosed to the customer that the affiliates intend to share such information, and the customer is given the right, prior to the sharing of any information, to 'opt-out' of the scheme.

6.6 The Reform Act also brings new privacy and disclosure rights with regard to the term 'firm offers' of credit or insurance products sent by banks. Section 2404(e) of the Act allows consumers to elect to have their names excluded from the lists that are used to generate firm offers of credit or insurance products. Consumers are given the right to see all information contained in a credit report and the right to request a free copy of the report from the user after an adverse action has been taken.

6.7 Under the Reform Act, furnishers of credit information are under a heightened duty to ensure that consumer credit report information is accurate, as well as a duty to update and correct such information when a consumer makes a request. The new standard of liability under the Reform Act is whether the furnisher of information knew or consciously avoided knowing that the information furnished was inaccurate. The furnisher of consumer credit information must therefore, upon learning that such information is inaccurate, contact the consumer credit reporting agency and make any necessary corrections to the information. Further, the furnisher of credit information may not thereafter furnish to the agency any of the information that remains incomplete or inaccurate. Upon notice of a dispute as to information provided to a reporting agency, the furnisher of the information must investigate the dispute within 30 days and must thereafter furnish corrected information to any national credit reporting agency to which it previously furnished inaccurate data.

Right to Financial Privacy Act 1978

6.8 The purpose of the Right to Financial Privacy Act (RFPA) is to protect the customers of financial institutions from unwarranted intrusion into their financial records while at the same time permitting legitimate law enforcement activity. Under this Act, the government may have access to, or obtain copies of, information contained in a customer's financial records from a financial institution only if:

- the customer authorises the disclosure;

- the government obtains an administrative or judicial subpoena or summons; and

- the records are sought pursuant to a search warrant or formal written request.

6.9 The RFPA provides for the procedural requirements that must be satisfied by the federal government prior to seeking a financial institution's customer records, as well as procedural requirements the institution must follow prior to disclosure.

The Financial Services Modernization Act 1999

6.10 The Financial Services Modernization Act (FSMA) or Gramm-Leach-Bliley Act is the major and most recent federal law governing the privacy of financial information.

6.11 Title V of FSMA entitled 'Privacy' states: 'It is the policy of the Congress that each financial institution has an affirmative and continuing obligation to respect the privacy of its customers and to protect the security and confidentiality of those customers' non public personal information'.

6.12 Section 6802 provides that financial institutions may not, without notice, directly or through any affiliate, disclose to a non-affiliated third party any non-public personal information.

Non-public personal information is defined as personally identifiable financial information:

- provided by a consumer to a financial institution;

- resulting from any transaction with the consumer or any service performed for the consumer; or

- otherwise obtained by the financial institutions.

6.13 Section 6802(b) provides that a financial institution may not disclose non-public personal information to a non-affiliated third party unless:

- Such a financial institution clearly and conspicuously discloses to the consumer, in writing or in electronic form or other form permitted by the regulations prescribed under s 6804 of this title, that such information may be disclosed to such third party.

- The consumer is given the opportunity, before the time that such information is initially disclosed, to direct that such information not be disclosed to such third party.

- The consumer is given an explanation of how the consumer can exercise that non-disclosure option.

6.14 This provision, basically, requires notice to be given to the consumer before disclosure can be made. The financial institution must also provide for the consumer to opt-out. The institution must notify the customer that it will be disclosing the information but the consumer cannot prohibit the disclosure. The Act also provides a series of exceptions to the general provision disallowing disclosure of financial information to a non-affiliated party: Among others, disallowing disclosure to non-affiliated third parties that perform services or functions on the institution's behalf, including for the marketing of its own products and services of those under a joint agreement with other financial institutions.

6.15 The other exceptions include disclosure of personal information necessary to effect, administer, or enforce a transaction requested or authorised by the consumer, or in connection with:

- servicing or processing a financial product or service requested or authorised by the customer;

- maintaining or servicing the customer's account with the financial institution, or with another entity;

- a proposed or actual securitisation, secondary market sale, or similar transaction related to a transaction of the consumer.

6.16 Disclosure to law enforcement agencies, secretary of treasury, a State insurance authority, self-regulatory organisations, and a consumer-reporting agency, are also exempted from the general rule. Interestingly, exception is created in situations where the disclosure is in connection with a proposed or actual sale, merger, transfer, or exchange of all or a portion of a business or operating unit. Anne Flanagan wrote, 'These very numerous and broad exceptions invite inquiry: What does the Act protect from disclosure to non-affiliated third parties? Perhaps little.'[1]

1   Anne Flanagan, 'Gramm-Leach-Bliley: Through the E.U. Data Protection Looking Glass' (2002) JIBL 237, 243.

6.17   Section 6803 of the FSMA requires financial institutions to disclose their privacy policy to the consumers. It provides:

'At the time of establishing a customer relationship with a consumer and not less than annually during the continuation of such relationship, a financial institution shall provide a clear and conspicuous disclosure to such consumer, in writing or in electronic form or other form permitted by the regulations prescribed under section 6804 of this tile, of such financial institution's policies and practices with respect to –

1.   disclosing non-public personal information to affiliated and non-affiliated third parties, consistent with section 6802 of this tile, including the categories of information that may be disclosed;

2.   disclosing non-public personal information of persons who have ceased to be customers of the financial institution; and

3.   protecting the non-public personal information of consumers.'

6.18   The disclosure shall include information on the following:

1.   the policies and practices of the institution with respect to disclosing non-public personal information to non-affiliated third parties; other than agents of the institution, and including –

    a.   the categories of persons to whom the information is, or may be, disclosed;

    b.   the policies and practices of the institution with respect to disclosing of non-public information of persons who have ceased to be customers of the financial institution;

2.   the categories of non-public personal information that are collected by the financial institution;

3.   the policies that the institution maintains to protect the confidentiality and security of non-public personal information.

6.19   Anne Flanagan, who assesses the Act based on the EU principles for fair and lawful processing, argues[1]:

• The Act governs only disclosure of data. Its notice requirements therefore relate only to the types of data collected and disclosed and the categories of parties to whom disclosed. The Act does not require notice as to how the collector or its affiliates, or indeed, the third parties will use the information.

• The choice of consent that is provided is, therefore, limited to the issue of disclosure, with no consent required as to use or further use. The Act's lack of choice for joint marketing programmes is criticised for failing to provide adequate protection. No one can opt-out of direct marketing by the institution, its affiliates or third parties in joint programmes.'

I   Anne Flanagan, 'Gramm-Leach-Bliley: Through the E.U. Data Protection Looking Glass' (2002) JIBL 246–247.

6.20   Anne Flanagan concludes that the Act provides several important new privacy protections to consumers of banks with its notice and disclosure require-ments, limitations on the sale of customer lists and the resale of credit header information. She further notes:'Despite these privacy protections that are some of the strongest accorded under US law, GLB (Gramm-Leach-Bliley) fails to comply with a majority of the EU principles for fair and lawful processing'[1].

I   Anne Flanagan, 'Gramm-Leach-Bliley: Through the E.U. Data Protection Looking Glass' (2002) JIBL 247.

Banking industry self-regulatory initiatives

6.21   Many of the industry efforts at self-regulation attempt to address a number of core principles that are typically considered to make up a model of 'fair information' practices. These include:

- Collection principles, which operate to limit the collection of personal information to that which is genuinely necessary.

- Transparency principles, which assure that individuals are informed about the manner in which information is to be collected, stored, and used by businesses and other organisations.

- Access and correction principles, which assures that individuals have access to, and the ability to correct information.

- Use principles, which govern how and under what circumstances businesses make use of personal information.

- Disclosure principles, which may require that some types of consent are granted by individuals to businesses and other organisations prior to the disclosure of such information to third parties.

6.22   The Bankers Roundtable, an industry group made of the US' 125 largest banking institutions, issued a 'Statement of Industry Principles' in November 1996 ('Bankers Roundtable Statement'), which addresses, among other topics, the issue of the privacy and confidentiality of consumer information. The Bankers Roundta-ble Statement treats privacy and security of consumer information as important public policy goals. Specifically, the statement recommends that Roundtable mem-bers should:

- Abide by all applicable federal and state laws regulating privacy issues.

- Train employees on bank requirements concerning consumer privacy, secu-rity, confidentiality, and data encryption, and address rule violations by employees promptly.

- Inform users of electronic financial services of consumer obligations and rights and methods for protecting their privacy.

- Act to maintain confidentiality of current and former customer information and protect customer confidentiality in all account and account transfer information outside of and within their institutions, except in cases where the member is compelled to meet legal requirements which compel otherwise or where disclosure is made at the request or with the consent of the customer.

- Develop and employ technologies that will enhance confidentiality in the transmission of consumer information.

- Disclose to their customers account and other information in conformance with all applicable banking laws.

6.23 The Consumer Bankers Association ('CBA') released its own set of principles ('Best Practices – Use of Customer Information') regarding the use of customer information in 1996. The CBA's principles include having members pledge to:

- Limit the use and collection of information about customers to what is necessary to administer our business, provide superior service, and offer opportunities to customers.

- Restrict employee access to customer information to those employees with a business need to know the information.

- Limit the instances in which the member will permit other companies to offer their products and services to the member's customers (i.e. when the member will provide customer information to third parties).

- Tell customers how to remove their names from telemarketing and mailing lists when they open accounts and maintain such information and provide it to customers upon request.

- Hire only those firms (e.g. to provide operational support to the member), which agree in writing to safeguard customer information according to the CBA's guidelines.

6.24 In September 1997, the American Bankers Association, Banking Industry Technology Secretariat and other banking organisations issued the following privacy guidelines:

- **Recognition of a Customer's Expectation of Privacy.** Financial institutions should recognise and respect the privacy expectations of their customers and explain principles of financial privacy to their customers in an appropriate fashion. This could be accomplished, for example, by making available privacy guidelines and/or providing a series of questions and answers about financial privacy to those customers.

- **Use, Collection and Retention of Customer Information.** Financial institutions should collect, retain, and use information about individual customers only where the institution reasonably believes it would be useful (and allowed by law) to administer that organisation's business and to provide products, services, and other opportunities to its customers.

- **Maintenance of Accurate Information.** Financial institutions should establish procedures so that a customer's financial information is accurate, current, and complete in accordance with reasonable commercial standards. Financial institutions should also respond to requests to correct inaccurate information in a timely manner.

- **Limiting Employee Access to Information.** Financial institutions should limit employee access to personally identifiable information to those with a business reason for knowing such information. Financial institutions should educate their employees so that they will understand the importance of confidentiality and customer privacy. Financial institutions should also take appropriate disciplinary measures to enforce employee privacy responsibilities.

- **Protection of Information via Established Security Procedures.** Financial institutions should maintain appropriate security standards and procedures regarding unauthorised access to customer information.

- **Restrictions on the Disclosure of Account Information.** Financial institutions should not reveal specific information about customer accounts or other personally identifiable data to unaffiliated third parties for their independent use, except for the exchange of information with reputable information reporting agencies to maximise the accuracy and security of such information, or in the performance of bona fide corporate due diligence, unless (1) the information is provided to help complete a customer-initiated transaction; (2) the customer requests it; (3) the disclosure is required or allowed by law (e.g. subpoena, investigation of fraudulent activity, etc); or (4) the customer has been informed about the possibility of disclosure for marketing or similar purposes through a prior communication and is given the opportunity to decline (i.e. 'opt-out').

- **Maintaining Customer Privacy in Business Relationship with Third Parties.** If personally identifiable customer information is provided to a third party, the financial institutions should insist that the third party adhere to similar privacy principles that provide for keeping such information confidential.

- **Disclosure of Privacy Principles to Customers.** Financial institutions should devise methods of providing a customer with an understanding of their privacy policies. Customers that are concerned about financial privacy will want to know about an institution's treatment of this important issue. Each financial institution should create a method for making available its privacy policies.

Conclusions

6.25 Concern over privacy violation is now greater than at any time in recent history. Uniformly, populations throughout the world express fears about the encroachment on online privacy. The customer of today has great expectations, which requires serious actions. Privacy is perceived as one of the key areas of electronic commerce. The price to ignore this issue is extremely high. As stated by PriceWaterhouseCoopers:

> 'Privacy issues drive – or drag – the information economy. Without privacy protections, there will be no consumer confidence in e-business. This is not an either/or situation. We must protect the rights of individuals, or e-business will suffer.'

6.26 This is evidence from the FTC's 2000 Report:

> '... [W]hilst the online market has grown at an exponential rate, an increased consumer concern regarding the collection and use (or misuse) of personal information by online businesses is turning into an apprehension, which is likely to translate into lost online sales. Studies have estimated that privacy concerns may have amounted to US$ 2.8 billion in lost online sales in 1999 for the United States alone, rising to a possible US$ 18 billion by 2002 should the consumer's privacy concerns not be addressed.'[1]

1 United States Federal Trade Commission, *Privacy Online: Fair Information Practices in the Electronic Marketplace: A Report to Congress* (May 2000).

6.27 Studies have shown that customers prefer legislation to a self-regulatory approach to protect their data. If it is true that customers are always right, it is just right for both the governments and private sectors to address the issue. The OECD believes that:

> 'In protecting privacy, the role of governments is to reaffirm the fundamental values considered as cornerstones of concepts about the protection of privacy and personal data, and to consider establishing a framework, which will encourage businesses to develop and adopt technological solutions to guarantee that these values are respected online and which will foster public education on these issues. The role of the private sector is to adopt transparent privacy policies and to develop technological solutions, which can be widely used.'

6.28 Ensuring the effective protection of privacy with regard to the processing of personal data on global information networks is necessary, as is the need to continue the free flow of information. Perhaps, the solution lies in a mix of regulatory and technology options that can achieve a comprehensive and balanced approach to online data protection across national borders, accommodating differing legal traditions, regulatory priorities and enforcement mechanisms.

CHAPTER SEVEN

EU Regulations Affecting Internet Banking and Implementation in the United Kingdom

Introduction

7.1   The European Parliamentary Financial Services Forum in its briefing notes[1] stated that retail banking in Europe has gone from being based on a range of limited products and lack of competition, to the development of new personalised IT-based products. Five trends are recognised and expected to dominate developments during the next decade. One of these is that technology will continue to transform financial services. This allows the industry to offer increasingly sophisticated, integrated and customised services at a lower cost of delivery. It has been acknowledged that the ability to respond rapidly to this opportunity will be an important determinant of future competitive performance, not just of individual players but also of European providers as a whole[2].

1   The briefing notes were prepared by the Industry Advisory Committee to the European Parliamentary Financial Services Forum, entitled 'Retail Financial Services: What Europe has to Offer' (22 November 2001).
2   *Ibid*, at p. 2.

7.2   In a broader context, the European Commission has put forward a Financial Services Action Plan, intended to create an integrated European market in financial services by 2005. A working party headed by Baron Alexander Lamfalussy, known as the 'Committee of Wise Men', has been established. The Committee has recommended the construction of the necessary EU regulatory framework for more responsive rules towards achieving the financial plan. Several pieces of legislation have been adopted while some are under serious consideration of the EU.

7.3   The Industry Advisory Committee made interesting observations on the EU legislative developments in this area. It states:

'Looking to the recent past the E-Commerce Directive, whilst being useful in setting out clearly a country of origin approach, has had only a limited liberalisation effect on retail financial services ... consumer contractual obligations were also excluded and as well as all financial services are in the nature of contractual obligations, then it is easy to see why the Directive has been limited to use retail financial service providers ... Looking forward, there is the Distance Marketing of Consumer Financial

Services Directive, the exact impact of which is still being debated in terms of what the political agreement reached by the Council really means and whether the Directive, with the various levels of harmonisation, is really going to be a useful instrument in providing legal certainty for banks operating cross-border and in enhancing consumers' protection[1].

1 The briefing notes were prepared by the Industry Advisory Committee to the European Parliamentary Financial Services Forum, entitled 'Retail Financial Services: What Europe has to Offer' (22 November 2001) pp 3–4.

The emergence of the Distance Marketing of Consumer Financial Services Directive 2002

7.4 It has been recognised that although a single European market has been under construction since 1973, the Union's financial markets have remained segmented. As a result, businesses and consumers are deprived of access to financial services beyond their national borders[1].

1 See Commission of the European Union, *Financial Services: Building a Framework for Action*, Communication to the Council and the European Parliament, COM (1998) 625, at p 1.

7.5 The 1996 European Commission's Green Paper, *Financial Services: Meeting Consumers' Expectations* drew attention to a number of particular problems encountered by consumers. The problems included the poor quality of service, lack of information and the activities of unregulated intermediaries[1]. Based on contributions received during consultations on this Green Paper, a report outlining measures to enhance consumer confidence in financial services within the single market was adopted. The European Commission concluded that further financial services initiatives are needed to meet adequately consumers' needs and expectations[2].

1 European Commission, 'Financial Services-Commission Adopts Communication on Enhancing Consumer Confidence', available at http://europa.eu.int/comm/internal_market/en/finances/consumer/566.htm.
2 *Ibid.*

7.6 The Communication, *Financial Services: Building a Framework for Action* concentrated on the removal of barriers to cross-border provisions of retail financial services in order to ensure consumer choice while maintaining consumer confidence and a high level of consumer protection[1]. The Commission concluded that EU financial services legislation needs to be enforced effectively but does not require radical surgery. However, new more flexible methods are required to adapt the rules to evolving market conditions and additional legislation is required in a few targeted areas including consumer redress[2]. In May 1999, a Communication entitled *Implementing the Framework for Financial Markets: Action Plan* was issued. This paper identified a daunting number of actions that were needed to complete the single market for financial services. It outlined a series of policy objectives and specific measures to improve the single market for financial services over the next five years.

---

1   European Commission, 'Financial Services: Commission Proposes Framework for Action', available at
    http://europa.eu.int/comm/internal_market/en/finances/general/fsen.htm.
2   *Ibid.*

7.7   The Action Plan suggested indicative priorities and time-scales for legislative and other measures to tackle three strategic objectives, namely, ensuring a single market for wholesale financial services, open and secure retail markets, and state-of-the-art prudential rules and supervision. The Action Plan also called for the adoption, before the end of 1999, among other things, of the Directive on Distance Selling of Financial Services.

7.8   On 14 October 1998, a proposal for a Directive to establish a clear regulatory framework for the marketing of financial services at a distance was presented by the EC. The Financial Services Commissioner, Mario Monti, commented that the proposal marked an important step towards improving the Single Market for Financial Services, and it will complement other initiatives to eliminate existing obstacles. The Consumers' Commissioner, Emma Bonino, regarded the proposal as safeguarding the interests of consumers at a high level of consumer protection:

> 'This proposal will safeguard the interests of consumers at a high level of consumer protection, and so help to build confidence in the use of the new technologies, while encouraging new market entrants, so that consumers should enjoy greater choice and more competitive prices.'

7.9   The Distance Marketing of Consumer Financial Services Directive (the Distance Marketing Directive (DMD)) aims to achieve a high level of consumer protection and enhance consumer confidence in distance selling. Recital 5 recognises that because of their intangible nature, financial services are particularly suited to distance selling and the establishment of a legal framework governing the distance marketing of financial services should increase consumer confidence in the use of new techniques for the distance marketing of financial services, such as electronic commerce.

7.10   The DMD justifies its existence on three grounds. First, the rules applicable to distance contracts for goods or services provided for in the 1997 Distance Selling Directive do not cover financial services[1]. Second, the consultations during the Green Paper showed that there is a need to strengthen consumer protection in this area[2]. Third, the necessity to enact common rules, as the adoption by the member states of conflicting or different consumer protection rules in this area could impede the functioning of the internal market and competition between firms in the market[3].

1   Recital 10.
2   Recital 11.
3   Recital 12.

7.11   The objective of the DMD is to establish the common rules on the distance marketing of consumer financial services. Specifically, the DMD is to approximate the laws, regulations and administrative provisions of the member states concerning the distance marketing of consumer financial services[1].

1 Article 1.

Scope and interpretation

7.12 The DMD builds on the existing Distance Selling Directive (DSD). It also implements the E-Commerce Directive (ECD), which was implemented in August 2002. The scope of the ECD, however, is in one respect wider, covering as it does a broad spectrum of commercial activity[1]. The DMD is confined to financial services and it is only the DMD and the DSD together which apply to a similarly wide spectrum of commercial activity. In another respect, however, it is the DMD which is wider. The ECD applies to transactions entered into over the Internet while the DMD (like the DSD) also applies to contracts concluded by a supplier who made exclusive use of other means of distance communication, such as the telephone, fax or mail[2].

1 See HM Treasury, *Implementation of the Distance Marketing of Consumer Financial Services Directive*, Consultation Document (July 2003) para 10.
2 *Ibid.*

7.13 The DMD covers all financial services liable to be provided at a distance[1]. It applies to both financial products and services (it refers to 'any service of banking, credit, insurance, personal pension, investment or payment nature'); and applies only to contracts entered into at a distance and only in relation to the formation of contracts with retail consumers[2].

1 Recital 14.
2 FSA, *Implementation of the Distance Marketing Directive: Proposed Rules and Guidance*, Consultation Paper (September 2003) para 2.3.

7.14 The Directive also applies to distance contracts for financial services concluded through an intermediary, but only after 'having regard to the nature and degree of that involvement'[1]. The logical (and obvious) conclusion to be drawn from this is that the DMD will only apply to contracts concluded through an intermediary where that intermediary is at a distance to the consumer, namely where there is no simultaneous physical presence[2]. In other words, there is a distance contract only if the intermediary is acting at a distance from the customer[3]. Where the financial services are provided through a chain of subsequent contracts the DMD will apply, but only to the initial contract[4].

1 Recital 19.
2 William Yonge, 'Legal Update: The Distance Marketing of Consumer Financial Services Directive' (2003) *Journal of Financial Services Marketing*, Vol 8, 80.
3 FSA, *Implementation of the Distance Marketing Directive: Proposed Rules and Guidance*, Consultation Paper (September 2003) para 3.30.
4 See art 1, and recital 16.

7.15 When a contract is entered into between a firm and a customer, the DMD requires the firm to provide the customer with prior information. Article 3 specifies the information to be provided to the consumer:

'In good time before the consumer is bound by any distance contract or offer, he shall be provided with the following information concerning the supplier, the financial service, the distance contract, and the redress.'

7.16 'Distance contract' is defined to mean any contract concerning financial services concluded between a supplier and a consumer under an organised distance sales or service-provision scheme run by the supplier, who, for the purpose of that contract, makes exclusive use of one or more means of distance communication up to and including the time at which the contract is concluded[1]. 'Means of distance communication' in turn, is defined as any means, which, without the simultaneous physical presence of the supplier and the consumer, may be used for the distance marketing of a service between those parties[2].

1 Article 2(a).
2 Article 2(e).

7.17 This requires parties to communicate exclusively through direct offer advertising or the use of, for example, telephone, facsimile, the Internet, electronic mail, post or interactive television. The key, therefore, to establishing and defining a distance contract is that all stages of the contract are carried out 'without the simultaneous physical presence of the supplier and consumer'[1]. In short, distance contracts are those the offer, negotiation and conclusion of which are carried out at a distance[2]. Thus, the DMD applies when the offer, negotiation and conclusion of a contract are carried out purely by distance as mentioned above.

1 Recital 15.
2 *Ibid.*

7.18 The DMD applies only to contracts between a 'supplier' and a 'consumer'. 'Consumer' is defined as 'any natural person who, in distance contracts covered by this Directive, is acting for purposes which are outside his trade, business or profession'[1]. This means that only private individuals are covered, and not individuals entering into contracts for business purposes as sole traders or members of a partnership[2]. 'Supplier' is defined as 'any natural or legal person, public or private, who acting in his commercial or professional capacity, is the contractual provider of services subject to distance contracts'[3].

1 Article 2(d).
2 See HM Treasury, *Implementation of the Distance Marketing of Consumer Financial Services Directive*, Consultation Document (July 2003) para 38.
3 Article 2(c).

7.19 As indicated earlier, 'financial service' means any service of a banking, credit, insurance, personal pension, investment or payment nature[1]. So, the impact of the DMD in the area of financial services is potentially wide-ranging. It affects substantially all the firms authorised by the FSA that deal with consumers[2].

1 Article 2(b).
2 FSA, *Implementation of the Distance Marketing Directive*, Discussion Paper (March 2003) para 2.9.

7.20 Recital 18 of the Directive explains, 'By covering a service-provision scheme organised by the financial provider', this Directive aims to exclude from its scope services provided on a strictly occasional basis and outside a commercial structure dedicated to the conclusion of distance contracts. This is reinforced by the use of the words 'under an *organised* distance sales' in the definition of the 'distance contract'. The FSA is of the view that few firms will be able to take advantage of this exclusion. If a firm provides even the most basic facilities for consumers to deal with it by post or telephone there is sufficient commercial structure for the DMD to apply. Similarly, if an organised scheme exists, even if this intended to supply other businesses, a one-off sale to a retail consumer will fall under the Directive[1].

1   FSA, *Implementation of the Distance Marketing Directive*, Discussion Paper (March 2003) para 3.12; see also the FSA's *Implementation of the Distance Marketing Directive: Proposed Rules and Guidance*, Consultation Paper (September 2003) para 2.19.

Pre-contract information

7.21   One of the main requirements of the DMD is disclosure before a customer is contractually committed. The Directive sets common standards for the information that must be supplied to consumers of financial services prior to a contract being concluded at a distance. Recital 21 of the Directive describes the rationale of this requirement:

'The use of distance communications should not lead to an unwarranted restriction on the information provided to the client. In the interests of transparency this Directive lays down the requirements needed to ensure that an appropriate level of information is provided to the consumer both before and after the conclusion of the contract. The consumer should receive, before conclusion of the contract, the prior information needed so as to properly appraise the financial service offered to him and hence make a well-informed choice.'

7.22   In a similar vein, the Treasury rationalises that this requirement will ensure that the consumer will not be misled into buying products on the basis of inadequate information[1].

1   See HM Treasury, *Implementation of the Distance Marketing of Consumer Financial Services Directive*, Consultation Document (July 2003) para 4.

7.23   As indicated earlier, art 3.1 of the DMD obligates the supplier to supply to the consumer a whole host of information on the supplier, the financial service, the distance contract and redress. This includes information about: the identity and the main business of the supplier; the geographical address at which the supplier is established; details of any professionals the consumer deals with instead of the supplier; a description of the main characteristics of the financial service; the total price to be paid, and notice of special risks; the existence or absence of a right of withdrawal; early termination right and penalties; out-of-court complaint; redress mechanism; guarantee funds or other compensation arrangements[1].

1   The DMD regards this as a right of the consumer to be provided with pre-contract information and under Article 12 this right and the right to withdraw from the distance contract cannot be waived by the consumers.

7.24 Apart from supplying the customer with the information, the supplier is required to inform the consumer that other information is available on request and the nature of such information[1]. Article 3.2 specifies that the information set out in art 3 shall be provided in a 'clear and comprehensible manner' in any way appropriate to the means of distance communication used, with due regard to 'the principles of good faith' in commercial transactions.

1 Article 3(3).

7.25 The importance that has been placed on the right to prior information is further evident in art 4 of the DMD, which provides a double-edge sword to suppliers. Not only will existing national information requirements, over and above those contained in art 3, continue to apply, but member states shall also be entitled to introduce national provisions that are more onerous than those contained in art 3[1]. Recital 13 reinforces this by providing that; 'Member States should not be able to adopt provisions other than those laid down in this Directive in the field it harmonises, unless otherwise specifically indicated in it'. The Directive is seen as an instrument where, 'a high level of consumer protection' is guaranteed, with a view to ensuring the free movement of financial services[2].

1 William Yonge, 'Legal Update: The Distance Marketing of Consumer Financial Services Directive' (2003) *Journal of Financial Services Marketing* Vol 8, 82.
2 See Recital 13.

7.26 If member states wish to introduce more stringent provisions, then the information requirements will have to be communicated to the Commission who shall, with a 'view to creating a high level of transparency', seek to ensure that this information is made available to both consumers and suppliers[1].

1 Article 4(3) and (4).

7.27 Article 5.1 requires that the information set out in art 3 and the full contractual terms and conditions be provided to the consumer on paper or on another 'durable medium' in good time before the consumer is bound by any distance contract or offer. 'Durable medium' is defined as 'any instrument which enables the consumer to store information addressed personally to him in a way accessible for future reference for a period of time adequate for the purposes of the information and which allows the unchanged reproduction of the information stored'[1]. Recital 20 explains that durable mediums include in particular floppy discs, CD-ROMs, DVDs and the hard drive of the consumer's computer on which the electronic mail is stored, but they do not include Internet websites unless they fulfil the criteria contained in the definition of a durable medium.

1 Article 2(f).

7.28 This means that information merely available on a website, is not likely to be a durable medium unless it can satisfy the definition 'durable medium' – capable of being stored personally in a way that is accessible for future reference[1]. A commentator has argued that an option for a consumer to click on a button on a website to download a copy of the terms and conditions would not amount to a durable medium because 'it leaves it to the consumer to decide whether or not to record that information'[2].

1 William Yonge, 'Legal Update: The Distance Marketing of Consumer Financial Services Directive' (2003) *Journal of Financial Services Marketing* Vol 8, 83.
2 Patricia Robertson, 'Distance Marketing of Financial Services', available at http://www.fountaincourt.co.uk/publications/pr_finservices_article1.htm.

7.29 Likewise, a link on an e-mail to a website containing the terms and conditions would not be a durable medium. The Internet and e-mail could prove to be rather a grey area in determining what falls within the definition of a durable medium[1]. It would seem to follow from the above that an e-mail attaching the terms and conditions to it would constitute a durable medium because they would be in the consumer's possession regardless of the consumer deciding whether to view the attached terms and conditions[2]. It is not known, however, whether this would be so where consumers view their e-mail on a website where the e-mail would not be saved to their hard disk: Would it be sufficient that the e-mail be saved on the consumer's Internet service provider's server?[3]

1 William Yonge, 'Legal Update: The Distance Marketing of Consumer Financial Services Directive' (2003) *Journal of Financial Services Marketing*, Vol 8, 83.
2 *Ibid.*
3 *Ibid.*

7.30 Article 5.2 of the DMD states that where the contract has been concluded at the consumer's request using a means of distance communication that does not allow the information to be provided before the conclusion of the contract, it must be provided immediately after the conclusion[1]. This allows a contract to be entered into through a single telephone call[2]. The FSA's view is that this provision[3]:

> 'Allows the consumer in some circumstances to conclude a distance contract at his own request without receiving certain information. But, this is not at the option of the supplier. So, provided the means of communication enables it, we would expect a firm to provide the article 3 information automatically as part of its normal selling process. Clearly, this will depend upon circumstances, but it appears to be facilitated by post, fax or Internet.'

1 The question that arises is how soon after the conclusion of the contract must the supplier provide the information? What interpretation is to be given to the words 'immediately after'?
2 FSA, *Implementation of the Distance Marketing Directive*, Discussion Paper (March 2003) para 5.4.
3 FSA, *Implementation of the Distance Marketing Directive: Proposed Rules and Guidance*, Consultation Paper (September 2003) para 4.6.

Right of withdrawal

7.31 The DMD provides a general right for a consumer to withdraw from a distance contract for a specified period after it has been concluded. Article 6 requires member states to ensure that the consumer shall have the right to withdraw from the contract without penalty and without giving any reason. The consumer will be entitled to a 14-calendar day period in which to withdraw from the contract. The exceptions are contracts for life insurance and personal pension operations where the consumers will be entitled to a 30-calendar day period[1].

1 Article 6(1).

7.32 The period for withdrawal shall begin from the day of the conclusion of the distance contract. For a life insurance contract, the period will begin from the time when the consumer is informed that the distance contract has been concluded. If the contract has been concluded but the consumer has not received the contractual terms and conditions and the art 3 information, the withdrawal period will begin from the day on which the consumer receives the terms and conditions as well as the information[1].

1 Article 6(1).

7.33 Article 6(2)(a) explicitly excludes certain types of financial services where the price depends on fluctuation outside the supplier's control from this right of withdrawal. These are services related to: foreign exchange, money market instruments, transferable securities, units in collective investment undertakings, etc. Article 6(2)(c) provides another exemption for contracts 'whose performance has been fully completed by both parties at the consumer's express request before the consumer exercises this right'. The FSA interprets this provision as including insurance contracts where a claim has been made, even though a policy may allow for more than one claim during its term[1]. The FSA also expects that withdrawal rights for many one-off execution-only and advisory services will fall away[2].

1 FSA, *Implementation of the Distance Marketing Directive*, Discussion Paper (March 2003) para 6.9.
2 FSA, *Implementation of the Distance Marketing Directive: Proposed Rules and Guidance*, Consultation Paper (September 2003) para 5.8.

7.34 The DMD, in art 6(3), confers discretion to member states to exclude other financial services from the right of withdrawal. These services include credit arrangements for the primary purpose of acquiring or retaining property rights in land or buildings and credit secured either by mortgage or other rights over immovable property.

7.35 Amongst the information on the distance contract set out by art 3, to be provided by the supplier to the consumer, is the practical instructions for the customer to exercise the right of withdrawal. This includes the address to which the notification of a withdrawal should be sent[1]. If a consumer wishes to exercise the withdrawal right, he should notify the supplier in accordance with the practical instruction. The notification must be done by means which can be proved in accordance with national law[2]. The DMD provides that the deadline shall be deemed to have been observed if the notification, if it is on paper or on another durable medium available and accessible to the recipient, is dispatched before the deadline expires[3]. Hence, the determining point is when the notification is dispatched and not when the supplier receives it.

1 Article 3(1)(3)(d).
2 Article 6(6).
3 *Ibid.*

7.36 Article 6(7) of the DMD provides that when a consumer cancels a distance contract then any 'attached contract' must also be automatically cancelled without penalty to the consumer. The 'attached contract' must be a financial services contract, whether attached by the supplier or by a third party with the supplier's agreement. Whether or not a contract is treated as attached will depend on the circumstances in each case[1].

1 FSA, *Implementation of the Distance Marketing Directive: Proposed Rules and Guidance*, Consultation Paper (September 2003) para 5.28.

Effect of withdrawal

7.37 Article 7(1) states that where a consumer exercises the right of withdrawal, he may only be required to pay for the service actually provided by the supplier up to the date of withdrawal[1]. The amount payable shall not:

- exceed an amount which is in proportion to the service already provided in comparison with full coverage of the contract; or

- in any case be such that it could be construed as a penalty.

1 Article 7(2) allows member states to legislate that consumers cannot be required to pay any amount when withdrawing from an insurance contract.

7.38 From the perspective of a supplier, the position is not as straightforward as one may think. Article 7(1) also provides that the performance of the contract may only begin after the consumer has given his approval. So, a supplier cannot demand any payment unless the performance of the contract, before the expiry of the withdrawal period, had been consented to by the consumer. Article 7(3) specifically states: 'In no case may he (the supplier) require such payment if he has commenced the performance of the contract before the expiry of the withdrawal period without the consumer's prior request'. Hence, if a supplier provides services, and he/she commenced the performance of the contract before the expiry of the withdrawal without the request from the consumer, and the consumer then exercises the withdrawal right, the supplier will not be able to recover the cost of the services that he has provided.

7.39 Also, art 7(3) does not allow the supplier to claim any payment if he/she cannot prove that the customer was duly informed about the amount payable as part of the pre-contract information. This reinforces the importance of the pre-contact information and its observance by the supplier. In this respect, the rule benefits not only the consumer but also the supplier alike. The word 'prove' in this article means that the supplier must keep a record that he has provided the consumer with the information, particularly, information required by art 3(1)(3)(a) about the amount payable by the consumer if he exercises the right to withdraw.

7.40 Practically, the supplier must comply with the pre-contract information requirements and ask for the consent of the consumer before performing the contract to be able to claim payment for services rendered in the case where a consumer withdraws from the contract. As mentioned earlier, if a supplier satisfies these requirements, the amount he/she can claim is subject to rules provided for in art 7(1).

7.41   There are obligations on both the supplier and consumer to return any sums they have received from each other in accordance with the distance contract. They must do so without 'undue delay' and no later than within 30 calendar days. For the supplier, the period begins from the day on which he receives the notification of withdrawal. As for the consumer, the 30-day period runs from the day on which he dispatches the notification. A consumer must also return any property he has received under the contract[1].

1   Articles 7(4) and (5).

Other provisions

7.42   The DMD seeks to protect consumers from unsolicited services and unsolicited communications. On the former, recital 25 explicitly states that consumers should be protected against unsolicited services. Article 9 obligates the EU countries to do so. It requires member states to take necessary measures to prohibit the supply of financial services without a prior request from the consumer. Member states are also required to take measures to exempt the consumer from any obligation in the event of unsolicited supplies, the absence of a reply not constituting consent.

7.43   On unsolicited communication, the DMD specifically prohibits the supplier from using automated calling systems and fax machines to market financial services without the consumer's prior consent. Regarding other types of distance communications, the communications shall not be authorised unless the consent of the consumers has been obtained ('opt-in'), or may only be used if the consumer has not expressed his manifest objection ('opt-out')[1]. This means that member states are provided with the discretion to choose an appropriate level of protection for consumers by adopting either an 'opt-in' or 'opt-out' policy.

1   Article 10.

British Bankers' Association Responses to FSA Discussion Paper

7.44   The British Bakers' Association (BBA) is of the view that the proposals set out in the Discussion Paper would have far-reaching consequences for the conduct of business regulation of deposit-based products which are currently regulated under the Banking Code and Business Banking Code (the Banking Codes). The Banking Code and the regulatory framework underpinning it were subject to a rigorous review in 2000/2001 by the Banking Codes Review Group. The Review concluded that the Banking Code was the appropriate regulatory mechanism for personal banking business in the UK. According to the BBA, Treasury ministers endorsed the Report's findings and accepted that it would not be appropriate to extend FSA conduct of business regulation to cover such business. The endorsement has received support from the ministerial colleagues at DTI. The BBA states, "We fear the proposals outlined in DP21 would undermine the Banking Code in a way not intended by Ministers and we fear for the future of the Banking Codes if the FSA's proposals are not substantially amended"[1].

Concerning scope of the DMD, the BBA states that they have considerable difficulty with FSA's proposal to include aspects of branch banking within the definition of a 'distance contract'. The BBA argues that the Directive was never intended to cover sales of financial services in branches. Nor is there anything in the Directive or it recitals that would support the FSA's view that branch sales be regarded as distance marketing. The BBA states, "We cannot agree with FSA's view that an example of a distance sale would be where a customer asks for leaflet, then it takes it home to complete and hands it back in the branch without seeking help from branch staff"[2]. FSA proposes that any transaction which does not include 'active involvement between a human agent of the firm and the customer' is a distance sale. The BBA respond is that, "This is not a requirement of the Directive and we fear that in this area, as in some others, the FSA is being super-equivalent o the Directive".

With regard to customers covered by the Directive, the BBA states that they are disappointed by the proposed removal of the expert/non private customer 'exemption' for distance sales. According to the BBA, the exemption is valued by customers who are expert or professional and do not need the full protection extended to other customers. The BBA is very concerned by the FSA's suggestion that it may seek to apply the DMD in respect of all customers covered by the definition of 'private customer'. Once again, the BBA argues that this would clearly be super-equivalent to the scope of the Directive. The BBA states, "It would create unnecessary complexity and confusion *vis a vis* the Business Banking Code if FSA implemented the DMD in respect of all 'private customers'. We consider it important that in implementing the Directive FSA should apply the DMD definition of customer and not be super-equivalent"[3].

On pre-contract information, the BBA is of the opinion that guidance will be needed on the definition of what constitutes 'in good time'. The timescales to be set by the FSA for the provision of pre-contract information will need to be realistic, taking into account of the means of distance communication and the nature of the product involved. Clear guidance is also needed on how 'explicit consent' can in practice be obtained and evidenced.

1 See BBA, Response to FSA Discussion Paper 21: Implementation of the Distance Marketing Directive, available at http://www.bba.org.uk/bba/jsp/polopoly.jsp?d=155&a=290.
2 *Ibid.*
3 *Ibid.*

7.45 The Treasury has made clear the Government's approach to implementation. The Government needs to ensure that *all* the financial services within the scope of the Directive comply with the requirements of the DMD[1]. There are two possible approaches. Firstly, to use the powers of the EC Act and make regulations covering *all* distance contracts concerning financial services. The alternative would be to incorporate the DMD requirements into the rules or other requirements of the competent authorities under the relevant existing legislation[2]. The Treasury prefers the second option primarily because it would be a more effective approach in terms of enforcement[3].

1 Treasury CP, para 43.
2 *Ibid*, paras 44 and 45.
3 *Ibid*, para 46.

7.46 Referring to Internet banking and the financial institutions providing the service, the FSA stated, 'Our proposed new rules will apply to deposit-taking and e-money issuance. Banks, building societies, credit union and e-money issuers will have to provide specified pre-contract information and give a retail consumer the right to cancel a distance contract'[1]. In fact, it is acknowledged that the impact of the implementation of the DMD will be greater on deposit-taking and e-money issuing than for many other types of regulated activity. This is because the current rules do not, in general, subject these activities to detailed conduct of business requirements[2]. The FSA further stated, 'But in order to implement the DMD in the United Kingdom as law, we are obliged to apply its requirements to deposit-taking'[3].

1 FSA CP, para 1.6.
2 *Ibid*, para 6.2.
3 *Ibid*.

7.47 The FSA proposes rules to require provision of pre-contract information for distance contracts, and to give relevant customers a rules-based right to cancel a contract once entered into (post-sale right to cancel)[1]. Specifically, the FSA proposes new rules to prescribe, often for the first time, or to change the detail of:

(a) the content of product documentation;

(b) the delivery of mechanisms for key features or other product documentations;

(c) cancellation rights that must be offered; and

(d) cancellation mechanisms[2].

1 FSA CP, para 1.6.
2 *Ibid*, para 2.15.

7.48 The instrument to be used to implement the new rules is the Banking Code. This is because, according to the FSA[1]:

'It is not evident to us that in order to secure our consumer protection objective there is a need substantially to overturn the current arrangements under the Banking Code. We are now proposing arrangements under which subscribers to the Code can look to it as providing an expression of what is required under the DMD.'

1 FSA CP, para 6.8.

7.49 The FSA believes that the Banking Code can act as a vehicle for the Directive requirements. This would mean that the FSA's Handbook would contain rules setting out the requirements for deposit-takers. It would also mean that the Banking Code would be amended to incorporate the DMD's requirements of pre-contract information and the right of withdrawal for deposit-taking by distance contracts. In terms of the supervision of the new rules, the FSA finds that there is no particular reason why the BCSB should not continue to monitor compliance with the Code[1].

1 FSA CP, para 6.11.

Distance contracts, customer and cancellation rights

7.50 Certain contracts will clearly be distance contracts, for example, where the consumer receives information through the post, through press, television, radio or Internet advertising and then deals with the firm solely by post, Internet, fax or telephone. Other contracts will clearly not be distance contracts, for example, where a consumer enters into a contract upon being given a face-to-face recommendation or advice from a firm or an adviser.

7.51 However, some cases will be less obvious and more difficult to interpret, for example, if the firms' branches provide leaflet and marketing literature describing their products and services and direct the customers to call centres or to off-site processing offices. The FSA has articulated three possible tests to determine whether or not a contract is a distance contract: (1) literal simultaneous physical presence test; (2) meaningful simultaneous physical presence test; and (3) face-to-face test. The FSA favours the second: under which a contract is not a distance contract if there is 'meaningful simultaneous physical presence' between the supplier and the consumer. The simultaneous physical presence of supplier and consumer is only 'meaningful' if the product or service it advertises is one on which the branch is able to advise and deal with the customer. So, where the entire branch staff, in response to a customer query, direct the customer to a means of communication such as a call centre, then there will be a distance contract[1].

1 FSA CP, para 3.14.

7.52 In a case where the customer receives information about a product or service in a leaflet picked up at the branch, but does not discuss it, and then deals with the branch by, say, telephone or post, the FSA's preliminary view is that there would be meaningful simultaneous presence in such a case, since the branch is equipped to deal with the product or service, even if it does not deal with the customer face-to-face. The FSA concluded, 'Given that face-to-face contact is not actually required by the DMD, we are inclined to think there should not be a distance contract here'[1].

1 FSA CP, para 3.15.

7.53 The FSA is of the view that the 'meaningful simultaneous physical presence test' provides the best fit with the intentions of the DMD and its definitions. It also believes that the test provides a practical and workable divide between distance contracts and others, for firms and consumers[1].

1 FSA CP, para 3.19.

7.54 There are differences between the DMD's definition of 'consumer' and the FSA's definition of a 'private customer'. For example, the FSA's rules allow for an individual acting in a private capacity but who is deemed expert in a particular field to be classified as an intermediate customer, whereas he would be treated as a consumer under the Directive. On the other hand, a small company classified as a private customer under the FSA's rules would not be a consumer for the purposes of the Directive[1].

1 See Freshfields Bruckhaus Deringer, 'Implementing the Distance Marketing Directive: Another Compliance Regime', briefing October 2003.

7.55 The FSA's solution is to vary the interpretation of 'private customers' in relation to distance contracts so that it includes all persons who are consumers for the purposes of the Directive. But the FSA prefers the term 'retail customer' instead of 'consumer' adopted by the Directive. This approach will continue to allow a private customer to be opted-out to intermediate customer status, but will require the firm to provide the customer with the additional information and appropriate cancellation rights that the Directive requires when concluding distance contracts with the customer[1].

1 See Freshfields Bruckhaus Deringer, 'Implementing the Distance Marketing Directive: Another Compliance Regime', briefing October 2003. See also FSA CP, para 4.19.

7.56 Article 6 of the DMD, in the FSA's view, requires a right of withdrawal for deposit-taking and e-money, for which there is currently no requirement in its Handbook. The FSA states[1]:

> 'So, we are persuaded that to implement the DMD we shall have to require firms to give cancellation rights for most deposit products entered into by distance means. We recognise that this could mean higher costs to firms or lower rates to consumers for some products, but we doubt there will be any significant effect.'

1 FSA CP, para 6.16.

7.57 Currently, under the FSA rules, firms have the option, in certain circumstances, to offer a pre-sale right to withdraw rather than a post-sale right to cancel the agreement. The DMD requires the consumer to be given a post-sale right to cancel a distance contract. The FSA is proposing to remove this option. Firms may continue voluntarily to offer a pre-sale right to withdraw as an additional right.

Pre-contract information requirements

7.58 The FSA acknowledges that for several reasons its current requirements do not provide a direct match with what the DMD requires. First, they do not require all the information that the DMD requires to be provided. Second, they do not apply to all products to which the DMD applies: for example, they do not extend to all deposits and deposit-based products. Third, the FSA's requirements about the timing of delivery of the information do not meet the DMD requirements in all circumstances, and, fourth, the FSA rules allow individuals to opt-out of receiving some of the information that would otherwise be required, but the DMD (art 12) does not allow consumers to opt-out of the protections it provides. To implement the DMD, the FSA proposes some changes regarding terms of business, information to be provided to expert customers, and direct offer financial promotions.

7.59 It is important to mention that firms will not automatically have to provide revised terms of business to existing customers. The FSA proposes to impose the additional pre-contract information requirement only in respect of distance contracts and it will only apply to new customers or existing customers when new services are being offered. Where a contract is concluded by electronic means, for example over the Internet, as discussed earlier, the information requirements imposed by the ECD (set out in the FSA's specialist sourcebook on the Directive) will also apply. The two sets of information requirements are similar, but not identical[1].

1   See Freshfields Bruckhaus Deringer, 'Implementing the Distance Marketing Directive: Another Compliance Regime', briefing October 2003.

Electronic Commerce Directive

Application to Internet banking

7.60 The Directive applies to 'information society services' (ISS), defined in art 2(a) as any service normally provided for remuneration, at a distance, by electronic means and at the individual request of a recipient of services. 'Any service normally provided for remuneration' means that it is not necessary that a service is paid for by the recipient. The costs of a service can also be covered by advertisement. For instance, free Internet providers fall under the scope of the Directive. 'At a distance' requires that the service should be provided without the parties being simultaneously present. 'By electronic means' requires that the service should be sent and received using electronic equipment. 'At the individual request of a recipient of services' means that the service should be delivered on demand. A visit to a website is always a service on demand, since the recipient 'request' the website by typing the URL or by following a link. So it is apparent that all forms of online financial services, including Internet banking fall within this definition. The FSA uses the term 'electronic commerce activity' (ECA) to describe an ISS delivering a financial service.

7.61 Furthermore, Recital 18 of the Directive states that information society services span a wide range of economic activities which take place online. Information society services are not solely restricted to services giving rise to online contracting but also, in so far as they represent an economy activity, extend to services which are not remunerated by those receiving them, such as those offering online information or commercial communications, or those providing tools allowing for search, access and retrieval of data.

7.62 The European Commission Communication of 7 February 2001, to the Council and the European Parliament on e-commerce and financial services stated: 'The e-commerce Directive is a horizontal framework directive that applies to all information society services (online services) and therefore also to financial services provided online'[1].

1   Available at http://europa.eu.int/scadplus/printversion/en/lvb/132044.htm.

7.63   On its website, when the Directive was proposed, the European Commission claimed that the proposal covers all sorts of Information Society services, both business to business and business to consumer, for example: online newspapers, online databases, online financial services, online professional services, online entertainment services such as video on demand, online direct marketing and advertising, and services providing access to the World Wide Web.

Country-of-origin principle

7.64   The European Commission aims to solve the problem of the multitude of applicable rules by adopting in the E-Commerce Directive the so-called 'country-of-origin' rule: ISS providers and their services will only have to comply with the rules of the country in which those service providers are established and from where the services therefore 'originate'. Enshrined within art 3 of the Directive, this much-debated principle means that online financial service providers will be subject to the regulations of the member state where the 'centre of activities', in the form of a fixed establishment, is located. Recital 22 of the Directive sets out the general principle and rationale of the rule:

> 'Information society services should be supervised at the source of the activity, in order to ensure an effective protection of public interest objectives; to that end, it is necessary to ensure that the competent authority provides such protection not only for the citizens of its own country but for all Community citizens; in order to improve mutual trust between Member States, it is essential to state clearly this responsibility on the part of the Member State where the services originate; moreover, in order to effectively guarantee freedom to provide services and legal certainty for suppliers and recipients of services, such information society services should in principle be subject to the law of the Member State in which the provider is established.'

7.65   Article 3 described as 'internal market' clause aims to ensure that there is free movement of information society services and is based on the general principle of free movement of services. Specifically, the new rules try to achieve a harmonised solution: financial services providers will be regulated only where they are established – so (in theory) each provider has to deal with only one regulator (e.g. the FSA for UK-based providers – financial services providers established in other EEA member states will be regulated by the laws of the particular member states from which they are operating). The FSA's regulated activities and financial services promotion regimes are generally disapplied to this extent[1].

1 See John Worthy, Nicholas Graham and Robert Finney, 'E-Commerce for Financial Services: Working with the New UK Rules', Computer Law & Security Report, Vol 19 no. 2 (2003) p 121.

7.66 Article 3, para 1, provides, 'Each Member State shall ensure that the information society services provided by a service provider established on its territory comply with the national provisions applicable in the Member State in question which fall within the co-ordinated field'. Paragraph 2 then provides that member states may not, for reasons falling within the co-ordinated field, restrict the freedom to provide information society services from another member state. These provisions read as a whole mean that the law of the country-of-origin will, as a general rule, apply to information society services provided by service providers[1]. This represents a major change in the regulation of financial services where they are provided electronically. Once the Directive has been implemented across Europe, ISS financial services providers will need to comply only with the laws of their home member state unless there is an applicable derogation.

1 See Lokke Moerel, 'The County-of-Origin Principle in the E-Commerce Directive: The Expected "One Stop Shop"'? (2001) CTLR 184.

7.67 One commentator argues that the 'internal market' clause of art 3(1) purports to eradicate restrictions relating to legal uncertainty as to the application of national law. He further states:

> 'That objective is served by requiring Member States in their capacity as "countries of origin" to ensure that firms established therein comply with national law. The obligation is addressed indistinctly to Member States and must be invariably implemented by national law-making, executive and judicial authorities'[1].

1 Apostolos Gkoutzinis, 'Online Financial Services in the European Internal Market and the Implementation of the E-Commerce directive in the UK', 18th BILETA Conference: *Controlling Information in the Online Environment* (April 2003) available at http://www.bileta.ac.uk/03papers/Gkoutzinis.html.

7.68 The 'co-ordinated field' is defined as requirements laid down in member states' legal systems applicable to information society service providers or information society services, regardless of whether they are of a general nature or specifically designed for them. The definition also provides explicitly that the co-ordinated field includes requirements, which the service provider must meet in relation to the start up of his activities (including qualification, authorisation or notification) and requirements in respect of the provision of the services (behaviour of the service provider, quality or content of the service, liability of the service provider).

7.69 As one commentator has said:

> 'To sum up, the European Union is seeking to create a dynamic environment for the evolution of the e-marketplace in financial services. More generally, the Directive is

the first, important step for the financial services industry down an exciting road which seeks ultimately to remove many of the barriers which currently exist in accessing and serving the needs of consumers of financial services in the whole of the EEA instead of only those in the provider's home jurisdiction. There will be many twists and turns to negotiate before the end of that road comes clearly into view'[1].

1   Joe Coffey, 'Financial Services and E-Commerce Directive', available at http://www.tjg.co.uk/topical/corp_gov/ecomm_directive.html.

7.70   In the UK, the implementation of the 'country of origin' rule has been affected by two statutory instruments: the Electronic Commerce (EC Directive) Regulations 2002 (the General Regulations) and the Electronic Commerce Directive (Financial Services and Markets) Regulations 2002 (the Financial Services Regulations). The General Regulations shall be regarded as the principal instrument of implementation. The General Regulations transpose into domestic law the 'internal market' clause vis-à-vis ISS and in relation to the 'co-ordinated field' by direct reference to the definitions made in the Directive[1]. The scope of application of the Financial Services Regulations is narrower. The Financial Services Regulations are solely concerned with the implementation of the 'internal market' clause in the field of financial services, specifically in relation to the FSMA 2000, the statutory instruments made thereunder and the rules issued by the FSA in exercise of its law-making powers[2].

1   Joe Coffey, 'Financial Services and E-Commerce Directive', available at http://www.tjg.co.uk/topical/corp_gov/ecomm_directive.html.
2   *Ibid.*

CHAPTER EIGHT

Regulating Internet Banking in the United Kingdom

General statutory framework

8.1   The Financial Services and Markets Act 2000 (FSMA 2000) confers extensive regulatory and supervisory powers over the financial services sector on the Financial Services Authority (FSA). The FSMA 2000 gives legal basis to the radical reform of the UK's system of financial regulation announced by the government soon after the May 1997 general election. The regulatory functions are conferred to the FSA with four statutory 'regulatory objectives' and seven 'regulatory principles' to guide it in discharging its 'general functions'. Michael Taylor, a Senior Economist at the International Monetary Fund (IMF), describes the significance of the impact of the FSMA 2000[1]:

> 'The obvious respect in which the Act is a radical measure is in providing statutory underpinning for the FSA, which combines the regulation of banking, securities and insurance business, and replaces no-fewer than nine pre-existing regulatory bodies. Indeed, the FSA is practically unique among agencies in the industrialised world in terms of the diversity of businesses regulated, and its very broad scope, encompassing both prudential and business regulation. A second respect in which the new Act is radical is in the range of enforcement powers it grants to the FSA. These go a significant way beyond the combined powers of the bodies which the FSA replaces.'

1   Michael Taylor, 'The Policy Background', in Michael Blair QC, Loretta Minghella, Michael Taylor, Mark Threipland and George Walker, *Blackstone's Guide to the Financial Services & Markets Act 2000* (2001) pp 2–3.

8.2   The FSA has been described as 'one of the most powerful financial regulators in the world in terms of scope, powers and discretion'[1]. Its scope is broad in three respects. First, it is cross-sectoral, covering the whole financial sector: banking, insurance, and investment business. Second, it regulates both the prudential and conduct (including market conduct) aspects of those businesses. Finally, it has enormous powers: authorising firms, legislating, monitoring, investigating, and enforcing the regime[2].

1   See the first report of the Joint Parliamentary Scrutiny Committee: Draft Financial Services and Markets Bill: First Report cited in E P Ellinger, E Lomnicka and R J A Hooley, *Modern Banking law*, (3rd edn, 2002) p 36.
2   E P Ellinger, E Lomnicka and R J A Hooley, *Modern Banking law*, (3rd edn, 2002) pp 36–37.

Regulatory objectives

8.3 The FSMA 2000 establishes a framework of objectives and principles within which the FSA is to carry out its general functions. Section 2(1) of the FSMA 2000 specifically provides that in discharging its general functions, the FSA must act in a manner which is compatible with the four regulatory objectives:

- market confidence;

- public awareness;

- the protection of consumers; and

- the reduction of financial crime.

8.4 These statutory objectives are high level and general. They are fixed, regardless of the environment in which the FSA operates[1]. According to Colin Mayer, these objectives have their basis in the market failures that afflict financial markets: market manipulation, systemic problems, asymmetric information, incomplete contracts and difficulties in the enforcement of contracts[2]. He argued 'while the regulation of banking is primarily concerned with systemic failures, the regulation of non-bank financial institutions is not'. The main market failures that afflict non-bank institutions are market manipulation, imperfect information and contract failure through poor performance. Therefore, the regulation of non-bank financial institutions hinges on information disclosure, monitoring and auditing and enforcement through the courts[3].

1 See Carol Sergeant of the FSA, 'Risk-based Regulation in the Financial Services Authority', (2002) *Journal of Financial Regulation and Compliance* Vol 10, No 4, 331.
2 Colin Mayer, 'Regulatory Principles and the Financial Services and Markets Act 2000', in Eilis Ferran and Charles A E Goodhart (eds) *Regulating Financial Services and Markets in the Twenty First Century* (2001) p 25.
3 *Ibid*, at pp 29–30.

8.5 The market confidence objective is identified as that of 'maintaining confidence in the financial system'. The term 'confidence' is generally used in the context of the regulation of securities markets, where the purpose of regulation is often said to be to provide investors and potential investors with confidence in the integrity and orderly conduct of the market. However, the objective as formulated in the FSMA 2000 goes beyond this relatively limited conventional sense in which regulation is concerned with market confidence. The objective refers to confidence 'in the financial system' which indicates a comparatively extended meaning[1]. The financial system is defined as 'the United Kingdom financial system, including: financial markets and exchanges; regulated activities; and other activities connected with financial market and exchanges'.

1 Michael Taylor, 'Accountability and Objectives of the FSA', in Michael Blair QC, Loretta Minghella, Michael Taylor, Mark Threipland & George Walker, *Blackstone's Guide to the Financial Services & Markets Act 2000* (2001) pp 2–3.

8.6 Although the banking sector is not specifically mentioned as an aspect of the financial system, during the passage through Parliament of the FSMA 2000, banking was said to be 'swept up' within the financial head of the definition of the financial system[1]. Moreover, accepting deposits is a regulated activity under s 5 of the Banking Act 1987. Thus, 'banking' is included in the definition of financial system.

1 David Toube, 'Introduction to the FSMA and the Financial Services Authority', in James Perry (ed) *The Financial Services and Markets Act: A Practical Legal Guide* (2001) p 11.

8.7 The FSA in its document *A New Regulator for the New Millennium* (FSA New Millennium) acknowledges that[1]:

'Market confidence is fundamental to any successful system; only if it is maintained will participants and users be willing to trade in financial markets and use the services of financial institutions. Maintaining this confidence involves, in our view, preserving both actual stability in the financial system and the reasonable expectation that it will remain stable.'

1 FSA New Millennium (January 2000) p 5.

8.8 According to the FSA this is achieved through preventing material damage to the soundness of the UK financial system caused by the conduct of, or collapse of, firms, markets or financial infrastructure; and explaining on what basis confidence in the UK financial system is justified. This includes stating explicitly what the regulator can and cannot achieve.

8.9 However, at the same time, the FSA recognises that maintaining market confidence does not, in the view of the FSA, imply aiming to prevent all collapses, or lapses in conduct, in the financial system[1]:

'Given the nature of financial markets, which are inherently volatile, achieving a 'zero failure' regime is impossible and would in any case be undesirable. Any such regime would be excessively burdensome for regulated firms and would not accord with the statutory objectives and principles. It would be likely to damage the economy as a whole and would be uneconomic from a cost-benefit point of view; it would stifle innovation and competition; and it would be inconsistent with the respective responsibilities of firms' management and of consumers for their own actions.'

1 FSA New Millennium (January 2000) p 7.

8.10 The FSA will aim to maintain a regime which ensures low incidence of failure of regulated firms and markets. This is especially failure which would have a material impact on public confidence and market soundness. If failures occur, the FSA will seek ways to minimise the impact of failures on market confidence. The FSA will retain and improve the mechanisms currently in place to protect consumers when firms collapse or fail to meet expected standards of conduct[1].

1 FSA New Millennium (January 2000) pp 6–7.

8.11 Fawcett provides the rationale of such an approach. She noted that stability or integrity in a market-place encourages investment, and maintaining confidence in a market requires the prevention of the development of (potential) systemic risks and, where prevention has not been possible or successful, the cure of such problems[1]. Maintaining the integrity of the market-place, however, does not mean preventing failure or 'negative' developments from occurring. A 'zero failure' approach would effectively inhibit forces from acting – it is to be expected that some products or companies will not succeed. A wide variety of factors may result in the failure of a product or company, only some of which will fall within the regulatory ambit. However, where the market failure of a product or company would pose a systemic risk, then maintaining the integrity of the market (or confidence in the market) may require a government or regulator to intervene to avoid damage to the system.

1 Amelia C Fawcett, 'Examining the Objectives of Financial Regulation – Will the New Regime Succeed? A Practitioner's View', in Eilis Ferran and Charles A E Goodhart (eds), *Regulating Financial Services and Markets in the Twenty First Century* (2001).

8.12 The FSMA 2000, in s 4, defines 'public awareness' as the promotion of public understanding of the financial system, including: promoting awareness of the benefits and risks associated with different kinds of investment or other financial dealing; and the provision of appropriate information and advice.

8.13 Recognising the problem that relates to this objective, the FSA stated:

'many consumers do not understand the financial system, the products and services offered and how they relate to their financial needs. Such consumers may not secure suitable products at fair prices; they may misunderstand the terms on which products are offered or may not realise the pros and cons of different product offerings'[1].

1 FSA New Millennium, p 7.

8.14 Under this 'public awareness' objective, the FSA will pursue two main aims: first, to improve general financial literacy; and, second, to improve the information and advice available to consumers. General financial literacy will be improved through programmes to help individuals acquire the knowledge and skills they need to be better-informed consumers of financial services. Under the second heading, the FSA will provide, or help others provide, generic information and advice to consumers and will encourage others to improve the availability and quality of their advice[1]. The priority will be given to filling a number of existing gaps in public understanding of retail financial products, in particular on the part of vulnerable and inexperienced consumers. Ultimately, the aim is to ensure that consumers have a better understanding of the risks and opportunities involved in investment markets[2].

1 FSA New Millennium, p 7.
2 *Ibid*, at p 8.

8.15 According to the FSMA 2000, the protection of consumers objective is securing the appropriate degree of protection for consumers[1]. In determining the appropriate degree of protection for consumers, the FSA is obliged to consider: the differing degrees of risk involved in different kinds of investment or other transactions; the differing degrees of experience and expertise that different consumers may have in relation to different kinds of regulated activity; the needs that consumers may have for advice and accurate information; and the general principle that consumers should take responsibility for their decisions[2].

1   FSMA 2000, s 5(1).
2   FSMA 2000, s 5(2).

8.16   The FSA identified the principal risks which consumers may face in their financial affairs. They are prudential risk, bad faith risk, complexity/unsuitability risk, and performance risk. Prudential risk refers to the risk that a firm collapses, because of weak or incompetent management or lack of capital. Bad faith risk involves the risk from fraud, misrepresentation, deliberate mis-selling or failure to disclose relevant information on the part of firms selling or advising on financial products. Complexity risk is the risk that consumers contract for a financial product or service they do not understand or which is unsuitable for their needs and circumstances. Performance risk concerns the risk that investments do not deliver hoped-for returns[1].

1   FSA New Millennium, p 8.

8.17   The FSA makes it clear that its role only relates to the first three risks. It states, 'The FSA has a role to play in identifying and reducing prudential risk, bad faith risk and some aspects of complexity/unsuitability risk. It is not the FSA's responsibility to protect consumers from performance risk, which is inherent in investment markets'[1]. The level of protection provided will depend on the sophistication of the consumer; professional counterparties need much less protection than retail consumers. It will also reflect the need that consumers have for advice and information, and the general principle that consumers should take responsibility for their decisions[2].

1   FSA New Millennium, p 8.
2   *Ibid*, at pp 8–9.

8.18   The fourth of the regulatory objectives is 'reduction of financial crime', which means 'reducing the extent to which it is possible for a business carried on by a regulated person, or in contravention of the general prohibition, to be used for a purpose connected with financial crime'[1]. 'Financial crime' is defined to include any offence involving fraud or dishonesty; misconduct in, or misuse of information relating to, a financial market; or handling the proceeds of crime[2]. An 'offence' includes an act or omission which would be an offence if it had taken place in the UK[3].

1   FSMA 2000, s 6(1).
2   FSMA 2000, s 6(3).
3   FSMA 2000, s 6(4).

8.19   According to the FSA, the three main types of financial crime which the FSA will play a significant role in seeking to prevent are: money laundering, fraud or dishonesty, including financial e-crime and fraudulent marketing of investments; and criminal market misconduct, including insider dealing[1]. For many other forms of financial crime such as credit card fraud, the FSA will play a secondary role, in co-operation with other organisations[2]. The FSA has sought to meet this regula-tory objective, principally in two ways. First, the FSA has a firefighting role; it is empowered to bring proceedings in relation to a broad range of criminal offences which fall within the definition of financial crime. Secondly, the FSA has a firewatching role and has integrated measures into the various rules, guidance and codes which it has produced and designed to ensure that regulated persons have adequate systems in place for the prevention and detection of financial crime[3].

1   FSA New Millennium, p 9.
2   *Ibid.*
3   David Toube, 'Introduction to the FSMA and the Financial Services Authority', in James Perry (ed) *The Financial Services and Markets Act: A Practical Legal Guide* (2001) p 14.

The principles of good regulation

8.20   In exercising it regulatory functions, the FSMA 2000 requires the FSA to have regard to a number of factors, known as the 'principles of good regulation': (1) the need for the FSA to use its resources in the most efficient and economic way; (2) the responsibilities of those who manage the affairs of authorised persons; (3) the principle that a burden or restriction which is imposed on a person, or on the carrying on of an activity, should be proportionate to the benefits, considered in general terms, which are expected to result from the imposition of that burden or restriction; (4) the desirability of facilitating innovation in connection with regulated activities; (5) the international character of financial services and markets and the desirability of maintaining the competitive position of the UK; (6) the need to minimise the adverse effects on competition that may arise from anything done in the discharge of those functions; and (7) the desirability of facilitating competition between those who are subject to any form of regulation by the FSA[1].

1   FSMA 2000, s 2(3).

8.21   In the FSA New Millennium paper, the FSA categorises these principles as efficiency and economy, role of management, proportionality, innovation, inter-national character of financial services and market and the desirability of maintain-ing the competitive position of the UK, and competition. This document also provides the FSA's interpretation of those principles.

8.22   The FSMA 2000 in the first principle requires the FSA to allocate and deploy its resources in 'the most efficient and economic way'. The FSA gives an undertaking that when addressing a specific risk, the FSA will aim to select the options which are most efficient and economic. The FSA also states that it will go beyond the statutory requirement to consult on fees and will consult on its budget. This will provide an opportunity for the FSA to explain how it plans to use the funds levied through regulated firms. Several mechanisms were identified to provide controls over its efficiency and economy. Interestingly, the Treasury under s 12 of the FSMA 2000 has the power to order independent reviews of the economy, efficiency and effectiveness with which the FSA has used its resources in discharging its functions.

8.23   The second principle relates to the corporate governance and the role of management. In this context, Michael Taylor argued[1]:

> 'A long-standing matter of concern in Britain and in many other countries has been that a regulatory regime might result in a shifting of responsibility from the firm's management to the supervisory authorities. No supervision, however effective, could – or should – ever replace sound management in the firm. It is important that supervisors and regulators do not become a kind of superior management board, and that sound corporate governance remains the depositors' and consumers' first and most important protection'.

1   David Toube, 'Introduction to the FSMA and the Financial Services Authority', in James Perry (ed) *The Financial Services and Markets Act: A Practical Legal Guide* (2001) p 35.

8.24   The FSA interprets the second principle to mean that a firm's senior management is responsible for its activities. The senior management is also responsible for ensuring that its business is conducted in compliance with regulatory requirements. According to the FSA, this principle is designed to guard against unnecessary intrusion by the regulator into a firm's business. More importantly, the FSA sees this principle as a basis for the FSA to hold senior management responsible for risk management and controls within firms[1].

1   FSA New Millennium, p 10.

8.25   The FSMA 2000, in the third principle, requires the FSA's regulation to be 'proportionate to the benefits, considered in general terms, which are expected to result from it'. The FSA interpret this to mean that the restrictions imposed on firms and markets should be in proportion to the expected benefits for consumers and the industry[1]. As an official of the FSA puts it, 'it means no rules can be imposed or changed without the FSA giving due consideration to the regulatory costs and benefits involved. It needs therefore to demonstrate to a reasonable level of satisfaction that the burden of any proposed rules or changes is proportionate to the expected benefit'[2].

1   FSA New Millennium, p 10.
2   Carol Sergeant of the FSA, 'Risk-based Regulation in the Financial Services Authority', *Journal of Financial Regulation and Compliance*' (2002), Vol 10, No 4. p 331.

8.26   Sections 155 and 157 of the FSMA 2000 require the FSA to carry out a cost-benefit analysis of proposed rules and guidance. Specifically, s 155(2)(a) obligates the FSA to have the draft of the proposed rule accompanied by the cost benefit analysis. Regulation must strike a cost/benefit balance: the most effective regulation may be the most inefficient if it exercises a significant negative influence on the entity or market regulated. Inefficient regulation will impact on the price of the products or services subject to (or provided by entities subject to) the regulation – a fact which may actually (unintentionally) distort the market or drive business elsewhere[1].

1   Amelia C. Fawcett of the FSA, 'Risk-based Regulation in the Financial Services Authority', *Journal of Financial Regulation and Compliance* (2002), Vol 10, No 4. p 331.

8.27 It has to be remembered, as mentioned by the FSA, that the restrictions imposed should be in proportion to the expected benefits, not only for the industry but also for consumers. The FSA gives the undertakings that it will take into account the costs incurred by firms and customers, it will carry out the costs and benefits' analysis of proposed regulatory requirements and the proportional approach will be reflected in the regulatory requirements[1].

1   FSA New Millennium, p 10.

8.28 Some are pessimistic about whether the cost/benefit analysis of the regulation can really be done. Professor Charles Goodhart, for example, remarked[1]:

> 'All in all I have great sympathy for those within the FSA who are charged with the responsibility of trying to undertake such cost/benefit analysis. The benefits are, for most practical purposes, simply not measurable. So it will be remarkably difficult to undertake any meaningful cost/benefit analysis, even though it is now required. Exactly how they will try to handle this impossible remit will be fascinating to see.'

1   Charles A E Goodhart, 'Regulating the Regulator-An Economist's Perspective on Accountability and Control', in Eilis Ferran and Charles A E Goodhart (eds), *Regulating Financial Services and Markets in the Twenty First Century* (2001) p 157.

8.29 On the fourth principle concerning innovation, the FSA states that it should facilitate innovation, for example by avoiding unreasonable barriers to entry or restrictions on existing market participants launching new financial products and services[1]. Under the fifth principle, it is recognised that the FSA will consider the impact on UK markets and consumers of the economic, industry and regulatory situation overseas. The FSA will also take into account the international mobility of much financial business. It will avoid damaging the competitive position of the UK. The final principle on competition requires the FSA to avoid unnecessarily distorting or impeding competition[2].

1   FSA New Millennium, p 11.
2   *Ibid.*

Objectives v principles

8.30 To Simon Gleeson, the creation of statutory objectives for the regulator represents one of the most important innovations of the FSMA 2000. He noted that the reason it was felt that statutory objectives were required goes back to the consequences of the ending of the self-regulatory framework[1]. To Alan Page, the device of statutory objectives is not new. However, the combination of objectives and principles, to him, represents the most ambitious attempt yet made to define the public interest in financial services regulation. He argued that the lack of any equivalent statement of objectives in the Financial Services Act 1986 was widely regarded as one of its major weaknesses, affording ample scope for disagreement about the purposes the Act was intended to serve[2].

1   Simon Gleeson, *Financial Services Regulation: The New Regime* (1999) p 13.

2   Alan Page, 'Regulating the Regulator-A Lawyer's Perspective on Accountability and Control', in Eilis Ferran and Charles A E Goodhart (eds), *Regulating Financial Services and Markets in the Twenty First Century* (2001) p 130.

8.31   The question that arises here is how much weight should be attached to the principles as against the objectives. The FSMA 2000 provides that the FSA 'must, so far as is reasonably possible, act in a way which is compatible' with the regulatory objectives. In relation to the principles, the wording of the FSMA 2000 is 'the Authority must have regard to'. The argument is that the FSA need only 'have regard' to the principles in discharging its general functions whereas the FSA must act in accordance with these objectives 'as far as is reasonably possible'.

8.32   As Alistair Alcock argued, 'the drafting does give the latter greater prominence'[1]. He further noted that it seems unlikely that any action of the FSA could be declared void just because it offended one of the principles. As the Economic Secretary said, defending the drafting[2]:

> 'We want something that requires the FSA to give proper weight to the principles and to ensure that it takes them properly into account but, at the same time, does not expose the regulators to tactical litigation on individual regulatory decisions. Exploration of these issues has led us to the conclusion that the current formulation strikes the right balance.'

1   Alistair Alcock, *The Financial Services And Markets Act 2000: A Guide to the New Law*, (2000) p 38.
2   Cited in Alistair Alcock, p 39.

8.33   Contrastingly, many expert commentators argued that if the FSA makes any rule which is clearly outside the statutory objectives, the rule will be declared void. Simon Gleeson, for example, is of the view that the question which a court must ask itself in considering these matters is whether the duty imposed (in this case, the FSA's duty to act in accordance with the objectives) is 'mandatory' – in which case an act done or rule made otherwise than in accordance with the duty will be void – or whether it is 'directory' – in which case the act or rule will remain valid[1]. The test as to whether a particular statutory provision is mandatory or directory is not a mechanical test of the form of words which is used in the statute; it involves the consideration by the court of 'the importance of the provision which has been disregarded, and the relation of that provision to the general object intended to be secured by the Act'. Given the fact that these provisions are at the very core of this Act it is extremely difficult to see how any Divisional Court could properly hold that they were intended to be merely minatory[2].

1   Alan Page, 'Regulating the Regulator-A Lawyer's Perspective on Accountability and Control', in Eilis Ferran and Charles A E Goodhart (eds), *Regulating Financial Services and Markets in the Twenty First Century* (2001) p 18.
2   *Ibid.*

8.34   However, in determining whether a particular act done in breach of a statutory requirement is void, the court will also look at the degree of discrepancy between the act done and the requirement invoked to avoid it. In cases where, although the requirement is clearly mandatory, the discrepancy, although real, is immaterial, the court will not declare the act concerned to be void[1]. The logical consequences of the application of these two principles is that rules made by the FSA which, although not directly within any of the four objectives, are within the penumbra, are unlikely to be struck down, but rules which are clearly outside any of the objectives almost certainly will be declared void[2].

1 Alan Page, 'Regulating the Regulator – A Lawyer's Perspective on Accountability and Control', in Eilis Ferran and Charles A E Goodhart (eds), *Regulating Financial Services and Markets in the Twenty First Century* (2001) p 18.
2 *Ibid.*

Principles for business

8.35 The FSA has articulated a series of high-level principles, rules and guidance. Some of them, which may have implications for Internet banking, directly or indirectly, are discussed here. The paper called *Principles for Businesses* (hereafter called Principles) was issued to provide a general statement of the fundamental obligations of firms under the new regulatory system. The Principles apply with respect to regulated activities generally. But in applying the Principles with respect to accepting deposits, the FSA will proceed only in a prudential context. It means, in this context, the FSA would not expect to exercise the powers brought into play by a contravention of a Principle unless the contravention amounted to a serious or persistent violation which had implications for confidence in the financial system, or for the fitness and propriety of the firm or for the adequacy of the firm's financial resources[1].

1 Principles, 1.1.3.

8.36 According to the FSA, breaching a Principle makes a firm liable to disciplinary sanctions. In determining whether a Principle has been breached it is necessary to look to the standard of conduct required by the Principle in question. Under each of the Principles the onus will be on the FSA to show that a firm has been at fault in some way. What constitutes 'fault' varies between different Principles[1]. The FSA lays down the following principles:

1. A firm must conduct its business with integrity.

2. A firm must conduct its business with due care, skill and diligence.

3. A firm must take reasonable care to organise and control its affairs responsibly and effectively, with adequate risk management systems.

4. A firm must maintain adequate financial resources.

5. A firm must observe proper standards of market conduct.

6. A firm must pay due regard to the interests of its customers and treat them fairly.

7. A firm must pay due regard to the information needs of its clients, and communicate information to them in a way which is clear, fair and not misleading.

8.   A firm must manage conflicts of interest fairly, both between itself and its customers and between a customer and another client.

9.   A firm must take reasonable care to ensure the suitability of its advice and discretionary decisions for any customer who is entitled to rely upon its judgment.

10.   A firm must arrange adequate protection for clients' assets when it is responsible for them.

11.   A firm must deal with its regulators in an open and co-operative way, and must disclose to the FSA appropriately anything relating to the firm of which the FSA would reasonably expect notice.

1   Principles, 1.1.7.

8.37   The FSMA 2000 empowers the FSA to take disciplinary measures against any authorised person who has contravened a requirement imposed on him by the FSA. The FSA is allowed to impose a penalty of such an amount, as the FSA considers appropriate, on such a person in respect of the contravention[1]. The FSA could also publish a statement that an authorised person has contravened a requirement (public censure)[2].

1   FSMA 2000, s.206.
2   FSMA 2000, s.205.

8.38   According to Daniel F Waters and Martyn Hopper, public censure or the imposition of financial penalties provides a powerful incentive to comply with regulatory requirements. They noted that, 'public discipline ensures that non-compliance is not profitable and that firms that invest in compliance are not at a disadvantage to those who do not'[1]. In this respect, they argued that disciplinary action assists in maintaining public confidence in the regulated industry by demonstrating that regulatory standards are being upheld and in promoting public awareness of regulatory standards through transparent communication of the nature and relative seriousness of failings[2].

1   Daniel F Waters and Martyn Hopper, 'Regulatory Discipline and the European Convention on Human Rights – A Reality Check', in Eilis Ferran and Charles A E Goodhart (eds), *Regulating Financial Services and Markets in the Twenty First Century* (2001) p 100.
2   *Ibid.*

Senior management arrangements, systems and controls

8.39   Another paper issued by the FSA is called *Senior management arrangements, Systems and Controls* (SYSC), which is relevant to the banks that provide Internet banking services. According to the FSA, the purposes of the SYSC are[1]:

●   to encourage firms' directors and senior managers to take appropriate practical responsibility for their firms' arrangements on matters likely to be of interest to the FSA because they impinge on the FSA's functions under the FSMA 2000;

- to increase certainty by amplifying Principle 3, under which a firm must 'take reasonable care to organise and control its affairs responsibly and effectively, with adequate risk management system; and

- to encourage firms to vest responsibility for effective and responsible organisation in specific directors and senior managers.

1 SYSC, 1.2.1.

8.40 Under the first heading, the main matters, which are likely to be of interest to the FSA, are those which relate to confidence in the financial system; to the fair treatment of firms' customers; to the protection of consumers; and to the use of the financial system in connection with financial crime. The FSA is not primarily concerned with risks which threaten only the owners of a financial business except in so far as these risks may have an impact on those matters[1].

1 SYSC, 1.2.2.

8.41 The SYSC, among other things, provides some rules and guidance on: (1) apportionment of responsibilities, (2) recording of apportionment, (3) systems and controls, and (4) 'areas covered by systems and controls'.

8.42 On the apportionment of responsibilities, the FSA requires that a firm must take reasonable care to maintain a clear and appropriate apportionment of significant responsibilities among its directors and senior managers in such a way that it is clear who has which of those responsibilities, and the business and affairs of the firm can be adequately monitored and controlled by the directors, relevant senior managers and governing body of the firm[1]. Also, a firm must appropriately allocate to one or more individuals, the functions of dealing with the apportionment of responsibilities; and overseeing the establishment and maintenance of systems and controls[2].

1 SYSC, 2.1.1.
2 SYSC, 2.1.3.

8.43 In relation to the recording of apportionment, a firm must make a record of the arrangements it has made to satisfy the apportionment and allocation requirements. A firm must take reasonable care to keep this record up-to-date. This record must be retained for six years from the date on which it was superseded by a more up-to-date record. A few guidelines are given on these rules. One of them is that where responsibilities have been allocated to more than one individual, the firm's record must show clearly how those responsibilities are shared or divided between the individuals concerned.

8.44 Under the heading of systems and controls, the rule is that a firm must take reasonable care to establish and maintain such systems and controls as appropriate to its business[1]. The nature and extent of the systems and controls which a firm will need to maintain will depend upon a variety of factors including[2]:

- the nature, scale and complexity of its business;

- the diversity of its operations, including geographical diversity;

- the volume and size of its transactions; and

- the degree of risk associated with each area of its operation.

1   SYSC, 3.1.1.
2   SYSC, 3.1.2.

8.45   The section on the 'areas covered by systems and controls' covers some of the main issues which a firm is expected to consider in establishing and maintaining the systems and controls appropriate to its business. It contains several rules and a series of guidance from the FSA on how a firm could ensure compliance with the rules. The rules are:

- A firm must take reasonable care to establish and maintain effective systems and controls for compliance with applicable requirements and standards under the regulatory system and for countering the risk that the firm might be used to further financial crime[1].

- A firm which carries on designated investment business with or for customers must allocate to a director or senior manager the function of having the responsibility for oversight of the firm's compliance and reporting to the governing body in respect of that responsibility[2].

- A firm must take reasonable care to make and retain adequate records of matters and dealings (including accounting records), which are the subject of requirements and standards under the regulatory system[3].

1   SYSC, 3.2.6.
2   SYSC, 3.2.8.
3   SYSC, 3.2.20.

Conduct of business

8.46   The FSA's rules and guidance are also found in the document *Conduct of Business* (COB). As mentioned by the FSA, 'most of the COB applies in relation to regulated activities, conducted by firms, which fall within the definition of designated investment business. In relation to deposits, the COB has only limited application[1]. The following, however, contains some guidance concerning the use of electronic communication to conduct business, which is relevant to Internet banking.

1   COB, 1.3.2.

8.47   Paragraph 1.8.2 of the COB provides some guidance in respect of electronic communication with or for customers. It states that for any electronic communication with a customer, a firm should:

(1)   have in place appropriate arrangements, including contingency plans, to ensure the secure transmission and receipt of the communication; it should

also be able to verify the authenticity and integrity of the communication; the arrangements should be proportionate and take into account the different levels of risk in a firm's business;

(2)   be able to demonstrate that the customer wishes to communicate using this form of media; and

(3)   if entering into an agreement, make it clear to the customer that a contractual relationship is created that has legal consequences.

8.48   The COB contains guidance on the use of the Internet and other electronic media to communicate financial promotions. Before using the Internet, digital or any other form of interactive television or other electronic media to promote its services a firm should refer to legislation such as the Data Protection Act 1998 and the Computer Misuse Act 1990, as well as to the COB chapter on the Internet and other electronic media[1].

1   COB, 3.14.4.

8.49   When designing websites and other electronic media, firms should be aware of the difficulties that can arise when reproducing certain colours and printing certain types of text. These difficulties could cause problems with the presentation and retrieval of required information[1].

1   COB, 3.14.4.

8.50   Some specific guidance is given to satisfy the rule that a direct offer financial promotion relating to a packaged product must contain certain information termed as 'contents of key features'[1]. On the key features and written contractual terms, the guidance is[2]:

•   A firm should make it clear that the information is available to a recipient of the direct offer financial promotion, and easily obtainable, before any application is made.

•   It is important that recipients should have the opportunity to view the full text of the relevant key features, terms and conditions, customer agreement and any other applicable risk information required by the rules.

•   This can be achieved through the use of a hypertext link, as long as it is not hidden away in the body of the text where a recipient could miss it when browsing through the pages.

•   Local printing of information by the user should be allowed, where feasible. Firms should endeavour to provide hard copy on request.

1   This rule is provided for in paragraph 3.9.10 of the COB, whereas the provision on the contents of key features is mentioned in paragraph 6.5 of the COB.
2   COB, 3.14.5.

Interim Prudential Sourcebook for Banks

8.51   Another important source of the rules and guidance for the financial industry in the UK is the *Interim Prudential Sourcebook for Banks* (IPSB) issued by the

FSA in 2001. It lays down a number of prudential techniques with no specific reference to electronic banking. Banking institutions are required to take reasonable care to organise and control their affairs responsibly and effectively, with an adequate risk management system. In assessing the fitness and propriety of a bank to perform a regulated activity, the FSA will have regard to a range of factors such as honesty, integrity and reputation, competence, capability and financial soundness.

8.52 Every bank must ensure that there is a clear apportionment of responsibilities at senior management level. Regarding outsourcing, the FSA requires that all outsourcing arrangements should be considered in the light of the requirement for sound and effective systems and controls. The FSA must be promptly informed of any outsourcing arrangement, the FSA and the external and internal auditors have access to information about the outsourced activity, and there is prior notification of all outsourcing arrangements regarding material units of the bank's operations. The bank will remain responsible to the regulator for the outsourced activity. Senior management is required to exercise rigorous surveillance over the affairs of the institutions.

8.53 The IPSB sets out the FSA's detailed prudential standards and related notification requirements applying to banks authorised under the FSMA 2000. The FSA articulated the purpose of the IPSB in this manner[1]:

> 'Banks are exposed by the nature of their business to risks including credit, market, liquidity and operational risks. Where these risks are not adequately managed, or where a bank otherwise suffers unexpected losses, a bank may be unable to meets its liabilities to depositors when they fall due or, in the case of a bank's insolvency, at all. Consumers could in such circumstances suffer loss and there could be adverse effects on market confidence.'

1   IPSB, 3

8.54 The purpose of the prudential standards set out in the sourcebook is to ensure that banks maintain capital resources commensurate with their risks and appropriate systems and controls to enable them to manage those risks. The IPSB applies to banks on an interim basis pending the preparation and implementation of a Single Prudential Sourcebook applying to all firms regulated by the FSA-termed the Integrated Prudential Sourcebook[1].

1   IPSB, 8.

8.55 As mentioned earlier, with no specific reference to Internet banking, the IPSB provides extensive rules and guidance on several issues – among other things, the maintenance of adequate capital, the achievement of sufficient liquidity, the exercise of consolidated supervision, the control of large financial exposure and concentration of risks, and many more.

8.56 On the issue of liquidity, the IPSB outlined the main prudential policies applying to banks: a bank must maintain adequate liquidity at all times; a bank must formulate a statement of its liquidity management policy; it should agree with the

FSA standards for adherence to this policy; a bank should have adequate systems for monitoring liquidity on a daily basis; and a bank should notify the FSA of any breaches of its liquidity mismatch guidelines as soon as they occur.

8.57 The FSA acknowledged that it is the responsibility of a bank's directors and management to take reasonable care to establish and maintain such systems and controls as are appropriate to the nature, scale and complexity of its business. The management is required also to ensure that the firm maintains adequate records which are appropriate to the scale, nature and complexity of its business. The FSA admitted that it does not prescribe a standard set of controls for all banks to follow. Rather, the FSA expects that each bank's records, systems and controls will be appropriate to the nature and scale of that bank's operations, and will develop with those operations. The FSA's role is to determine in the light of the information which it reviews whether the firm is in compliance with the Principles and Rules.

8.58 The FSA raised several concerns on 'systems and control weaknesses', which are divided into the headings of: general, segregation of duties, possible conflict of interest, employees, the back of the office, and payment system. Under the first heading, according to the FSA, 'many of the cases supervisors have observed that have given rise to actual cases of fraud, or exposed banks to opportunities for fraud, relate to inadequate internal controls'. On segregation of duties, the FSA acknowledged:

> 'Segregation of duties can only achieve its objective if it is effectively performed. A theoretical control does not stop abuse. In supervisors' experience, procedures which appeared adequate on paper have failed in practice when faced by a determined individual or weak operatives. So a control system can only be judged by whether it operates in practice under stress, no matter how efficient it may seem in theory'[1].

1   IPSB, 3.2.

8.59 On the payments systems, the FSA raised its concern that 'significant risks can arise from weaknesses in controls over the major payment systems used in banks. There have been instances where internal controls over *electronic payments systems* and tested telex payments have been breached'. In this context, the FSA requires that a bank should regularly review its controls over all systems which could enable significant funds to be transferred to unauthorised third parties.

8.60 The FSA recognised that the scope and nature of adequate control systems should take account of the matters covered in the SYSC and: the amount of control by senior management over day-to-day operation; and the degree of centralisation and *the extent of reliance on information technology*. A system of internal control should be designed and operated to provide reasonable assurance that[1]:

- all the bank's revenues accrue to its benefit;

- all expenditure is properly authorised and disbursed;

- all assets are adequately safeguarded;

- all liabilities are recorded;

- all statutory requirements relating to the provision of accounts are complied with and all prudential reporting conditions are adhered to.

I   IPSB, 3.3.

8.61   The high level controls are the controls which are primarily exercised at director and senior manager level. The high level controls typically include: the setting of strategy and planning; approval of risk policies; establishment and review of the organisational structure; the system of delegation; review of high level management information; and maintaining the framework for monitoring and/or review of risk management and detailed control systems and for the implementation of action points following such a review. The FSA insisted that its requirements for adequate internal control systems apply to high level as well as to detailed control systems[1].

I   IPSB, 3.3.

8.62   The FSA does not believe it is appropriate to prepare a comprehensive list of control procedures which would then be applicable to any bank, nor is it possible to prepare a detailed list of particular procedures which should be undertaken, where appropriate, by all banks. Nonetheless, internal control systems should provide reasonable assurance that[1]:

- the business is planned and conducted in an orderly and prudent manner in adherence to established policies;

- transactions and commitments are entered into in accordance with management's general or specific authority;

- management is able to safeguard the assets and control the liabilities of the business;

- there are measures to minimise the risk of loss from irregularities, fraud and error, and promptly and readily identify them when they occur;

- the accounting and other records of the business provide complete and timely information;

- management is able to monitor on a regular and timely basis, among other things, the adequacy of the bank's capital, liquidity, profitability and the quality of its assets;

- management is able to identify, regularly assess and, where appropriate, quantify the risk of loss in the conduct of the business so that the risks can be monitored and controlled on a regular and timely basis; and appropriate provisions can be made for bad and doubtful debts, and for any other exposures both on and off the balance sheet;

- management is able to comply with the FSA's reporting rules; and

- the bank is able to comply with the other notification requirements under
  the FSMA 2000.

I   IPSB, 3.3.4.

8.63   The FSA recognised that the scope and nature of the specific control
objectives which should be adopted for the business to be conducted in a prudent
manner should be commensurate with a bank's needs and particular circumstances,
and should have regard to the manner in which the business is structured,
organised and managed, to its size and the nature, volume and complexity of its
transactions and commitments[1].

I   IPSB, 3.3.5.

8.64   Once again, the FSA believes that it is not appropriate for it to provide an
exhaustive and prescriptive list of detailed control requirements which should
apply to all banks. However, the FSA considers that each bank should address the
following control objectives: organisational structure; risk management; monitoring
procedures; segregation of duties; authorisation and approval; completeness and
accuracy; safeguarding assets; and personnel[1].

I   IPSB, 3.3.5.

8.65   The FSA specifically recognised the importance of banks' information held
in electronic form and the need to protect it[1]:

> 'The information held in electronic form within a bank's information systems is a
> valuable asset that needs to be protected against unauthorised access and disclosure.
> It is the responsibility of management to understand the extent to which a bank relies
> upon electronic information, to assess the value of that information and to establish
> an appropriate system of controls.'

I   IPSB, 3.3.6.

8.66   The FSA considered that the control objectives described above apply
equally to operations undertaken in both manual and electronic environment.
However, the FSA recognised that there are additional risks associated with
electronic environments. The protection of the information can be achieved by a
combination of manual and automated controls, the balance of which will vary
between banks, reflecting the need for each to address its particular risks in a
manner which is cost effective[1].

I   IPSB, 3.3.6.

8.67   According to the FSA, 'the types of risk most often associated with the use
of information technology in financial systems may be classified as follows: fraud
and theft; errors; interruption; and misinformation'. On the first category, the FSA
stated that access to information and systems can create opportunities for the
manipulation of data in order to create or conceal significant financial loss.
Additionally, information can be stolen, even without its physical removal or

awareness of the fact, which may lead to loss of competitive advantage[1]. The FSA recognised that unauthorised activity can be committed by a person with or without legitimate access rights.

1 IPSB, 3.3.6.

8.68 On 'interruption', the FSA acknowledged, 'the components of electronic systems are vulnerable to interruption and failure, without adequate contingency arrangements this can lead to serious operational difficulty and/or financial loss'[1].

1 IPSB, 3.3.6.

8.69 The FSA requires management to be aware of its responsibility to promote and maintain a climate of security awareness and vigilance throughout the organisation. In particular, management should give consideration to: IT security education and training, designed to make all relevant staff aware of the need for, and their role in supporting good IT security practice and the importance of protecting company assets; and IT security policy, standards, procedures and responsibilities, designed to ensure that arrangements are adequate and appropriate[1].

1 IPSB, 3.3.6.

8.70 Regarding outsourcing, the FSA requires that all outsourcing arrangements should be considered in light of the requirement for sound and effective systems and controls. Banks are required to adequately record and control their business. Where a bank has outsourced an aspect of its operation to another part of the group, or to an external supplier, it should ensure that its records and controls adequately cover that business. Banks should put in place procedures for monitoring and controlling the outsourced operation.

The FSA's new approach to regulation

8.71 Section 2(4) of the FSMA 2000 lays down the general functions of the FSA: to make rules, to prepare and issue codes, to give general guidance, and to determine the general policy and principles by reference to which it performs particular functions. Apart from these, the FSA oversees the performance of regulated activities and enforces all legal requirements[1], issues statements and codes with regard to the conduct expected of all authorised persons and takes disciplinary action in cases of compliance with imposed requirements[2].

1 FSMA 2000, ss 56–63 and Sch 1, s 6.
2 FSMA 2000, ss 205–211.

8.72 With respect to Internet banking, as far as the FSMA 2000 is concerned, the clearest indication of the nature and scale of prudential standards imposed on credit institutions is offered by Sch 6 to the FSMA 2000, which specifies the threshold conditions that an institution must satisfy at all times in order to be granted and maintain permission by the FSA to engage in regulated activities.

8.73 Specifically, the FSMA 2000 requires that the resources of the person concerned must, in the opinion of the FSA, be adequate in relation to the regulated activities that he/she seeks to carry on. In reaching this conclusion, the FSA may consider the means by which the institution in question manages the incidence of risk associated with the profile of its business. The bank must also satisfy the FSA that it is a fit and proper person to conduct the regulated activity, having regard to all the circumstances, including the nature of the activity and the need to ensure that the bank's affairs are conducted soundly and prudently.

8.74 As mentioned by Kirstene Baillie, to date, the UK financial services regulators have[1]:

- stated that all existing rules could apply and their jurisdiction extends to all websites which may be accessed in the UK;

- avoided creating specific rules for Internet business;

- issued guidance clarifying how existing regulations apply; and

- developed a realistic enforcement policy.

1 Kirstene Baillie, 'Financial Services', in Michael Chissick and Alistair Kelman, *Electronic Commerce: Law and Practice* (3rd edn, 2002) p 227.

8.75 The FSA's declared aim is to be a world-leading regulator, respected for its effectiveness, integrity and expertise both at home and abroad. The FSA's goal is to maintain efficient, orderly and clean financial markets and help retail consumers achieve a fair deal. The FSA acknowledged that it would do this in a number of ways: getting a fair deal for consumers, improving industry performance, flexible and proactive regulation, and maximising its effectiveness[1].

1 FSA New Millennium, 11–12.

8.76 At the heart of the FSA's approach to regulation is the concept of 'risk'. By risk, the FSA specifically means risk to their statutory objectives. In short, the FSA sees its approach to regulation as moving away from an individualised and isolated focus on regulatory problems presented by specific institutions to a holistic methodology premised upon identifying and pre-empting risks to the regulatory objectives as a whole. In 2000, the FSA identified 15 risks to their statutory objectives[1]. *Financial Risk Outlook 2002*, identified some of the risks for that year, which were:

- firms' and consumers' response to a less benign economic environment;

- the impact of unexpectedly low or volatile returns on consumer behaviour;

- changing expectations of obligations on firms and consumers;

- the changing legal environment for consumer products and the legal risk associated with some high impact, often innovative, product structures;

- financial crime, including the impact and aftermath of terrorist attacks;

- legal and regulatory changes arising from international fora; and

- firms' responses to the FSMA 2000.

I   See David Toube, 'Introduction to the FSMA and the Financial Services Authority', in James Perry (ed) *The Financial Services and Markets Act: A Practical Legal Guide* (2001) p 15.

8.77   Strategic aims have been set for each of the key spheres in which the FSA operates – in relation to consumers, firms, financial markets and regulatory regimes. In the words of an official of the FSA, 'taken together, the aims support the statutory objectives'[1]. The aims are[2]:

- *Consumers:* 'consumers are better able to make informed choices and achieve fair deals in their financial dealings'. This aim supports two statutory objectives – consumer protection and promoting public understanding.

- *Firms:* 'regulated firms and their senior management understand and meet their regulatory obligations'. This aim supports the statutory objectives to secure consumer protection, maintain market confidence and reduce the scope for financial crime.

- *Market:* 'consumers and other participants have confidence that markets are efficient, orderly and clean'. This aim supports the objectives to maintain market confidence and reduce the scope for financial crime.

- *The regulatory regime:* 'an appropriate, proportionate and effective regulatory regime is established in which consumers, firms and other stakeholders have confidence'. This aim supports the objectives to maintain market confidence and promote public understanding.

I   Carol Sergeant of the FSA, 'Risk-based Regulation in the Financial Services Authority', *Journal of Financial Regulation and Compliance*' (2002), Vol 10, No 4. p 332.
2   *Ibid.*

The FSA and electronic commerce

8.78   The FSA has been keen to rule out the introduction of specific require-ments, which would solely regulate the conduct of online banking operations. Carol Sergeant, the then Director of Banks and Building Societies, FSA, stated[1]:

> 'The FSA intends to be e-neutral. Our current legislation, the Banking Act and the Building Societies Act, provide us with the powers we need and our current range of supervisory tools are perfectly adequate although we may need to deploy some with different degrees of intensity … So, we have no special regime for e-banks and we see no reason why we should not be able to authorise any new e-banks provided they meet our minimum prudential standards.'

I   Carol Sergeant, 'E-Banking: Risks and Responses', available at http://www.fsa.gov.uk/pubs/speeches/sp46.

8.79   A key paper that summarises the position of the FSA on electronic commerce, the *FSA's Approach to the Regulation of E-Commerce* (FSA E-Commerce) was circulated in June 2001. It has significant implications for Internet banking.

According to the FSA, apart from the four statutory objectives, the FSA's approach to e-commerce takes into account the principles of good regulation. Particularly relevant to e-commerce are[1]:

- the role of senior management in meeting the challenges of e-commerce;

- facilitation of innovation by avoiding unnecessary barriers to launching new financial products and services;

- the need to have regard to the international character of financial services and markets and the desirability of maintaining the competitive position of the UK;

- the minimisation of any adverse effects of regulatory decisions on competition; and

- a proportionate regulatory approach.

1 FSA E-Commerce, 1.4.

8.80 The other guiding principles for e-commerce regulation are: the fundamental principles of regulation remain the same whatever the medium; regulators should not unnecessarily impede the legitimate use of the Internet by market participants and markets; and regulators should strive for transparency and consistency regarding how their regulations apply in an Internet environment[1].

1 FSA E-Commerce, 3.7.

8.81 The FSA has also adopted a policy of technological, or delivery channel, neutrality. The policy means that the FSA will not discriminate in its approach on the basis of delivery channel alone, unless the risks to the statutory objectives from different channels justify it. According to the FSA, technological neutrality does not mean that the same specific requirements must be imposed on all delivery channels, since the risks related to doing business via telephone, Internet, or post may be different[1].

1 FSA E-Commerce, 3.12.

8.82 The policy of technological neutrality, according to the FSA, does not prevent it from discriminating in its approach – for example in rule making, intensity of supervision or in consumer focused work – solely on the basis of delivery channel, if the risks to the FSA's statutory objectives justify it. The FSA stated that this has four implications for its approach[1]:

- non-discrimination does not suggest the imposition of the same requirements on all delivery channels, since the risk and/or control environments of delivery channels may differ and may therefore require recourse to different regulatory approaches. Nor does it prevent the FSA from taking medium-specific action to address a risk arising from the use of a particular communications channel. But it does require the FSA to be able to justify any differences by reference to the features of the specific medium;

- in pursuing the approach of technological neutrality the FSA will have to consider, for example the effect that a general requirement may have on different delivery channels. It is not enough to impose a general requirement that applies to all media, since this may be discriminatory. Delivery channel specific cost/benefit analysis will, therefore, need to be considered wherever it appears that the compliance cost of meeting a general requirement in one delivery channel may be significantly greater than in others;

- the FSA will need to provide for the same overall risk-based intensity of supervision, investigation, enforcement and consumer focused work regardless of delivery channel. So, for example, it would not be technologically neutral to devote greater levels of regulatory attention to a particular channel, solely because it was easier to monitor activities in cyberspace. To do so would adversely affect competition. Whereas, paying greater attention to a medium because the risks were greater would be in line with a technologically neutral approach;

- operating a policy of technological neutrality involves the FSA in identifying the particular risks associated with a specific technology, assessing the impact and probability of a risk crystallising, seeing how cost effectively such risks are currently addressed by the FSA, and taking whatever action might be needed to ensure that appropriate standards are maintained.

1   FSA E-Commerce, 3.12.

8.83   According to the FSA, technological neutrality is not its new aim. Technological neutrality is achieved at the statutory level, in that an activity which triggers a requirement for authorisation will do so whether the activity is performed face-to-face, by post, telephone, or in cyberspace[1].

1   FSA E-Commerce, 3.13.

8.84   The FSA has identified and prioritised 17 risks associated with e-commerce. For some of them, the ways the risks can become material are also identified. In relation to other risks, in addition to identifying how they can become material, the FSA has identified which of its statutory objectives will be at risk if those identified priority risks are not addressed.

8.85   The FSA divided the risks into two main categories. First, risks arising within the industry, for example, availability problems with e-commerce systems leading to consumer loss, or significant crime via e-commerce delivery channels. Second, risks arising within the FSA which, if left unmanaged, could affect the ability of the FSA to meet its statutory objectives[1]. The risks, among others, are[2]:

- A breakdown of controls related to the development of e-commerce business leads to consumer detriment, failure or significant loss in a firm or firms.

- Problems with an outsourced function, or a heavy dependence on a third party for material aspects of an e-commerce service leads to consumer detriment, failure or significant loss in a firm or firms.

- Prolonged problems in the availability of firms' key e-commerce systems leads to consumer detriment, failure or significant loss in a firm or firms.

- Firms' problems with the customer-driven scale of demand lead to consumer detriment, failure or significant loss in a firm or firms.

- Criminals commit fraud using information gathered from consumers' PCs.

- There is significant financial crime via e-commerce channels.

- Major e-crime or security incidents lead to a loss of confidence in the Internet as a medium, and subsequently to major disruption of a market or financial sector.

- Criminal or terrorist attacks on payments and settlement systems lead to major disruption and/or financial crime.

- Consumers suffer detriment as a result of making choices based on false assumptions about the status of information or the quality of a firm's analysis of their circumstances, gained via e-commerce delivery channels.

- Misuse and/or compromise of electronic signatures leads to consumer detriment, failure or significant loss in a firm or firms.

1   FSA E-Commerce, 5.6 and 5.7.
2   FSA E-Commerce, Box 1.

8.86   On consumer security, the FSA remarked that it has an interest in ensuring that information to help consumers to protect their data is accessible to the public. The FSA noted[1]:

> 'Ultimately, consumers are responsible for keeping financial and other important data secure where it is in their control to do so. But in order to do this they need reliable and comprehensible information on what steps to take. The FSA has an interest in such information being accessible to the public, since it is directly relevant to the statutory objectives of reducing financial crime, protecting consumers and promoting their understanding of the financial system.'

1   FSA E-Commerce, 7.5.

8.87   The FSA acknowledged that security is an ongoing challenge both in the physical and online worlds. And consumers have always had a role to play. Interestingly, in this respect, the FSA continued by stating, 'Their responsibility does not change merely because they are operating online'. Arguably, this would mean that the obligations on the part of consumers are the same, whether they do business offline or online[1].

1   FSA E-Commerce, 7.6.

8.88   According to the FSA, there are three IT security risks that customers are facing. First, a criminal finds or correctly guesses passwords and other data, uses them to log-on to a site of a financial institution and steals money. Second, a criminal sends an e-mail containing a malicious computer program which is able to collect consumer data. This data is then used by the criminal to access the customer's account. Third, a consumer is directed to a dummy or look-alike site, or falls victim to an online scam[1].

1   FSA E-Commerce, 7.7.

8.89   The FSA is of the view that security is a shared endeavour. Financial service firms, the computer industry and regulators all have a role to play. So does the public. Several ways were suggested by the FSA to improve consumer security: promoting good password practice; protecting the computer from attack by software programs; and avoiding dummy and fraudulent sites as well as those promoting scams. The FSA's suggestion concerning good password practice is noteworthy. The FSA recognised that[1]:

> 'It is possible for financial firms to enforce good password practice. They might, for example, require the password to be changed at certain times. They might install systems that reject passwords which are easy to guess. On the other hand, forcing people to choose passwords which are difficult to remember, especially when these accounts are not accessed everyday and have to be changed regularly, may increase the risk that a password will be written down – a careful balance needs to be struck.'

1   FSA E-Commerce, 7.18.

8.90   The FSA has been at the forefront in identifying the risks arising from e-commerce and responding to them. The document outlined existing FSA regulatory work in the areas of authorisation, banking supervision, authorisation enquiries, enforcement, consumer relations, etc. In the area of banking, supervisors have reviewed firms' e-commerce services on a risk basis in a number of ways, including meetings with management and IT staff, the use of a systems question-naire, on-site visits by the FSA's IT risk review specialists, and reports on IT systems and controls commissioned from external audit firms[1].

1   FSA E-Commerce, A.6.

8.91   The FSA acknowledged that, 'Firms which operate wholly or to a material extent via the Internet are *highly* vulnerable to the technology on which their business is based. A series of IT failures, or a single serious one, could do significant commercial damage to a firm's reputation and consumer base. It might threaten the firm existence'[1].

1   FSA E-Commerce, A.2, emphasis added.

8.92   In relation to granting the authorisation to firms, the FSA has to be satisfied that the firm meets the relevant minimum threshold conditions for authorisation. According to the paper, for the past two years, the FSA has required firms applying for authorisation and intending to provide services via the Internet or similar electronic means to complete a detailed e-commerce business and systems questionnaire, which has been developed by the FSA. The questionnaire focuses firms on all aspects of IT systems and controls and the way in which their systems are managed. The areas covered by the questionnaire include: project management; systems security; IT recovery procedures; system availability; and change of control procedures[1].

1   FSA E-Commerce, A.3.

Cracking the codes for banking customers

8.93   The banking industry produced 'The Banking Code' in 1992 with the aim of setting minimum standards of good practice to be followed by banks (and building societies) in their relations with personal customers. It has been in existence for over a decade, and the current edition, which is its sixth version, came into effect on 1 March 2003. The Code has evolved from a practitioner-facing document to a consumer-facing one. However, it has grown more detailed with each revision as the breadth and depth of coverage has increased and as consumers and practitioners have sought additional clarification[1]. Before examining its content, it is useful to trace the developments that led to the formulation of the current version of the Code.

1   Banking Services Consumer Codes Review Group, *Cracking the Codes for Banking Customers* (May 2001) para 2.22.

8.94   In March 2000, Don Cruickshank published his report to the Chancellor of the Exchequer on *Competition in UK Banking*. As part of its response to this Report, in November 2000, the Government set up the Banking Services Consumer Codes Review Group, which was chaired by DeAnne Julius. Cruickshank felt it was 'inappropriate for the banks to determine the standards against which complaints against them are judged'. Among other things, the terms of reference of the Review Group were to examine[1]:

● whether the voluntary codes are delivering sufficiently strong benefits to consumers;

● what scope there is to introduce greater independence and consumer representation in the drawing up of codes; and

● whether greater information disclosure can be achieved without the need for further regulation.

1   Banking Services Consumer Codes Review Group, *Cracking the Codes for Banking Customers* (May 2001) para 1.17.

8.95   In May 2001, the Review Group published a report *Cracking the Codes for Banking Customers* containing some findings and recommendations concerning the Banking Code and Mortgage Code. Here, the focus of the discussion was on the findings and recommendations in relation to the Banking Code. In its assessment, the Review Group noted[1]:

'The background to the establishment of the Code Review Group was the perception of widespread public discontent with the standards of banking services in the UK.

Our Group did not find strong evidence for this. We did find evidence of consumer detriment in some well-known areas, but this needs to be seen in the context of the large number of transactions that take place in these markets, the vast majority of which are conducted satisfactorily. The percentage of bank customers whose complaints are unresolved by their own banks' procedures is very low.'

I   Banking Services Consumer Codes Review Group, *Cracking the Codes for Banking Customers* (May 2001) para 3.1.

8.96   The Review Group, however, remarked, 'It did find some continuing problems in banking services'. The absolute size of consumer detriment, according to the Review Group, is not really possible to quantify in any robust way[1]. On the Banking Code, the Review Group stated that there is broad consensus that service standards in banking can be effectively dealt with by self-regulation. The Group said, 'Indeed, our consultation exercise revealed that many feel the Banking Code, while not perfect, is an exemplar of self-regulation'[2].

I   Banking Services Consumer Codes Review Group, *Cracking the Codes for Banking Customers* (May 2001) para 3.3.
2   *Ibid*, para 3.8.

8.97   According to the Review Group, the four areas of customer benefit that successive revisions to the Code have delivered are: abolition of unlimited loan guarantees; limitation of card liability to £50; pre-notification of bank charges; and customer self-selection of PINs. Despite the overall satisfaction, the Review Group has raised some concerns about the process for drawing up the Code, notably:

- consultees do not have a sufficiently clear idea of the structure of the review process, including the timetable for review;

- feedback from those conducting the reviews is not systematic or transparent enough; and

- decisions on final Code content are not seen to have sufficient independent scrutiny.

8.98   The Review Group raised two specific concerns regarding the content of the Banking Code: on account switching and dealing with people in financial difficulty. On the account switching, the Review Group reported, 'the latest edition of the Banking Code includes commitments to co-operate if customers decide to move their current accounts. However, there are still considerable barriers which prevent those dissatisfied with their account from moving …'[1]

I   Banking Services Consumer Codes Review Group, *Cracking the Codes for Banking Customers* (May 2001) paras 3.10, 3.11.

8.99   In relation to dealing with people in financial difficulty, the Review Group recognised that there is evidence that financial institutions do not deal appropriately with the individuals burdened with financial difficulties. Specific problems include the imposition of punitive and unexpected charges, and a lack of respect for consumers' right to first appropriation. In this respect, particularly about the content of the Code, the Review Group's concern is that the Code at present provides little guidance on what the commitment to deal 'sympathetically and positively' with customers in financial difficulties means[1].

1 Banking Services Consumer Codes Review Group, *Cracking the Codes for Banking Customers* (May 2001) para 3.12.

8.100 The overall assessment of the Group is that the voluntary code for banking has delivered benefits to consumers and it should be updated to deal with new concerns and changes in the competitive and regulatory environment. However, the Group noted that the consultation process revealed that many customers feel inadequately equipped to make sound financial decisions. In the words of the Group:

> 'they do not find it easy to get the information they need when they need it and in a form they can understand. They are often not aware of the protections and remedies provided by the relevant consumer codes. As a result, they are reluctant to change banks, even when they are dissatisfied.'[1]

The Group recognised that Codes cannot resolve all of these problems, but codes can go some way further towards empowering consumers to act in their own best interest[2].

1 Banking Services Consumer Codes Review Group, *Cracking the Codes for Banking Customers* (May 2001) para 3.28.
2 *Ibid.*

8.101 The Review Group proposed twelve recommendations. The main seven of them are to enable benefits to be delivered in the four areas: easier account switching; better customer information; clearer code review process; and more information on code compliance. The rest are further recommendations, which relate to several areas. The seven recommendations are:

• *Recommendation 1: A new standard for switching accounts.*
  When a personal customer wants to switch their current account to a new bank, the old bank should provide a five day guarantee to transfer customer information to the new bank. All banks should publish the average time it takes them to complete the transfer process for a new customer and they should commit to a five week target for the end to end process by the end of 2002. The BCSB should monitor compliance with this new 'five-day start – five-week finish' standard.

• *Recommendation 2: A portable credit history*
  At the customer's request, their current bank should provide their 'positive data' credit history to any other bank that the customer specifies.

• *Recommendation 3: Customer Annual Summary Statement*
  Every bank customer should receive a personal statement summarising the total charges paid and interest received on their current accounts, saving accounts, personal loans and credit cards for each tax year (ending 5 April) before the end of June.

- *Recommendation 4: Three code formats*
  Codes should be produced in three formats: a leaflet, the full code and guidance notes. The leaflet should be distributed biennially to all current account and mortgage holders, while the full code and guidance notes should be readily available to any one who wants them.

- *Recommendation 5: Biennial code reviews*
  The code review process should be formalised, made more transparent, and led by an independent 'Reviewer'.

- *Recommendation 6: Published aggregate compliance data*
  Aggregate data on compliance with key code provisions should be published by the monitoring bodies.

- *Recommendation 7: Published individual compliance data*
  The monitoring boards should develop an objective formula to rate code compliance by individual institutions and publish the results.

8.102 Concerning recommendation 4 relating to the full code, the Review Group acknowledged that it should be largely a principle-based document and be seen as a reference document for customers to run to if they feel they have a complaint. More importantly, the Group considered that it should be available wherever accounts, etc can be opened, including the Internet[1]. This would mean that the bank should provide the Banking Code to a consumer who wants to subscribe to Internet banking services.

1 Banking Services Consumer Codes Review Group, *Cracking the Codes for Banking Customers* (May 2001) para 4.33.

8.103 The other recommendations of the Review Group include that all banking services providers should sign up to the relevant code(s)[1]. Specifically relating to the Banking Code, it is recommended that the guidance note to the Code should be revised to spell out key practices which are consistent with the Code principles on treatment of people in financial difficulties. The revised Guidance should have been re-issued to subscribers by November 2001[2].

1 Banking Services Consumer Codes Review Group, *Cracking the Codes for Banking Customers* (May 2001) para 4.64, recommendation 8.
2 *Ibid*, para 4.70, recommendation 11.

Responses to the Report of Review Group

8.104 The British Bankers' Association (BBA) has responded to the Report and made comments on each of the recommendations. The BBA supported the thrust of the recommendations and the positive and constructive way in which they have been presented. The BBA considered that the Report, 'represents an endorsement of the current self-regulatory framework under the Banking Code'[1].

1 British Bankers' Association, 'Cracking the Codes for Banking Customers', response to the Report by the Banking Services Consumer Codes Review Group, available at http://www.bba.org.uk/public/newsroom/35451/44411?view=Print.

8.105 In relation to recommendation 1, the BBA stated that in the vast majority of cases the process of closing an existing current account and opening a new one is completed well within five weeks. Against this background, according to the BBA, 'the targets proposed by the Julius Group should be achievable within the timescale proposed in the Report'[1]. The BBA plans to introduce service standards for both the 'old' bank and the 'new' bank. The BBA outlined the standards to implement the Group's recommendation and stated that the Banking Code Standard Board (BCSB) will monitor these standards and failure to comply will be a breach of the Code and dealt with accordingly[2].

1 British Bankers' Association, 'Cracking the Codes for Banking Customers', response to the Report by the Banking Services Consumer Codes Review Group, available at http://www.bba.org.uk/public/newsroom/35451/44411?view=Print p 2.
2 *Ibid.*

8.106 The BBA does not agree with the Group's finding concerning the portable credit history, which was the basis of recommendation 2. The BBA noted[1]:

'We are not aware that the absence of a portable credit history has created a barrier to account switching. Neither the BCSB study, nor Cruickshank, identified this as an issue and the Julius Group's assertion that it is a problem is not backed by any supporting evidence.'

1 British Bankers' Association, 'Cracking the Codes for Banking Customers', response to the Report by the Banking Services Consumer Codes Review Group, available at http://www.bba.org.uk/public/newsroom/35451/44411?view=Print p 3.

8.107 The BBA has raised four concerns in relation to recommendation 3. They relate to cost-benefit, content, timing of delivery to customers, and implementation date. Among other things, the BBA is not convinced about the need for annual statement information to be delivered between April and the end of June each year and that the proposed implementation date in the Report of June 2002, according to the BBA is not realistic[1].

1 British Bankers' Association, 'Cracking the Codes for Banking Customers', response to the Report by the Banking Services Consumer Codes Review Group, available at http://www.bba.org.uk/public/newsroom/35451/44411?view=Print p 4.

8.108 The BBA supported recommendations 4 and 6 and the thrust of recommendation 11. It gave its endorsement to recommendation 8. With regard to the latter, the BBA acknowledged that it cannot force firms to subscribe. It feels that the Treasury and FSA could do more to encourage firms, where appropriate, to adhere to the relevant codes and the BBA would be interested to know what the Treasury and FSA intend to do in this regard[1].

1 British Bankers' Association, 'Cracking the Codes for Banking Customers', response to the Report by the Banking Services Consumer Codes Review Group, available at http://www.bba.org.uk/public/newsroom/35451/44411?view=Print p 6.

8.109 On recommendation 5, the BBA supported 'wholeheartedly' the need for transparency of process and substance. It accepted that the involvement of an independent Reviewer would help to demonstrate to the public that the process for reviewing the Codes is fair and objective. In the BBA words, 'the industry has nothing to hide in this regard'[1].

1 British Bankers' Association, 'Cracking the Codes for Banking Customers', response to the Report by the Banking Services Consumer Codes Review Group, available at http://www.bba.org.uk/public/newsroom/35451/44411?view=Print p 5.

8.110 Recommendation 7 according to the BBA is a source of considerable concern to its members. The BBA believes that if this recommendation is implemented fully, it would erode industry support for the Banking Code. The BBA argued that if the BCSB is to be obliged to publish compliance data for each firm, it would need to be far more rigorous and prescriptive in its compliance monitoring. The BBA argued further that if the BCSB is to publish data for all subscribers, it will need to be in a position to defend in public its rating of every firm and will need to equip itself against potential legal challenges from subscribers who dispute the regulator's rating. This means that the BCSB would need extra resources and eventually the costs of regulation under the Banking Code would greatly increase[1]. According to the BBA, the main impact of these changes would be that the relative attractiveness to the banks of the Banking Code would be diminished vis-à-vis the main alternative[2]. The BBA also questioned the benefit to consumers of the publication of compliance data. The BBA remarked[3]:

'In short term the alternative for firms would be to avoid any form of conduct of business regulation of their banking business, by dropping out of the banking Code framework and we fear some subscribers might elect to do this. In the longer term, FSA regulation is likely to be an alternative ... It is an alternative that Banking Code subscribers could expected to take seriously if the nature of BCSB regulation changed as implied by the Report.'

1 British Bankers' Association, 'Cracking the Codes for Banking Customers', response to the Report by the Banking Services Consumer Codes Review Group, available at http://www.bba.org.uk/public/newsroom/35451/44411?view=Print p 6.
2 *Ibid.*
3 *Ibid.*

8.111 The Economic Secretary, Ruth Kelly endorsed the Banking Code and in her response to the Review Group Report welcomed the industry's constructive response to the recommendations. Acknowledging that the majority of the recommendations were accepted, she said[1]:

'DeAnne's review highlighted areas where improvements should be made to benefit banking customers. There has been a very constructive response with the majority of the recommendations being accepted by industry. The measures being taken forward will benefit customers ...'

1 See HMT Press Release 140/01 on 12 December 2001, available at http://www.hm-treasury.gov.uk/ newsroom_and_speeches/press/2001/press_140_01.cfm.

The Review of the Banking Code

8.112 As mentioned earlier, one of the key recommendations of the Review Group was for biennial code reviews and that the Code review process be formalised, made more transparent, and led by an independent 'Reviewer'. Following this recommendation, in January 2002, Professor Elaine Kempson was appointed by the BBA to review the Banking Code. It is the first time that someone outside the industry has been appointed to do the job – previously it had been done by the industry itself. In 2002, Kempson published her report with several specific recommendations. Among other things, the recommendations are:

- The wording of the Code should be delivery-channel neutral.

- All subscribers should provide their customers with generic copies of the Code.

- The Code should be re-ordered so that the sections relating to lending and financial difficulties are grouped together and placed later in the Code.

- The Key Commitments should be collapsed to four overall commitments, to:
  1. act fairly and reasonably in all our dealings with you;
  2. help you to understand how our financial products and services work;
  3. deal with things that go wrong quickly and sympathetically;
  4. publicise this Code, have copies readily available and ensure that our staff are trained to implement it fully.

- Several sections require more substantial revision.

- A new clause should be inserted into the Code giving overall commitments to complete transfer of accounts quickly and without errors.

- A new clause should be added to the Code giving a commitment by both the new and the existing bank or building societies to waive any bank charges that might otherwise be incurred if they are the result of errors made by the bank or building society or any undue delays caused by them.

- The Review Group's proposals on portable credit history and Customer Annual Summary Statements should not be taken further in their present form.

8.113 The Kempson Report has received support from the BBA, the Building Societies Association, and the BCSB. Ian Mullen, the Chief Executive of the BBA said[1]:

> 'Concerns of the unexplained can undermine any relationship. Hence, with the ever-increasing complexity of financial products, it is crucial that banks are transparent and open. The banking relationship is open on trust and Professor Kempson's recommendations will help to make that trust stronger. They make sense and we are pleased to adopt them.'

1 See BBA Press Release, 18 November 2002, 'Independent Review Promises Clearer Communication for Bank Customers', available at http://www.bba.org.uk/public/newsroom/pressreleases/ 61785?version=1.

8.114 Similarly, the Building Society Association and BCSB were pleased with planned changes. Seymour Fortescue, the Chief Executive of the BCSB said that the planned changes will improve protection for personal customers and the BCSB will continue to carry out rigorous, independent monitoring and enforcement of bank's and building societies compliance with the Code[1].

1 See BBA Press Release, 18 November 2002, 'Independent Review Promises Clearer Communication for Bank Customers', available at http://www.bba.org.uk/public/newsroom/pressreleases/61785?version=1.

The Banking Code 2003

8.115 The most recent edition of the Banking Code is effective from 1 March 2003. The voluntary Code sets standards of good practice for financial institutions to follow when they are dealing with 'personal customers', which excludes sole traders, partnerships, companies, clubs, and societies. It applies to all the products and services listed in the Code, which include current accounts, including basic bank accounts; card products and services; loans and overdrafts; savings and deposit accounts, etc.[1] The Code contains banks' 'key commitments' to customers[2]. Banks promise to 'act fairly and reasonably in all dealings' by:

- meeting all the commitments and standards in the Code, in the products and services the banks offer, and in the procedures bank staff follow;

- making sure products and services meet relevant laws and regulations;

- having secure and reliable banking and payment systems; and

- considering cases of financial difficulty sympathetically and positively.

1 The Banking Code 2003, s 1.1.
2 *Ibid*, s 2.

8.116 Banks promise to help customers understand how financial products and services work by giving information about the products and services in plain English, explaining their financial implications, and helping consumers to choose the one that meets their needs. Banks also promise to deal with things that go wrong quickly and sympathetically[1].

1 The Banking Code 2003, s 2.

8.117 The 'commitments' section is followed by a section on 'information', which aims at helping the customer to choose appropriate products and services by providing information both before and while the service is provided. Before and after one has chosen an account, the information to be provided to him/her, among other things, includes: information explaining the key features of the services and products; information about how the account works; information about interest rates, changes in interest rates, and charges for the day-to-day running of the account; and cash-machines charges etc[1].

1 The Banking Code 2003, ss 3, 4, and 5.

8.118 On the terms and conditions, the Code provides that all written terms and conditions will be fair and will set out the customers' rights and responsibilities clearly and in plain language. Legal and technical language will only be used if necessary. Banks will inform customers before making any changes to the terms and conditions. If the change is to the customers' advantage, the banks will make changes immediately and inform the customers within 30 days. If the change is to customers' disadvantage, a 30-days notice will be given before the bank makes any changes[1].

1   The Banking Code 2003, s 6.

8.119   Special mention is made of advertising and marketing. Banks will make sure that all advertising and promotional material is clear, fair reasonable and not misleading. Section 8.3 states, 'unless you specifically give your consent or ask us to, we will not pass your name and address to any company, including other companies in our group, for marketing purposes. We will not ask you to give your permission in return for standard account services'. The Code defines 'standard account services' as opening, maintaining and running accounts for transmitting money. Banks may tell customers about another company's services or products, and if a customer says that he is interested, that company may contact the customer directly[1]. Banks will give customers the opportunity to say that they do not want to receive marketing approaches. At least once every three years, banks will remind customers that they can ask the banks not to be contacted for marketing purposes[2].

1   The Banking Code 2003, s 8.4.
2   *Ibid,* s 8.5.

8.120   The rules on liability for losses are provided for in ss 12.9 and 12.10 of the Code. Section 12.9 provides, 'If you act fraudulently, you will be responsible for all losses on your account. If you act without reasonable care, and this causes losses, you may be responsible for them'. This may apply if customers do not follow the Code's advice on how to help protect their accounts and prevent fraud as listed out in s 12.4. Section 12.10 states that:

> unless we can show that you have acted fraudulently or without reasonable care, your liability for the misuse of your card will be limited as follows:
> * If someone else uses your card before you tell us it has been lost or stolen or that someone else knows your PIN, the most you will have to pay is £50.
> * If someone else uses your card details without your permission for a transaction where the cardholder does not need to be present, you will not have to pay anything.
> * If your card is used before you receive it, you will not have to pay anything.

8.121   It is interesting to note that the Code has a section on 'Financial difficulties – how we can help', which sets out how the banks intend to deal with financial difficulties and complaints. Banks states that they will consider cases of financial difficulty sympathetically and positively. The first step will be to try to contact you to discuss the matter[1].

1   The Banking Code 2003, s 13.10.

CHAPTER NINE

Data Protection and Internet Banking in the United Kingdom

Introduction

9.1   The world today is about who controls information. As more and more users flood the Internet, more information is being collected, processed, used and stored by more and more organisations. As one commentator said, 'Personal data is a valuable commodity. Seeking, sharing, selling and exploiting personal information are major functions of the New Economy'[1]. In his book *The Road Ahead*, Bill Gates acknowledged that information is already being collected about us each day by private and public authorities, and that we often do not know it is being used or how accurate it is. He recognised that privacy is one of the important issues that requires greater attention.

1   David Aaron, former United States Under Secretary of Commerce.

9.2   Banking is a data-intensive business, dependent on computer systems and telecommunication networks for the provision of financial services at national and international level. As a custodian of funds, a bank's business is dependent on the trust in which its customers hold it. Combining banking and the Net creates opportunities and challenges. Using the Internet to provide banking services brings tremendous benefits in increasing competitiveness, but its very openness also makes it vulnerable to privacy and security threats. People continue to voice concern about giving personal information over the Internet. As Internet banking grows, the concern over privacy attracts greater attention. Indeed, the Basel Committee E-Banking Group has identified privacy as one of the issues that need to be addressed when banking and the Internet are brought together.

Online banking in the United Kingdom

9.3   In early 1990s a number of banks experimented with their own intranet services. The first major financial institution to offer a web-based banking service in the UK was Nationwide Building Society's Online Banking website, launched in May 1997. The first bank to offering current account services over the Internet was the Royal Bank of Scotland hard on the Nationwide's heels in June 1997[1]. Today, there are currently 23 banks and building societies offering online banking services.

Among the big hitters are Barclays Online with some 1.5 million registered users and Egg with about 960,000 banking customers with Internet access. Other important players are Lloyds TSB (700,000), Bank of Scotland (600,000), Nation-wide (430,000), NatWest (425,000), Royal Bank of Scotland (300,000), First Direct (250,000) and Smile (200,000)[2].

1 See moneyextra, 'Online Banking – What is it?' available at http://www.moneyextra.com/faqs/bankingfaq1.html.
2 See thegoodwebguide, 'The Good Web Guide Website Review: Online Banking', available at http://www.thegoodwebguide.co.uk/chan_mone/wwwreviews.php3?chapter_id=000030.

9.4 The UK online banking sector is growing fast. Market analyst Datamonitor reported that there were 10 million online accounts in 2002. The number has risen to 11.5 million in 2003. By 2005, it could grow to 17 million, according to Internet consultant Forrester Research. According to the Guardian Unlimited, 'Part of the increase may be down to the fact that the sector is no longer just made up of Internet-only bank customers. All the big high street banks now have online operations, and it was the online operations of the high street banks that made the most progress in 2003[1].

1 Sarah Crown, 'Online Banks "Get Top Marks" ', Guardian Unlimited (13 January 2004) available at http://money.guardian.co.uk/onlinebanking/story/0,13813,1122232,00.html.

9.5 Essentially, there are two kinds of services, PC banking and Internet banking. PC banking as mentioned in Chapter One enables customers to operate their accounts from their PC, loaded with the bank's dedicated software. Internet banking gives customer access from any computer linked to the Internet. Most online banking services enable customers to view their balance and statement, transfer funds, pay bills and apply for a number of products. However, a more limited number allow customers to set up standing orders and direct debits, and amend overdrafts. Interestingly, the Good Web Guide commented[1]:

'Internet banking still does not permit cash withdrawals and deposits. Nor does this look remotely imminent although the technology is well advanced. The absence of electronic cash handling facilities is a major shortcoming of the system and reduces Internet banking to a revolution of convenience rather than of substance.'

1 See moneyextra, 'Online Banking – What is it?' available at http://www.moneyextra.com/faqs/bankingfaq1.html.

9.6 In terms of customer satisfaction, the results from the Virtual Online Banking Survey, published in January 2004, finds that online banking customers are increasingly enthusiastic about their method of banking, with 70% now rating the service as excellent or very good. The survey asks customers to rate their banks on a scale of one to five. The average rating out of five achieved by the UK's online banks rose from 3.6 in 2002 to 3.9 in 2003. The survey found that the greatest improvements were in the speed of the online banks' systems and the ease of use. Ratings have also improved considerably for the payment of standing orders and direct debit functions[1].

1 Sarah Crown, 'Online Banks "Get Top Marks" ', Guardian Unlimited (13 January 2004) available at http://money.guardian.co.uk/onlinebanking/story/0,13813,1122232,00.html.

9.7   The survey also showed that customers of the most popular online banks generally rate the service they receive below average. Lloyds TSB, Barclays, HSBC, NatWest and First Direct are used by more Internet banking customers than other online banks, yet only two of them – First Direct and HSBC – scored above average for customer satisfaction between July and September 2003[1]. Virtual Surveys' online banking survey asked the opinions of over 4,000 online banking customers in the third quarter of 2003, and found that while Bank of Scotland and Abbey provided the least satisfactory service, Smile, First Direct and Nationwide made their customers the happiest[2].

1   See Lisa Bachelor, 'Bi Banks Beaten by Online Rivals', Guardian Unlimited (14 October 2003) available at http://money.guardian.co.uk/onlinebanking/story/0,13813,1062714,00.html.
2   *Ibid.*

Privacy, confidentiality, and first data protection principle

9.8   Privacy is often confused and used interchangeably with confidentiality. Do they mean the same thing? Privacy is not confidentiality. Privacy is about fair information practices: how a company collect or gather, use, disclose, and destroy information about an identifiable individual. So, it is about management of information and a much broader area than confidentiality.

9.9   There is some degree of interaction between the two. The action for breach of confidence, however, is characterised as a *sui generic* hybrid cause of action that springs from multiple roots in equity and the common law. The action relies upon contract, equity and property law concepts to enforce the policy of the law that confidences be respected[1]. Duties of confidence may exist in situations in which privacy related principles also apply. As well, laws which protect privacy in particular circumstances may depend upon the presence of a 'reasonable expectation of privacy' for the existence of the legal right[2]. However, other principles related to privacy, such as those related to fair information practices which have statutory force in the public sector and in the public sector in certain jurisdictions do not depend on information being confidential or even there being present any reasonable expectation of privacy. In fact, it is the public availability of personal information and the ease with which such information may be collected, analysed and reused which often creates privacy concerns[3].

1   Sookman, *Computer, Internet and Electronic Commerce* (2000) paras 8.5 and 8.6.
2   *Ibid.*
3   *Ibid.*

9.10   The duty of confidentiality was established in the case of *Tournier v National Provincial and Union Bank of England*[1]. The Court of Appeal held unanimously that a bank does owe a duty of confidentiality to its customers, that the duty is a legal one which arises from contract, and that the duty is not absolute but subject to certain qualifications. Lord Justice Bankes LJ set out the qualifications to the duty of confidentiality as follows:

●   where disclosure is under compulsion by law;

- where there is a duty to the public to disclose;

- where the interests of the bank require disclosure;

- where the disclosure is made by the express or implied consent of the customer.

1 [1924] 1 KB 461.

9.11 In 1987, 63 years after the landmark decision of *Tournier*, the UK Treasury, in association with Bank of England, set up a Committee to review the law relating to banking services. The Review Committee, under the Chairmanship of Professor R B Jack. The issue of the banker's duty of confidentiality was considered to be sufficiently important to justify an entire chapter in the lengthy and detailed report. The Jack Committee recommended several proposals, among others, that the duty of confidentiality should be codified in statute and at the same time the exceptions to the rule should be updated. This recommendation to codify the *Tournier* rule and other recommendations were rejected by the government of the day[1].

1 See the government White Paper, *Banking Services: Law and Practice* (Cm 1026, 1990).

9.12 The government took the view that adoption of the rule in a voluntary Code of Banking Practice, published in December 1990 (3rd edn), effectively from July 1997 would safeguard the position of customers. Where a breach of the duty of confidentiality is threatened by the bank the customer can obtain an injunction to prevent the bank from disclosing information relating to the customer's affairs but where disclosure has already been made without authorisation the only remedy available to the customer is to sue for damages for breach of contract.

9.13 The *Tournier* rules became the accepted common law position, not only in the UK, but also in many common law jurisdictions worldwide. This case, in the absence of any statutory provisions, still represents the legal status of the duty in the UK despite the fact that the banking industry has undergone major changes since 1924. The *Tournier* rules have been incorporated into the banking codes. The latest Banking Code (March 2003), for example, provides[1]:

'We will treat all your personal information as private and confidential (even when you are no longer a customer). We will not reveal your name and address or details about your accounts to anyone, including other companies in our group, other than in the following four exceptional cases when we are allowed to do this by law.
- If we have to give the information by law.
- If there is a duty to the public to reveal the information.
- If our interests require us to give the information (for example, to prevent fraud) but we will not use this as a reason for giving information about you or your accounts (including your name and address) to anyone else, including other companies in our group, for marketing purposes.
- If you ask us to reveal the information, or if we have your permission.

1 The Banking Code (March 2003) para 11.1.

9.14 The UK Data Protection Act 1998 (DPA 1998) came into force on 1 March 2000, and replaced the Data Protection Act 1984. It was implemented in the UK in order to comply with the EU Data Protection Directive (95/46/EC). As data controllers, banks are obliged to comply with a number of broadly stated rules formulated as eight data protection principles set out in Sch 1. Each principle also has detailed statutory guidelines. The first principle is that personal data shall be processed *fairly* and *lawfully* and, in particular, shall not be processed unless at least one of 'the conditions for processing' (in Sch 2) is met; and in the case of sensitive personal data, at least one of 'the conditions for processing sensitive data' (in Sch 3) is also met.

9.15 In the Ninth Report of the Data Protection Registrar (now Information Commissioner) to Parliament in June 1993, the Registrar published his views on the requirements of the First and Second Data Protection Principles to obtain, hold and process personal data lawfully. The Registrar considers unlawful to mean: '... something which is contrary to some law or enactment or is done without lawful justification or excuse'. The Registrar's view is that standards of fairness and lawfulness must be objectively assessed and applied. To assess the proper standards, the yardstick to be used is the standpoint of the 'common man'. A bank might be in contravention of the first principle even though the bank did not intend to be unfair and did not consider itself to be acting unfairly.

9.16 On 27 January 1994, the Registrar issued a paper, *Personal Data Held within the Finance Industry: Some Implications of the First Data Protection Principle with regard to Confidentiality* designed to advise and inform the industry on the duty of confidence[1]. The Registrar states[2]:

> 'In circumstances where an obligation of confidence arises between a data user and a data subject in the finance industry, it is the Registrar's view that it is *unlawful* for a data user to use data for a purpose other than that for which the information was provided except in certain circumstances permitted by law, such as with the consent of the data subject. Where such a use involves the processing of personal data, then this may entail *unlawful* processing within the meaning of the First Data Protection Principle.'

1 See Data Protection Report 14 (August 1994) Appendix 1.
2 *Ibid*, para 4.

9.17 The Registrar's view is that financial institutions are subject to an obligation to maintain details of relationships and financial transactions between themselves and those individuals with whom they deal as confidential. Confidentiality policies and procedural instructions should be made available to, and practiced by, members of staff. The most usual basis for the disclosure of personal data by financial institutions to third parties (including companies in the same commercial grouping) is that the individual has consented to such disclosure: the fourth of the *Tournier* exceptions[1]. Proper records of consent must be maintained. If consent has not been given, it is possible that the disclosures are unlawful unless other lawful reasons for disclosure can be demonstrated. In general, if a financial institution gives an individual notice of what it intends to do with personal data about that person, and s/he does not respond, the financial institution would not be entitled to assume that s/he had impliedly consented to the use of the information. In other words it is impossible to infer consent from silence alone[2].

1   See Data Protection Report 14 (August 1994) para 9.
2   *Ibid*, para 10.

9.18   On the use of personal data for marketing, the Registrar is of the view that whether or not a disclosure is involved, the duty of confidence also restricts the *use* of data. Customer information cannot lawfully be either disclosed, or used, for marketing purposes by third parties, including companies in the same commercial grouping, without the consent of the customer[1].

1   See Data Protection Report 14 (August 1994) para 20.

9.19   The Registrar is mindful of the imbalance in power that exists between financial institutions and individual consumers and the fact that in a modern society individuals are effectively constrained to make use of the products and services which those institutions provide. The Registrar is concerned that a customer may have no choice but to give such consent as more and more institutions seek to impose the same conditions of trade[1]. It may be *unfair* to process information to be used for third party marketing purposes or in order that that information may be exchanged with other institutions without the consent of customers given freely. In considering whether a breach of the fair processing requirement of the First Principle arises in a particular case, the Registrar will consider, *inter alia*, the degree of choice generally available to the individual and the nature of the product or service which he or she seeks[2].

1   See Data Protection Report 14 (August 1994) para 29.
2   *Ibid*.

9.20   In order to ensure that banks and other financial institutions do not breach the fair and lawful requirements of the First Data Protection Principle, the Registrar recommended several standards to be adopted, some of which are[1]:

- Individuals be told each time information to be contained in personal data is requested from all the non-obvious uses to which data about them and their accounts may be put. This includes what data may be disclosed to whom, and in what circumstances.

- Personal data should not be made available to third parties, either by direct disclosures or by the use of host mailing techniques, without consent.

1   See Data Protection Report 14 (August 1994) para 30.

Data security in Internet banking

9.21   As mentioned by the FSA, 'the decision to buy a financial product or service may expose the consumer to greater risk. The purchase of a financial product or service may require disclosure of more information. Consumers conducting financial transactions online may therefore require greater security and trust in the online financial firm'[1]. The FSA recognises that total security does not exist in either the offline or online world; however, adequate security can exist[2]. Security is a shared endeavour. Banks, the computer industry, regulators, consumers, and the general public all have a role to play.

1 FSA, 'The FSA's Approach to the Regulation of E-Commerce' (June 2001) para 7.4(b).
2 *Ibid*, para 7.6.

9.22 The requirements on the security of personal data are set out in the seventh data protection principle which states that appropriate technical and organisational measures shall be taken against unauthorised or unlawful processing of personal data and against accidental loss or destruction of, or damage to, personal data. The DPA explains that an 'appropriate' level of protection is one that is adequate in all the circumstances of the case. In determining what is adequate a data controller should consider; (1) the nature of the data to be protected (2) the state of technological development (3) the cost of implementing security measures, and (4) the harm that might result from unauthorised or unlawful processing or from accidental loss, destruction and damage of the personal data. The Information Commissioner's *Legal Guidance* points out that the level of security must be 'appropriate' and therefore a risk-based approach in determining the proper level of security is advised. The areas which banks should consider include security management, controlling access to information, ensuring business continuity, staff selection and training, and detecting and dealing with breaches of security. Given the financial importance of the information that banks process, the ability of banks to finance the cost to implement security measures, and the harm that might result from the security failure, the measures would have to be fairly extensive.

9.23 In 2001, the FSA warned Internet banks that they were not doing enough to protect themselves or their customers against fraud. Since then, many banks have reported tightening up their security arrangements, although the FSA refused to be drawn on whether it felt that the measures were sufficient. Dave Eacott, spokesman for the FSA, said:

'We do have conversations with the institutions about how they address the issue of Internet security. The reason we do that is because in our rules there is a requirement to have good systems and that extends into the IT area as well'[1].

1 See Marianne Curphey, 'Friend or Foe?' Guardian Unlimited (24 September 2003) available at http://money.guardian.co.uk/onlinebanking/story/0,13813,1029640,00.html.

9.24 The Information Commissioner states that the British Standard on information security management BS7799[1] provides a helpful framework by which an organisation can implement an effective information security policy. In practice, most banks should be able to meet the requirements of this standard. Although compliance with this standard is not a guarantee against action by the Commissioner in relation to security, it can act in mitigation by demonstrating that an organisation has exercised all reasonable care in the circumstances.

I   This standard identifies three categories of information security: confidentiality; integrity-protecting information against tampering; and availability. It has been argued that a comprehensive security policy should address all of these.

9.25   Section 18(2)(8) of the DPA 1998 requires a bank to notify the Commissioner with 'a general description' of the measures to be taken for the purpose of complying with the Seventh Data Protection Principle. Simply put, the notification to the Commissioner must include a general description of security measures to protect personal data. One commentator argues, 'Yet that description is insufficient for the Commissioner to determine whether the measures that firms intend to take will indeed be "appropriate", given the nature of the data and the processing to which it will be subject'[1]. He further argues[2]:

'UK law falls short of requiring any measurable standard of information security, so businesses cannot refer to legislation to determine whether their information security is appropriate. Apart from firms operating in particular regulated industries, it is unlikely that action would be taken against a company for failure to implement adequate information security unless the risks against which it is supposed to guard actually occur. It is clear, however, that managing information security is now accepted to be good business practice, and it is this standard against which firms will be judged if litigation ensues. Directors who are personally culpable for failing to ensure that information security strategy is implemented may be found liable for failing to exercise proper skill and care if business data is destroyed or falls into the wrong hands.'

I   David Griffiths, 'Treat IT Security as if the Law Required it', ComputerWeekly.com (23 April 2003) available at http://www.computerweekly.com/Article121041.htm. He is a partner specialising in information security at the international law firm Clifford Chance.
2   *Ibid.*

9.26   Banks have been unwilling to allow independent experts to examine their systems, justifying this by claiming that they need to keep design and operation of their systems secret in order to protect them from attack[1]. This approach, known in security circles as 'security through obscurity', is now widely discredited because any advantages provided by secrecy are offset by the fact that this secrecy allows serious faults to exist in systems for long periods without being discovered.

I   Nicholas Bohm, Ian Brown, and Brian Gladman, 'Maintaining Consumer Confidence in Electronic Payment Mechanisms', available at http://www.cs.ucl.ac.uk/staff/I.brown/payment_fraud.html.

9.27   Security is at the heart of the banking industry. Nick Gill of NatWest Bank said, 'We are not complacent about the subject but we would not launch a service unless we are confident about the security aspects'[1]. Some banks explicitly state that they deploy specific security technologies such as the Secure Socket Layer (SSL) and Secure Encryption Technology (SET) for their Internet banking services. However, it is accepted throughout the industry that whilst software is designed to perform specific functions, experts – and these include hackers and crackers – can make it do other things, and perfect software does not exist as all software contains bugs – coding errors in computer programs[2].

1 Moneyextra, 'Online Banking – Guide to Online Security', available at http://www.moneyextra.com/faqs/bankingfaq4.html.
2 Eduardo Gelbstein and Ahmad Kamal, *Information Insecurity: A Survival Guide to the Uncharted Territories of Cyber-threats and Cyber-security* (2002) p 16.

9.28 One of the biggest challenges is that of overcoming an organisation's 'comfort zone': the belief that their arrangements are adequate and appropriate because a security incident has not occurred in the past or has not been detected. Statements such as 'we have a firewall', 'we use a 128 bit encryption key', etc. are, by themselves, no substitute for a set of robust security policies, tools, measures, controls and a determined approach to compliance[1].

1 Eduardo Gelbstein and Ahmad Kamal, *Information Insecurity: A Survival Guide to the Uncharted Territories of Cyber-threats and Cyber-security* (2002) p 17.

Data sharing

9.29 The second principle requires that personal data shall be obtained only for one or more specified and lawful purpose(s) and shall not be further processed in any manner incompatible with that purpose or those purposes. The use of the word 'incompatible' suggests a use that is contradictory, to rather than simply different from, any originally specified purpose or purpose[1]. If this is the correct interpretation then it is open to the bank to contend that processing which was not specified at the time of the collection of the data not inconsistent with the original specified lawful purposes does not fall foul of this provision as long as the bank subsequently specifies it.

1 Rosemary Jay and Angus Hamilton, *Data protection: Law and Practice* (2nd edn, 2003) p 162.

9.30 As indicated earlier, the Banking Code 2003 forbids the disclosure of personal data to other companies, including companies in the group[1]. Also, as already mentioned in Chapter Eight, banks have promised that they will make sure that all advertising and promotional material is clear, fair, reasonable and not misleading[2]. And they will not pass customers' information to any company, including other companies in their group for marketing purposes unless customers have given their consent[3].

1 The Banking Code (March 2003) para 11.1.
2 The Banking Code (March 2003) s 8.1.
3 *Ibid*, s 8.3.

9.31 The Registrar is of the view that customer information cannot lawfully be either disclosed, or used, for *marketing purposes*, without the consent of the customer. It is also *unfair* for information to be exchanged with other institutions without the consent of customers given freely. In other words, using data collected for Internet banking purposes for direct marketing, without the consent of the customers might be in breach of the First Principle. The position is the same if the data is to be passed to third parties, whatever may be the purpose or purposes.

9.32 Principle two prohibits a bank from using data for purposes incompatible with the purpose(s) that it was collected for. In relation to the disclosure to and use of data by the credit reference agencies, the Registrar's view is that[1]:

'Individuals may be invited to consent to their account details being passed to credit reference agencies when such information does not constitute black data[2]. The disclosure of white data and default data that does not yet meet the black data situation *should only be disclosed to credit reference agencies with consent.*'

1 See Data Protection Report 14 (August 1994) para 30(d).
2 Information about bank loans where an individual has fallen three months in arrears and has at that time received a communication from the bank warning that if no measures are taken to deal with the situation within a further 28 days.

9.33 According to the Registrar, this consent should not be made a condition of an agreement but should be the free choice of the individual, although financial organisations are at liberty to point out the advantages of allowing white data to be disclosed to credit reference agencies and the disadvantage of not so doing. The disclosure of data to credit reference agencies, and retention of data by such agencies, according to the Registrar, must be notified to the individual at the time of the application.

9.34 In the Banking Code 2003, the banks state that when a customer opens an account, banks will inform the customer when they may pass the account details of the customer to credit reference agencies. With regard to 'black information' the attitudes of the banks towards the disclosure of this type of information is reflected in section 13.6 of the Code. It provides:

We may give information to credit reference agencies about the personal debts you owe us if: (i) you have fallen behind with your payments; (ii) the amount owed is not in dispute; (iii) you have not made proposals we are satisfied with for repaying your debt, following our formal demand.

The banks will give at least 28 days' notice that they plan to give the information to credit reference agencies. What is the legal justification for the release of such information? One commentator argues[1]:

'There is no doubt that banking practice, prior to the introduction of the Code, had been to release "black information", but it is difficult to understand what legal justification existed for what appears to be a breach of the duty of confidentiality. This continues to be the case. It can only be assumed that the banks have been relying on either exception (b), public interest, or on (c) that the interests of the bank require disclosure. It is arguable that they have no entitlement to divulge such information under the common law. The safest, and proper, course of action for the banks to adopt would be to ensure that loan documentation specifically gives permission for such information to be released to registered credit reference agencies.'

1 Andrew Campbell, 'Bank Confidentiality and the Consumer in the United Kingdom', in Peter Cartwright (ed) *Consumer Protection in Financial Services* (1999) p 93.

9.35   The Banks also stated in the Banking Code that they might give credit reference agencies *other information* about the day-to-day running of a customer's account if he/she has given the bank permission to do so[1].

1   The Banking Code (March 2003) s 13.8.

Use of cookies

9.36   The use of cookies is fundamental to e-business. Many banks use cookies for their Internet banking services. In fact, the British Bankers Association (BBA) regards the use of cookies as an essential part of a service. The BBA states, 'There are occasions where a cookie is an essential part of a service, such as for e-banking or security'[1]. On the other hand, use of cookies amounts to collection of data and this has data protection implications. The most significant implications are on the requirement that personal data must be collected fairly and lawfully as provided for in the first data protection principle. Certain information must be provided to the data subject at the point of data collection and consent of the data subject must be obtained. The problem with the use of cookies are that many users are unaware of cookies and the fact that their information is being collected, without knowledge or consent of the user, and the information collected is being used to make offers – direct marketing – and customers will be bombarded with unsolicited commercial e-mail (spam).

1   See BBA, *Response to the DTI's Consultation Paper on: Implementation of the Directive on Privacy and Electronic Communications*, available at http://www.bba.org.uk/public/newsroom/35451/137695?version=1, para 18.

9.37   The Privacy and Electronic Communications (EC Directive) Regulations 2003, implementing the EU Directive on Privacy and Electronic Communications (E-Privacy Directive) sets out some rules on the use of cookies. Regulation 6 of the Regulations, which came into force on 11 December 2003, provides:

'(1)   Subject to paragraph (4), a person shall not use an electronic communications network to store information, or to gain access to information stored, in the terminal equipment of a subscriber or user unless the requirements of paragraph (2) are met.

(2)   The requirements are that the subscriber or user of that terminal equipment:
(a)   is provided with clear and comprehensive information about the purposes of the storage of, or access to, that information; and
(b)   is given the opportunity to refuse the storage of or access to that information.

(3)   Where an electronic communications network is used by the same person to store or access information in the terminal equipment of a subscriber or user on more than one occasion, it is sufficient for the purposes of this regulation that the requirements of paragraph (2) are met in respect of the initial use.

(4)   Paragraph (1) shall not apply to the technical storage of, or access to, information:

(a) for the sole purpose of carrying out or facilitating the transmission of a communication over an electronic communications network; or

(b) where such storage or access is strictly necessary for the provision of an information society service requested by the subscriber or user.'

9.38 This means that a bank and other web operators must not store information or gain access to information stored in the terminal equipment of a user unless the user is: (1) 'provided with clear and comprehensive information about the purposes of the storage of, or access to, that information' and (2) 'given the opportunity to refuse the storage of or access to that information'.

9.39 The Information Commissioner has published guidance that provides his interpretation of the rules of the Regulations[1]. He reminded the service providers of the implications of cookies on data protection. The Information Commissioner states:

'Where the use of a cookie type device does involve the processing of personal data, service providers will be required to ensure that they comply with the additional requirements of the DPA 1998. This includes the requirements of the third data protection principle which states that data controllers shall not process data that is excessive'[2].

1 Information Commissioner, *Guidance to the Privacy and Electronic Communications (EC Directive) Regulations 2003, Part 2: Security, Confidentiality, Traffic and Location Data, Itemised Billing, CLI and Directories*, pp 4–7.
2 *Ibid*, para 2.1.

9.40 On information to be provided to the user before cookies can be used, as required under reg 6(2)(a), the Information Commissioner states[1]:

'The Regulations are not prescriptive about the sort of information that should be provided but the text should be sufficiently *full* and *intelligible* to enable individuals to gain clear appreciation of the potential consequences of allowing storage and access to the information collected by the device should they wish to do so. This is comparable with the transparency requirements of the first data protection principle.'

1 Information Commissioner, *Guidance to the Privacy and Electronic Communications (EC Directive) Regulations 2003, Part 2: Security, Confidentiality, Traffic and Location Data, Itemised Billing, CLI and Directories*, para 2.2.

9.41 The BBA is more specific and insists that the information provided to users should be made in plain language, in terms appropriate to their service so as to inform a user *what a cookie is* and *how it might be used*, without causing concern or alarm. The explanation should also describe, in general terms, the potential implications of disabling a cookie, e.g. the service cannot be provided at all or the user may have to input the same details each time they visit the site[1]. The Directive requires that the methods for giving information; offering a right to refuse or requesting consent should be made as user-friendly as possible[2].

1   See BBA, *Response to the DTI's Consultation Paper on: Implementation of the Directive on Privacy and Electronic Communications*, available at http://www.bba.org.uk/public/ newsroom/35451/137695?version=1, paras 14–15.
2   See Recital 25 of the Directive.

9.42   According to the BBA, users should also be advised that they may set various levels of cookie controls on their browser which will either accept all cookies, some cookies or notify them whenever a cookie is about to be placed on their computer. However, the BBA believes that other than directing users towards their own computer's handbook for specific instruction, it should not be the operator's responsibility to give detailed step-by-step guidance on how to disable cookies[1].

1   Information Commissioner, *Guidance to the Privacy and Electronic Communications (EC Directive) Regulations 2003, Part 2: Security, Confidentiality, Traffic and Location Data, Itemised Billing, CLI and Directories*, para 16.

9.43   The Directive seems to provide little guidance as to what information needs to be provided to the user. Article 5(3) provides that member states shall ensure that the use of electronic communications networks to store information or to gain access to information stored in the terminal equipment of a subscriber or user is only allowed on condition that the subscriber or user concerned is provided with clear and comprehensive information *in accordance* with Directive 95/46/EC, *inter alia* about the purposes of the processing. The Data Protection Directive (Directive 95/46/EC) is specifically referred to in this provision and many other provisions of the Directive. So the information provided to the users must be sufficient to enable a user to make an informed decision as to the use of cookies.

9.44   The second part of art 5(3) of the Directive states:

> 'This shall not prevent any technical storage or access for the sole purpose of carrying out or facilitating the transmission of a communication over an electronic communications network, or as strictly necessary in order to provide an information society service explicitly requested by the subscriber or user'.

What interpretation to be given to this provision? Perhaps, it is an exception or exemption given to the general rule regarding the two conditions attached to the use of cookies. In other words, these two conditions, to provide: (1) clear and comprehensive information to the user, and (2) opportunity to refuse the use of cookies, do not apply if the sole purpose is to carry out or facilitate the transmission of communication, or that it is 'strictly necessary' to provide an information society service explicitly requested by the user. This seems to be the interpretation adopted by the UK, which is reflected in reg 6(1), (2), and (4). However, Recitals 24 and 25 of the E-Privacy Directive seem to suggest the contrary.

9.45   Recital 24 recognises the use of cookies is part of the private sphere of the users requiring protection under the European Convention for the Protection of

Human Rights and Fundamental Freedoms. It then states, 'The use of such devices should be allowed *only* for legitimate purposes, with the knowledge of the users concerned'. While Recital 25 states:

'However, such devices, for instance so-called cookies, can be a legitimate and useful tool ... where such devices, for instance cookies, are intended for a legitimate purpose, *such as to facilitate the provision of information society services,* their use should be allowed on condition that users are provided with clear and precise information in accordance with directive 95/46/EC about the purposes of cookies or similar devices ... Users should have the opportunity to refuse to have a cookie or similar device stored in their terminal equipment'.

This means that a cookie is only allowed for legitimate purposes and the two conditions must be satisfied. It is difficult not to accept this interpretation as the last sentence of Recital 25 mentions the *acceptance* of a cookie for legitimate purpose, 'Access to specific website content may still be made conditional on the well-informed acceptance of a cookie or similar device, if it is used for a legitimate purpose'.

9.46 Concerning the refusal of cookies, the Information Commissioner stresses the importance of the mechanism which is uncomplicated, easy to understand and accessible to all. The mechanism by which a subscriber or user may exercise their right to refuse should be prominent, intelligible and readily available to all, not just the most computer literate or technically aware. Where the relevant information is to be provided in a privacy policy, the policy should be clearly signposted at least on those pages where a user may enter a website. The relevant information should be appearing in the policy in a way that is suitably prominent and accessible and it should be worded so that all users and subscribers are capable of understanding, and acting upon it, without difficulty[1]. There is nothing to prevent service providers from requiring users to 'opt-in' to receipt of the cookie as opposed to providing them with the opportunity to 'opt-out'[2].

1   Information Commissioner, *Guidance to the Privacy and Electronic Communications (EC Directive) Regulations 2003, Part 2: Security, Confidentiality, Traffic and Location Data, Itemised Billing, CLI and Directories,* para 2.2.
2   *Ibid,* para 2.4.

9.47 The BBA does not agree that consumers should be given a chance to refuse in relation to all cookies, especially where they involve the processing of anonymous or session-specific data. The organisation argues, 'Where no personal data are disclosed and a living individual cannot be identified, then there would appear to be no data protection-related reason for giving consumers the chance to refuse'[1].

1   Information Commissioner, *Guidance to the Privacy and Electronic Communications (EC Directive) Regulations 2003, Part 2: Security, Confidentiality, Traffic and Location Data, Itemised Billing, CLI and Directories,* para 17.

9.48 The Information Commissioner interprets the term 'strictly necessary' to mean that such storage of or access to information should be essential, as opposed to reasonably necessary, for the exemption to apply. Also, it is be restricted to what is essentially for the provision of the service requested by the user, rather than what might be essential for any other uses the service provider might wish to make of that data. One commentator argues[1]:

> 'No doubt the interpretation of this exception – when is a cookie necessary as opposed to desirable – will be a key issue in its implementation. One of the most interesting of this is how this process is managed in cases where either a computer has multiple users (individual living persons) or where a subscriber has "consented" to the use of cookies but individual users have not (or *vice versa*). This is important because a cookie recognises or attaches itself to specific computers rather than specific users or subscribers. The Government looks like it will duck this issue, as the Regulations do not seek to deal with possible conflict between multiple users/subscribers having access to the same machines.'

1 Mark Crichard, 'Telecoms Privacy Directive – UK Implementation', Computer Law & Security Report Vol 19 no.4 (2003) p 301.

9.49 What exactly constitutes this strict necessity is not made clear. Several of the sites surveyed took this tack, stating that if users wished to disable cookies they would be unable to use the features of the site-effectively. In other words, they are saying, 'If you don't like cookies, go elsewhere'[1].

1 Ian Thomas, quoted in the Web Abacus press release.

Other data protection principles

9.50 Apart from the important requirements that personal data must be processed 'fairly and lawfully', banks and financial institutions are required to observe other data protection principles in processing their customers' information (principles 2–8):

● Personal data shall be obtained only for one or more specified and lawful purpose, and shall not be further processed in any manner incompatible with that purpose or those purposes.

● Personal data shall be adequate, relevant and not excessive in relation to the purpose or purposes for which they are processed.

● Personal data shall be accurate and where necessary, kept up-to-date.

● Personal data processed for any purpose or purposes shall not be kept for longer than it is necessary for that purpose or those purposes.

● Personal data shall be processed in accordance with the rights of the data subject under the DPA.

● Appropriate technical and organisational measures shall be taken against unauthorised or unlawful processing of personal data and against accidental loss or destruction of, or damage to, personal data.

- Personal data shall not be transferred to a country or territory outside the EEA unless that country or territory ensures an adequate level of protection for the rights and freedoms of data subjects in relation to the processing of personal data.

Collecting personal data online

9.51 The EU has stressed the importance of ensuring that adequate means are put in place to guarantee that individual Internet users get all the information they need to place their trust, in full knowledge of the facts, in the sites with which they enter into contract, and if need be, to exercise certain choices in accordance with their rights under European Legislation[1]. To supplement the EU Data Protection Directive, the Working Party has adopted on 17 May 2001, the *Recommendation on Certain Minimum Requirements for Collecting Personal Data Online in the European Union*. It provides concrete indications on how the rules set out in the Directive should be applied to the most common processing tasks carried out via the Internet. The indications are intended to identify the concrete measures to be put in place by the players concerned for ensuring that processing is fair and lawful (application of articles 6, 7, 10 and 11 of the Data Protection Directive). The *Recommendation* is considered as the first initiative to spell out the European level of a minimum set of obligations that can be followed by controllers operating websites.

1   See WP 37 (5063/00): Working Document – Privacy on the Internet – An integrated EU approach to online data protection. Accessed on 21 November 2000. Available at http://europa.eu.int/comm/internal_market/en/media/dataprot/wpdocs/wp37n.htm.

9.52 The Working Party states that any collection of personal data from an individual via a website implies prior supply of certain information. In terms of content, compliance with this obligation makes it necessary, among other things[1]:

- to state clearly the purpose(s) of the processing for which the controller is collecting data via a site. For example, when data are collected both to execute a contract (Internet subscription, ordering a product, etc) and also for direct marketing, the controller must *clearly state these two purposes*;

- to list the recipients or categories of recipients of the collected information. When collecting any data, the sites should state whether the collected data will be disclosed or made available to third parties – such as business partners, subsidiaries etc. in particular – and why (for purposes other than providing the requested service and for the purposes of direct marketing).

    If this is the case, Internet users must have a real possibility of objecting to this online by clicking a box in support of disclosure of data for purposes other than providing the requested service. The Working Party is of the opinion that where there is no mention of recipients, this is equivalent to the controller undertaking not to communicate or disclose the information collected to third parties whose name and address have not been provided.

- to point out the security measures guaranteeing the authenticity of the site, the integrity and confidentiality of the information transmitted over the network taken in application of the national legislation applicable;

- to state clearly the obligatory or optional nature of the information to be provided; and

- to mention clearly the existence of automatic data collection procedures (cookies), before such a method to collect any data.

1 See WP 37 (5063/00): Working Document – Privacy on the Internet – An integrated EU approach to online data protection. Accessed on 21 November 2000. Available at http://europa.eu.int/comm/ internal_market/en/media/dataprot/wpdocs/wp37n.htm, para 2.1.

9.53 The Working Party considers that the following information should be shown *directly on the screen* before the collection in order to ensure fair processing of data. The information concerns the identity of the controller, the purpose(s), the obligatory or optional nature of the information requested, the recipients or the categories of recipients of the collected data, the existence of the right of access and rectification, the existence of the right to oppose any disclosure of the data to third parties for purposes other than the provision of the requested service and the way to do so, the information which must be supplied when using automatic collection procedures, and the level of security during *all* processing stages including transmission[1].

1 See WP 37 (5063/00): Working Document – Privacy on the Internet – An integrated EU approach to online data protection. Accessed on 21 November 2000. Available at http://europa.eu.int/comm/ internal_market/en/media/dataprot/wpdocs/wp37n.htm, para 2.2.

9.54 Also, the Working Party considers that complete information on the privacy policy should be directly accessible on the home page of the site and anywhere where personal data are collected online. The title of the heading to click on should be sufficiently highlighted, explicit and specific to allow the Internet user to have a clear idea of the content he/she is being sent.

9.55 Other recommendations of the Working Party include:

- collect data only as far as necessary in view of achieving the purpose specified;

- ensure that data is processed only in so far as it is legitimate on the basis of one of the criteria enumerated in art 7 of the Data Protection Directive;

- ensure effective exercise of the right to access and to rectify;

- implement the 'finality' or 'purpose' principle, which requires personal data only be used where necessary for a specific purpose;

- fix a storage period for the data collected; and

- take the steps necessary to ensure data security during processing including *transmission*[1].

1 See WP 37 (5063/00): Working Document – Privacy on the Internet – An integrated EU approach to online data protection. Accessed on 21 November 2000. Available at http://europa.eu.int/comm/internal_market/en/media/dataprot/wpdocs/wp37n.htm, para 3.

9.56 The Working Party *reiterates* its view that e-mail addresses picked up in public areas of the Internet such as news groups without the informed knowledge of the individual are not lawfully collected. They can thus not be used for any other purpose than the one for which they have been made public, in particular not for direct marketing. More importantly, in the context of Internet banking, the Working Party recommends[1]:

> 'Use of e-mail addresses for direct marketing solely where these have been collected fairly and lawfully. Fair and lawful collection implies that the data subjects have been informed of the possibility of this information being used for commercial direct marketing and that they have been placed in a position to consent to such use directly at the time the information is collected (click box online). The sending of e-mail of a promotional nature under these conditions must also be accompanied by the possibility of online withdrawal from the mailing list used.'

1 See WP 37 (5063/00): Working Document – Privacy on the Internet – An integrated EU approach to online data protection. Accessed on 21 November 2000. Available at http://europa.eu.int/comm/internal_market/en/media/dataprot/wpdocs/wp37n.htm, para 4.

Unsolicited commercial e-mail

9.57 The 2003 Regulations implement the E-Privacy Directive's provisions concerning unsolicited commercial e-mail. Regulation 22 prohibits the sending of unsolicited commercial e-mail without prior consent unless the exception applies. This regulation, however, only applies to the transmission of unsolicited communications by means of electronic mail to *individual* subscribers. 'Individual' is defined to mean a living individual and includes an unincorporated body of such individual. This means that it is legal for a company or spammer to send spam to corporate e-mail addresses. The All Party Parliamentary Internet Group (APIG) believes that it is a very serious mistake in not prohibiting unsolicited business-to-business e-mail[1]. According to the Department of Trade and Industry (DTI), the decision was taken so that 'legitimate business-to-business communication' was not hampered. The DTI insists that during its consultation on the new Directive, many businesses said that they did not want to lose e-mail as a marketing tool.

1 All Party Parliamentary Internet Group (APIG), *Spam: Report of an Inquiry by All Party Internet Group* (October 2003).

9.58 Regulation 22(2) states:

> 'a person shall neither transmit, nor instigate the transmission of, unsolicited communications for the purposes of direct marketing by means of electronic mail unless the recipient of the electronic mail has previously notified the sender that he consents for the time being to such communications being sent by, or at the instigation of, the sender.'

9.59 'Electronic mail' is defined as any text, voice, sound or image message sent over a public electronic communications network which can be stored in the network or in the recipient's terminal equipment until it is collected by the recipient, and includes messages sent using a short message service. While direct marketing is regarded by the Information Commissioner as covering a wide range of activities which apply not just to the offer for sale of goods or services, but also to the promotion of an organisation's aims and ideals. This would include a charity or a political party making an appeal for funds or support[1].

1 Information Commissioner, *Guidance to the Privacy and Electronic Communications* (*EC Directive*) *Regulations 2003. Part 1: Marketing by Electronic Means,* p 3. Section 11 of the Data Protection Act 1998 refers to direct marketing as the communication (by whatever means) of any advertising or marketing material which is directed to particular individuals.

9.60 It is interesting to note that the legislation does not only prohibit the transmission of electronic mail for direct marketing purposes without prior consent but also the instigation to transmit the electronic mail. There is no guidance either from the DTI or the Information Commissioner as to the interpretation of 'instigate the transmission'.

9.61 'For the time being', according to the Information Commissioner, should not be interpreted to mean that consent must inevitably lapse after a certain period. Consent, once given, will not inevitably last indefinitely[1]. However, it will remain valid until there is good reason to consider it is no longer valid, for example, where it has been specifically withdrawn or it is otherwise clear that the recipient no longer wishes to receive such messages. The initial consent will remain valid where there are good grounds for believing that the recipient remains happy to receive the marketing communications in question, for example, where the recipient has responded positively to previous, reasonably recent marketing e-mails[2]. Simply put, 'for the time being', does not mean that such consent will inevitably lapse after a certain period, but neither does it mean that it will last indefinitely.

1 Information Commissioner, *Guidance to the Privacy and Electronic Communications* (*EC Directive*) *Regulations 2003. Part 1: Marketing by Electronic Means,* p 3. Section 11 of the Data Protection Act 1998 refers to direct marketing as the communication (by whatever means) of any advertising or marketing material which is directed to particular individuals.
2 *Ibid.*

9.62 Regulation 22(2), which provides for the soft opt-in scheme, allows a business/person to send or instigate the sending of electronic mail for the purpose of direct marketing where:

(a) that person has obtained the contact details of the recipient of that electronic mail in the course of the sale or negotiations for the sale of a product or service to that recipient;

(b) the direct marketing is in respect of that person's similar products and services only; and

(c) the recipient has been given a simple means of refusing (free of charge except for the costs of the transmission of the refusal) the use of his/her contact details for the purposes of such direct marketing, at the time that the details were initially collected, and, where he/she did not initially refuse the use of the details, at the time of each subsequent communication.

9.63 The implication of this section is interestingly put in the guidance issued by the Information Commissioner:

'... if you satisfy these criteria, you do not need prior consent to send marketing by electronic mail to individual subscribers. If you cannot satisfy these criteria you cannot send marketing by electronic mail to individual subscribers without their prior consent.'

9.64 The DTI has taken a liberal approach by allowing the sending of electronic e-mail not only when the details of the recipient have been obtained in the course of the sale but also in the course of *negotiations* for the sale of a product or service. The justification for taking this position is based on the DTI views that[1]:

'The most important safeguards here are that contact details are fairly collected and subscribers are clearly informed of, and given a chance to object to, use of their data for direct marketing by that same business. As long as these conditions are met, and there is a direct relationship of some kind between the two parties, it does not seem necessary to insist that there must have been actual purchase for this exemption to apply.'

1 See the DTI public consultation document on how to implement the DPEC, Chapter 6, p 37.

9.65 According to the Information Commissioner, a sale does not have to be completed for the condition to apply. He, however, recognises that it may be difficult to establish where negotiations may begin. The guidance given is that where a person has actively expressed an interest in purchasing a company's products and services and not opted-out of further marketing of that product or service at the time their details were collected, the company can continue to market them by electronic mail unless and until that person opts-out of receiving such messages at a later date[1].

1 Information Commissioner, *Guidance to the Privacy and Electronic Communications (EC Directive) Regulations 2003. Part 1: Marketing by Electronic Means*, p 3. Section 11 of the Data Protection Act 1998 refers to direct marketing as the communication (by whatever means) of any advertising or marketing material which is directed to particular individuals.

9.66 The Commissioner does not consider that 'negotiation for the sale of a product or service' includes the use of cookie technology to identify a person's area of interest when they are browsing a company's website. Unless that person has expressly communicated their interest to the company/entity by, for example, asking for a quote, no 'negotiation' can be said to have taken place for the purpose of these Regulations[1].

1 Information Commissioner, *Guidance to the Privacy and Electronic Communications (EC Directive) Regulations 2003. Part 1: Marketing by Electronic Means*, p 3. Section 11 of the Data Protection Act 1998 refers to direct marketing as the communication (by whatever means) of any advertising or marketing material which is directed to particular individuals.

9.67 How should the 'similar products' rule in (b) be interpreted? The intention of this provision, according to the Information Commissioner, is to ensure that an individual does not receive promotional material about products and services that they would not reasonably expect to receive. The Information Commissioner adopts a purposive approach. For example, someone who has shopped online at a supermarket's website (and has not objected to receiving further e-mail marketing from that supermarket) would expect at some point in the future to receive further e-mails promoting the diverse range of goods available at that supermarket[1].

1   Information Commissioner, *Guidance to the Privacy and Electronic Communications (EC Directive) Regulations 2003. Part 1: Marketing by Electronic Means*, p 3. Section 11 of the Data Protection Act 1998 refers to direct marketing as the communication (by whatever means) of any advertising or marketing material which is directed to particular individuals.

9.68 The DTI seems to suggest that a business can only direct market the kind of products that the addressee would have reasonably expected the business to market at the time they gave or agreed to the use of their contact details. So a business could market the products available at the time, but not necessarily those of a business that it took over, or a substantially new product range. Once again, the DTI places the emphasis on the key safeguard that addressees' contact details are fairly obtained[1].

1   Information Commissioner, *Guidance to the Privacy and Electronic Communications (EC Directive) Regulations 2003. Part 1: Marketing by Electronic Means*, p 3. Section 11 of the Data Protection Act 1998 refers to direct marketing as the communication (by whatever means) of any advertising or marketing material which is directed to particular individuals.

9.69 As the E-Privacy Directive requires, use of electronic mail for direct marketing purposes where the identity or address of the sender is concealed, sometimes referred to as hard-core spam[1] is totally prohibited. Regulation 23 provides:

> 'A person shall neither transmit, nor instigate the transmission of, a communication for the purposes of direct marketing by means of electronic mail:
> (a)   where the identity of the person on whose behalf the communication has been sent has been disguised or concealed; or
> (b)   where a valid address to which the recipient of the communication may send a request that such communications cease has not been provided.'

1   See e.g. Stewart Room, *Hard-core Spammers Beware?* [2003] NLJ 1780.

9.70 The Regulation applies to any subscribers, individual and corporate alike. This means that a business/entity cannot transmit or instigate the transmission of electronic mail for direct marketing purposes where the identity of the sender has been disguised or concealed or a valid address to which the recipient can send an opt-out request has not been provided. In an online environment, 'valid address' could be a valid e-mail address. The provision of a premium rate, national rate or freephone number would not satisfy this obligation[1].

1   Information Commissioner, *Guidance to the Privacy and Electronic Communications (EC Directive) Regulations 2003. Part 1: Marketing by Electronic Means*, p 3. Section 11 of the Data Protection

Act 1998 refers to direct marketing as the communication (by whatever means) of any advertising or marketing material which is directed to particular individuals.

Prior consent and the soft opt-in scheme

9.71 As already mentioned, the use of unsolicited commercial e-mail is allowed only if the subscribers have given their prior consent. According to art 2(f) and Recital 17, 'consent of a user or subscriber, regardless of whether the latter is a natural or a legal person, should have the same meaning as the data subject's consent as defined and further specified in Directive 95/46/EC' (Data Protection Directive). This Directive defines the data subject's consent as 'any freely given specific and informed indication of his wishes by which the data subject signifies his agreement to personal data related to him being processed'. The E-Privacy Directive 2002 does not specifically provide the actual method to collect the consent. Recital 17 reaffirms this. It states that consent may be given by any appropriate method enabling a freely given specific and informed indication of the user's wishes, including ticking a box when visiting an Internet website.

9.72 The Working Party is of the opinion that without prejudice to other applicable requirements, methods whereby a subscriber gives prior consent by registering on a website and is later asked to confirm that he/she was the person who registered and to confirm his/her consent seem to be compatible with the Directive. Other methods, according to the Working Party, may also be compatible with legal requirements. The Working Party states[1]:

'In contrast, it would not be compatible with Article 13 of the Directive 2002/58/EC simply to ask, by a general e-mail sent to recipients, their consent to receive marketing e-mails, because of the requirement that the purpose be legitimate, explicit and specific. Moreover, consent given on the occasion of the general acceptance of the terms and conditions governing the possible main contract must respect the requirements in Directive 95/6/EC, that is, be informed, specific and freely given. Provided that these latter conditions are met, consent might be given by the data subject for instance, through the ticking of a box.'

1 See Opinion 5/2004 on Unsolicited Communications for Marketing Purposes under Article 13 of the Directive 2002/58/EC adopted on 27 February 2004.

9.73 According to the Working Party, implied consent to receive such mails and pre-ticked boxes are not compatible with the definition of consent of Directive 95/46/EC. The Working Party insists[1]:

'The purpose(s) should also be clearly indicated. This implies that the goods and services, or the categories of goods and services, for which marketing e-mails may be sent should be clearly indicated to the subscriber. Consent to pass on the personal data to third parties should also be asked where applicable. The information provided to the data subject should then indicate the purpose(s), the goods and services (or categories of goods and services) for which those third parties would send e-mails.'

210

1   *Ibid.*

9.74 Paragraph 2 of art 13 provides for an exception to the opt-in rule which is implemented in the UK by reg 22(2). Recital 41 of the E-Privacy Directive provides useful elements to help interpret art 13(2):

> 'Within the context of an existing customer relationship, it is reasonable to allow the use of electronic contact details for the offering of similar products or services, but only by the same company that has obtained the electronic contact details in accordance with Directive 95/46/EC. When electronic contact details are obtained, *the customer should be informed about their further use for direct marketing in a clear and distinct manner*, and be given the opportunity to refuse such usage. This opportunity should continue to be offered with each subsequent direct marketing message, free of charge, except for any costs for the transmission of this refusal.'

9.75 The Working Party stresses that this exception is limited in several ways and must be interpreted restrictively. Article 13(2) uses the words *sale* and *its customer* and Recital 41 reinforces this using the phrase *existing customer relationship*. E-mails may only be sent to customers from whom electronic contact details for electronic mail have been obtained, in the context of the sale of a product or a service, and in accordance with the Data Protection Directive. This latter requirement for instance includes information about the purposes of the collection. Only the same natural or legal person that collected the data may send marketing e-mails. The Working Party states, '*Subsidiaries or mother companies are not the same company*'. The exception only applies to the marketing of similar products and services. The opinion of the Working Party is that, while this concept of 'similar products and services' is not an easy concept to apply in practice and justify further attention, similarity could be judged in particular from the objective perspective (reasonable expectations) of the recipient, rather than from the perspective of the sender.

Enforcement

9.76 Regulation 30(1) allows any parties to bring an action for damages. It provides:

> 'a person who suffers damage by reason of any contravention of any of the requirements of these Regulations by any other person shall be entitled to bring proceedings for compensation from that other person for that damage'.

The Regulations also provide for the defence. Regulation 30(2) states that in proceedings brought against a person by virtue of this regulation it shall be a defence to prove that he had taken such care as in all circumstances was reasonably required to comply with the relevant requirement.

9.77   Clive Gringras pointed out that a single individual would be unlikely to show that they had suffered substantial losses as the result of spam. However, groups of individuals, or ISPs on their behalf might be in a better position to be able to show the true level of damage that had been incurred. He suggested that 'super complaint' should be permitted, such as those that can be made by consumer organisations to the Office of Fair Trading under the Enterprise Act 2002[1].

1   See Opinion 5/2004 on Unsolicited Communications for Marketing Purposes under Article 13 of Directive 2002/58/EC, adopted on 27 February 2004 para 46.

9.78   By virtue of reg 31, the enforcement powers are vested in the Information Commissioner and the remedies for breach are contained in Part V of and Schs 6 and 9 to the Data Protection Act 1998 (DPA 1998). Under s 40 of the DPA as amended by this regulation, the Information Commissioner is empowered to serve an enforcement notice on any person that the Commissioner is satisfied has contravened or is contravening any of the requirements of the Regulations. A person who fails to comply with the enforcement notice is guilty of an offence[1] and punishable by a maximum fine of £5,000 in the magistrates' court, unlimited in the Crown Court.

1   DPA 1998, s 47(1).

9.79   Where it is alleged that there has been a contravention, reg 32 allows either the Office of Communications (OFCOM) or a person aggrieved by the contravention of the requirements of the Regulations to request the Commissioner to exercise his enforcement functions. However, this does not mean that the enforcement function of the Commissioner can only be exercised upon request. It is exercisable whether or not there is a request.

9.80   As s 40 of the DPA 1998requires, the Information Commissioner must be *satisfied* that a person has contravened or is contravening the requirements of the Regulations. It implies that there must some kind of formal investigation before an enforcement notice is issued. Schedule 1 to the Regulations requires that the words 'or distress' in s 40 be omitted. The implication is that there is no need for the Information Commissioner to consider whether the contravention with the requirements of the Regulations has caused or is likely to cause distress to any person in deciding whether to serve an enforcement notice. Perhaps this is recognition that spam causes distress and no proof is needed.

9.81   In deciding whether to serve an enforcement notice, the Commissioner must consider whether the contravention has caused or is likely to cause any person damage[1]. This, however, does not mean that the Commissioner can only issue an enforcement notice in cases where damage has occurred. What it will probably mean in practice is that the Commissioner will feel more inclined to issue such a notice in the presence of damage and less inclined to do so in the absence of it. If this interpretation is incorrect, at minimum the provision will make it mandatory for the Commissioner to take into account whether the contravention has caused or is likely to cause any person damage.

1   DPA 1998, s 40(2).

9.82 The UK Registrar's Guideline No 7 issued in 1994 pertaining to the enforcement and appeals in relation to the 1984 DPA 1998 provides some guidance on the issuance of an enforcement notice. Paragraph 2.5 of the Guideline states that the decision to serve an enforcement notice is at the discretion of the Registrar who must consider, in making that decision, whether the breach has caused, or is likely to cause, anyone damage. However, the fact that there is no evidence of this does not prevent the Registrar from serving an enforcement notice.

9.83 The Guideline states that usually the Registrar will have had some contacts with the data user before an enforcement notice is served, and that, in many cases, it should be possible to resolve problems by informal discussions and negotiations without serving a notice. Where a problem cannot be resolved informally then, unless special circumstances prevent it, the data user will receive a formal letter advising that service of an enforcement notice is being considered and inviting representations as to why the notice should not be served. These representations will usually be made in writing but, in an appropriate case, the Registrar indicates that he may be prepared to hear oral representations. Having considered any representations, the Registrar will decide whether to serve the notice.

9.84 The Registrar has stressed his concern that the enforcement notice procedure is a *last resort* – except for those registered persons who are unwilling to co-operate with the Registrar in his obligation to promote observance of the data protection principles. The Registrar's normal process will be consultative and advisory, rather than directive. It is disputable whether this approach and attitude can be adopted in relation to an enforcement notice against spammers.

9.85 Many argue that the Information Commissioner, enforcement notices and criminal penalty for the failure to comply are not the answers to spam. Some consider an enforcement notice will be too little too late[1]. The APIG's finding deserves attention[2]:

'We are very concerned by the evidence we heard with regard to enforcement and the Information Commissioner's own comments upon the DTI's new Regulations. We do not believe that he has been given the ability to act quickly and decisively to stop the sending of spam. We do not believe that waiting for an enforcement notice to be breached before financial penalties are applied is anything other than a recipe for spammers to 'try it on' until the authorities catch up with them.'

1   See e.g. Mike Butler, Hammonds, *Spam – the Meat of the Problem*, Computer Law and Security Report (20 03) Vol 19 No 5, p 388.
2   All Party Parliamentary Internet Group (APIG), *Spam: Report of an Inquiry by All Party Internet Group* (October 2003) para 53.

9.86 The APIG recommends that the DTI urgently review the ability of the Information Commissioner to police the new Regulations on the sending of spam and provide appropriate powers to deal with what will inevitably be rapidly changing situations.

Compliance and observance by the industry in general

9.87 This part of the chapter assesses the extent that the industry in general, and banks specifically, comply and observe the data protection principles as well as the rules of the 2003 Regulations. It looks at businesses' general compliance with the DPA 1998 and of the rules concerning cookies and unsolicited commercial e-mail as set out in the 2003 Regulations. This chapter concludes with the assessment, specifically, of the compliance of banks with these rules and regulations. Based on their privacy policies, the current practices of the banks are critically examined.

Compliance with the Data Protection Act 1998

9.88 In 2002, the Office of the Information Commissioner commissioned the University of Manchester Institute of Science and Technology (UMIST) to conduct a study of compliance with the DPA 1998. One of the main aims of the study was to assess the degree to which the operation of UK websites is in compliance with the DPA 1998. The study included making in excess of 3,000 URL visits; many of these were not active sites despite being listed as such. The study team spoke to at least 900 companies and organisations. 180 interviews were conducted. 170 websites were evaluated.

9.89 The study finds that there is good general awareness of the DPA 1998 across both large and small companies. Most view customer confidentiality as important and 'good for business'. The level of compliance is variable depending on the size of the company and the extent to which the business is regulated by an outside body[1]. The study reports that[2]:

> Larger and/or companies within regulated industry sectors exhibit a high level of compliance. Regulated companies are those such as insurance companies whose business is regulated by the Financial Services Authority. Banking and insurance company websites exhibit some of the best examples of compliance. Most of the larger companies have 'Compliance Units' who are responsible for setting up company internal processes to ensure compliance. The best examples of Compliance Units set controls for web developers and for web content.

1   UMIST and Office of the Information Commissioner, *Study of Compliance with the Data Protection Act 1998 by UK Based Websites, Final Report* (May 2002).
2   *Ibid*, para 2.1.

9.90 Smaller and/or companies operating within unregulated industry sectors exhibit a low level of compliance. Those who were compliant tended to be so more by accident than by design. There is a general level of awareness of privacy issues but only in as much as they might impact on the interests of the business. There were some exceptions but even the best examples were not 100% compliant, the key areas for concern being those of data retention and data security[1]. The study also found that there was generally a low level of company internal security. Most small companies do have good intentions and are often not aware of the danger of unintentional misuse of data or of the potential for external attack.

1   UMIST and Office of the Information Commissioner, *Study of Compliance with the Data Protection Act 1998 by UK Based* Websites, *Final Report* (May 2002).

9.91   According to the survey:

> 'it appears that many organisations do not fully understand what is meant by "data collection". They assume that if they haven't explicitly asked for the data then they haven't "collected" it. Particularly worrying in this respect is the collection of free form data (i.e. where the user can enter whatever information they choose) as used in e-mails, chat rooms and discussion groups.'[1]

Half of the sites surveyed carried either a privacy policy or fair collection notice. 42% of sites did not post any form of privacy information. Small business sites are much less likely to carry privacy information than those of a larger business. The study finds[2]:

> 'Privacy notices and explanations may be written in such a way as to be misleading or unclear to the ordinary visitor who may not be familiar with the exact terms of the law. Alternatively, the position on the website may be such that it is effectively unavailable, whether intentionally or unintentionally. Only 5% of privacy statements reached the recommended level of intelligibility to the average reader ... Financial and Insurance sites faired worse while children's sites, travel and retail sites scored better.'

1   UMIST and Office of the Information Commissioner, *Study of Compliance with the Data Protection Act 1998 by UK Based* Websites, *Final Report* (May 2002).
2   *Ibid*, para 3.1.

9.92   Almost half of the organisations surveyed place a cookie on the user's computer. In almost a quarter of these cases, a third party places a cookie on the users' computer. Approximately 35% of all sites surveyed state that information collected from users may be used for direct marketing or other purposes. Of those sites with privacy policies 61% stated this[1]. This suggests that sites with privacy policies are more likely to inform users that information they divulge may be used for direct marketing. Only 35% of all sites surveyed gave users a choice about whether they wanted to be contacted by the organisation for marketing or other purposes. Of these, 50% adopted an opt-out policy and 28% adopted an opt-in policy[2].

1   UMIST and Office of the Information Commissioner, *Study of Compliance with the Data Protection Act 1998 by UK Based* Websites, *Final Report* (May 2002) para 3.2.
2   *Ibid*.

Compliance with rules and regulations on cookies

9.93 Recent research carried out by web analyst and marketing measurement specialist WebAbacus has revealed that a shocking 98% of the UK's top e-commerce sites are not ready for these new Regulations[1]. In a survey of 90 of the UK's top e-commerce websites carried out the day before the legislation was due to come into force, WebAbacus discovered that only 2% of the sites examined conformed to the best practice of providing users with a 'simple and easily understood' mechanism for refusing cookies. But even more shockingly, 24% had no privacy at all. The full results of the survey were as follows:

• 24% had no privacy policy;

• 12% had a privacy policy, but did not include information about cookies;

• 53% had a privacy policy with information about cookies (this might have included a reference to blocking cookies through a browser);

• 8% had a privacy policy, with information about cookies and detailed instructions for blocking cookies through a browser;

• 2% had a singe click opt-out (compliant).

[1] See WebAbacus Press Release (11 December 2003) 'WebAbacus Research Reveals 98% of Top UK E-Commerce Sites Not Compliant With New Legislation'.

9.94 Ian Thomas, strategic development Director for WebAbacus, commented[1]:

'The findings show that companies are either not aware of the legislation, or are ignoring it. Providing website users with a single click opt-out is very simple, so there is no excuse. Cookies are a tremendously useful tool to help websites offer a more personalised service. Used responsibly, they pose no threat to user privacy. The new regulations take us a little closer to encouraging best-practice use of cookies, but ultimately the industry needs to set its own standards and make those standards clear, so that individuals can easily identify websites that are behaving responsibly with their data.'

[1] See WebAbacus Press Release (11 December 2003) 'WebAbacus Research Reveals 98% of Top UK E-Commerce Sites Not Compliant With New Legislation'.

9.95 A simple way to comply with the requirements of the Regulations is to provide the Internet users with a privacy policy, a privacy policy statement, terms and conditions, data protection notice, or combination of any of these. The privacy policy or notice if used properly can meet the Regulations requirements. As mentioned by the BBA, it would be the responsibility of corporate subscribers to set their own policy and make their users aware of that policy.

9.96 The Directive and the Regulations do not make a distinction between permanent and session cookies. Indeed whereas permanent cookies remain on the terminal equipment after closing of connection, session cookies which may indeed in some cases be necessary for the functioning of the website, disappear at the end of the session. According to the Belgian Data Protection Commission, whereas the use of session cookies may be considered in some cases as necessary and complying with the data protection principles, this is not always the case as regards the use of permanent cookies[1].

1 Sophie Louveaux and Maria Veronica Perez Asinari, 'New European Directive 2002/58 on the Processing of Personal Data and the Protection of Privacy in the Electronic Communications Sector – Some Initial Remarks' (2003) CTLR 135.

Compliance with rules relating to unsolicited commercial e-mail

9.97 The Regulations distinguish between 'private' and 'business' spam, which creates loopholes in the process. The enforcement is left to the overworked and under-resourced Information Commissioner. The fine of £5,000 for breaking the Regulations is too low. It is illegal to send spam to private e-mail addresses, but legal to send spam to the employees of businesses. The SPAMHAUS criticises the Regulations[1]:

'Britain's much anticipated anti-spam law has been rendered toothless and will now do very little if anything to stop spam in the UK, instead it will create more confusion and misery for British businesses with spammers now insisting that spamming anything that sounds like a business address is legal.'

1 SPAMHAUS, *Britain Bungles Anti-Spam Law*, available at http://www.spamhaus.org/news.lasso?article=11.

9.98 The Information Commissioner acknowledges that the fine is not big enough to deter dedicated spammers who are causing the biggest problems. Assistant Information Commissioner, Phil Jones, said that it is hard to find the perfect regulatory process for spam. The Commission admits that there could be a lot of extra pressure on them, which is likely to increase as the amount of spam does. Phil Jones said[1]:

'We are not under any illusion that regulation is the answer, although regulation does have a part to play in enforcement. We see regulation being as important for the formal badge of disapproval and reinforcing the grounds for industry co-operation. I don't think the supposed dedicated spammers are going to be quaking in their boots at the fine.'

1 See Synergy Professional Solutions Limited, 'Anti-Spam Laws Lack Bite' (28 September 2003) available at http://www.synergyprofessional.com/articles.php?aid=2.

9.99 Regardless of the criticism, the real test for the legislation is whether of not the number of unsolicited commercial e-mails can successfully be reduced and to what extent the rules are being observed. Ironically, according to a survey by the Institute of Directors (IoD), more than a third of all UK businesses are unaware of the new anti-spam legislation. Although the legislation went through three months of consultation, the snapshot poll of 118 IoD members found that 35% were unaware of the new legislation. Of those respondents whose companies engage in e-mail marketing, a worrying 29% said they did not know about, or understand, what the new legislation means for them[1].

1 Daniel Thomas, *Widespread Ignorance Over UK Anti-Spam Laws*, ComputerWeekly.com (11 December 2003) available at http://www.computerweekly.com/Article127153.htm.

9.100   The new law, according to SPAMHAUS has led to a boom in British-based spam. Criminal gangs, as well as established marketing firms, are taking advantage of the new Directive, to make Britain one of the world's fastest growing sources of spam[1]. Steve Linford of SPAMHAUS said that the fact that business e-mail addresses are exempt from the law has given spammers a justification for claiming that their unregulated sales pitches are solely intended for business in-boxes. He further stated[2]:

> 'For the first time, Britain is among the top ten originators of spam, which now accounts for 15 billion daily e-mails around the world ... The British problem has only just come to our attention in the past few weeks.'

1 See David Rowan, *Britain is Flooding the World*, Times Online (24 January 2004) available at http://www.timesonline.co.uk/article/0,,2–974830,00.html.
2 *Ibid.*

Banks' current practices

9.101   The Bank of Scotland has the most comprehensive privacy policy, especially, on how the bank uses the customers' information[1]. The privacy policy says, 'Essentially, we use your information to look after your accounts or provide a particular service. *Occasionally we may contact you about other things* that may interest you or save you money, but of course you can opt-out by informing your nearest branch'. In addition, the privacy policy specifically states[2]:

> 'Occasionally, members of our group of companies may contact you by letter, telephone, e-mail or otherwise to inform you about other products and services that may interest you. We try to limit our customer contact programme to acceptable levels, but if you wish to exercise your right to opt-out simply inform your local branch or let us know by any means convenient for you.'

1 Available at http://www.bankofscotlandhalifax.co.uk/security/privacy.shtml.
2 *Ibid*, at p.3.

9.102   As far as e-mail is concerned, the bank states that it will keep a record of customers' e-mail address and any messages that customers send to the bank. However, the bank's privacy policy states, it 'may contact you unless you ask us not to'. Several issues may arise here. First, whether the bank is allowed to use the data to contact its customers about other things. As discussed above, under the second data protection principle, data collected for certain purpose(s) can only be used for that/those purpose(s) Second, for the collection and processing of data to be fair and lawful under the first principle, the bank should clearly specify the 'other things'. Furthermore, the Working Party has recommended that the data controller should state clearly the purpose(s) of the processing for which the controller is collecting data via a site[1]. Third, the bank adopts an opt-out approach whereas reg 22(2) requires the bank to obtain the prior consent of the customer before sending an e-mail (opt-in).

1   See WP 37 (5063/00): Working Document – Privacy on the Internet – An integrated EU approach to online data protection. Accessed on 21 November 2000. Available at http://europa.eu.int/comm/ internal_market/en/media/dataprot/wpdocs/wp37n.htm.

9.103   The bank can rely on the soft opt-in exception provided all the elements are satisfied:

(a)   the contact details have been obtained in the course of the sale or negotiations for sale of a product or service;

(b)   the direct marketing is in respect of similar products and services;

(c)   the customers have been given a simple way to refuse their contact details be used for direct marketing.

As for the latter element, the customers can opt-out by informing the nearest branch or by any means convenient to the customers. It is questionable and debatable whether informing the nearest branch is a simple means.

9.104   The privacy statement quoted above and elsewhere seems to indicate that the Bank of Scotland discloses and shares customers' information with the companies in its group. The words 'members of our group of companies may contact you' suggest that the information given by the customer to the bank will be passed on to its group of companies. Elsewhere in the privacy policy document, the bank explicitly states, 'Your information may also be shared by other members of our group to keep their records up to date and administer your relationship with them ... unless you have given us your consent, we will not provide information about you to companies outside our group to use for their own marketing purposes', and 'We don't sell or reveal your details to any companies outside our group for their marketing purposes without your consent'. There is no mention of the customers' consent which is required by law before data is disclosed and shared with third parties. It is not wrong to presume that the bank discloses and shares customers' information with its members in its group without obtaining their consent. Indeed, it is a practice which is in contravention with the first data protection principle and the Banking Code[1].

1   See topic on data sharing above as well the footnotes to paras 9.13 and 9.18.

9.105   The Royal Bank of Scotland (RBS) in its terms and conditions[1] of use of its website states[2]:

'By agreeing to be bound by these terms and conditions, you are consenting to us collecting and storing certain personal data about you. This data will be used to provide the service applied for and may be stored by the RBS Group to keep you informed of products and services which may be of interest to you. This data will not be used other than in the normal course of our business. If you do not wish to receive such information, all you need to do is to write to let us know.'

To some extent, the policy is commendable as the information collected is to be used to provide the service applied for. However, this data may also be used to market other products and services. Like the Bank of Scotland, the RBS adopts an opt-out scheme instead of opt-in as required by law.

1   Available at http://www.rbs.co.uk/legal_info/default.htm.
2   *Ibid*, at para 7.

9.106   The HSBC privacy statement is drafted in a very general manner. The bank simply says that the data collected will be handled in accordance with the UK's Data Protection Legislation[1]. There is a need for a more elaborate privacy policy as recommended by the Working Party[2]. Definitely, it is not sufficient to say that the bank processes customers' data in accordance with the DPA 1998. Not every customer knows the principles and rules in that legislation. The HSBC's privacy policy may change at any time without notice. Citibank states, 'Keeping customer information secure, and using it *only* as our customers would want us to, is a top priority for all at Citigroup'[3]. The bank promises to safeguard the confidentiality of the information and limit the collection and *use* of customer information to the minimum. The bank promises that it will not reveal customer information to any external organisation unless the customers have previously been informed by disclosure or agreement, the bank has been authorised by the customer or is required to do so by law. The bank also promises, 'We will always maintain control over the confidentiality of our customer information. We may, however, *facilitate relevant offers from reputable companies*. These companies are not permitted to retain any customer information unless the customer has specifically expressed interest in their products or services'. What does facilitate relevant offers means? Who are reputable companies? Once again, for the processing of data to be fair and lawful under the first principle, the process must be transparent and the privacy policy must reflect the transparency. The bank should be more specific and clear about 'facilitate relevant offers'. Perhaps this means that the bank discloses and shares customers' data with outside companies. As already mentioned, this can only take place if the customers have given their consent. The bank should list the companies that it discloses and shares the information with.

1   Available at http://www.ukpersonal.hsbc.co.uk/public/ukpersonal/personal_banking/legal_and_co.
2   See footnotes for paras 9.48, 9.49 and 9.51.
3   Available at http://www.citibank.com/uk/priavcy/index.jsp.

9.107   Lloyds TSB, like other banks, shares customers' information with other companies in its group[1]. The information collected by the Lloyds TSB Bank plc and other companies in the group are kept in the Lloyds TSB database and this information will be used by the bank and other companies in the group. The privacy policy of Lloyds TSB states, 'You agree that we and other companies in the Lloyds TSB Group may *use* and update this centrally held information'. The purposes, among others, are 'to provide you with other services' and 'to identify other products and services which might be suitable for you and send you information about them'.

220

1   Available at http://www.lloydstsb.com/privacy_policy.asp.

9.108   Lloyds TSB and Citibank explicitly state that they may disclose customers' information to credit reference agencies. In the context of the former, it is a condition for the customers to agree on when they subscribe to the Internet banking services. The Citibank says it will exchange customers' information with reputable clearinghouse services and reference sources. There is no mention about consent which needs to be obtained before the information can be disclosed to credit reference agencies[1].

1   See Data Protection Report 14 (August 1994) para 30(d).

9.109   On cookies, all the banks examined use cookies in their operation. As already discussed, the 2003 Regulations prohibit a bank from storing information or gaining access to information stored in the terminal equipment of a user unless the user is provided with *clear* and *comprehensive* information about the purposes of the cookies and given the opportunity to refuse the storage of or access to that information.

9.110   It has to be reminded that the Commissioner is of the view that the explanation should be sufficiently *full* and *intelligible* to enable individuals to gain clear appreciation of the potential consequences of allowing storage and access to the information collected by the device. The BBA insists that the information provided to users should be made in plain language in terms appropriate to their service so as to inform a user *what a cookie is* and *how it might be used*. The explanation should also describe, in general terms, the potential implications of disabling a cookie.

9.111   The purposes of using cookies vary from establishing and maintaining banking sessions to trading purposes to enhancing customers' visit to the website, etc. The NatWest and the Royal Bank of Scotland use all types of cookies. Their privacy policies and provisions on cookies are almost similar, perhaps prepared by the same lawyer/s. The banks state:

> 'We currently use a combination of first party, third party, permanent and temporary cookies in the following ways: to collate general non-personal management informa-tion; to evaluate the effectiveness of our advertising and promotions on third party websites; and as a flag to help us recognise when we have already asked you to participate in any online market research'.

The banks also explain what a cookie is and provide an opportunity for the users to refuse the use of cookies (opt-out). However, there is no explanation on the implications of disabling the cookies. Barclays makes use of transient (or per-session) cookies as well as persistent (or permanent) cookies. In the author's view, the Lloyds TSB and HSBC explanations on cookies are rather too brief. It is doubtful whether they satisfy the requirement of the 2003 Regulations that information must be clear; which the Information Commissioner has interpreted to mean that the explanation should be sufficiently full and intelligible to enable individuals to gain a clear appreciation of the potential consequences of allowing storage and access to the information collected by the device.

9.112 Abbey National plc uses a third party measurement tracking code to collect core information on the usage of the Abbey website[1] (third party cookies). The information collated includes the number of page views that occur on the website and the number of unique visitors and common ways of arriving at or leaving the website. The purposes are to enable Abbey National to review its content and improve site navigation. The institution states:

> 'This information is collected and aggregated, and in no way does this unique *identifier identify a user personally*. Abbey *does not* and *will not* marry any data collected by these third parties with any personal information collected on the website.'

Unlike Abbey, the Citibank may combine the information. Its privacy policy says so:

> 'Our cookies typically do not gather personally identifiable information. However, if your web browser is set to accept cookies, we may combine our cookie data with personally identifiable information which you provide to us (such as your e-mail address), so that you may receive marketing offers specifically suited to your needs.'

1 The privacy statement is available at http://www.abbey.com/privacy_statement.htm.

9.113 Simply put, the information is combined and then used to send unsolicited commercial e-mail (spam). As discussed earlier, this is not allowed without prior consent (opt-in) or if it falls under the exception. Even under the exception of offering of similar products or services where the customer information has been obtained in the context of a sale, customers should be given an opportunity to opt-out.

9.114 The Abbey National states, 'In no way does this unique identifier identify a user personally'. While the Citibank says that their cookies typically do not gather personally identifiable information. The issue is whether this information which does not and would not, as claimed by the banks, identify the user personally, would amount to personal data. The Information Commissioner takes the view that if a cookie allows an organisation to collect information which allows the organisation to distinguish the user from other users then this will amount to personal data, even if traditional identifiers – such as name and address – are not collected[1]. The Commissioner states, therefore, that profiles based on cookies that are used to deliver targeted marketing messages to particular individuals are to be treated as personal data[2].

1 The Information Commissioner Website FAQs, FAQ 14, paras 6.002 and 6.021 quoted in Hazel Grant, 'Data Protection', in Simon Stokes and Rob Carolina (eds) *Encyclopedia of E-Commerce* (2003) pp 6–35.
2 *Ibid*, paras 6.006 and 6.007.

9.115 Barclays Bank uses cookies to maintain session integrity and protect financial information as well as personal detail. The bank explicitly states that its online banking uses cookies *as part of its normal service* to enable information about customers and their preferences to be stored and to prevent unauthorised access to the customers account online. The bank makes it a condition for the online banking services; 'It is a condition of service for Barclays online banking that users accept cookies. Without them we cannot ensure your data is secure. Therefore we're unable to extend service to users who have selected to reject cookies'[1]. In other words, if one does not like cookies, he/she cannot subscribe to the Internet banking services from Barclays. He/she needs to go elsewhere.

1 Available at http://www.barclays.com/privacy/cookies.html.

9.116 The HSBC's personal Internet banking services use session cookies. The bank explains what a cookie is and its functions. It is argued that if consumers choose to have the Internet banking services with the bank, the consumers do so with the informed consent to the use of cookies. As stated above, the problem lies in the fact that the HSBC's privacy policy may change at any time without notice. Such consent, arguably, would no longer be valid in a situation where there is a unilateral change to the policy.

Concluding remarks

9.117 It is essential for businesses to manage customers' data in accordance with the rules and regulations. Otherwise, consumers will loose confidence in e-commerce. Perhaps, UK businesses need sometimes to change their practices to comply with the new Regulations. They should already be starting to do so. However, there is no justification for not observing the data protection principles as the law has been in existence since 1984. Furthermore, several guidelines and recommendations have been issued both at the European and national levels to provide guidance and ensure compliance by businesses[1]. As Elizabeth France, the former Information Commissioner, puts it[2]:

> 'Ensuring compliance with the data protection standards is not simply an issue of operating within the law; it is also about effective handling of personal information and respecting the interests of individual data subjects.'

1 Apart from what have been mentioned in this chapter and elsewhere in the book, the Information Commissioner has issued the *Guide to Data Protection Auditing* in 2002.
2 News release on 9 January 2002 during the launching of the Guide.

CHAPTER TEN

Apportionment of Liability in Internet Banking in the United Kingdom

Introduction

10.1   William Blair QC wrote[1]:

> 'English law has been slow to recognise that the customer of a bank needs any protection over and above established rules as to misrepresentations, undue influence and the like. In this as in other fields, freedom of contract has been the order of the day. But in recent times recession and unprecedented levels of problems of domestic debts have contributed to growing political pressure for greater sensitivity … As one leading banker has put it, the 1990s will be a caring decade, where the power of the consumer will require banks to be more responsive to the needs of their customers. Its response to these pressures is one of the major challenges presently facing the banking industry'.

As stated by the Report of the Review Committee, 'banking is intimately concerned with people's personal financial affairs, necessarily a matter of concern to all of us. The law has to find a balance between the reasonable requirement of any bank for freedom to operate commercially, and the no less reasonable requirement of its customer, perhaps with weaker bargaining power, for the basic protections the law should give him in the ordering of his private affairs'[2].

1   In Ross Cranston (ed) *European Banking Law: The Banker-Customer Relationship* (2nd edn, 1999) p 22.
2   *Banking Services: Law and Practice, Report by the Review Committee* (February 1989) para 2.35.

10.2   This chapter examines the issue of apportionment or allocation of liability among the stakeholders in Internet banking, particularly, between the banks and customers. The primary focus is when customers suffer losses due to fraud committed by third parties, and losses caused by systems failure or malfunction. The existing rules applying to conventional transactions are discussed, the recommendations of the Review Committee are revisited, and the practices of the banks, once again, are analysed, based on their terms and conditions.

Liability due to fraud

Forged cheques and fraud involving the use of credit cards

10.3 In conventional transactions, if a bank debits a customer's account with payment of a cheque that was not signed by the customer, the bank has no mandate to do so and must credit the amount charged. However, a cheque is a bill of exchange and s 24 of the Bills of Exchange Act 1882 will apply, which provides:

> 'Where a signature on a bill is forged ... the forged ... signature is wholly inoperative, and no right to retain the bill or to give a discharge therefore or to enforce payment thereof against any party thereto can be acquired through or under that signature, unless the party against whom it is sought to retain or enforce payment of the bill is precluded from setting up the forgery ...'

10.4 Simply put, where a signature on a bill is forged, there is no right to retain the bill or to give a discharge, unless the party against whom it is sought to retain or enforce payment of the bill is precluded. The Bills of Exchange Act 1882 did not introduce new law. It codified the contemporary common law, and reflected the more general rule which still prevails in English law[1]. This rule is that if A wishes to enforce a document against B on the basis that B is bound by it because he has signed it, and if B denies that he signed it, then it is for A to prove that the signature it bears was made or authorised by B. It is not for B to prove that it was not.

---

1 Nicholas Bohm, Ian Brown, and Brian Gladman, 'Electronic Commerce: Who Carries the Risk of Fraud', *Journal of Information, Law and Technology* (31 October 2000) available at http://elj.warwick.ac.uk/jilt/00–3/bohm.html.

10.5 If the fraud involves the use of a credit card, as indicated above, the rules in ss 83, 84 and 171 of the Consumer Credit Act 1974 will apply. These rules cease the liability of the customer at the point where he/she notifies the loss to the bank. In this case, the customer has a limited liability of £50 for any fraudulent transaction carried out by the use of his/her card before informing the bank. Furthermore, the Consumer Credit Act 1974 makes the customer liable to any extent for the use of a credit card by a person who acquired possession of it with his consent.

Recommendations of the Review Committee

10.6 As already mentioned in 1987 an independent review into banking services law and practice was set up by the UK Treasury and the Bank of England. The Review Committee completed its report in December 1988. The remit of the Review Committee was wide ranging and included matters of banking practice as well as law. It gave priority to four objectives: the need for fairness and transparency in the banker-customer relationship; to maintain confidence in the security of the banking system; to promote the efficiency of the banking system, and to preserve and consolidate the bankers' duty of confidentiality to customers.

10.7   The Report contained a valuable examination of many aspects of modern domestic banking law, with its diverse legal and practical problems, and a lengthy list of recommendations. Some of these recommendations would require enabling legislation to give effect to them, and others were to be incorporated in a new code of banking practice. As already mentioned in the previous chapter, the government of the time, firmly of the opinion that building on competition within a flexible regulatory framework was the most helpful protection for the customer, responded cautiously to the Report, but it supported the idea of a voluntary code of practice[1].

1   See Joan Wadsley and Graham Penn, *The Law Relating to Domestic Banking* (2nd edn, 2000) p 79.

10.8   There is a need to revisit the Report for several reasons. The most important of all is the fact that the report is an outcome of a committee which was asked to examine the law and its practical implications from the points of view of banker, customer and the general public interest in the availability, reliability, security and efficient and effective operation of payment, remittance and other banking service. The other reason is that the Review Committee has given serious consideration to the development in banking and payment systems. Indeed, the Committee's term of reference was 'to have regard to current and prospective developments in banking and payment systems, including developments in electronic data processing and electronic funds transfer technology'.

10.9   According to the Committee, there is an initial question about the customer's right of action in a disputed EFT, which applies to ATM networks jointly operated by a number of banks and to EFT-POS systems, in which a number of parties are contractually related. The Committee remarked[1]:

> 'If banks have chosen of their own volition to introduce new and more complex payment systems, it should not be the customer who suffers, by comparison with the standards he has come to expect under paper-based systems ... Banking, we again recall, is not the customer's business, but the bank's.'

1   *Banking Services: Law and Practice, Report by the Review Committee* (February 1989) para 10.36.

10.10   The Review Committee is of the view that there is a need for regulation to govern EFT[1]:

> 'It is difficult not to conclude, from this brief survey of the arguments on either side, that there is a pressing need for EFT to be subject to some degree of regulation ... Leaving EFT solely to contractual arrangement does not appear to meet the case, when there is widespread doubt as to whether the allocation of duties and liabilities among the provider and users of EFT systems is totally equitable. The arguments against any sort of regulations have been shown to be partly suspect and, for the rest, less than conclusive.'

1   *Banking Services: Law and Practice, Report by the Review Committee* (February 1989) para 9.29.

10.11   The Committee was concerned with the situation where both parties accept that fraudulent use of card and PIN in a customer-activated EFT system has led to financial loss, and there is no dispute about the underlying facts. The Committee states, 'At present, in the absence of any legal framework, each bank sets its own terms and conditions on the matter, which vary from bank to bank, and customers have no choice but to abide by them, or change their bank'[1]. The Review Committee states[2]:

> 'There is a clear case, in our view, for introducing legal rules on the allocation of liability in cases of loss through fraud, and for keeping them broadly in line with those in the Consumer Credit Act 1974. In a day and age when the usage of different kinds of payment cards is tending to converge, there are strong arguments for consistency in the legal treatment of payment cards, wherever possible. That consideration apart, it is plainly inequitable that a customer's liability for loss through fraud should be limited by law in the case of credit cards, but the banks are free to set their own rules in the case of cash cards and debit cards.'

1 *Banking Services: Law and Practice, Report by the Review Committee* (February 1989) para 10.37.
2 *Ibid*, para 10.41.

10.12 The Review Committee recommended that a provision in statute law, applicable to any customer-activated EFT system, should set the limits of legal liability for loss due to fraud on the principles established in ss 83 and 84 of the Consumer Credit Act 1974. The main provisions are that a customer should normally be liable for any losses incurred up to the point where he/she notifies his/her bank, subject to a financial limit currently fixed as £50; the bank should be liable for any losses incurred thereafter. Where gross negligence on the part of either party could be demonstrated, the party should be liable for any amount up to the full amount of the loss. The bank's duty should be in any event to its customer, but the bank should have a right of relief against a third party who could be shown to have contributed to loss by fraud through an EFT system[1].

1 *Banking Services: Law and Practice, Report by the Review Committee* (February 1989) recommendation 10(10).

Distribution of liability in cases of fraudulent transaction: banks practices

10.13 There is a link between fraud and computer systems. Fraudulent transactions may occur due to weaknesses in computer systems. Commentators assert that, 'Although UK banks have denied that weaknesses in their computer systems are responsible for the alleged fraudulent transaction, the evidence ... highlights failings in such systems which can have serious impact on customers'[1]. According to them:

> 'The banks have been unwilling to allow independent experts to examine their systems, justifying this stance by claiming that they need to keep the design and operation of their systems secret in order to protect them from attack. This approach, known in security circles as "security through obscurity", is now widely

discredited, because any advantages provided by secrecy are offset by the fact that this secrecy allows serious faults to exist in systems for long periods without being discovered.'

1   Nicholas Bohm, Ian Brown, and Brian Gladman, 'Electronic Commerce: Who Carries the Risk of Fraud', *Journal of Information, Law and Technology* (31 October 2000) available at http:// elj.warwick.ac.uk/jilt/00–3/bohm.html.

10.14   In 2001, the FSA warned Internet banks that they were not doing enough to protect themselves or their customers against fraud. Since then, many banks have reported tightening up their security arrangements. Dave Eacott spokesman for the FSA, said[1]:

'We do have conversations with the institutions about how they address the issue of Internet security. The reason we do that is because in our own rules there is a requirement to have good systems and that extends into the IT area as well.'

1   See Marianne Curphey, 'Friend or Foe?', available at http://money.guardian.co.uk/onlinebanking/story/ 0,13813,1029640,00.html.

10.15   The Banking Code 2003 only covers the situation where customers suffer losses due to their own fraudulent act or they act without reasonable care. Paragraph 12.4 of the Code requires a customer to take care of his cards, electronic purse, PINs and other security information. Paragraph 12.9 places the responsibility on the customer if losses occur. It states, 'If you act fraudulently, you will be responsible for all losses on your account. If you act without reasonable care, and this causes losses, you may be responsible for them'. 'Act without reasonable care' may mean the failure on the part of a customer to follow the advice given in para 12.4 on how the customer can help prevent fraud and protect his account.

10.16   The crucial situation is when fraud is committed by a third party and the customer is at no fault at all. In the absence of any legal framework, banks have adopted different approaches. As one commentator says, 'British banks have a variety of policies in place outlining their policies if a security breach or fraud occurs – but the fact that there are no standard guidelines in place is leaving customers confused'[1]. Stuart Cliffe, the Director of the National Association of Bank Customers (NABC), argues that[2]:

'Online banks should make a definite guarantee to their customers that if anything goes wrong, the money will be refunded immediately to their account. Banks can easily stand the loss of a few hundred or thousands of pounds but it would be difficult for the customer.'

1   Pia Heikkila, 'E-banks Told to Carry the Can for Online Fraud', available at http://www.silicon.com/ management/itdirector/print.htm?TYPE=story&AT=1101943.
2   *Ibid.*

10.17   According to Nicholas Bohm, Ian Brown, and Brian Gladman, the terms in use tend to cover both telephone banking and online banking where access is provided by a computer. Two distinct trends are emerging. Some banks are using terms closely based on those used for card transactions, so that the customer is bound by fraudulent instructions but liability is limited to £50[1]. Among those adopting this approach are the Co-operative Bank and Lloyds TSB. But other banks provide for the customer to be bound by fraudulent instructions, and provide no limit on the resulting liability. Among those in this group are Prudential Banking plc, the Halifax and the Bank of Scotland. In this respect, they argue that the customer's protection rests wholly on the secrecy of the security information, without any physical indication (such as loss of a card) to alert the customer to any compromise of the secrecy[2]. The commentators are very critical of the practices of banks in the UK[3]:

'We argue that the approach taken by banks is unfair to their customers in some cases, fails to encourage the development of adequate security measures, and prevents the banking system from playing its proper part in the development of electronic commerce in the United Kingdom.'

1   Nicholas Bohm, Ian Brown, and Brian Gladman, 'Electronic Commerce: Who Carries the Risk of Fraud', *Journal of Information, Law and Technology* (31 October 2000) available at http://elj.warwick.ac.uk/jilt/00–3/bohm.html.
2   *Ibid.*
3   *Ibid.*

10.18   Ahmad Azzouni observes that there are three different approaches adopted by the banks in relation to liability due to fraud: (1) some banks are using terms closely based on those used for card transactions; (2) others have chosen to carry the whole risk of fraud unless they can prove that the customer acted fraudulently; and (3) banks which exclude all liability in case of fraudulent transactions (until they are notified)[1]. In respect of the first group of banks, the conditions stated by the Co-operative Bank are the best example[2]. Condition 3 complies with the provisions of the Consumer Credit Act 1974 as it states that:

'If you suspect that someone knows your Customer Security Codes, please notify the bank immediately. When we receive notification, your liability will cease. Until then, you may be liable for up to £50 of any loss. If unauthorised use of your Customer Security Codes is due to your negligence, fraud, disclosure or misuse, you will probably be liable for all losses ...'

1   Ahmad Azzouni, 'Internet Banking and Law: A Critical Examination of the Legal Controls over Internet Banking in the UK and Their Ability to Frame, Regulate and Secure Banking on the Net', [2003] J.I.B.L.R., 351 at 360.
2   The terms and conditions are available at www.co-operativebank.co.uk.

10.19   In respect of the second group of banks, which carry the whole risk of fraud until it is proved that the customer has acted fraudulently, the HSBC's approach is the best example. It is provided in clear terms that the bank will carry the whole risk of fraudulent use unless the bank can prove that the customer acted fraudulently or with gross negligence or failed to observe the required precautions against disclosure of security information[1]. Clause 2.4 of the HSBC's terms and conditions requires a customer to inform the bank immediately of any unauthorised access to their Internet banking service, any unauthorised transaction or instruction, or if the customer suspects that someone else knows their security number. Once a customer has notified the bank of any of these, Clause 4.2 states, 'you will not be responsible for any unauthorised instructions carried out *after* we have had reasonable time to suspend the Internet banking services in respect of your account(s) unless we can show you have acted fraudulently'. However, a question may arise as to the position of an unauthorised instruction or fraud which takes place before the bank is able to suspend the account?

1   Ahmad Azzouni, 'Internet Banking and Law: A Critical Examination of the Legal Controls over Internet Banking in the UK and Their Ability to Frame, Regulate and Secure Banking on the Net' [2003] JIBLR 351, 361.

10.20   The bank states, 'You will be responsible for all losses (including the amount of any transaction carried out without your authority) if you have acted with gross negligence so as to facilitate that unauthorised transaction, or you have acted fraudulently. For the purposes of Clause 4, gross negligence shall be deemed to include failure to observe any of your security duties referred to in these Terms'[1]. David Howarth, the UK's Internet banking manager said that the terms and conditions were intended to highlight possible security holes to customers, not to give HSBC 'an easy opt-out' in the event of a problem with an account[2].

1   HSBC Internet Banking Terms and Conditions, available at http//www.ukpersonal.hsbc.co.uk/hsbc/personal_banking/personal-internet-banking/terms.
2   See Lucy Sheriff, 'HSBC Online Lets Users Take Blame for Security Issues', The Register, available at http://www.teheregister.co.uk/2000/08/22/hsbc_online_lets_users_take/print.html.

10.21   It is interesting to note that Barclays adopts an 'Online Banking Guarantee' in cases of fraud. It states:

'We take security seriously at Barclays. As an online banking customer you auto-matically benefit from our Online Banking Guarantee, giving you 100% protection. We promise to protect you. In the unlikely event that you suffer Internet fraud on your account, we guarantee to cover any losses no matter what the amount.'[1]

This is reinforced by condition 3.5 of the bank which says that they will do all that they reasonably can to prevent a breach of security which may result in unauthorised access to the customers' account and information. The bank will accept liability for any loss or damage to customers from any breach of security provided that customers have not breached condition 3.3 which requires custom-ers to do all that they reasonably can to ensure the secrecy of the security procedure at all times.

1   Online Banking Guarantee is available at http://www.personal.barclays.co.uk/BRC1/jsp/brccontrol?task=articlegroup&site=pfs&val.

10.22   Clause 3.4 of Barclays' terms and conditions requires that a customer must tell the bank as soon as he/she can if he/she thinks someone else may know the security procedures. The bank further states:

'Until you tell us, you will be responsible for all instructions that we receive and act on even if the instruction was not given by you. Unless we can show that you have been fraudulent, grossly negligent or have not complied with condition 3.3 we will refund your account with any payments we make after you tell us. We will have no further liability to you'.

10.23 Barclays uses the broad term of Internet fraud in its 'Online Banking Guarantee', while the HSBC is more specific: 'We will refund you the amount of transaction carried out in accordance with *any instruction where your security number has been used without your authority'*. The HSBC says that where they are liable for any unauthorised transaction, they will credit the customer account with any money lost up to the amount of the transaction, and any related interest and charges'[1]. The HSBC will credit not only the amount of transaction involved but also interest and charges.

1   Clause 4.1.

10.24 Interestingly, the Alliance & Leicester admits liability for losses if instructions are not given by a customer. The exceptions are when the customer has acted fraudulently; has failed to exercise reasonable care; or has failed to comply with the legal terms including the safeguards; or the instruction was made by someone else with the customer's permission. This liability however is subject to limitations in clause 10.3. It provides:

> 'Any liability we may have to you will be limited to the value of the transaction during the course of which such liability arose. We shall not be liable to you in any circumstances for any loss or damage (other than that which cannot be excluded in law) which is not direct; or is beyond our reasonable control; or which we could not reasonable foresee'.

If a customer suffered losses due to fraud by a third party, are these losses direct? Is this a loss that the bank could or could not reasonably foresee? There are too many exceptions to the company's liability.

10.25 According to Ahmad Azzouni, the approach of the last group of banks, which excludes all liability in case of fraudulent transactions (until they are notified), is the most widely adopted in the UK. Among these banks are Halifax, the Royal Bank of Scotland, Bank of Scotland, and Lloyds TSB. These banks provide for the customer to be bound by fraudulent instructions and provide no limit on the resulting liability. Like other banks, the Bank of Scotland obligates the customer to take all reasonable precautions to ensure that the secured input is not disclosed to anyone else. Should the customer suspect that the secured input has become known to an unauthorised person or suspects any misuse of or breach of confidentiality or secrecy in respect of the secured input the customer shall immediately contact the bank[1]. Clause 6 of the bank's terms and conditions states:

> 'Once the customer has told the Bank of any misuse of or breach of confidentiality or secrecy in respect of secured input the Bank will take steps to prevent the secured input being used to access any account. Until the Bank has been told of this, the customer will be responsible for any authority or instruction given using the

customer's secured input, even it was not given by the customer or a nominated user. *The Bank will not be liable for having acted on such instructions.'*

I   The terms and conditions are available at http://www.bankofscotland.co.uk/business/waysofbanking/internet/terms.html, clause 5.

10.26   Another point concerns the phrase 'Until the bank has been told of this, the customer will be responsible for any authority ... even it was given by the customer'. As argued by Bohm, Brown and Gladman, the customer's protection rests wholly on the secrecy of the security information, without any physical indication (such as loss of a card) to alert the customer to any compromise of the secrecy[1].

I   Pia Heikkila, 'E-banks Told to Carry the Can for Online Fraud', available at http://www.silicon.com/management/itdirector/print.htm?TYPE=story&AT=1101943.

10.27   As already mentioned, the Alliance & Leicester admits liability if instructions are not given by a customer. However, it disclaims liability in several circumstances set out in clause 10.1[1]. It provides:

'We shall not be liable to you for any loss or damage (other than that which cannot be excluded in law) which you may suffer as a result of:
1.   our having acted upon your instructions received using security information or following receipt of any information from you;
2.   any misuse or abuse of the Alliance & Leicester Internet banking service by you;
3.   your security information having been disclosed by you to someone else;
4.   our system for any reason being unavailable.'

I   Available at http://www.alliance-leicester.co.uk/internetbanking/index.asp?page=home&ct=primary meu.

10.28   The problem may arise concerning point 1. For example, if through fraud, a third party managed to get hold of the security information of a customer and then used the security information to give an instruction to the bank to withdraw money from the customer's account, is the instruction given by the customer? If yes, the Alliance & Leicester will not be liable. If not, the Alliance & Leicester admits its liability.

10.29   It is worth mentioning the condition of the Nationwide Building Society (NBS) in relation to an instruction or transaction which was not carried out by the customer[1]. Clause 3.6 of the NBS's terms and conditions states, 'You will not be liable for an Internet banking transaction on one of your accounts which was not carried out by you or for access to or use of your account by someone else'. The customer is not liable, and the terms and conditions are silent on the liability of the NBS. Who is liable then?

I   The terms and conditions are available at http://www.ntionwide.co.uk/Demos/InternetBankingDemo/termsandconditions.htm.

10.30   The principles of proportionality and equity must control banks' assertion that they are excluded from responsibility. It is true that technical risks or risks related to third parties such as hackers cannot be attributed to the banks if they take all reasonable possible steps to protect themselves[1]. However, if the damage suffered by the customer is great; if the customer did not commit any offence; and if the bank has sufficient resources to make good the damage without falling into serious financial difficulties, the institutions must bear partial damages in all cases[2]. It would indeed be unjust to make a diligent customer sustain huge damages. This is particularly true in the sensitive field of telebanking, where damage could have very serious consequences for the customer (for example, a loss of 85% of a retired employee's fortune − saved all his life − when the retiree has made no error)[3].

1 See Cedric J. Magnin, 'Telebanking Contract in Swiss Law' [2001] *ILSA Journal of International & Comparative Law*, Vol 8:61, 128.
2 *Ibid.*
3 *Ibid.*

Liability for systems malfunction

10.31   When considering the potential liability of banks for technical malfunctions, it is possible to divide the malfunctions into two categories: those which are beyond the control of the bank and those which are within its control. Depending on the nature of the electronic fund transactions, different parties control certain systems. In the case of money transfer though the ATM or POS system, the bank, or the group of banks, which manages the system, is the customer's sole contact. In contrast, the Internet banking customer is a subscriber of a telecommunication company. The customer procures the necessary equipment and also the use of the services supplied by the telecommunication company. Like the customer, the bank is simply a user of the telecommunications service and the technical aspects of the system may be beyond the bank's control. There are many others involved between the bank and its customers; the telecommunications company, Internet service providers (ISP) and certification authorities (CA). Fairness requires the apportionment of liabilities among all parties involved − CAs, banks, ISP, hardware/software providers, and consumers − depending on the relative degree of fault.

10.32   A bank is under a duty to act in accordance with its customer's mandate and to carry out its services with reasonable care and skill. Should a bank fail to act correctly on a payment order received from its customer, then a bank may be liable for breach of those duties. Its liability, as mentioned earlier, will depend on whether the cause of the failure is within or outside the bank's control. Banks normally limit their liability for the latter type through the use of widely drafted *force majeure* provisions which expressly exclude liability for technical failure which is beyond the reasonable control of the bank.

10.33   If the failure arises because of the malfunction of a bank's systems, the bank may be held liable if the customer can show that the failure has been caused by the negligent operation, choice or maintenance of the system by the bank. Some commentators argue that the duty of banks for technical failure is closer to an absolute standard[1]. Section 13 of the Supply of Goods and Services Act 1982 reads:

'In a contract for the supply of a service where the supplier is acting in the course of a business, there is an implied term that the supplier will carry out the service with reasonable care and skill'. Here, the liability might arise due to the failure of the bank to comply with the implied contractual duty to perform its services with reasonable care and skill imposed by the statute. The standard of reasonable care and skill is to be adjudged by using the objective standard set by the reasonably competent banker. Banks commonly seek explicitly to limit their liability for technical failure in their standard terms and conditions.

1 See A Arora, *Electronic Banking and the Law* (1988).

10.34 System failure may also trigger a decision from a regulatory authority to pursue an action against the bank. Schedule 3, para 4(7) of the Banking Act 1987 states that: 'an institution shall not be regarded as conducting its business in a prudent manner unless it maintains … *adequate systems of control of its business and records*'.

10.35 The Citibank case in 1994 provides an interesting case study in this respect. The Citibank system, called the 'Financial Institutions Citibank Cash Manager' (FICCM), provided large institutional customers with dial-in access from any geographic location to the online service, based on a computer in Parsipenny, New Jersey. Once the service had been accessed, customers could carry out a range of financial transactions, including the execution of credit transfers between accounts.

10.36 Access to the Citibank system required the customer to input two control numbers and passwords. However, the passwords were fixed, which gave rise to the risk that such data could be intercepted at some point during the communication process and re-used. Subsequently, Citibank has implemented a new authorisation procedure involving the use of dynamically-generated, encrypted passwords, based on a smart-card. It was clear that the accused, Vladimer Levin was able to monitor FICCM-initiated transactions over a period of time before choosing from which accounts to make unauthorised transfers, as well as the amounts involved.

10.37 The Review Committee is very critical of the practice of the banks of disclaiming liability arising as a result of system malfunction[1]:

> It will be seen that it is normal practice for banks to disclaim liability for any loss whatsoever suffered as a consequence of failure equipment … it was understandable that, in the very early days of EFT equipment when performance was uncertain, banks should have wished to protect themselves in this kind of way. But the reliability of most systems is well tested now, and is indeed the subject of proud claims by banks. Banks cannot have it both ways: in today's conditions, their standard terms and conditions must be construed as somewhat unfair on customers. It needs to be recalled that it is the banks who have chosen to introduce new technology: it is unreasonable that the customer, who had no part in that decision, should be penalised for its consequence, except in special circumstances.'

---

1   *Banking Services: Law and Practice, Report by the Review Committee* (February 1989) para 10.45.

10.38   The Review Committee recommended that a provision in statute law, applicable to any EFT system, should make the bank normally liable to the customer for any direct, or clearly consequential, loss due to the failure of EFT equipment to complete a transaction, notwithstanding the terms of any contract to the contrary. Compensation may be reduced if the failure is due to causes beyond the bank's control, or if intent or gross negligence on the customer's part has contributed to the fault. If, in the case of a customer-activated system, the customer should have been aware that the equipment was unavailable for use of malfunctioning, the bank's liabilities should be limited to the correction of any errors on the customer's account, and the refund of any charges or fees imposed on him/her as a result. It should be for the bank to resolve with third parties any question of liability on their part[1].

1   *Banking Services: Law and Practice, Report by the Review Committee* (February 1989) recommendation 10(11).

10.39   According to the Committee, a provision in statute law should apply, notwithstanding the terms of any contract to the contrary, to the apportionment of any loss arising from a transaction carried out through a customer-activated EFT system, where it is in dispute whether or not that transaction was authorised. *It should require that loss to be apportioned on an equitable basis*, by reference to the extent to which the acts or omissions of the parties have contributed to the loss. Apportionment of the loss should take into account such factors as (i) the steps taken by the customer to protect the security of his/her card and PIN, (ii) the extent to which the system provided by the bank protects the customer against unauthorised transactions on his/her account, and (iii) the relative weight of the evidence adduced by the parties in support of their respective contentions that the transaction was, or was not, authorised[1].

1   *Banking Services: Law and Practice, Report by the Review Committee* (February 1989) recommendation 10(12).

Distribution of liability in system failure: banks practices

10.40   As already mentioned, it is possible to divide the malfunctions into two categories; those which are beyond the control of the bank and those which are within its control. Banks normally limit their liability for the former type through the use of widely drafted *force majeure*. They may also attempt to exclude or restrict liability for systems failure within their control.

10.41   It is normal for a bank not to want to be held liable for the faults of a third party or system malfunction which is beyond its control. Clause 5.3 of the HSBC's terms and conditions provides an example where the bank disclaims liability for losses arises as a result of technical breakdown or system failure. The condition states:

'We shall not be liable to you for any loss you suffer due to any event or circumstances *beyond our control* which leads to the Internet Banking Service being wholly or partly unavailable such as, but not limited to, technical breakdown, strikes or other industrial action (whether or not involving our employees) or communications or power failure. You may be able to reduce your loss by telephoning us instead.'

10.42 Citibank Online in condition 4.1 states that the bank agrees to make reasonable efforts to ensure full performance of Citibank Online. The bank will not be liable for any failure to provide the service or to comply with the terms and conditions for any cause that is *beyond its reasonable control*. The bank will not be liable for any losses or delays in the transmission of instructions caused by any Internet service provider or by software failure or for any indirect or consequential loss[1]. What is the position if the software belongs to and is under the control of the bank?

1 See Citibank Online Terms and Conditions available at http://www.citibank.com/uk/aboutcitibank/general/termsandconditions/internetbanking.jsp, see also condition 27 of the bank's General Terms and Conditions which is available at http://www.citibank.com/uk/aboutcitibank/general/termsandconditions/general.jsp.

10.43 In another document called *Terms, Conditions, Caveats and Small Print* (TCCSP), Citibank adopts the following terms:

'In no event will Citicorp be liable for any damages, including without limitation direct or indirect, special, incidental, or consequential damages, losses or expenses arising in connection with this site or use thereof or inability to use by any party, or *in connection with any failure of performance*, error, omission, *interruption*, defect, delay in operation or transmission, computer virus or line or *system failure*, even if Citicorp, or representatives thereof, are advised of the possibility of such damages, losses or expenses'[1].

There is no indication whether this covers system failure within or beyond the control of the bank. A more important question is how to reconcile this with the specific condition 4.1 of Citibank Online. As indicated above, apart from the specific Citibank Online Terms and Conditions (COTC), the bank adopts the Citibank Account General Terms and Conditions. If there any differences between them the specific terms override the General terms[2]. How about differences between specific COTC and TCCSP?

1 See the *Terms, Conditions, Caveats and Small Print* which is available at htpp://www.citibank.com/uk/terms/index.jsp.
2 See clause 1 of the Citibank Online Terms and Conditions.

10.44 Cahoot explicitly mentions instances whereby it will not be liable and this is followed by more general terms. The company states, 'We will not liable to you if we are unable to perform our obligations to you because of failure of any machine, data processing system or transmission link or because of any industrial dispute or due to any other cause which is outside our control or the control of anyone working for us or on our behalf'[1].

1   See condition 10 of the Cahoot internet banking terms and conditions, available at http://www.cahoot.com.

10.45   Xavier Thunis argues that the inclusion of the phrase such as this unquestionably broadens the concept of *force majeure*. He is of the opinion that the bank should in principle have access to back-up equipment which is sufficient to permit the system to continue to operate[1].

1   Xavier Thunis, 'Recent Trends Affecting the Banks' Liability During Electronic Fund Transfer Operations', [1991] 8 JIBL 297, 299.

10.46   It seems that the Bank of Scotland disclaims liability not only for system failure which is beyond its control but also system failure within its control. Clause 12 of the terms and conditions provides:

'Subject to any terms implied by law or by the rules of any regulatory body and which cannot be excluded, the Bank shall not be liable in contract, tort (including negligence), delict or otherwise:

…

(b)   for any downtime, unavailability, failure, malfunction, distortion or interruption to the Service, whether caused by a failure in the Websites, or any communications means or otherwise;

…

(e)   for force majeure, including, without limitation, industrial disputes, any act or omission by any third party or the revocation of any licence held by the Bank in connection with the Service or any other act or omission outside of the Bank's control.'

10.47   By using the terms *force majeure* and *outside of the Bank's control* the intention of clause 12(e) is very clear – to cover circumstances beyond the bank's control. Clause 12(b) may open to different interpretations. Common sense and logic tell us that it may seek to cover system failure or malfunction within the control of the bank. If this argument is right, it cannot be fair for the bank to disclaim liability in this situation and to have the expression of intention stated in its terms and conditions. The good practice is for this bank and other banks to admit liability for losses suffered by the customer due to the banks' system failure or malfunction and/or system failure within their control. This should be clearly stated in the terms and conditions.

CHAPTER ELEVEN

Internet Banking in Australia: Law and Practice

Introduction

11.1 Australia has emerged as one of the information economy world leaders, with 41% of its total population accessing the Internet as at May 2000. The story of Internet banking in Australia dates back to 1994 when Adelaide Bank launched a simple website providing product and services information. In December 1995, Advance Bank launched an Internet banking site. In early 1997, the Commonwealth Bank, the first of the Big Four banks, launched Internet banking with its NetBank. Adelaide Bank, adding transactional functionality, followed this; Westpac and St George launched Internet banking in early 1998. In May 1999, ANZ and National Australia Bank introduced Internet banking[1]. At present, all the major banks and some smaller banks are providing Internet banking services.

1   See Milind Sathye, 'Case Study 1 – Growth of Internet Banking in Australia'.

11.2 The growing use of Internet banking is evidenced by the rise in Internet banking and online bill payment by 810% between May 1998 and May 2000[1]. According to research carried out by Nielsen NetRating, 3.7 million people visited an online website in December 2002, an increase of 16.2% over the number of visitors in December 2001. The Australian Bankers' Association (ABA) stated that customers in Australia want innovation to continue in the ways to conduct banking transactions. The take up rate of Internet banking is faster than ATM or phone banking. There are six million customers now registered, with an estimated 5,000 people a day registering for Internet banking. The ABA states that less than 10% of transactions are carried out in bank branches, the bulk of transactions are now done electronically through ATMs, EFTPOS, telephone and online banking[2].

1   NOIE (National Office of Information Economy) (2000) The Current State of Play, NOIE (November 2000).
2   Australian Bankers' Association, 'New Ways Of Banking' Fact Sheet (February 2003).

11.3 The future of Internet banking in Australia looks bright. In response to a survey in 1999 by the Angus Reid Group, 98% of Australians banking online said they would continue to do so. The same survey suggests that 32% of Australian Internet users not currently using Internet banking intend to start online banking in the near future. The leading online banks in Australia are the Commonwealth Bank of Australia (CBA), ANZ, National Australia Bank (NAB) and Westpac Corporation.

11.4   This chapter examines the legislative and regulatory framework of Internet banking in Australia. It outlines the rules and regulations relating to Internet banking in the country. Being the most significant one, the new EFT Code, receives special treatment. The focus of the discussion is on the rules concerning allocation of liability and protection of customers' privacy. An attempt is made to examine the terms and conditions of some of the banks that provide Internet banking services in the effort of assessing the levels of compliance with the rules and regulations, particularly, the EFT Code.

The legislative and regulatory framework

Financial Services Reform Act 2001

11.5   The government launched a major inquiry into the regulation of Australia's financial system by establishing the 'Wallis Financial Sector Inquiry'. The report was released in March 1997, recognising that the financial system was undergoing continuous and rapid change including amongst other things, convergence, increased openness, increased competition and globalisation. Three interlinked forces primarily drive these changes: changing customer needs; new technologies and skills; and changes to regulation across a broad spectrum. The report concluded that:

> 'In the financial system, specialised regulation is required to ensure market partici-
> pants act with integrity and that consumers are protected. The financial system
> warrants specialised regulation due to the complexity of financial products, the
> adverse consequences of breaching financial promises and the need for low-cost
> means to resolve disputes.'

11.6   The Australian government accepted this view. On 11 March 2002, the Financial Services Reform Act (FSRA) came into effect, making extensive amendments to the Corporations Act and other legislation covering the financial sector. The FSRA implements the Wallis report proposals. The three key features of this new regulatory and legislative regime are to provide: a harmonised approach to licensing of financial services providers, including a disclosure and conduct framework; a single statutory regime for financial product disclosure; and the licensing of financial markets and clearing and settlement facilities. The FSRA makes extensive amendments to the Corporations Act and other legislation covering the financial sector.

11.7   While the FSRA is primarily aimed at developing the financial services industry and boosting competition, it also aims to ensure there is a fair deal for consumers. In particular, it is noted that consumer sovereignty is a guiding principle for the reforms, and the Act aims to build a regulatory framework that enhances consumer protection and promotes market integrity. The new framework was set up with one agency responsible for each of the main kinds of regulation applied to the financial system. In the words of the Treasurer, 'we have adopted in Australia a model of regulation which is known as the "twin peaks" doctrine. One regulator to deal with prudential supervision, APRA, another to deal with corporate enforcement, ASIC'[1]. According to him, the ASIC's ability to use a civil penalty regime has enabled it to move quickly and successfully to enforce the laws. And this is where a major step forward has been made in relation to corporate regulation, in the use of a civil penalty regime. He quoted Professor Hall, who said recently:

> '... the regulatory technique in Australia I think is at the forefront of using banning orders. Europe is looking at using them and is paying close attention to what is happening in Australia.'

1 Peter Costello, the Australian Treasurer address to CCH forum, 'Australia's Financial Services Reform Agenda' (17 July 2003).

11.8 Although credit products and services are not affected by the FSRA, the ASIC now has a new consumer protection role in credit matters. The ASIC can investigate complaints about misleading or deceptive conduct, or unconscionable conduct by credit providers. Section 792A of the Corporations Act as amended by the FSRA provides for the general obligations of the market licensee. Among other things, a market licensee must:

(a) to the extent that it is reasonably practicable to do so, do all things necessary to ensure that the market is a fair, orderly and transparent market; and

(b) comply with the conditions on the license; and

(c) have adequate arrangements for supervising the market, including arrangements for;
   (i) handling conflicts between the commercial interests of the licensee and the need for the licensee to ensure that the market operates in the way mentioned in paragraph (a); and
   (ii) monitoring the conduct of participants on or in relation to the market; and
   (iii) enforcing compliance with the market's operating rules; and

(d) have sufficient resources to operate the market properly and for the required supervisory arrangements to be provided; and

(e) ensure that there are approved compensation arrangements in relation to the market; and

(f) take all reasonable steps to ensure that no disqualified individual becomes, or remains, involved in the licensee.

11.9 Under s 792B, a market licensee is required to give written notice to the ASIC, as soon as practicable, if a market licensee becomes aware that it may not be able to meet, or has breached, an obligation under s 792A. Failure to comply with this requirement is an offence. Section 792F obliges a market licensee to submit an annual report regarding its compliance with the obligation to the ASIC. It provides that a market licensee must, within three months after the end of its financial year, give ASIC an annual report *on the extent to which the licensee complied with its obligation as market licensee.* Failure to comply with this requirement is an offence.

11.10 Section 794C empowers the ASIC to do an assessment of how well a market licensee is complying with any or all of its obligations as a market licensee. Also, the ASIC is given the power to give directions to a market licensee. Section 794D provides that if ASIC is of the opinion that it is necessary, or in the public interest, to protect people dealing in a financial product or class of financial products by giving a direction to a market licensee to suspend dealings in the financial product or class of financial products; or giving some other direction in relation to those dealings.

11.11 Part 7.10 of the FSRA deals with market misconduct and other prohibited conduct relating to financial products and services. Breaches of some of these misconduct provisions will amount to a criminal offence and attract civil pecuniary penalties. Section 1041E prohibits a person from making a statement or disseminating information that is false or materially misleading and, as a result, is likely to: induce persons to apply for, dispose of or acquire financial products; or have the effect of increasing, reducing, maintaining or stabilising the price for trading in financial products on a financial market.
Section 1041F prohibits a person from inducing another person to deal in financial products through the following means:

- by way of publishing a statement, promise or forecast if they know it to be misleading, false or deceptive;

- by a dishonest concealment of material facts; or

- by the recording or storing of false or materially misleading information with the expectation that the information will be available to the other person or a class of persons that will include that person.

11.12 Section 1041G prohibits people, in the course of carrying on a financial services business, from engaging in dishonest conduct in relation to a financial product or service. Section 1041H prohibits people from engaging in conduct that is misleading or deceptive or likely to mislead or deceive, in relation to a financial product or service. Interestingly, the FSRA allows persons who have suffered loss or damage as a result of the conduct of another person contravening ss 1041E, 1041F, 1041G or 1041H to seek compensation under s 1041I.

11.13 Apart from these, s 991B requires financial services licensees to give priority to clients' order, and s 991A prohibits a financial services licensee from engaging in unconscionable conduct in relation to the provision of a financial service. If as a consequence of unconscionable conduct a person suffers loss or damage, that person will be able to recover the amount of the loss or damage against the licensee.

11.14 Another key element of the FSRA regime is product disclosure. The FSRA applies consistent disclosure requirements for all 'financial products', coupled with flexibility in the legislation that allows for significant differences between products. These requirements consist of a point of sale disclosure through a Product Disclosure Statement, ongoing disclosure and periodic reporting requirements, advertising requirements and an obligation to provide confirmation of transactions. The new disclosure requirement will generally only apply to dealings with retail clients[1].

1   P S B Hutley, A E Bennett and P A Russell, An *Introduction to the Financial Services Reform Act 2001* (2nd edn, 2003) p 2.

11.15 In general, the disclosure regime is divided into three distinct stages, and the documentation required at each stage must be sequentially numbered in order to assist a consumer to recognise whether they have received the disclosure document that is relevant to the transaction they are entering into. The three documents required are: Financial Services Guide (FSG), Statement of Advice (SoA), and Product Disclosure Statement (PDS). The FSRA contains details concerning these documents. The FSG is a document that contains basic information that any retail client is entitled to receive before obtaining any financial advice or service. The financial service providers must provide an FSG at the outset of dealing with retail clients unless one of the five exceptions applies[1]. The SoA is required when personal advice is given to retail clients, either as the means by which advice is provided or as a record of advice, while the PDS applies to all financial products that are issued in the course of a business of issuing financial products[2].

1   P S B Hutley, A E Bennett and P A Russell, An *Introduction to the Financial Services Reform Act 2001* (2nd edn, 2003) p 29.
2   *Ibid*, at pp 32 and 34.

Trade Practices Act 1974

11.16 The Australian government has passed several laws aimed at preserving competition and at the same time protecting consumers. The courts have declared some invalid. The Australian Industries Preservation Act 1906 (Cth) was declared invalid in *Huddart Parker & Co Pty Ltd v Moorehead*[1]. The Trade Practices Act 1965 (Cth) was declared invalid in *Strickland v Rocla Concrete Pipes & Co*[2].

1   (1909) 8 CLR 330.
2   (1971) 124 CLR 468.

11.17 The current federal law in this area is the Trade Practices Act 1974. One of the key provisions, s 52 provides, 'a corporation shall not, in trade or commerce, engage in conduct that is misleading or deceptive or likely to mislead or deceive'. The term 'misleading or deceptive' is not defined in the Act. However, courts' decisions seem to define this expression as, 'to lead astray in action or conduct, to cause to err, to make believe what is false'[1].

1   For example, *McWilliams Wines Pty Ltd v McDonald's System of Australia Pty Ltd* [1980] ATPR 40–188.

11.18 It is not necessary under s 52 that there should have been an intention to mislead or deceive or that any person should in fact have suffered loss or damage as a result of the conduct or should even in fact have been misled or deceived. All that is necessary is that conduct of the relevant quality ('misleading or deceptive') should have been engaged in. But in determining whether the test is satisfied it is necessary to ask 'misleading or deceptive of whom?' And it has been suggested that the answer is 'customers'[1]. The courts' decisions seem to suggest that what must be considered is the effect on those likely to be affected by the conduct, for example, those to whom advertising is addressed.

1 See S J McMillan, 'Supply of Goods and Services', in R B Vermeesch and Justice K E Lindgren, *Business Law of Australia* (9th edn, 1998) p 971.

11.19 In the specific context of electronic commerce and Internet banking, perhaps the position in the US may be relevant and is worth noting. Section 45(a)(1) of the Federal Trade Commission Act forbids 'unfair or deceptive acts or practices in or affecting commerce'. In GeoCities[1], the FTC charged GeoCities with failing to observe its privacy promise. GeoCities offered free website hosting services, with sites organised thematically into virtual communities. GeoCities – which was subsequently acquired by Yahoo!, and continued operating under the name of Yahoo!GeoCities – provided its members (which it dubbed 'homesteaders') with space on its web server, accessed through a URL of the form 'www.geocities.com/member_name/...' . To become a member, a user had to provide GeoCities with certain types of personal information, including first name, zip code, e-mail address, gender, and date of birth. In its privacy notice, GeoCities stated: 'We will not share this information with anyone without your permission'.

1 FTC Docket No C-3850 (5 February 1999).

11.20 The complaint alleged that, contrary to this privacy statement, GeoCities 'sold, rented, or otherwise marketed or disclosed the information, including information collected from children, to third parties who have used the information for purposes other than those for which members have given permission'. The complaint also alleged that GeoCities represented that it collected certain identifying information from children, when in fact the information was collected by undisclosed third parties operating through GeoCities' website. The complaint alleged that these were deceptive misrepresentations, in violation of the FTC Act. GeoCities consented to entry of an order that prohibited future misrepresentations, required it to post a website privacy policy containing specified categories of information, and required it to obtain 'express parental consent' before collecting personal identifying information from children.

11.21 One important lesson from this case is that the existing law can be invoked if a website makes representations in its privacy policy concerning its handling of site visitors' personal information, but fails to honour its promises. Perhaps, the time would come for the Australian courts to decide whether the provisions of the Australian Trade Practices Act and the FSRA could successfully be used in a case such as this.

The Best Practice Model 2000

11.22 The Australian government has developed some guidance for the industry and consumers in ensuring that consumers are adequately protected and have confidence in making online transactions. In 2000, the treasury published a document called *Building Consumer Sovereignty in Electronic Commerce – A Best Practice Model for Business* (the Best Practice Model), which is a voluntary code of practice for B2C electronic commerce.

11.23 The Best Practice Model focuses on areas where the online environment's special characteristics necessitate business practices different to those in the offline world. These include: the distance between the business and the consumers; the speed at which transactions can be completed online; the need for authentication; and information collection practices. The objective is to guide businesses on matters concerning fair business practices; advertising and marketing; disclosure of a business's identity and location; disclosure of a contract's terms and conditions; the implementation of mechanisms for concluding contracts; the establishment of fair and effective procedures for handling complaints and resolving disputes; adopting privacy principles; using and disclosing information about payment, security and authentication mechanisms; and the processes and policies necessary to administer a code based on the Best Practice Model.

11.24 Clause 18 of the Best Practice Model states, 'businesses should adopt fair business practices when engaging in B2C electronic commerce'. The fair practices in accordance with the legislation in Australia, among others, require businesses: not to engage in conduct that is misleading or deceptive or is likely to mislead or deceive; not to make false or misleading representations about the goods or services they supply; not to engage in unconscionable conduct; and to ensure that services supplied will be rendered with due care and skill.

11.25 On advertising and marketing, businesses should make sure advertising is clearly identifiable and can be distinguished from other content. Businesses should also make sure their business is identifiable from advertising, and be able to back up their advertising or marketing claims. Businesses should not send commercial e-mail except to people with whom they have an existing relationship or to people who have already said they want to receive commercial e-mail. Businesses should have simple procedures so that consumers can let them know when they do not want to receive commercial e-mail.

11.26 The Best Practice Model gives a significant emphasis to information to be provided to customers before they enter into a contract. Clause 29 provides that businesses engaged in e-commerce should provide enough information about the terms and conditions and costs of a transaction to enable customers to make informed decisions. This information should be clear, accurate and easily accessible. It should be provided in a way that gives consumers an adequate opportunity for review before entering into the transaction and to retain a record of the transaction. Information about terms and conditions should be clearly identified and distinguished from advertising material. More importantly, businesses should give consumers a clear and complete text of the transaction's terms and conditions. This information should be clear enough so that the consumer can access and retain a record of that information, for example, by printing or electronic record.

11.27   Regarding privacy, the Best Practice Model requires the businesses to respect consumers' privacy when dealing with personal information. As a minimum they must comply with the benchmark standards for handling personal information set out in the Privacy Commissioner's *National Principles for the Fair Handling of Personal Information*. Businesses should also provide consumers with clear and easily accessible information online about the way they handle personal information.

11.28   Businesses should make sure consumers have access to information about the security and authentication mechanisms the business uses, in clear, simple language that helps consumers assess the risk in relying on those systems. Businesses should provide security appropriate for identification and authentication mechanisms to be used by consumers. There is an obligation to update the security and authentication mechanisms to make sure the security offered is maintained, at an appropriate level. Also, there is a prohibition on trying to contract out the responsibilities for losses arising from the misuse or failure of authentication mechanisms. The Best Practice Model encourages the establishment of the internal complaint handling procedures as well as an external dispute resolution mechanism.

The New Code of Banking Practice

11.29   The Australian Bankers' Association (ABA) wrote and published the Code of Banking Practice (the Code) in November 1993. The Code became fully operational on 1 November 1996. Membership of the Code is voluntary but the Code is binding once adopted. Each bank currently operating in Australia with significant retail operations has formally adopted the Code. On 12 May 2000, the ABA appointed an external consultant to conduct a review of the Code.

11.30   Following an initial round of consultations and submissions, an issue paper was released in March 2001. It came to the conclusion that: the Code had not been seriously supported by the banking industry; there had been no sense of the banking industry wanting to enhance the Code or use it as a means of dealing with new issues; the Code had not succeeded in improving bank–customer relationships; and the Code had been largely irrelevant to both banks and customers[1]. After further consultations and follow-up submissions, a final report was issued in October 2001. The Final Report made 61 recommendations for improving the protection available to consumers under the Code and broadening its coverage. Significant recommendations included:

- Committing Code Members to the overriding principle of fairness in their dealings with the customers.

- Removing provisions that overlapped with the reform made by the Financial Services Reform Act 2001 or the Uniform Consumer Credit Code.

- Improving internal complaints handling; extension of the Code to small business customers.

- Measures designed to assist older people, those on lower incomes and those with a disability.

- Establishing a Code compliance body with the power to publicly name Code Members who, after being warned, do not comply with the Code.

1   See Bruce Whittaker, Stephen Cavanagh and Jackson Lam, 'The New Australian Code of Banking Practice', (2003) JIBLR 231, 233.

11.31   The new Code of Banking Practice was launched by the ABA in August 2002 and will come into effect in August 2003. As of 13 August 2003, four banks (Adelaide Bank Limited, BankSA – a division of St. George Bank Limited, Commonwealth Bank of Australia and St. George Bank Limited) have subscribed to this new Code. David Bell, the Chief Executive of the ABA commented[1]:

'This Code meets and beats similar codes in other countries such as the United Kingdom, Canada, New Zealand and Hong Kong. The ABA's Code of Banking Practice stands out both in scope and the specific customer benefits it provides ... The revised Code is a major step forward by Australian banks in listening to community concerns and delivering change. This Code reinforces and complements Australia's world class banking system and bank customers have a Code that will bring a new dimension to their freedom of choice in banking services.'

1   ABA Media Release (1 August 2003).

11.32   Impressively, the Code was drafted in simple language and in a user-friendly manner. The provision on the application of the Code provides: 'This Code is a voluntary code of conduct which sets standards of good banking practice for us to follow when dealing with persons who are, or who may become, our individual and small business customers and their guarantors'. The word 'us' is defined as the banks that an individual or small business deals with who have adopted the Code. A small business means a business employing less than 100 full-time (or equivalent) employees if the business is or includes the manufacturer of goods, or in any other case, less than 20 full-time (or equivalent) employees. The Code applies to individual as well as small business customers. By the definition of the words 'banking service', in terms of products, the Code applies to financial services provided by a Code Member whether they are supplied to a customer directly or through an intermediary. It also applies to the distribution or supply of a financial service or product of a third party by the Code Member. But this does not apply to that product or service itself. In this respect, the scope of the New Code is much broader than the old one.

11.33 The Code outlines the banks' key commitments and general obligations to customers, which states that banks will:

- continuously work towards improving the standards of practice and service in the banking industry;

- promote better informed decisions about their banking services;

- provide general information about the rights and obligations that arise out of the banker and customer relationship in relation to banking services;

- provide information to customers in plain language;

- monitor external developments relating to banking codes of practice, legislative changes and related issues.

11.34 It is interesting to note that the Code contains a commitment by the banks to act in fairness. It provides, 'we will act fairly and reasonably towards you in a consistent and ethical manner. In doing so we will consider your conduct, our conduct and the contract between us'. The wording of this provision falls short of the recommendations made in the issues paper, which recommended that Code Members should be required to consider whether the circumstances of the case might justify not applying the strict terms of the contract[1]. By giving weight to the contract between the Code Member and the customer in assessing fairness, it is possible that this formulation may result in conduct only being regarded as unfair or unreasonable if the conduct is not expressly authorised by the contract, but not otherwise. Ultimately, Code Members must ensure that they act in an ethical and consistent manner towards their customers but it appears that there is nothing in the New Code to preclude them from enforcing the law and their contract rigidly[2].

1   ABA Media Release (1 August 2003).
2   *Ibid.*

11.35 Other commitments and general obligations of the banks include to have regard to their prudential obligation in meeting the commitments, compliance with all the relevant laws relating to banking services, compliance with the Code, commitment concerning review of the Code, to enhance the access of the elderly and disabled customers to transaction services, commitment to train staff to enable them to discharge their functions competently and efficiently and to have adequate knowledge of the provisions of the Code, to promote the Code and make it available to customers.

11.36 The New Code lists out the matters to be included in the terms and conditions of the banking service. These include the standard fees and charges which apply, notification of changes to the terms and conditions, how the interest is calculated, etc. In terms of the form, the terms and conditions will be distinguishable from marketing or promotional materials, be in English and any other language if appropriate, and be consistent with the Code, etc.

11.37 The Code Member will expeditiously provide the customers, or any person, upon request, with the terms and conditions of any ongoing banking service that they offer. The terms and conditions will be provided at the time of or before the contract for an ongoing banking service is made. The exception is where it is impractical for the banks to do so, in which case the terms and conditions will be provided as soon as practicable afterwards. There are contractual consequences for failing to provide terms and conditions before the service is used. The issue is whether sufficient notice has been given of the terms and conditions, and sufficient opportunity given to reject them and withdraw them.

11.38 In the context of Internet banking, as the Australian Banking Industry Ombudsman (ABIO) stated:

> 'as a technical solution to the legal problem of giving adequate and effective notice of terms and conditions, a website usually requires the user to view and accept terms and conditions before proceeding, to ensure that the terms and conditions become part of the contract'[1].

The ABIO argues that while this is an important step, and one that is in a consumer's interest, it is difficult to make this palatable to users. It can also underline to them their inability to do anything other than accept the terms and conditions or not to receive the service – terms and conditions should always be read carefully by customers but in human terms it is easier to put to one side a printed booklet of terms and conditions than it is to ignore on-screen text that refuses to leave the screen until it is accepted[2].

1   ABIO Special Bulletin on Electronic Commerce: Emerging Issues in Electronic Banking Disputes, Bulletin No 35, p 10.
2   *Ibid.*

11.39 The New Code will establish a Code Compliance Monitoring Committee (CCMC) to monitor the level of compliance by Code Members and to investigate allegations of breach of the Code. Under the Code, the CCMC may receive complaints about breaches of the New Code from 'any person'. This would include complaints not only from customers but also from consumer organisations and state regulatory agencies. More importantly, under clause 34, the CCMC is empowered to publicly name Code Members in connection with a breach of the Code. It must be shown that Code Members have: (i) been guilty of *serious* or *systematic* non-compliance; (ii) ignored the CCMC's request to remedy a breach or failed to do so within a reasonable time; (iii) breached an undertaking given by the CCMC; or (iv) not taken steps to prevent a breach reoccurring after having been warned that Code Members might be named. Several questions may arise here; firstly, how serious is serious? Secondly, what would amount to systematic non-compliance? Specifically, how many breaches can be considered as systematic non-compliance? Also, it is unclear whether the provisions are to be read disjunctively or conjunctively. The word 'or' in between paragraphs (iii) and (iv) seems to suggest that (i), (ii) and (iii) should be read together but separately from (iv).

The new EFT Code: its impetus and emergence

11.40   On 5 April 2001, the ASIC released the new Electronic Funds Transfer Code of Conduct. This new Code aims to create a world-best practice consumer protection regime in a technology-neutral form for users of electronic banking and payment products. The new Code becomes operative on 1 April 2002 but may be adopted by banks before that date. The decision to adopt the Code is voluntary but once adopted the Code is contractually binding on banks and financial institutions. On the day of its release, Ms Jillian Segal, Deputy Chair of the ASIC, said[1]:

> 'ASIC believes that this new Code is the first anywhere in the world to give such comprehensive protection to users of electronic banking. The new Code protects Australian consumers, regardless of how they do their banking.'

1   See ASIC's Media and Information Releases (5 April 2001) available at www.fido.asic.gov.au.

11.41   The new Code will apply to virtually all types of electronic funds transfer performed by consumers, other than those requiring the user's manual signature to authenticate the user's authority to perform the transaction[1]. Ms Jillian Segal stated that consumers have new and important protections under the revised code for their electronic banking, especially for Internet and telephone banking. The Code sets out fair rules for who is liable for what if there is an authorised transaction on an account[2].

1   The definition of 'access method' in clause 1.5 of Part A limits the application of the Code.
2   Media and Information releases on 20 August 2001.

11.42   According to a local security expert, Leif Gamertsfelder, the new Code that aims to minimise the risks involved in electronic banking is a one of its kind in the world and a big win for the consumer. The Code, he asserts, brings two main benefits to Australian consumers. First, it gives the consumer an extremely clear understanding of when they are liable for unauthorised transactions. Second, which he describes as a 'huge bonus for consumers', is that in the event of a dispute the Code puts the evidentiary onus on the institution. He continued, stating[1]:

> 'There's no precedent for this in Australia or elsewhere. It's not implicit, it's making everything very explicit for the consumer to say this is a safe zone. The new EFT Code should be the catalyst for the rapid uptake of electronic banking in this country because from a realistic perspective the risks have been taken out of the online banking equation.'

1   See ZDNet Australia, 'Code Sets Aust E-Banking Apart From Rest of the World' (27 March 2002) available at http://www.zdnet.com.au/newstech/ebusiness/story/0,2000048590,20264285,00.htm.

11.43   The old Code deals with specific electronic means of remotely accessing an account at a financial institution for transferring funds. Clause 1.1 of the Code limits its application to transactions intended to be initiated by an individual through an electronic terminal by the combined use of an EFT card and a personal identification number (PIN). Because of this technological limitation, the old Code, in practice applies only to using EFT cards with PINs at ATM and EFTPOS terminals. It does not cover most (and perhaps all) current remote electronic access to accounts via telephone, computers (including Internet access) and other electronic equipment. This is because these services do not use a card and PIN for access but usually require one or more identifiers or codes without a card[1].

1 ASIC, Discussion Paper on an Expanded EFT Code of Conduct, July 1999, p 14.

11.44 It is also unclear whether telephones, personal computers and televisions are 'electronic terminals' within the meaning of the old Code. Nor does the Code cover; first, using a stored value card to access an account unless the card requires a PIN for access, second, using a stored value card to make a payment by transferring stored value where no PIN is required or where no transfer of funds to or from a financial institution account is involved, and third, deposits, withdrawals and payments utilising digital representations of value such as digital cash and digital cheques[1].

1 ASIC, Discussion Paper on an Expanded EFT Code of Conduct, July 1999, p 14.

11.45 These limitations led the Treasury/the Australian Competition and Consumer Commission (ACCC) taskforce on the operation of the EFT Code of Conduct, which reported in March 1998, to recommend that a working party be established to consider the real and potential impact of telephone and computer banking and the potential problems arising from those technologies. It was recommended that the Working Group propose either appropriate changes to the old EFT Code to accommodate those technologies or develop a separate mechanism for apportioning liability and resolving disputes arising out of those technologies[1].

1 ASIC, Discussion Paper on an Expanded EFT Code of Conduct, July 1999, p 14.

11.46 The Government accepted the recommendation and asked the ASIC to convene the Working Group. The ASIC did this in April 1999. At its first meeting, the Working Group made several decisions on the scope of its project. In particular it was decided that as stakeholders are familiar with the old EFT Code and compliance levels are high it would expand the old EFT rather than develop a new mechanism. It was also decided that any expanded code should be technology neutral in its drafting and seek to cover all forms of electronic funds transfers be they, for example, via telephone or computer banking or involving stored value products. Finally, it was agreed that the working group would not seek to reopen the general policy behind the old EFT Code as the ACCC and the Treasury had only just reviewed this. Rather, the project, with two exceptions, would be confined to considering the amendments necessary to expand the coverage of the Code to deal with new electronic funds transfer technologies[1].

1 ASIC, Second Draft Expanded EFT Code of Conduct and Commentary (January 2000) p 14.

The relevant and important provisions of the new Code

Scope and coverage

11.47 The ASIC noted when the Code was launched, that:

'the revised EFT Code covers all forms of electronic fund transfers, including ATM and EFTPOS transactions, telephone and Internet banking, all credit card transactions (other than those intended to be authenticated by a manual signature), and stored value products such as smart cards, pre-paid telephone cards and digital cash'[1].

1   Extract from ASIC Media Release dated 5 April 2001.

11.48   Part A of the Code applies to 'EFT transactions' and governs the rights and obligations of both users and account institutions. The Code adopted a wide definition of electronic fund transactions. Clause 1.1(a) of the Code defines EFT transactions as funds transfers initiated by giving an instruction, through electronic equipment and using an access method, to an account institution (directly or indirectly) to debit or credit an EFT account maintained by the account institution. And clause 1.2 defines a 'fund transfer' as the transfer of value to or from an account or between accounts. The phrase 'to or from an account' has been inserted to make it clear that withdrawals and deposits from or to an account are covered (whether in the form of currency, electronic stored value, or prepaid physical payment instrument such as a bank cheque or traveller's cheque). A credit card transaction initiated through electronic equipment using only information such as the card number, name and expiry date is a funds transfer covered by the Code[1].

1   ASIC, Discussion Paper on an Expanded EFT Code of Conduct, July 1999, p 22.

11.49   'Electronic equipment' is defined to include an electronic terminal, computer, television and telephone. 'Access method', in turn, is defined in clause 1.5 as a method authorised by an account institution for use by a user and accepted by the account institution as authority for it to act on an instruction given through electronic equipment to debit or credit an EFT account and comprises the use of one or more components, including (but not limited to) devices, identifiers, codes or a combination of these; and does not include a method requiring the user's manual signature where the comparison of the appearance of that manual signature with a written specimen signature is the principal intended means of authenticating a user's authority to give the instruction (whether or not that means is used in a particular transaction).

11.50   An 'account institution' is defined in clause 1.4 as an institution which subscribes to the Code and maintains EFT accounts for account holders. 'EFT account' is defined to mean an account maintained by an account institution which belongs to an identifiable account holder who is a customer of the account institution and where the account institution permits a user to initiate a fund transfer from or to the account using an access method through electronic equipment.

11.51   Clause 1.1 has been clarified so that instead of applying to 'transaction', which was an undefined term under the old EFT Code, it now applies to 'fund transfers' which is clearly defined in clause 1.2. It has been expanded to cover funds transfers rather than being limited to transactions through an electronic terminal by the use of a card and PIN. The technology neutrality and broader coverage of the new Code are also achieved through the definitions of the words of 'electronic equipment' replacing 'electronic terminal', 'access method' replacing 'EFT card' and 'PIN' and 'Code' replacing 'personal identification number' or 'PIN'. The effect of these changes, in the words of ASIC, is to extend the coverage of the Code to all funds transfers made through a wide variety of electronic equipment using a wide variety of access methods approved by an account institution.

11.52 Simply, EFT transactions under the new Australian Code are fund transfers initiated by giving an instruction through electronic equipment and using an access method. This means that the Code applies to virtually all types of electronic funds transfers performed by consumers, other than those requiring the user's manual signature to authenticate the user's authority to perform the transaction. As Mark Sneddon stated, the new Code has a much broader scope as it covers[1]:

- all means of remote access to accounts, for example, telephone, Internet, kiosk, television;

- all types of access methods, for example, magnetic strip card, chip card, customer ID number, password, PIN, digital signatures and biometric identifiers;

- credit card and charge card payments by telephone and over the Internet;

- transactions involving the use of stored value facilities, including stored value on chip cards and digital coins used for Internet payments.

1 Mark Sneddon, 'Electronic Funds Transfer – The New Code of Conduct' The Magazine of the Melbourne PC User Group.

Liability for unauthorised transactions

11.53 The Code sets out detailed rules regarding allocation of liability in cases of losses due to unauthorised transactions. It was admitted that this is one of the contentious areas in remote electronic account access. According to the Working Party a genuine unauthorised transaction profits a third party and leaves a loss to be distributed between two relatively innocent parties – the account institution and the user. There are two guiding principles which underlie the Code's allocation of liability. First, liability should be allocated to the party or parties that can reduce the incidence of losses at the lowest cost. Second, liability allocation rules should be simple, clear and decisive so as to minimise the costs of administering them. The view adopted is that a regime for allocating losses from unauthorised EFT transactions should share those losses between the user and the account institution, according to the circumstances of the loss. Clause 5.2 of the Code provides that the account holder will not be liable for losses that:

- are caused by the fraudulent or negligent conduct of the employees or agents of the account institution;

- relate to forged, faulty, expired or cancelled access methods;

- occur before the device or code has been received by the user, where a code or device is required for the user to use the access method; or

- are caused by the same transaction being incorrectly debited more than once to the same account.

11.54   In any dispute about receipt of a device or code, it is to be presumed that the user did not receive the item, unless the account institution can prove otherwise. The account institutions can establish that a user received a device or code by obtaining an acknowledgement of receipt from the user. If a device or code was sent by mail or e-mail, the account institution is not to rely only on proof of delivery to the user's correct address as proof that the user received the device or code. Also, account institutions will not have any terms or conditions that deem a device or code sent to the user's correct address to have been received by the user.

11.55   Under clause 5.3, the account holder will also not be liable in respect of any losses resulting from unauthorised transactions that occur after the account institution has been notified that any device forming part of the access method has been misused, lost or stolen or that the security of any code forming part of the access method has been breached. For this purpose, it is an obligation of the account institution to provide an effective and convenient means by which users can notify a lost or stolen device or unauthorised use of a device or breach of security of a code. Under clause 5.4, an account holder has no liability for losses resulting from unauthorised transactions where it is clear that the user has not contributed to such losses.

11.56   Clauses 5.5 and 5.6 set out the circumstances in which an account holder will be liable for losses resulting from unauthorised transactions:

- Where the account institution can prove on the balance of probability that the user's fraud or the breaching of certain security requirements by the user in relation to the user's secret codes contributed to the losses.

- The account institution can prove on the balance of probability that the user contributed to the losses by unreasonably delaying notification of the misuse, loss or theft of a device or breach of the security of secret codes.

- Where a secret code was required to perform the transaction and neither of the first two circumstances applies, the account holder is liable for no more than $150 of the losses.

11.57   In other words, if a code is needed to perform a transaction, a no-fault regime will apply. The account holder will be liable for the lower of $150, the balance of the accounts accessed or the actual loss at the time of notification. The account holder will only be liable for a greater amount where the account institution can prove on the balance of probability either of the first two circumstances. The account holder is liable for the *actual losses* that occur before the account institution is notified in cases that fall under the first situation. In situations which fall under the second bullet point, the account holder is liable for actual losses that occur between when the users became aware (or should reasonably have become aware of lost or stolen device) and when the account institution was actually notified.

11.58 The final part of clause 5.5(a) clarifies that where an access method includes more than one code; and the account institution proves that the user contravened the requirements of clause 5.6 by voluntarily disclosing or by keeping a record of one or more codes but not all the codes in the access method; the account holder is only liable if the account institution also proves on the balance of probabilities that the user's contravention of clause 5.6 was the dominant contributing cause of the losses. The endnote 16 further clarifies that 'the dominant contributing cause of the losses' is the cause that is more than 50% responsible for the losses when assessed together with all contributing causes.

11.59 What would amount to breaching of security requirements? First, by voluntarily disclosing one or more of the secret codes to anyone, including a family member or friend. Second, by indicating one or more of the secret codes on an access device or keeping a record of one or more of the secret codes (without making a reasonable attempt to protect the security of the code records) such that they are liable to loss or theft simultaneously. Third, by self-selecting a secret code which represents the user's birth date or a recognisable part of the user's name after having been warned by the account institution not to select such a code. Fourth, by acting with extreme carelessness in failing to protect the security of all the secret codes. Under clause 5.6 of the Code, a user contravenes the security requirements if his/her action or inaction falls under any of these circumstances. 'Extreme carelessness' means a degree of carelessness with the security of the codes, which greatly exceeds what would normally be considered careless behaviour. For example, storing the user's username and password for Internet banking in a diary or personal organiser or computer (not locked with a PIN) under the heading 'Internet banking codes'[1].

1   See the endnotes of the EFT Code.

Liability in cases of systems failure

11.60 Clause 6.1 of the Code provides that account institutions will be responsible to their users for loss caused by the failure of an institution system or institution equipment to complete a transaction accepted by an institution system or institution equipment in accordance with the user's instructions.

11.61 The terms 'institution equipment' and 'institution system' are used in an attempt to fairly apportion responsibility. The terms are defined in clause 1.4 to cover electronic equipment, electronic systems, communications systems or software controlled or provided by or on behalf of an account institution to facilitate EFT transactions. The thinking and rationale behind this is that account institutions should only be responsible for malfunction of systems or equipment over which they have some direct or indirect control, because in Internet banking and other EFT, the system and/or equipment may be controlled or provided by several parties; the banks, the customer or the third parties such as the Internet providers.

11.62   Interestingly and importantly, the new Code in clause 8.2 provides that an account institution cannot avoid its obligation to its users by reason only of the fact that they are party to a shared EFT system and that another party to the system has actually caused the failure. This means that account institutions need to ensure that their agreements with other parties in relation to shared EFT systems enable them to recover any loss they incur as a result of any act or omission of any such party that results in the account institution failing to meet the obligations it owes to its users[1].

1   Alan Peckham and Juan-Jose Zentner, 'The New EFT Code of Conduct' (2001) JIBL 2443.

11.63   The new Code also prohibits the account institutions from denying the right of the user to make claims due to systems failure. Clause 6.2 states that the account institution is not to deny, implicitly or explicitly, a right to the user to make claims for consequential damage which may arise as a result of a malfunction of institution systems or institution equipment, however caused. The only exception is that where the user should have been aware that the system or equipment was unavailable for use or malfunctioning. In this situation, the account institution's responsibilities may be limited to the correction of any errors in the account, and the refund of any charges or fees imposed on the account holder as a result.

Variation of the terms and conditions of use

11.64   The new Code requires the account institutions to provide written notice to users if they wish to vary their terms and conditions of use. Clause 3.1 provides that account institutions wishing to vary or modify the EFT terms and conditions to impose or increase charges relating solely to the use of an access method, or the issue of an additional or replacement access method; increase an account holder's liability for losses relating to EFT transactions; or impose, remove or adjust a daily transaction limit or other periodic transaction limit applying to the use of an access method, an account or electronic equipment; will provide written notification to the account holder, and allow a period of notice of at least 20 days before the changes take effect.

11.65   For other changes, the account institutions are required to give notice at the following times: in time to comply with any applicable legislative requirements for a particular period of notice in advance of the date the change takes effect; or where there is no such legislative requirement, in advance of the date the change takes effect. The account institutions will have to provide notice of other changes in the manner required by applicable legislation, or if there are no such requirements, in a manner that is likely to come to the attention of as many account holders as possible. Advance notice need not be given when changes are necessitated by an immediate need to restore or maintain the security of the system or individual accounts.

Privacy and data protection

11.66 Clause 21.1 of the Code provides 'from 21 December 2001 Code subscribers will comply with the National Privacy Principles in the Privacy Act 1988 (Cth) or with Codes to which the Code subscriber has also subscribed which are approved and operative under that legislation'. This means that account institutions will comply with the ten National Privacy Principles (NPPs). Clause 21.2 provides some guidelines to assist in interpreting the NPPs and applying them to EFT transactions:

- Where surveillance devices (including visual, sound or data recording) may be used by or on behalf of an account institution to monitor EFT transactions, account institutions should notify users before the commencement of each transaction or of each session of transactions, that the transaction may be recorded by surveillance devices and the nature of the surveillance.

- Account institutions shall take reasonable steps to ensure that no institution equipment or institution system is capable of providing any information concerning an account unless the correct access method for that account has been used.

- Transaction receipts should not disclose information which would reveal the full account number, name or address of the account holder.

- Clear privacy policies should be made available at or through electronic address of the account institutions. The privacy policy should be provided to a user by electronic communication if the user so requests. This means the banks must provide their privacy policy on their websites.

In deciding whether a Code subscriber has complied with the relevant principles, the terms of the principles and not the guidelines are determinative.

Implementation of the EFT Code

11.67 The new EFT Code does not apply to that part of a funds transfer which is the debiting of and transfer of value from; or that part of a funds transfer which is the receipt of value and the crediting of that value to; an account that is designed primarily for use by a business and established primarily for business purposes. The new Code will therefore have a limited application with respect to electronic funds transfers from or to a business account[1]. The implementation of Part A of the Code:

- requires that account institutions prepare and provide users with clear and unambiguous terms and conditions applicable to EFT transactions which reflect the requirements of the Code;

- imposes notification obligations on account institutions in relation to changes to the terms and conditions;

- requires that transaction receipts be issued setting out a range of information;

- requires that statements of account be issued at least every six months containing certain required information and warnings;

- apportions liability for unauthorised transactions and for system failure;

- requires account institutions to ensure that their EFT transaction system generate sufficient records to enable transactions to be traced and checked and to enable errors to be identified and corrected; and

- requires the account institutions to establish internal complaint investigation and resolution procedures that comply with Australian Standard AS426–1995.

1   Alan Peckham and Juan-Jose Zentner, 'The New EFT Code of Conduct' (2001) JIBL 2443.

11.68   As a result, account institutions need to make a number of necessary changes to their practices and documentation to implement Part A of the new Code. The changes include; preparing new terms and conditions, reviewing and updating notification procedures, updating computer systems, providing an effective means to enable users to notify the lost or stolen device or unauthorised transaction, reviewing and amending internal dispute resolution procedure, reviewing and updating statements of account and providing account holders with a summary of access method security guidelines, etc. In short, almost the whole systems, documentation and practice need to be revamped in accordance with the requirement of the new Code. It is interesting to examine whether the banks in Australia observe this new rule of the game.

The new EFT Code in action

Liability for unauthorised transactions and systems failure

11.69   The official start up date for the Code was 1 April 2002. The ASIC, however, encouraged the institutions to adopt it as soon as it was released. As of 3 April 2002, according to the ASIC, 205 institutions have signed up to the Code. Ms Jillian Segal said, 'While the code is voluntary, we are expecting all institutions that offer electronic funds transfers to sign up to it as was the case with the old code'. Impressively, all the Australian banks offering Internet banking services in this study have opted to subscribe to the Code and incorporated its rules into their terms and conditions.

11.70   The Internet banking service of the Commonwealth Bank of Australia (CBA), NetBank, provides a detailed explanation of the electronic banking conditions of use. It begins with a statement, 'we warrant that we will comply with the

EFT Code'. Uniquely, part of the conditions of use was drafted and presented in a less formal and customer-friendly manner. It is in the form of questions and answers. Adhering to the EFT Code, the provision on apportionment of liability for unauthorised transactions is a very comprehensive one.

11.71   It is interesting to note that the conditions of use contain a definition of 'an unauthorised transaction'. Clause 11.1 defines an unauthorised transaction as one which is not authorised by the account holder. A transaction carried out by the account holder or with the account holder's consent is not an unauthorised transaction. It also states, 'we are entitled to treat any transaction carried out by any other user as authorised by you unless, prior to the transaction, you have told us to cancel that user's access method and the device is destroyed'. This means that the presumption applies here that any transaction carried out by another user is a transaction authorised by the account holder. The burden is on the account holder to rebut this presumption by asking the bank to cancel the user's access method before the transaction takes place, and the device is destroyed.

11.72   Clause 11.2 lists out the circumstances where the account holder will not be liable for unauthorised transactions. The account holder will not be liable for:

- any loss arising out of an unauthorised transaction which a user did not contribute to;

- any loss arising after the user has notified the institution of the misused, lost or stolen access method;

- any loss caused by the fraudulent or negligent conduct of the bank's employees or agent;

- any loss as a result of any component of an access method being forged, faulty, expired or cancelled;

- any loss that arose prior to the user receiving the access method or code; and

- any loss caused by the same transaction being incorrectly debited more than once to the user account.

11.73   Clause 11.3 provides the detailed situations in which the user will be liable for unauthorised transactions. In all the circumstances the burden is on the bank to prove on the standard of balance of probability that the account holder contributed to the loss. First, the transaction and the loss occurs before the bank was notified of the misused, lost or stolen access method or that the security of the codes has been breached which arose via fraud on the part of the user – or via any user voluntarily disclosing their code – or where the access method also utilises a device and the user indicates one or more of the codes on the outside of the device, or the user keeps a record of one or more of the codes without making any reasonable attempt to protect the security of the codes, or the user keeps a record of one or more of the codes in a manner that is liable to loss or theft simultaneously with the device.

11.74   Second, where the user keeps a record of *all* of the codes without making any attempt to protect the security of the codes, they are liable to loss or theft simultaneously with the device. Third, where the bank has specifically instructed the user not to select a code that represents the user's date of birth, or a recognisable part of his/her name, the bank has brought to the user's attention the consequences of selecting such a code and yet the user has still selected such a code. Fourth, the user acts with extreme carelessness in failing to protect the security of all their codes. Fifth, the loss is a result of the unreasonable delay on the part of the user to notify the bank of the misuse, loss or theft of a device forming part of an access method or unreasonable delay in notifying the bank that the security of all the codes forming part of the access method has been breached.

11.75   The extent of the user's liability is clearly set out in clause 11.4. The user will be liable for the actual loss in any of the first to fifth circumstances which occur before the bank was notified of the misused, lost or stolen device forming part of the access code or of the security breach. Interestingly, for a situation where the loss occurs due to the user voluntarily disclosing his/her code, this clause provides that the user will not be liable unless such breach is the dominant cause of the loss. This is a positive attitude and fair practice from the customers' point of view. Where none of the above circumstances apply, the user will be liable for the least of $150 or the balance of those accounts or the actual loss at the time the bank was notified of the misuse, loss or stolen device or security breach (excluding the portion of the losses incurred on any day which exceed any applicable daily transaction or other periodic transaction limits).

11.76   Other positive features of the NetBank's conditions of use are found in clauses 11.5 and 11.6. In the former, where the bank expressly authorise any conduct on the part of a user or where the bank expressly or impliedly promote, endorse or authorise an account access service, no conduct, disclosure, recording or storage of an access will breach any of the requirements of all of the circumstances of the first to fourth limbs mentioned above. This does not apply in cases involving fraud on the part of a user. Of course, the bank may impose conditions on any authorisation. In the latter, in certain circumstances, the bank or an external dispute resolution body may decide to reduce the users' liability. The circumstance is when the user alleges that a transaction is unauthorised and the bank has not placed a reasonable daily or periodic limit. In deciding to reduce the users' liability, the following factors will be taken into account: first, whether the security and reliability of the means used by the bank to verify the relevant transaction authorised by the user adequately protected the user from losses in the absence of reasonable daily or other periodic transaction limits protection. Second, if it relates to a funds transfer that involved drawing on a line of credit accessible by the access method, whether at the time of making the line of credit accessible by the access method, the bank had taken reasonable steps to warn the user of the risk of the access method being used to make unauthorised transactions on that line of credit.

11.77   The NetBank conditions of use on systems failure is in the form of a question, what happens if the electronic equipment does not work properly? In clause 7, the bank states:

> 'We undertake to make all reasonable efforts to ensure that the electronic equipment operates during hours they are usually open but we are not liable to you if the electronic equipment does not accept instructions from you or any other user or if your or any other user's access method does not activate the electronic equipment. If the electronic equipment accepts instructions from you or any other user, we are liable to you for loss caused if the transaction is not completed in accordance with those instructions.'

11.78   The ANZ Internet banking strictly observes the rules of the EFT Code. Clause 15.2 of its terms and conditions outlines the circumstances where the bank and account holder are liable. More impressively, it begins with the provisions on the bank's liability itself:

> 'ANZ will be liable (and the Account Holder will not be liable) for losses incurred or suffered by the Account Holder that:
> - are caused by the fraudulent or negligent conduct of ANZ's employees or agents or companies involved in networking arrangements or of merchants or their agents or employees;
> - relate to any forged, faulty, expired or cancelled component or part of the Internet Banking service (for example, a CRN, Password or Code);
> - arise from transactions that require use of any Password or Code forming part of your Internet Banking service that occur before you have received or selected the Password or Code (including a reissued or reselected Password or Code);
> - result from the same Internet Banking transaction being incorrectly debited a second or subsequent time to the same Linked Account;
> - result from an unauthorised transaction that occurs after you have notified ANZ that the security of your Password or Code has been breached; or
> - result from an unauthorised transaction if it is clear that you have not contributed to the losses.'

11.79   The terms and conditions provide that if it is not clear whether the account holder has contributed to the loss caused by an unauthorised transaction, the amount of the account holder's liability will be limited to the least of $150; the actual loss at the time ANZ is notified that the security of a Password or Code has become breached; or the balance of the linked account.

11.80   Paragraph (c) of clause 15.2 provides for the circumstances where an account holder is liable. It states if ANZ can prove on the balance of probability that an account holder contributed to the loss arising from the unauthorised transaction, an account holder is liable for the actual loss which occurs before ANZ is notified that the security of the password or code had been breached. The situations are:

- through an account holder's fraud;

- by voluntarily disclosing a password or code to anyone, including a family member or friend;

- by making no attempt to protect the security of the recording of a password or code;

- by using the birth date or an alphanumeric code as a password or code; or

- acting with extreme carelessness in failing to protect the security of a password or code.

11.81   It also provides that if ANZ can prove on the balance of probability that an account holder has contributed to a loss caused by an unauthorised transaction by unreasonably delaying notification that the security of the password or code has been breached after the account holder becomes aware of the loss, theft or breach, the account holder will be held liable to ANZ for actual losses incurred between:

- the time the account holder became aware of the event; and

- the time ANZ is actually notified of the relevant event.

11.82   Regarding the loss due to systems failure, the ANZ's terms and conditions provide that:

'ANZ is responsible to you for any loss caused by a failure of an EFT Institution's Equipment to complete a transaction accepted by an EFT Institution's Equipment in accordance with your instructions. However, if you were aware, or should have been aware, that the EFT Institution's Equipment was unavailable for use or malfunctioning, ANZ's responsibility will be limited to correcting errors in the account and refunding any charges or fees imposed as a result'.

11.83   The terms and conditions of the Westpac Banking Corporation begin with the following statement, 'from 1 April 2002 the Electronic Funds Transfer Code of Conduct will apply. This Code will give personal customers even more protection. (Westpac has adopted this Code from 1 April 2002)'. The account holder of Westpac will not be liable for losses resulting from unauthorised transactions that:

- are caused by fraudulent or negligent staff or agents of Westpac or companies involved in networking arrangements;

- happen before the user receives or selects their Access code;

- happen after Westpac has been notified that an access code has been misused, lost or stolen or security of access code has been breached;

- are the results of the same transaction being incorrectly debited more than once to the same account.

11.84   Interestingly, Westpac pledges that in the above situations, 'we will credit the amount of the unauthorised transaction to your account'. Clause 4.1 of the terms and conditions also states that the account holder will not be liable for losses resulting from unauthorised transactions where it is *clear* that the user has not contributed to the loss.

11.85   Under clause 4.2, the account holder will be liable for losses resulting from transactions which are carried out by the user, or by another person with the user's knowledge and consent. The account holder will be liable for actual losses resulting from unauthorised transactions caused by the user engaging in fraud; or voluntarily disclosing any of their access codes to anyone, including a family member or friend; or keeping a record of an access code without making a reasonable attempt to disguise it or to prevent unauthorised access to it in accordance with the Product Document for Internet Banking. The account holders will also be liable if they write their access Codes or a disguised record of their access codes on the electronic equipment or select an access code which represents their birth date, or being an alphabetical code which is a recognisable part of their name, after the bank has asked them not to select such an access code and told them of the consequences of doing so or act with extreme carelessness in failing to protect their access codes.

11.86   The account holder will also be liable for actual losses resulting from unauthorised transactions caused by the user unreasonably delaying notifying the banks of the misuse of their access codes, loss of their access codes, or their access codes become known to someone else. In these cases an Internet banking account holder's liability will only extend to losses which occur between the time when the user became aware (or should reasonably have become aware) of such misuse, loss or theft and when the bank was actually notified.

11.87   Clause 4.3 provides for the circumstances for the limited liability of the account holder. The account holder will only be liable for losses resulting from unauthorised transactions to a limited extent, in circumstances where an access code was required to perform the transaction and it is unclear whether the user contributed to the loss. The account holder's liability in such cases will be the least of $150.00 or the balance of the account(s), including any pre-arranged credit, or the actual loss at any time the bank is notified of the misuse, loss or the access codes becoming known to someone else (excluding that portion of the loss incurred on any one day which exceeds the applicable daily transaction limit).

11.88   There is no specific provision on allocation of liability in cases of systems failure or malfunction. Perhaps clause 4.5 is intended by the bank to cover these situations. Among other things, it provides that the bank will not be liable for: (1) any failure or delay of Internet banking to provide information or perform operations requested; (2) indirect or special loss or damage *howsoever* caused, including negligence; (3) consequential loss or damage that the account holder suffers as *a result of using Internet banking*; and (4) unavailability of Internet banking and events beyond the control of the bank such as but not limited to Internet connection. Except for the second part of limb (4), arguably, this is not in line with the Code. As discussed above, clause 6.1 of the Code requires the bank to take responsibility for loss caused by the failure of an institution system or institution equipment to complete a transaction accepted by an institution system or institution equipment in accordance with the user's instructions. For example, under limb (1), the situation may arise where the account holder suffers damage or loss due to the failure of the bank to perform the operation requested because of the banks' system or equipment failure. It is also argued that the wordings of limbs (2) and (3) are too wide and may cover systems failure or malfunction.

11.89 Like other banks, the terms and conditions of the National Australia Bank (National) adopted the rules set by the new Australian EFT Code. The account holder is not liable, among other things, for losses that are caused by the fraudulent or negligent conduct of the National's employees or agent, losses arising because the security device or password is forged, faulty, expired or cancelled, losses after notification that the security of the security device or password has been breached and where it is clear that the user has not contributed to such losses.

11.90 The account holder is liable for losses resulting from unauthorised transactions where the National can prove on the balance of probability that the user contributed to the losses. This may happen due to either the user's act of fraud or contravention of the security requirement. The account holder is also liable where the National can prove on the balance of probability that the user contributed to the losses resulting from unauthorised transactions because the user unreasonably delayed to notify the National that the security device or password has been breached.

11.91 The National terms and conditions makes no mention of its liability except in the case of system failure. Clause 27.4 of the terms and conditions states that the National will be liable to users for losses users suffer caused by the failure of the National's equipment or National's system to complete a personal EFT transaction accepted by the National's system or the National's equipment in accordance with the user's instructions.

11.92 However, where the user should have been aware that the National's equipment or the National's system was unavailable for use or malfunctioning the National's responsibilities will be limited to the correction of any errors in the account holder's account and the refund of any charges or fees imposed on the account holder as a result. The National will also not be liable for any losses caused by the failure of the National's equipment or the National's system where the National's system or National's equipment had not accepted the personal EFT transaction.

Privacy and data protection

11.93 All the four banks in this study adopt a privacy policy that is quite comprehensive and elaborative in nature. The degree of comprehensiveness varies between one bank and another. The banks explain what information is collected from the customers, the purposes of collection, and how they handle the information. Westpac even elaborates on how it collects and uses the information. It is common among the banks to have the provision on information sharing, with entities in the same group as well as with third parties. With regard to sharing of information with the third parties, positively, all the banks list out the parties that they may exchange personal information with. The other common feature of the privacy policies of all the banks examined in this study is the statement concerning the commitment of the banks to observe and ensure compliance with the National Privacy Principles (NPPs) of the Privacy Act. In this respect, CBA, ANZ and NAB adopt the general statement to the effect that they are bound by the NPP. The Westpac Group goes slightly beyond just a mere general statement. It states, 'our policies, processes and systems have been developed to ensure we comply with all our obligations under the Privacy Act'. This one-sentence statement has a broad meaning. It carries a positive, appealing and powerful message for the customers. The CBA, NAB, and Westpac have a special section in their privacy policy statements, the provisions relating to Internet privacy.

11.94 There are some different rule of practice adopted by the banks with respect to information sharing between members in a group and between banks and third parties. There are two issues here; first, regarding the consent of the customer before the bank can disclose the information to the third parties. Second, how the bank can ensure that third parties protect and handle the information in accordance with the existing rules and regulations. The CBA insists that it will obtain the customer's consent before disclosing the information. In terms of ensuring that third parties protect the information, the CBA states in general terms that it takes its obligations to protect customer information *very seriously* and it makes every effort to deal *only* with parties who share and demonstrate the same attitude. Where the third parties know personal information, there are *confidentiality* arrangements in place.

11.95 Several points may arise here. First, is it practical for the bank to deal only with such parties? Second, privacy and data protection is not confidentiality – they are not the same. Since privacy and data protection are much wider than confidentiality, it is not good enough just to protect confidentiality. Whatever may be the intention of the bank, the word 'confidentiality' does not represent privacy and data protection. Third, the word 'arrangements' is a bit too general. Fourth, how serious is 'very seriously'? The bank specifically mentioning the specific mechanism, such as contract, can avoid some of these concerns and uncertainty. It is specific and reflects the seriousness of the bank in protecting the customers' information. The CBA limits the use and subsequent disclosure of the information by the third parties.

11.96 Westpac adopts a more stringent rule. First, the bank will only disclose the information if they are allowed to or obliged to do so by law or where consent, expressly or impliedly, has been obtained. Second, the bank will bind the third parties through contract. Westpac states, 'we will only disclose your personal information where we are allowed to or obliged to do so by law or where we have your express or implied consent'. It also states that the bank will limit the disclosure to the information that is needed by the third parties to perform their services. More importantly, the bank insists, 'we bind these companies through contractual arrangements to the same standard of care as we uphold ourselves'.

11.97 The ANZ will only disclose personal information to third parties with express or implied consent, or where the bank is entitled or required to do so. There is nothing mentioned about ensuring that third parties observe certain standards in dealing with the information.

11.98 The NAB's privacy policy makes no mention about the requirement of consent or other justifications as preconditions to disclosure. However, it ensures that third parties will observe the rules and regulations in dealing with the information. The privacy policy statement says:

> 'where your personal information is disclosed we will seek to ensure that the information is held, used or disclosed consistently with the National Privacy Principles, any relevant Health Privacy Principles under state legislation and other applicable privacy laws and codes'.

11.99 To some extent, comparatively, Westpac provides good practice concerning information sharing between banks and third parties. The customer's consent will be obtained before disclosure. The bank will disclose only information required by third parties to perform their duties as agreed upon. This means that the bank will exercise this limitation on itself. Contrastingly, the CBA states, 'contractors, agents and outsourced service providers are not able to use or disclose personal information for any purposes other than our own'. The limitation here relates to the wider issues of use and subsequent disclosure by third parties. Since the ultimate aim is to exercise control on third parties dealing with the information, arguably, the mechanism adopted by Westpac is better able to perform this function. Lastly, Westpac will enter into a contract with third parties to obligate them to protect the information with certain conditions.

11.100 On the sharing of information within a company, there are differences in the practice of all the four banks. The first issue is concerning consent. The banks should obtain the consent of the customers before disclosing and sharing the information with other members in the group. Second, for what purpose(s) is the information to be used by other companies in the group other than the purpose(s) for which it was collected? The ANZ specifically mentions that they will obtain customers' consent to share personal information within ANZ. The information will only be used for the purposes which are agreed by the customers.

11.101 As mentioned earlier, Westpac will only disclose information to another person or organisation where customers have given their express or implied consent. The bank specifically states that they share personal information with members of the Westpac Group. Westpac may also use the information for other purposes than Internet banking, for example, to market their new products and services. In another words, the information may be used for direct marketing purposes. The privacy policy states, 'we may use your information to offer you products and services that we believe meet your needs. However, you can notify us at any time if you do not wish to receive these offers'. This means, unless the bank receives notification from the customers, it will use the information, such as name, address, and phone number to promote the offers. This 'opt-out' approach is not good practice. An 'opt-in' approach is more sensible. The customers should be allowed to agree before receiving any promotional materials concerning any offers from the bank.

11.102   The NAB privacy policy mentions consent in an indirect manner and specifically in the context of direct marketing. The NAB may disclose and share the personal information with other member companies within the group. The privacy policy states, 'in line with modern business practices common to many financial institutions and to meet your specific needs we may disclose your personal information to an organisation described below'. This includes group organisations offering: banking and finance products or services: financial planning, broking services or personal investment products; trustee or custodial services; and life insurance or general insurance products. It is questionable whether the information provided by the customers for Internet banking purposes can be disclosed to and shared with other member companies offering those products and services.

11.103   The requirement of consent is mentioned in an indirect manner, and specifically in the context of direct marketing. The bank states:

'it is our practice to seek your consent to use or disclose your personal information to let you know about, and develop, products and services from across the Group that might better serve your financial, e-commerce and lifestyle needs or promotions or other opportunities in which you may be interested. This may be done after an initial marketing contact. We assume we have your consent to use service providers to assist us with this, unless you tell us otherwise'.

11.104   The Commonwealth Bank, to some extent, has good rules and practice pertaining to the sharing of information among members within a group. The privacy policy statement provides:

'Members of the Commonwealth Bank Group (the Group) that have collected personal information are permitted by the Privacy Act to disclose personal information to other members of the Group. This enables the Group to have an integrated view of its customers. Any such disclosure is controlled by the Privacy Act, and members of the Group with whom you do not have a relationship will not use that information for the purpose of contacting you. Without your consent, other members of the Group may not use or disclose your personal information for purposes other than for which your information was originally collected. All members of the Group observe the same standard of privacy and information handling practices.'

11.105 The privacy policy statement also provides the list of members of the Commonwealth Bank Group, together with a brief description of the services they provide. As indicated above, the bank will obtain the customers' consent before disclosing and sharing the information. There is a guarantee that any members of the group with whom customers do not have a relationship will not contact customers. For example, it is against the Group's policy for Commonwealth Securities Limited (CommSec) to use the personal information of Commonwealth Bank customers to identify and direct market to people who do not already have a relationship with CommSec. However, the Commonwealth Bank itself may inform a customer of the services available from itself or from CommSec or other members of the group, provided that the customer has given his consent and has not instructed the bank not to direct market.

11.106 There is also a guarantee that the information provided to a company for certain purposes, for example for Internet banking, would not be used by other members of the group for some other purposes, without the consent of customers. The list enables customers to have a clear idea and knowledge about who, possibly, the bank may disclose to and share the information with, provided consent is obtained.

11.107 According to the privacy policy statement of the Commonwealth Bank Group, customers may indicate that they do not want to receive information on products and services offered by or through the collecting member by 'ticking the box' on the form they sign when they take out a product or service; or contacting the collecting member at any time to indicate that they wish to 'opt-out' of receiving such information. As mentioned earlier, this 'opt-out' scheme is not a good practice.

11.108 On variation of terms and conditions of use of Internet banking, the new EFT Code, as mentioned earlier, requires at least 20 days' notice before changes take place if they involve important matters. The Commonwealth Bank Internet banking service, NetBank, however, will give 30 days' notice. All the other three banks state that they will give 20 days' notice.

Compliance with the EFT Code

11.109 As stated by Ms Jillian Segal, Deputy Chair of the ASIC, consumers will receive far broader protection for all their electronic banking under the new EFT Code. It delivers protection by detailing: the disclosure consumers must receive before they first use a new form of electronic banking; the information consumers must receive on receipts; liability for unauthorised transactions and system or equipment malfunction; protection of a consumer's privacy; that, when the customer agrees, electronic communications rather than paper ones are allowed; and complaints investigation and dispute resolution processes. Institutions will have to meet a higher standard of proof before a consumer can be held liable for an unauthorised transaction. It also imposes obligations on consumers to protect the security of the codes they use to access electronic banking.

11.110   As at July 2002, there were 50 authorised banks in Australia, of which 36 were foreign owned and 14 were domestic. At the end of March 2001, 10 banks in Australia were providing transactional Internet banking services. There is no doubt that the financial market in Australia is of a world-class standard. *The World Economic Forum 2001 Global Competitiveness Report* ranked Australia's banking sector second in the world for soundness of banks and also second in the world for financial market regulation and supervision.

11.111   Perhaps, at the time of writing, it is too early to make a comprehensive assessment of the level of industry compliance with the new EFT Code. According to the ASIC, the next report of 2004, which will be the first monitoring of the new EFT Code, importantly will provide complaint data broken down by payment mechanisms. So there will be separate statistics for ATM, EFTPOS, Internet and telephone banking.

11.112   However, the track records relating to compliance with the EFT Code could provide some indications of the future. In March 2003, the ASIC published a report on financial institutions, *Compliance with the Payments System Codes of Practice and the EFT Code of Conduct, April 2001 to March 2002*. There were 199 institutions which subscribed to the EFT Code. The ASIC stated;

> 'To the best of our knowledge, all financial institutions in the period under consideration that provided retail EFT transactions (as defined by the EFT Code) complied with the Code. This is pleasing as it ensures that all consumers will be governed by the same set of rules, and entitled to an appropriate minimum level of protection'[1].

The ASIC also reported that there has been a significant decrease in the reported instances of non-compliance with the EFT code in the reporting period. Two Code subscribers reported full compliance with every clause of the EFT Code. Of the remainder, most institutions were compliant with all but one or two of the clauses[2].

1   ASIC, Compliance with the Payments System Codes of Practice and the EFT Code of Conduct (April 2001–March 2002) p 52.
2   *Ibid*, at p 53.

11.113   In total there were 286 instances of non-compliance with Code provisions reported to the ASIC. This compares with 316 instances of non-compliance reported in the previous year. The provision that had the highest rate of non-compliance was one requiring the institutions to publicise the availability of the institution's terms and conditions and the provision to annually provide a self-contained statement of card and PIN security requirements. The second of these breaches, in particular, is a matter of urgency since the liability of consumers under the code is directly linked to their compliance with code PIN security requirements[1].

1 ASIC, Compliance with the Payments System Codes of Practice and the EFT Code of Conduct (April 2001–March 2002).

11.114 The report noted that between April 2001 and March 2002:

- the overall number of complaints had increased, but it must be noted that the number of transactions had increased by over 140 million;

- the incidence of complaints per million transactions remained constant for all subscribing financial institutions (not just banks) at 81 complaints per million transactions;

- the total number of complaints had risen to just under 9%. Complaints relating to system malfunction rose by 18.6%, however, complaints about unauthorised transactions fell by 6.2%;

- the number of complaints made to major banks had decreased from 17 to 11 complaints per million transactions, and for the minor banks it had decreased from 11 to 8 complaints per million transactions;

- from the monitoring statements received relating to compliance, six institutions reported receiving a complaint regarding privacy.

11.115 The Chief Executive of the Australian Bankers' Association (ABA), David Bell, commenting on the report said[1]:

'I am pleased to see that ABA member banks have achieved high levels of compliance with the Code of banking Practice and EFT Code of Conduct. These self-regulatory codes set out the banking industry's key commitments and obligations to customers on standards of practice, disclosure and principles of conduct for their banking services. This 'good report card' from ASIC is testimony that self-regulation is working for the benefit of bank customers.'

1 Australian Bankers' Association Media Release, 'Asic Report shows Banks' High Level of Compliance with Code of banking Practice and EFT Code of Conduct', available at http://www.bankers.asn.au/ABA/adminpages/AdminViewAnArticle.asp?ArticleID=477.

11.116 It has to be remembered that the old EFT Code covered consumer transactions intended to be initiated through use of card and a PIN, which include ATM cash transactions, electronic payments such as EFTPOS and transactions made through terminals before a teller with the use of a card and PIN. The new code is the revised version of the old one, extending its scope to cover phone banking as well as Internet banking. Like the old one, the new code regulates the rights, obligations and liability of the parties. The requirements concerning handling of disputes, disclosure of certain information to customers, privacy and security obligations are maintained in the new code. Based on these facts, it can be argued that this most recent report of the ASIC is able to give a good indication that the banks offering Internet banking services in Australia will achieve a high level of compliance with the new EFT Code. Nevertheless, it is exciting to wait and read the next 'report card' of 2004.

Customer satisfaction

11.117   Arguably, the number of Internet banking customers and their levels of satisfaction may also be used as the yardstick to assess the compliance of the institutions with the Code. The ACNielsen.consult Online Banking Study, conducted between July and December 2001, found that two-thirds of all Australian Internet users do their banking online. Nearly three million people, including a high proportion of women and under-25s, make financial transactions on the Internet, up 70% on the previous year. It is stated that the figures confirmed that Internet banking has rapidly become the 'killer application' in online financial services.

11.118   The Australian Prudential Regulation Authority (APRA) stated, 'The most rapid growth is occurring in online, or Internet financial services, especially banking. Australia now ranks as one of the world leaders in online banking, comparable with the United States, but behind Northern European countries like Finland'[1]. The Reserve Bank of Australia in its latest bulletin noted[2]:

> 'Paper instruments such as cheques have been replaced to a significant extent by more efficient electronic alternatives. The Internet has begun to have an impact on how Australians conduct their banking and payments activities ... Based on preliminary data for 2002, these Internet-banking-initiated credit transfers made up 5% of the value and 16% of the number of all credit transfers.'

1   APRA Insight (1st Quarter 2001) p 4.
2   Reserve Bank of Australia, 'The Changing Australian Retail payments Landscape' (July 2003) pp 1 and 5.

11.119   In terms of customers' satisfaction, there are statements by some banks that their customers are satisfied with the Internet banking services. In 2001, Westpac stated that 95% of its 1,094,024 registered Internet banking customers are 'satisfied or very satisfied' with the service. The ANZ spokesperson said, 'We survey our customers regularly and the overall satisfaction level is 89%'[1]. Commenting on the ACNielsen's study, the Chief Executive Officer, Ramin Marzbani remarked[2]:

> 'The major banks appear to have done a good job educating customers to the benefits of banking online and in reinforcing messages about the security of the experience. This has created a large and widening pool of people quite comfortable with banking, transacting and transferring their money over the Internet. As well as seeing growth in the number of people using online banking, we're also seeing an increase in those satisfied with their experience. Satisfaction levels are running at about 91%, which is good news for an industry being put under increasing pressure to deliver to a rapidly growing online customer base.'

1 See ZDnet, 'Banks Unite in Rejection of Net Banking Report', available at http://www.zdnet.com.au/newstech/ebusiness/story/0,200004890,20262376,00.htm. These statements were made in refuting the findings of a report that slated Internet banking and phone banking as negative experiences for many Australians. The Westpac was reported as saying that the survey spoke to 175 people out of a population of 18 million and that was 35 people per bank.

2 See ACNielsen, 'Online Banking Wins Plenty of Fans in Australia, NZ', available at http://asiapacific.acnielsen.com.au/newsletter_story.asp?newsID=98storyID=16.

11.120 If the past could be used to predict the future and assuming that the widespread acceptance of Internet banking could be regarded as one of the measurements of compliance, it is fair to say that high levels of compliance with the New EFT Code could be expected. The 2004 report would prove this argument is right or wrong. One of the drafters of the Code noted:

> 'the close involvement of industry and user representatives in the drafting of the Code is likely to ensure a high degree of adoption by financial institutions and other organisations as a way of enhancing customer confidence in the wide array of new payments technologies that are being offered, and will be offered, to consumers'[1].

1 See the endnotes of the EFT Code.

11.121 The FSRA allows a two-year period for the industry to make the transition to the new regime. It would also be fascinating to know the levels of adoption and compliance of the banks with 2003's Code of Banking Practice. It goes without saying that Australia has been very active in the exercise of developing a better legal and regulatory environment for the financial industry.

CHAPTER TWELVE

Internet Banking in Malaysia: Law and Practice

Introduction

12.1 In 1998, two years before the introduction of Internet banking in Malaysia, the Prime Minister, Mahathir Mohamad, recognised the importance of Internet banking and the need to review the existing financial, regulatory and legal system. He emphasised the need to address the issues of assignment of liability, consumer protection, and privacy in e-commerce[1]:

> 'The fundamental requirement for the successful take-off of E-Commerce is trust, and the guarantee that transactions can take place safely and securely. Among the prevalent issues associated with E-Commerce are financial-related issues such as electronic payment systems, Internet banking and Internet stock broking. These need to be reviewed within the context of each country's existing financial, regulatory and legal system ... Cyber laws, for instance, need to address issues relating to the assignment of liability of those involved in E-Commerce transaction. The issue of consumer protection and privacy also needs to be addressed.'

1 Address at the Economist Roundtable on Electronic Communities in Asia (13 February 1998).

12.2 This chapter analyses the legislative and regulatory framework of Internet banking in Malaysia. An attempt is made to assess whether the existing legal and regulatory requirements are fully observed and implemented by the banks in their day-to-day operation. It points out the conflicts between some of the provisions of the regulations. The discussion in this chapter is based on the assumption that the Personal Data Protection Act (PDPA) has been passed and is in force in its current form. It also based on the argument that the BNM/GP 11 – *Guidelines on Consumer Protection on Electronic Fund Transfer* and the *Code of Good Banking Practice* do not apply to Internet banking. This is because of the very restrictive interpretation of the term 'electronic funds transfer' in the Guidelines[1], while the Code only applies to banking institutions that provide financial services by means of 'plastic cards'. Arguably, the Code is solely meant for ATM transactions.

1 Paragraph 4 states that the Guidelines cover electronic fund transfers carried out through or by means of telegraphic transfer, point-of-sale terminal, stored value card terminal, cash dispensing machine, telephonic instruments, or debit card.

12.3 Reference is made to the rules and regulations, as well as cases concerning data protection in the UK. There are two main reasons for such an attitude. First, the PDPA is modelled upon the English Act. Second, inevitably, in this new area of law, the courts in Malaysia would seek guidance from other jurisdictions. It is highly likely that the position in the UK would be referred to.

Internet banking in Malaysia: present and future

12.4 In May 2000, the Central Bank, Bank Negara Malaysia (BNM) made an announcement that domestic banking institutions would be allowed to offer Internet banking services effectively from 1 June of that year. Locally incorporated foreign banks, however, had to wait until 1 January 2002 before doing so. The first local bank offering Internet banking services was the Maybank, the largest in terms of assets as well as network distribution, when it launched its portal, maybank2U.com on 15 June 2000. Maybank2U.com, since then, has received several awards; Best of e-commerce Interactive Marketing Innovations (2002), Best Consumer Internet Banking in Malaysia (2002), Best Consumer Online Securities Trading in Asia Pacific (2002), Best Internet application Website (2001), Best Internet Bank in Malaysia (2001), and PIKOM Computimes Award for E-commerce Site of the Year 2000. Today, Maybank2u.com has 650,000 registered customers and logged over 16 million transactions. The popular transactions are online banking, online bill payments and online share trading. In April 2003, Maybank launched the country's first Internet banking kiosk.

12.5 In December 2000, Hong Leong Bank commenced its Internet banking operation 'E-banking' through its website, www.hlbb.hongleong.com.my. This was followed by Southern Bank and Alliance Bank. The newcomer is the Bank Islam Malaysia Bhd which launched its Internet banking services known as bankislam.biz in January 2003. The bank hopes to get 100,000 users or 10% of its cardholders to use the Internet banking services by 2005. Since the launch more than 2,000 customers had registered to use bankinislam.biz.

12.6 According to the International Telecommunication Union, 'Malaysia has reached an enviable level of ICT development considering its per capita income'. At the end of 2000, Malaysia ranked 30th in the world in Internet penetration, above several more developed nations. By December 2000, there were approximately 1.2 million Internet subscribers in the country translating to an estimated four million users, or 17.2% of the population[1]. Another report, by the Malaysian Communication and Multimedia Commission stated that there were two million Internet subscribers at June 2001. The government has set up a national objective of raising Internet subscriber penetration to 25% of the population by 2005. The International Data Corporation's current predictions, however, indicate that by 2005, the number of Internet subscribers in Malaysia is expected to reach 4.5 million.

1   International Telecommunication Union, Multimedia Malaysia: Internet Case Study (March 2002).

12.7 The IDC Market Research Sdn Bhd, in its study published in 2001, predicted that users of local Internet and Intranet based online banking services would reach 1.1 million by the year 2004, with the total number of online banking accounts reaching 1.6 million, or 23% of all local Internet users that year[1]. According to the IDC's survey, 'customers preferred to conduct their banking transactions via the ATM or by visiting their bank's branch, rather than through the Internet'. The study found that the main reason for not conducting Internet banking was due to the fact that users felt no need for such a service. Other reasons include the lack of knowledge of Internet banking, lack of interest in such services and fear of online fraudulence.

1   The Star (30 January 2001). In-Tech/3.

12.8 According to the Association of Banks in Malaysia, the statistics show that less than 2% of customers access Internet banking services in Malaysia compared to 9% in Singapore, South Korea and Japan, and 8% in Hong Kong. In May 2003, the Malaysian banks launched a three-month campaign to encourage customers to switch to Internet banking.

12.9 The Governor of the Central Bank stated that as of May 2003, 12 domestic and foreign banks were offering Internet banking services. According to her, there were an estimated one million Internet banking customers in Malaysia. She urged banks to be more proactive and innovative in payment services to 'accelerate our progress on this front'. The Governor believes that education could increase consumer acceptance. She said[1]:

> 'Internet banking, for example, is a fast and convenient mode of conducting banking transactions that has yet to gain widespread acceptance amongst banking consumers. With greater access to information on this, consumers can be better informed on the advantages of this form of banking. Any fears or apprehension on this mode of banking may be removed thus allowing for greater convenience derived from banking via desktops in the comfort of the home and office.'

1   The Governor's opening remarks at the Launch of the Consumer Education Programme (30 January 2003).

The legislative and regulatory framework

12.10 The Central Bank, Bank Negara Malaysia (BNM) refers to Internet banking as banking products and services offered by banking institutions on the Internet through access devices, including personal computers and other intelligent devices. There are three types of Internet banking websites; informational, communicative, and transactional. An informational website enables the dissemination of information about the banking institution and is used to advertise its products and services. A communication site allows some interaction between a banking institution and its customers. Customers may transmit information and make enquiries about their accounts. Fully-fledged Internet banking is in operation when a bank has a transactional website allowing customers to execute transactions such as bill payments and money transfers.

12.11 In March 2001, the BNM launched the Financial Sector Master Plan, a ten-year blue print to develop the financial sector through a six-pronged approach[1]. This Master Plan highlights the need to give greater attention to the development of information and communications technology (ICT) by the financial service sector. It is acknowledged that modern technology will continue to be a key driver that will shape future development and competition in the financial services. ICT is affecting every aspect of banking in unprecedented ways. It is facilitating radical change in the operations and structure of financial markets, in roles and relationships among service providers, intermediaries and investors, as well as regulators. In terms of the approach on regulatory control, the BNM noted[2]:

> 'An important element in achieving an efficient and innovative market is for BNM to move from the traditional "regulator knows best" approach to a "'supervised market approach". As BNM moves towards a supervised market approach, it will be essential for banking institutions to understand the regulatory philosophy of "What is not forbidden is allowed". BNM will focus on greater supervision with minimal regulation.'

1 The aim of the Master Plan is to improve the efficiency and effectiveness of the financial sector before opening it up to greater foreign competition.
2 Bank Negara Malaysia, Financial Sector Master Plan, (2001) p 11–12.

12.12 The BNM, under s 35 of the Central Bank of Malaysia Act 1958, has a legal duty to use its best endeavours, in co-operation with other banks, to promote and maintain banking and financial services for the public. More importantly, it has a legal duty to foster higher standards of banking and finance in Malaysia

12.13 Section 119(1) of the Banking and Financial Institutions Act 1989 (BAFIA) prohibits any institutions from providing the electronic fund transfer (EFT) system without the approval of the BNM. It provides that no person shall commence to operate any EFT system, or where such person has been operating any EFT system immediately before the effective date, continue to operate such system for a period exceeding 90 days after the effective date, or such period as the BNM may specify, unless he has submitted for the approval of the BNM the scheme of the operations of the system, and the rules, contract, bye-laws or other documents relating to the rights, duties and liabilities of the persons participating in the system, and obtained the authorisation in writing of the BNM to operate the system.

12.14 In essence, this section prohibits the commencement or continuance of any EFT operations unless the BNM has given written authorisation to do so. To enable the BNM to make a decision to grant or not to grant the authorisation, this provision requires the submission of the scheme of the operations of the system, and the rules, contract, by-laws and other documents concerning the rights, duties and liabilities of the persons participating in the system.

12.15   Electronic Fund Transfer (EFT) is defined in s 2(1) of the BAFIA to mean, 'any transfer of funds (other than a transaction originated by cheque, draft or similar instrument) which is initiated, activated or commenced, regardless of at which stage it was initiated, activated or commenced, through an electronic terminal, telephonic instrument or computer or magnetic tape or other storage device so as to order, instruct or authorise any person to debit or credit an amount, and includes point-of-sale transfers, direct deposits or withdrawals of funds, automated teller machine transactions, and transfers initiated, activated, commenced or transmitted by telephone'.

12.16   The three elements of the EFT are: first, there must be a transfer of funds, second, the transfer must be initiated, activated or commenced through the apparatus mentioned in the definition, which includes computers, and third, an instruction is given to another person to debit or credit a sum of money. Internet banking falls within this definition and is considered as an EFT.

12.17   Under s 119(2) of the BAFIA, before making any decision to allow any bank to offer Internet banking services, in addition to the documentation mentioned above, the BNM may require the person seeking the authorisation to submit to the BNM, any such other information and particulars relating to the system. The BNM may also make an inspection of the premises, equipment, machinery, books or other documents, or accounts and transactions, relating to the system[1].

1   BAFIA, s 119 (2).

12.18   Section 119(3) provides:

> 'BNM may approve or reject a scheme submitted under subsection (1) and the rules, contract, by-laws or other documents relating thereto and submitted therewith, or may approve the same subject to such modifications and alterations to the scheme, or to any or all of the documents as aforesaid submitted therewith, as it may deem necessary, desirable or expedient, and may in giving any authorisation under this section, impose such restrictions, limitations or conditions as it may deem fit'.

12.19   To enable the Central Bank to achieve its objective, s 116 gives power to the BNM to make regulations. Section 116(2)(e) allows the BNM to make regulations to provide for the imposition of duties, liabilities, responsibilities, restrictions, limitations, prohibitions or sanctions, or the conferment of rights, privileges, benefits or indemnities on directors, officers or shareholders of the licensed institutions or holding companies of licensed institutions or the parties to any electronic fund transfer system set up, or operating in Malaysia. More specifically, in the context of Internet banking, s 116(2)(f) empowers the BNM to make regulations to provide for the setting-up, operation, or administration of, or any other matter whatsoever relating to electronic fund transfer systems.

12.20   Section 119(4) obligates banks to comply with the regulations of the BNM. Section 126 gives power to the BNM to issue guidelines, circulars or notes in respect of the conduct of the banks. There is a penalty for non-compliance. Under ss 103 and 104 of the BAFIA, any person who contravenes any specification or requirements made, or any order in writing, directions, instructions, or notice given, or any limit, term, condition or restriction imposed, or anything howsoever done, in the exercise of any power conferred under, pursuant to, or by virtue of any provision of the Act shall be guilty of an offence and shall be liable to be punishable with a fine not exceeding 500,000 Ringgit. In the case of a continuing offence, the person, shall, in addition, be liable to be punished with a daily fine not exceeding 1,000 Ringgit for every day during which the offence continues.

12.21   Section 27 of the BAFIA prohibits advertisements for deposits unless they are issued by the licensed bank, a licensed finance company, a licensed merchant bank or a licensed discount house. This means that only licensed financial institutions are allowed to advertise for deposits on Internet websites. This also means that only institutions licensed under the BAFIA can own informational or communicative Internet banking websites. Section 35 allows the BNM to take corrective and remedial actions against false, deceptive, offensive or misleading advertisements.

The Minimum Guidelines on the Provision of Internet Banking Services by Licensed Banking Institutions

12.22   Using the powers granted by the legislations, the BNM issued the *Minimum Guidelines on the Provision of Internet Banking Services by Licensed Banking Institutions* (Guidelines) in May 2000. It sets out minimum guidelines that licensed banking institutions in Malaysia should observe in providing Internet banking. Banking institutions are free to adopt more stringent measures. The Guidelines cover several areas: Internet banking risks, active oversight by the board of directors and senior management, risk management practices, security requirements, consumer protection and privacy issues, and compliance with other regulatory requirements. As mentioned earlier, it is an offence for any person to contravene any of the provisions of the Guidelines[1]. 'Person' is defined in the BAFIA to include an individual or any corporation[2]. It is beyond the scope of this chapter to examine the Guidelines in their entirety. The focus is on the selected issues of risk management, allocation of liability, and protection of consumers' data. These issues are crucially important for the success of Internet banking.

1   BAFIA, ss 103 and 104.
2   BAFIA, s 2.

12.23   The Guidelines classified Internet banking services into three types. The levels of risks and the efforts to mitigate them are identified. First, an informational site, intended to distribute general information about the banking institution and to advertise its products and services. There is no interactive capability. According to the Guidelines the risk is relatively low, as the information on the website is not linked to the banking institution's internal computer systems that store information databases of the banks.

12.24 Second, a communicative site, which allows some interaction between the banking institution's systems and the customer. Customers may send information and make enquiries about their accounts. The communication may take the form of e-mail, online forms, account inquiries, or static file updates. The Guidelines require banks to put in place the appropriate controls to prevent, monitor and alert management of any unauthorised attempt to access the bank's internal networks and computer systems, apart from implementing virus protection measures.

12.25 Third, a transactional site, which allows customers to execute transactions. The risk is the greatest and strongest level of protection is required. The Guidelines recognise that Internet banking risks can adversely impact on the banking institution's earnings and capital. It categorises the risk into the following sets of risks:

- Strategic risk, which arises from adverse business decisions, improper implementation of decisions or lack of response to industry changes.

- Transaction risk, which arises from deficiencies in system design, implementation or ineffective monitoring, resulting in fraud, error and the inability to deliver banking products and services.

- Compliance risk, which arises from violation of, or non-conformance with, laws, rules, regulations, prescribed practices, or ethical standards. Compliance risk can lead to a diminished reputation, limited business opportunities and lack of contract enforceability.

- Reputation risk, which arises when systems or products do not work as expected and cause widespread negative public reaction.

- Traditional banking risk, such as credit risk, interest rate risk, liquidity risk, price risk, and foreign exchange risk.

12.26 The BNM outlines the role and responsibilities of the board of directors as well as of the senior management. The board of directors, among others, should approve the Internet banking strategy of the bank to ensure that it is consistent with the bank's strategic and business plan. It is the responsibility of the board of directors to ensure that the Internet banking systems are operated in a safe and sound manner.

12.27 The board of directors has the ultimate responsibility for ensuring that an adequate system of internal control is established and maintained. The board is also required to demonstrate an active oversight of the management of Internet banking risk by receiving periodic briefings that identify the material risks. Senior management, among others, should take the steps necessary to identify, monitor and control Internet banking risks and monitor the effectiveness of the internal control system. Senior management should ensure that the Internet banking system is designed and operated in a manner that complies with all relevant laws and monitor developments and changes in consumer and banking laws, regulations, and interpretive rulings and take adequate measures to comply with them.

12.28   The Guidelines place an emphasis on risk management practices. The risk management process should be subject to appropriate oversight by the board of directors and senior management. The proper implementation of the Internet banking system requires the senior management to establish control, policies and procedures, training and testing, contingency planning, and proper oversight of any outsourcing.

12.29   The board of directors should review, approve and monitor Internet banking technology-related projects. The board of directors should also ensure that appropriate policies and procedures are in place to manage Internet banking-related risks. Senior management is required to conduct periodic security risk assessments to identify internal and external threats. The security measures instituted should be current and properly implemented. Banks are required to establish specific reporting requirements for security breaches.

12.30   As far as outsourcing is concerned, banks are allowed to outsource their Internet banking systems to *resident* service providers and software vendors. However, the following conditions must be satisfied:

- the processes to be outsourced do not take away the decision making function of the bank and do not threaten strategic flexibility and the process control of banks;

- the outsourcing arrangement would not impair the image, integrity and credibility of the bank; and

- there are cost savings in outsourcing such functions.

12.31   The BNM requires banks to be able to manage the risk associated with outsourcing and to ensure that the appropriate oversight programme is in place to monitor the outsourcing vendor's controls, conditions and performance. The details of the outsourcing arrangements should be forwarded to the BNM, at least two weeks before entering into an agreement with the service provider. Interestingly, the Guidelines specify a list of conditions to be satisfied by the banks in managing outsourcing arrangements. Prior approval from the BNM is required if a bank wishes to outsource to non-resident outsourcing service providers.

12.32   Under product transparency, banks are required to ensure that the products and services offered on the Internet are fairly and accurately disclosed. The terms and conditions and fees are to be made transparent to consumers in plain language. In the event of any variation being made to terms and conditions, which would have the effect of increasing charges to the customer, or increasing the customer's liability for losses, banks are under an obligation to provide advance notice to the customers.

12.33   The terms and conditions of Internet banking services must include duties of the bank and the customers, contractual arrangements for liability arising from unauthorised or fraudulent transactions, mode of notification of changes in terms and conditions, and information relating to the lodgement of complaints, investigations and dispute resolution procedures.

12.34 Internet banking still requires face-to-face interaction with customers in two situations. First, where a customer opens an account, and, second, where a customer seeks an extension of credit. In such cases, banks are required to meet their customers in line with the BNM's 'Know Your Customer Policy'.

Protection of consumers' data under the Personal Data Protection Act

12.35 At the heart of the Malaysia's PDPA are the data protection principles. The PDPA, which is very much based upon the UK Data Protection Act 1984, provides nine data protection principles to be observed by data users including banking institutions providing Internet banking services. Principle 1 states that personal data shall be collected fairly and lawfully.

12.36 Neither 'fairly' nor 'lawfully' is explicitly defined in the legislation. However, 'fairly' is subject to extensive interpretative provisions in paragraphs (2), (3), and (4). Paragraph 2 provides that in determining whether personal data are collected, held or processed fairly, regard is to be had to the method by which the personal data are obtained, including in particular whether any person from whom the personal data are obtained is deceived or misled as to the purposes for which the personal data are collected, held, processed or used.

12.37 Paragraphs 3 and 4 contain some other guidelines in deciding fairness. Paragraph 3 provides that personal data are to be treated as obtained fairly if the personal data consist of information obtained from a person who is authorised by or under any law to supply it; or is required to supply it by or under any convention or other instrument imposing an international obligation on Malaysia.

12.38 Paragraph 4 requires data users to inform data subjects whether it is obligatory or voluntary to provide the information to data users. It states that where personal data are or are to be collected from the data subject, all practicable steps shall be taken to ensure that he/she is explicitly informed, on or before collecting the personal data, of whether it is obligatory or voluntary for him/her to supply the personal data. If it is obligatory to supply the personal data, the data subject must be informed of the consequences for the failure to do so.

12.39 A consumer would be informed explicitly of the purpose/purposes (in general or specific terms) of collection, and the class of persons to whom the personal data may be transferred. He must also be informed of his/her right to access the personal data as well as his/her right to request for the correction of personal data.

12.40 In the UK, in the case of *CCN Systems Ltd and CCN Credit Systems Ltd v Data Protection Registrar*[1], the Data Protection Tribunal highlighted two important points in determining fairness. First, regard has to be made to the purpose of the legislation – to protect the rights of the individual about whom data is obtained, stored, processed or supplied. Second, the standard is one of objective fairness. It means that the matter of whether or not the data user had the motive or intention to breach the data protection principles is irrelevant.

1   Encyclopaedia of Data Protection, fn. 85, paras 6–055–6–056.

12.41 In *Innovations (Mail Order) Limited v Data Protection Registrar*[1], the Tribunal had to decide whether information has been obtained fairly in relation to direct marketing purpose. In addition to supplying goods, Innovation Ltd derived the significant amounts of its income by trading in lists of customer names and addresses and making these lists available to other companies for direct marketing purposes (list rental).

1   Case DA/9231/49/1, Encyclopaedia of Data Protection, fn.85, paras 6–176–6–178.

12.42 Innovation Ltd obtained its customers by orders from their catalogues and in response to advertisements placed in the media. Customers ordering directly from the catalogues were advised of the possibility of their details being made available for other purposes, but those responding to the advertisements did not receive this information until after they had placed an order, that is, after they had supplied their personal details in response to the advertisement. The company argued that it was not practicable to provide notice of this practice in all other media advertisements, because of time and space constraints, and that later notification was more appropriate, as it would allow customers to be given more choice over the potential use of their information. The Registrar, on the other hand, argued that, if the obtaining was to be fair, the customer had to be aware of all the potential uses of personal details at the time that the order was made. The company appealed against the notice. The Tribunal stated:

> 'We have reached a conclusion that the words "fairly obtained" in the first data protection principle direct attention to the time of obtaining, not to a later time. We do not ignore the facts and circumstances of what happens thereafter. They may provide evidence of the purpose or purposes for which the data was in fact obtained and may provide evidence of the intention of the data user when he has sought, received, collected and obtained the personal information. We conclude in the facts and circumstances of this case that a purpose for which personal information is obtained, namely, list trading, is not obvious, unless clearly stated before it is obtained. The purpose that is obvious is the supply of goods. We conclude the personal information will not be fairly obtained unless the data subject is so told of the non-obvious purpose before the information is obtained.'

12.43 The House of Lords, in *R v R*[1] considered the term 'unlawful' and held it to mean 'something which is contrary to some law or enactment or is done without lawful justification or excuse'. The Ninth Report of the UK's Registrar observed that the effect of this broad definition is that a data user must comply with all relevant rules of law in relation to the purposes for which he holds personal data, and the ways in which he obtains and processes it. The Registrar also suggested certain areas for concern, which might be fertile ground for breaches of the first and second data protection principles. They are confidentiality, the *ultra vires* rule, excess of delegated powers and the concept of legitimate expectations.

I   [1991] 3 WLR 767.

12.44   In considering whether information has been fairly and lawfully obtained, the UK's Registrar takes into account all the circumstances and considers issues such as:

- Was it reasonable to expect the person supplying information to appreciate, without any further explanation by the data user, the identity of the data user and the purposes for which the information would be used or disclosed? If not, why did the data user not explain them to the person?

- If the data user did explain why the information was required and why it might be used or disclosed, was the explanation complete and accurate?

- Did the person ask about uses and disclosures of the information and, if so, what reply was made?

- Was the person supplying the information under the impression that it would be kept confidential by the data user? If so, was the impression justified by the circumstances and did the data user intend to preserve that confidence? (Is a data user who puts data online still preserving that confidence? This depends both upon the extent of that data user's registration and the extent of security arrangements.)

- Was any unfair pressure used to obtain the information; for example, were any unjustified threats or inducements made or offered?

- Was the person improperly led to believe that he or she must supply the information, or that failure to provide it might disadvantage him or her?

- Did the data user have any particular knowledge about the person from whom the information was obtained, either because the person was one of a specific group, for example young people, or because the data user had a personal relationship with the person? If the data user had such knowledge, would the explanation given by the data user concerning the collection and intended uses be understood by the ordinary man in the street?

12.45   Principle 2 of the PDPA, on purposes of collection, provides that personal data shall be held only for one or more specified and lawful purposes. Personal data shall not be collected unless: the personal data are collected for a lawful purpose directly related to a function or activity of the data user who is to use the personal data; the collection of the personal data is necessary for, or directly related to that purpose; and the personal data are adequate, relevant but not excessive in relation to that purpose.

12.46 The data must be held for one or more 'specified' and 'lawful' purposes. The position with regard to lawful purposes is analogous to that relating to lawful collection under the first data protection principle. A bank must make sure that they obtain enough data, but not too much, and not irrelevant data. A bank needs to ascertain the minimum amount of information which it requires in order to carry out the purpose for which the data is to be held. In other words, it leaves a great deal of discretion to the bank to decide the amount of data required for the purpose of providing Internet banking services.

12.47 The UK's Data Protection Tribunal in *Runnymede Community Charge Registration Officer v Data Protection Registrar*[1], in considering the similar provisions of the UK Data Protection Act 1984, held that where information is required in relation to certain individuals, it is not reasonable to hold such additional data in relation to all individuals. As the Registrar in her *Guidelines* under the 1984 Act (November 1994 issue) said:

> 'Where a data user holds an item of information on all individuals, which will be used or useful only in relation to some of them, the information is likely to be excessive and irrelevant in relation to those individuals in respect of whom it will not be used or useful and should not be held in those cases. *It is not acceptable to hold information on the basis that it might possibly be useful in the future without a view of how it will be used.* This is to be distinguished from holding information in the case of a particular foreseeable contingency which may never occur, for example, where a data user holds blood groups of employees engaged in hazardous occupations.'

1   [1990] RVR 236.

12.48 Principle 3 provides that personal data held for any purpose shall not, *without the consent of the data subject*, be used for any purpose other than the purpose for which the personal data were to be used at the time of the collection of the personal data; or a purpose directly related to that purpose. Basically, data can only be used for the purpose for which they were collected. The exception is when the data subject has given his consent. The determining point is the purpose specified by the data user at the time of the collection of the data. However, data can be used for another purpose, provided it is directly related to the specified purpose.

12.49 Difficulties may arise in interpreting 'directly related'. The question is whether the data collected by a bank for the purpose of providing Internet banking services can be used for other purposes, for instance, to promote other products and services of the bank and its subsidiaries. The safest way for the bank is to obtain the consent of the consumers before doing so. Alternatively, the bank can rely on the argument that the purpose is directly related to the Internet banking purposes. It must be emphasised, however, that the words used in the PDPA are 'directly related' and not just 'related'. This means that the purpose(s) concerned must have a close nexus with the Internet banking purposes.

12.50 The PDPA prohibits the disclosure of personal data to a third party without the consent of the data subject. Principle 4 provides that personal data shall not, without the consent of the data subject, be disclosed, unless:

(a)   the disclosure of the personal data is done for the purpose in connection with which the personal data was obtained or is directly related to the purpose in connection with which the personal data was obtained; or

(b)   in the case of the registered data user, disclosed to a person of a description entered in a register under this Act.

12.51 The word 'disclose' is defined to include 'disclosing information extracted or inferred from the personal data'. Data are only disclosed if they are acquired (whether intentionally or accidentally) by someone outside the user's organisation or a registered unit of the user's organisation. Disclosure is therefore contrary to the Act where data which are non-exempt are used or disclosed to an unregistered person or for an unspecified or unregistered purpose or both.

12.52 A bank can only disclose personal data to third parties for the purposes of providing Internet banking services and/or for the purposes connected to it. Being a registered data user, the disclosure can only be done to persons registered under the Act. This means that banks must register the institutions or persons to whom they expect to disclose the data.

12.53 Principle 5, which has significant impact on Internet banking, relates to the accuracy of data. It states;

> 'all practicable steps shall be taken to ensure that personal data are accurate, complete, relevant, not misleading and up-to-date, having regard to the purpose including any directly related purpose for which the personal data are, or are to be used'.

This principle is not to be regarded as being contravened by reason of any inaccuracy in personal data which accurately record information obtained by the data user from the data subject or a third party in a case where:

(a)   having regard to the purpose for which the personal data were obtained and further processed, the data user has taken reasonable steps to ensure the accuracy of the personal data; and

(b)   the data subject has notified the data user of the data subject's view that the personal data are inaccurate and the personal data indicate that fact.

12.54 'Inaccurate' is defined in the Act to mean incorrect, misleading, incomplete, or obsolete. Paragraph (2) provides some guidance on the interpretation of the principle, particularly, in relation to accuracy. The interpretation provisions in paragraph (2) allow that there will be no breach of the accuracy requirement where the data is, in fact, inaccurate but where the data user has accurately recorded the information from a data subject or third party *and*:

(a)   has taken reasonable steps to ensure accuracy (having regard to the purpose or purposes for which the data were obtained and further processed); and

(b)   has recorded the data subject's view as to inaccuracy within the relevant data, where such views have been conveyed.

12.55   The requirement on the data user to accurately record information obtained from the data subject or third party, presumably means that the data user may not claim the benefit of this exemption. This is so where the data user themself is responsible for the inaccuracy. However, it only applies where the user accurately records erroneous information where the error originates from the data subject or the third party. It is doubtful whether this is applicable to banks where there is a duty on their part to know their customers.

12.56   The requirement to take reasonable steps 'having regard to the purpose or purposes for which the data were obtained and further processed' is presumably an acknowledgement that inaccuracies in certain types of data (e.g. as to creditworthiness) may have more severe consequences than in others, and that consequently more stringent accuracy checks would be required.

12.57   In the UK, when considering compliance with the accuracy requirement, the Commissioner will examine whether the data controller has taken steps necessary to ensure inaccuracies do not occur in the data in deciding what action to take. Factors to be taken into account are[1]:

● The significance of the inaccuracy. Has it caused or is it likely to cause damage or distress to the data subject?

● The source from which the inaccurate information was obtained. Was it reasonable for the data user to rely on information from that source?

● Any steps taken to verify the information. Did the data user attempt to check its accuracy with another source? Would it have been reasonable to ask the data subject, either at the time of collection or at another convenient opportunity, whether the information was accurate?

● The procedures for data entry and for ensuring that the system itself does not introduce inaccuracies into the data.

● The procedures followed by the data user when the inaccuracy came to light. Were the data corrected as soon as the inaccuracy became apparent? Was the correction passed on to any third parties to whom the inaccurate data may already have been disclosed? Did the inaccuracy have any other consequences in the period before it was corrected? If so, what has the data user done about those consequences?

1   See Susan Singleton, *Data Protection – The New Law* (1998) p 19.

12.58   Under the PDPA, the obligation to keep data up-to-date seems to be unqualified – 'all practical steps shall be taken to ensure that personal data are up-to-date'. Whereas in the UK, the provision is qualified – data need only be kept up-to-date where 'necessary'. In this respect, the Commissioner will be concerned to see:

- whether any record has been kept of the date when the information was recorded or last updated;

- whether those involved will be aware or will have been made aware that the data do not necessarily reflect the current position;

- whether the data controller will take steps at regular intervals to update data and whether those steps are adequate; and

- whether the fact that data may be out-of-date is likely to cause damage or distress to the data subject[1].

1   See Susan Singleton, *Data Protection – The New Law* (1998) p 19.

12.59   Principle 6 concerning the duration of retention of personal data does not allow personal data held for any purpose be kept for longer than is necessary for that purpose. Obviously, this principle requires data users to review data regularly and delete what is no longer required. This provision reinforces the obligation in s 44, requiring a data user to erase any personal data held by him/her where the personal data are no longer required for the purpose. There is no such obligation if such erasure is prohibited under any law, or it is in the public interest (including historical interest) for the personal data not to be erased. A bank must erase the information given by a customer for Internet banking purposes when no longer has an account with the bank.

12.60   Principle 7 requires data users to take the rights of data subjects into account, when personal data are processed. The specific rights reinforced in the principle are the right of access, the right to be informed of the logic in relation to automated decision practices and the right to have the data corrected. This principle must be read together with s 33 of the Act, which specifies the maximum time period for the data user to comply with the data access request – not later than 45 days after receiving the request.

12.61   Principle 8 obligates the data user to take all practicable steps to ensure the security of personal data. It provides, 'all practicable steps to ensure security shall be taken against unauthorised or accidental access, processing or erasure to, alteration, disclosure or destruction of, personal data and against accidental loss of personal data'. The practicable steps to be taken shall have regard to: the nature of the personal data and the harm that would result from such access processing, erasure, alteration, disclosure, loss or destruction; the place or location where the personal data are stored; the security measures incorporated (whether by automated means or otherwise) into any equipment in which the personal data are stored; the measures taken for ensuring the reliability, integrity and competence of personnel having access to the personal data; and the measures taken for ensuring the secure transmission of the personal data.

12.62 This principle explicitly states 'all practicable steps'. Does this mean that each and every data user must take all steps? It should be noted that the expression 'practicable' is the qualification. The data user must take measures commensurate with the risks represented by processing and the nature of the data having regard to the cost of implementation. Therefore, a balance is to be struck between the seriousness of the consequences of a failure in security and the costs involved.

12.63 Principle 8 specifically mentions that regard must be had to the nature of the data and the harm that would result. The law imposes a fairly high duty of care between certain persons – for example, between doctor and patient, solicitor and client, bank/bankers and client – so the greater the damage which could result if data was wrongfully processed, arguably therefore the greater the level of security to be adopted.

12.64 With the current development of technologies for certain industries, passwords are no longer sufficient and should be supplemented by other security devices, such as encryption and firewalls. Where personal data is particularly sensitive or confidential or where the harm resulting from the unauthorised access or processing, etc is great, it may be argued that these eight data protection principles will not be deemed to be complied with, without the use of cryptography or other security technologies.

12.65 Security should not be an issue as it is in the interests of every organisation to implement, maintain and monitor adequate levels of security. However, the Act will apply also to data on paper and this will require organisations to consider security aspects in relation to paper files, card indexes and the like. Bearing in mind that security in principle 8 covers accidental loss or destruction, there could be a significant upturn in demand for lockable fireproof cabinets.

12.66 Principle 9 relates to information to be generally available. It requires that all practicable steps be taken to ensure that a person can ascertain a data user's policies and practices in relation to personal data and be informed of the kind of personal data held by a data user. This principle implies that data users should formulate policies and practices in managing the processing of personal data. Data users also shall take all practicable steps to ensure that individuals can be informed of the kind of personal data held by them. A bank should formulate policy concerning its practice in managing personal data and the policy should be made available to consumers.

Interaction between PDPA and the Guidelines

12.67 The Guidelines contain provisions which reflect the policy of the BNM and its attitude towards the privacy and protection of customers' information. The Guidelines also provide some specific rules and regulations that banks must observe. The BNM considers the privacy of consumer personal information to be an important element of public trust and confidence in Malaysia's banking system[1]. It states that it is fundamental for banking institutions to promote customers' trust in the institutions and to reassure customers that they recognise and respect the privacy expectations of the customers[2]. Banking institutions are expected to maintain awareness of the emerging consumer online privacy concerns and take the necessary steps to address them[3].

1   Clause 4.1 of the Privacy Policy in the BNM Minimum Guidelines.
2   Clause 4.2.
3   Clause 4.3.

12.68   The Guidelines require banks to adopt responsible privacy policies and information practices. They must disclose those policies and practices to increase consumer knowledge and understanding. Banks are also required to take other prompt and effective actions necessary to provide consumers with privacy protection in the online environment. What 'other prompt and effective actions' are not mentioned.

12.69   The privacy policy statements of the banking institutions should be clearly stated and readily understandable by consumers. The referencing points or icons for the privacy policy statement should be highly visible at specific locations on the banking institutions' websites where they may be most meaningful to the customers. Banking institutions should, at the minimum, prompt customers to refer to the banking institutions' privacy policy statements prior to or at the time that individually identifiable information is collected.

12.70   Clause 4.8 of the Guidelines regarding 'privacy policy statements' provides that the privacy policy statement must:

(i)   identify the types of information the banking institution collects about customers or consumers and how the information is used;

(ii)   provide a brief description of the kind of security procedures that are in place or clearly state that sufficient safeguards have been put in place to protect the loss, misuse or alteration of information under the banking institution's control including limiting employee access to information and handling information about customers who have ended their customer relationship with the banking institution;

(iii) identify with whom the banking institution shares this information, including agents, affiliated and non-affiliated third parties and how the banking institution ensures that the confidentiality of information is maintained;

(iv)   explain the choices available to customers regarding collection, use and distribution of the information including the customers' right to opt-out of disclosures that are not mandatory;

(v)   explain how banking institutions maintain the accuracy of information and how customers or consumers can correct any inaccuracies in the information; and

288

(vi)   explain how banking institutions handle consumer questions or complaints about the handling of personal information.

12.71   How do the PDPA and the Guidelines interact? It seems that conflict is inevitable. The PDPA provides an opportunity for a data subject to consent to, or withhold consent for, the collection, disclosure, use or processing of personal data. Consent is defined in s 2 to mean 'any *express* consent given by data subject or a relevant person'. In the case of *Bell v Alfred Franks & Barlett Co Ltd*[1], Shaw LJ stated that consent must involve a positive and demonstrative act, something of an affirmative kind. It is not to be implied. Simply, consent is an 'opt-in' action. Clause 4.8 (iv) of the Guidelines, however, provides for an 'opt-out' approach.

1   [1980] 1 All ER 356.

12.72   An opt-in requires the data subjects to let the data users know that the data subjects consent to the subsequent use of personal data; that is, data subjects have to say 'count me in' if they allow the transfer or disclosure. Without such positive indication, banks assume that the data subjects do not wish to have their information given to other companies for other purposes. It means that if the data subjects have not provided them with prior consent, the data subject information could not and should not be disclosed to the third parties.

12.73   An opt-out means that the data subject has to inform the data users of their wish *not* to have their information passed on to others, usually by checking a box. If a data subject does not check the box – if they do not say 'count me out' – the data users are free to use the information in any way they wish. The criticism of opt-out is that it puts the default in the wrong place. The reality of opt-out is that most users do not read and study privacy policies. Thus, most users will not in fact opt-out. This does not mean that they have actually consented to the data policies of the bank, just merely that they have not read the privacy policy. Thus, it can be argued that if websites were really respectful, they would not go about the disclosure and use of user data for other purposes unless they had actual consent from the consumer.

12.74   Banks may argue with some plausibility, however, that opt-in is unduly restrictive in that most consumers do not mind having their data collected and used by their websites. Thus, opt-in would place an artificially high burden on all those users who prefer receiving the benefits that various websites and banks have to offer but who do not bother to read privacy policies[1]. Banks may also argue that it is actually doing a favour to have opt-out instead of opt-in as the former policy will promote efficiency. This example nicely illustrates the important point that one's view regarding the proper scope of the demands of privacy respect may turn on one's higher level normative theory. From a deontological perspective, however, respect will not be defined in terms of efficiency but rather independently, or as part of an interrelated set of moral concepts such as autonomy. To respect people is to treat them as autonomous beings. For adherents to everyday Kantian morality, this may entail a prohibition on using their data without explicit notice and consent, even if it may be productive of social utility, or for that matter, a particular user's utility, to do so[2].

1   See Steven Hetcher, 'Changing the Social Meaning of Privacy in Cyberspace', Harvard Journal of Law and Technology, Vol. 15, No. 1 (Fall 2001) pp 190–191.
2   *Ibid.*

12.75   Clause 4.8(iii) of the Guidelines requires banks to identify with whom the banking institutions share the information. The question is whether banks can share the information with others. Sharing information would mean that the data would be disclosed to a third party. Principle 4 of the PDPA prohibits this unless there is consent of the data subject. There are exceptions to this rule. First, if the disclosure of the personal data is done for a purpose in connection with which the personal data was obtained. Second, the purpose is directly related to the purpose in connection with which the personal data was obtained.

12.76   It is important to note that principle 4 does not prohibit the banks from disclosing data to the third parties. This is impractical and unrealistic. The banks are required to obtain the consent of the customer prior to the disclosure. However, as mentioned earlier, if the disclosure is for other purposes directly connected to the providing of Internet banking services, consent is not required. The banks should ensure that third parties maintain the privacy of the data. Practically, this would mean that the banks have an obligation that third parties will protect the data. For this purpose, some banks would enter into a contract with third parties, others would insist that third parties have the same data protection policy as the banks.

12.77   Clauses 4.8(ii) and (iv) go a step ahead of principles 8 and 5 of the PDPA respectively. Principle 8 only requires the bank to take all practicable steps to ensure the security of the personal data. Clause 4.8(ii) requires banks to provide a brief description of the kind of security procedures taken by them to protect the security of the personal information. Similarly, under principle 5 banks are obliged to take all practicable steps to ensure the accuracy of the personal data, and the Guidelines, in clause 4.8(v), require banks to give an explanation as to how they maintain the accuracy. All these must be mentioned in the privacy policy statement of the bank.

Practices of banks

12.78   All the banks examined, to one degree or another provide a privacy policy. The Hong Leong Bank (HLBB) adopts two sets of privacy policy. One applies to the accessing of its website, and another, specifically, is for Internet banking services. The former is very detrimental and unfair to the Internet users. It is also in contravention with the PDPA. The bank's terms of access provide:

> Any information sent to Hong Leong Bank Berhad through the use of this site will be deemed not to be confidential and be deemed to remain the property of HLBB who

shall be free to use, copy, publish, reproduce, distribute and/or transmit all such information at Hong Leong Bank Berhad's absolute discretion for any purpose, any ideas, concepts, know-how or technique contained.

12.79 There is no privacy on the data of the users who use the Internet to access the bank's website. The irony is plain to see. The bank claims the visitors' information as its property. It is also against fair information practices and the PDPA for the bank to use the information without the consent of the visitors. In short, the visitors are at the mercy of the bank as far as their data is concerned. This might discourage consumers to visit the bank's website to find out about the services offered by the bank. These consumers could potentially be the customers of the bank. Policy such as this would keep consumers away from the bank.

12.80 For its Internet banking services, Hong Leong Online, the privacy policy states the types of information it collects, the purposes of collection, employee access, security measures to protect the information, accuracy of information, and customers' complaints. It is interesting to note that the information collected is not only used for the purpose of providing Internet banking services but also for other purposes, such as to evaluate customers' creditworthiness, to prevent fraud and to offer additional products or services of the bank and its related companies etc. The bank assumed that its related companies could also use the information. There is also the possibility that the information will be disclosed to and shared with third parties. The privacy policy, among others, states:

'your data may be used by HLB and/or its related companies for the purpose of researching, designing, launching, promoting and marketing existing and improved banking, financial and other services and products of HLB, *its related companies* or *selected third parties* and monitoring the provision, operation and use of such services or products'.

The customers' data collected by the bank will also be used for the purpose of forwarding *publicity materials* or *other information* from HLB or its related companies or such other third parties from time to time. As discussed below, these practices if done without the consent of the customers are in contravention of the international rules and the rules of the PDPA alike.

12.81 It must be remembered that the PDPA does provide for civil as well as criminal penalties if a data user contravenes the data protection principles. Section 88 provides that an individual who suffers any damage or distress by reason of a contravention of a requirement under the Act shall be entitled to compensation from the data user for such damage or distress. 'Requirement' is defined in s 2 as the 'compliance or contravention of the data protection principle'. As far as criminal penalties are concerned, contravention of the data protection principle is not in itself an offence. However, if a data subject has made a complaint to the Commissioner and an enforcement notice has been issued, the failure to comply with the enforcement notice will amount to a criminal offence under s 89(3)(b) of the PDPA. In other words, the contravention of the data protection principle could lead to a criminal offence. The data user is liable to a fine not exceeding 200,000 ringgit or to an imprisonment for a term not exceeding three years or to both, if convicted.

12.82   Bankislam.biz provides separate statements on privacy and security. It does explain the procedures to protect the security of personal information and types of data collected from customers. However, the main document of the terms and conditions of bankislam.biz contains provisions, which arguably, might be in contravention of the PDPA. Paragraph 16.3 of the terms and conditions of the bank states:

> 'Whilst the Bank will use its best endeavours that all information transmitted or *received* using the Bank's Internet Banking Services is secure and cannot be accessed by unauthorised third parties, the Bank does not warrant the security of any information transmitted by the Customer using the Bank's Internet Banking Services. Accordingly, the Customer hereby accepts the risk that any information transmitted or *received* using the Bank's Internet Banking Services may be accessed by unathorised third parties and the *Customer agrees not to hold the Bank liable for any such unauthorised access or any loss or damage suffered as a result thereof.*'

12.83   It is acceptable for the bank not to warrant the security of customers' data during its transmission from the customers to the bank. It is an acceptable fact, given the open nature of the Internet, that third parties might be able to intercept the information. It is however, unacceptable, for the bank to place the risk onto the customers for the information that the bank has received and stored in its system. Arguably, if it is proved that the unauthorised access or loss of data is due to the failure of the bank to protect its system, the bank might be in contravention of principle 8. As discussed earlier, this principle obligates the bank to take all practicable steps to protect the security of the information from unauthorised access by third parties, alteration, destruction etc. Furthermore, paragraph 16.3 negates the effect of s 88 of the PDPA, which gives the data subject the right to bring a civil suit and claim compensation from the data user, if he/she suffers losses resulting from an unauthorised access of his/her data.

12.84   Paragraph 16.4 of the terms and conditions of the bank states:

> 'the Customer further agrees that neither the Bank nor any of its officers shall be liable for any loss or damage suffered by the Customer as a result of disclosing, divulging or revealing of any information concerning the Customer Account(s) with the Bank as provided for in item 15.1 above'.

Unlike the criminal remedy, the Act is silent on whether customers could hold the officers of a company liable in the civil action[1]. Perhaps it may be argued that the principle of agency would apply here. If this argument is right, the officers of the bank, being the agents of the company, can be held liable, when an action is successfully brought against the bank.

1   Section 92 of the PDPA allows the officers of a company to be charged severally or jointly for the criminal offence and where the company is found guilty of the offence, the officers of the company shall be deemed to be guilty of the offence. They can escape liability if it is proved that the offence was committed without their knowledge, consent or connivance and the officers have taken all reasonable precautions and had exercised due diligence to prevent the commission of the offence.

12.85   Like HLB, other banks assumed that they could share customers' information with their group of companies. Many banks assumed that they could share the information with third parties, as well. The privacy policy of the Maybank2u.com, for example, states:

> 'Besides sharing information between members of the Maybank Group, we do not disclose your information to any third party or external organisation. This is in view of our strict compliance to the BAFIA.
> However to ensure that you benefit from a full range of products and services, your non-financial information may from time to time, may be provided to our alliance partners, suppliers and/or any other parties.
> If you do not wish to share your information with other entities, or you do not want to be solicited for products or services offered by the Maybank Group, or entities it provides information to, please write in or email us.

12.86   The question arises as to whether the bank could share the information with the members of its group. The disclosure of information, under principle 4 of the PDPA, requires the bank to obtain the consent of the data subject. The exceptions are: the disclosure for the purpose of providing Internet banking services; and the disclosure for purposes directly connected to Internet banking. Furthermore, principle 2 allows a bank to hold data *only* for one or more specified and lawful purpose. Specified purposes are purposes as registered in the register of the Commissioner. Principle 3 explicitly prohibits data to be used for any other purposes except with the consent of customers. This means that data collected by a bank for the purpose of providing Internet banking services could not be used for other purposes. If a bank wishes to do so, prior consent of the data subject must be obtained.

12.87   The banks may argue that the disclosure to and sharing of information with their group of companies does not amount to the disclosure to or sharing with third parties. The validity of this argument depends very much upon the status of the holding company and of other companies in the group. Are they separate and several data users or one data user? The Act is silent on this[1]. However, an analogy can be drawn from the status of government departments under the PDPA. Section 3 provides that the Act shall bind the government. It further states, 'for the purpose of this Act, each government department shall be treated as a government department separate from any other government department'. If government departments are to be considered as separate data users, the position could not be different for companies. This means that a holding company could not and should not disclose or share customers' information with companies in their group without the customers' consent. The consent should always be given through an 'opt-in' or affirmation action as required by the PDPA. In contrast, the

Maybank2u.com's privacy policy and the privacy policies of all other banks examined, provide for an 'opt-out' mechanism.

1   The English Act adopts the term 'data controller' and the Information Commissioner is of the opinion that individual companies who are controllers must notify separately.

12.88   Like other banks, the AmBank Group, in its privacy policy, assumes that the information it collects from customers could be shared and disclosed to members in its Group. The privacy policy states that personal information supplied by customers shall be used to provide AmBank Group's services. However, it further states:

> 'AmBank Group may also use your personal information to market AmBank Group's products and services to you based on your interests and to mainly assist AmBank Group in customising and delivering its services and products that may be of interest to you.'

12.89   The RHB Bank privacy policy, to some extent, provides a good model. It makes statements informing customers that the information received shall only be used in the course of providing financial services. It states, 'We shall strive to ensure that security measures are exemplary and that *all confidential information received shall only be used in the course of providing financial services to you*'. However, it would be better if the bank could be more specific, stating for the purpose of 'Internet banking services' rather than 'financial services'. The RHB Bank and the Bumiputra-Commerce Bank Berhad (BCBB) recognise that the banks will only transfer data if the customers consent to it. This is in line with the requirement of principles 3 and 4 of the PDPA. Paragraph 3(a) of the privacy policy of the RHB states:

> 'We assure you that whole and any part of the information received from you shall not be divulged, reproduced or used for any purpose other than that as stated in this privacy policy, or unless duly authorised by you or in the restricted circumstances permitted by law.'

12.90   Meanwhile, clause 6 of the privacy policy of the BCBB states:

> 'We shall, at all times, endeavour to safeguard the privacy of your information and accordingly, we do not disclose the same to any third party or external organisations. Notwithstanding this and for the purposes of helping us serve you better, your non-banking and non-financial information may be provided to our third party vendors, advertisers, affiliates or relevant third party subject to *your consenting* to the same'.

The BCBB's policy on the use of information in clause 3 states that the information is generally meant to be used in the ordinary course of business. It further states;

> 'Our use of your information may also extend to other purposes ... to prepare demographics concerning our customers' use of our products and services which

may, at our sole discretion, be made available to our third party vendors, *advertisers*, affiliates or relevant third parties in aggregate or demographic form'.

12.91   Practically, this provision has to be read together with clause 6. Before third parties can use the information, there must be the disclosure from the bank to the third parties. Under clause 6, the bank will obtain the consent of the customers before doing so. This is a fair practice and is in line with the PDPA. The problem is, however, that consent is assumed. In other words, it is the pre-condition for the Internet banking services. This argument could not be wrong because of the fact that customers will have to notify the bank if they wish to withdraw the consent. The bank has adopted the 'opt-out' approach, as provided for in the rest of clause 6. Once a customer subscribes to Internet banking, he is assumed to have given his consent to the bank for the information collected for Internet banking purposes to be disclosed and shared with third parties, including advertisers. The obligation is on the customer to withdraw his consent if he wishes.

12.92   The Public Bank Berhad (PBB), like other banks, thought that it could share the customers' data with the companies in its groups. Clause 2 of the privacy policy statement states, '... and apart from sharing of information between members of the PBB Group, *the PBB will not disclose the Customer's information to any third party or external organisations*'. Nevertheless, the second part of the policy statement is very much in compliance with the PDPA and the international rules.

12.93   The RHB Bank disallows the retention of its customers' information by third parties. It states that such third parties with whom RHB Bank shares the information, are not permitted to retain any customer information unless the customers have specifically expressed interest in their products or services and/or have authorised the same'. This means that third parties will have to eliminate the information after the purpose or purposes for which the information was received have been completed.

Apportionment of liability

12.94   There is a wide range of risks or incidents relating to Internet banking. They can be classified into three categories. First, there is no order from the authorised customer. This may be attributable to an error by the bank, usually the result of fraud, whereby a third party uses the means of access of a customer in order to make a transfer. Second, the authorised customer correctly issues the order, but the transfer proves to be irregular, either in terms of the amount or identity of the transferee. This can either be due to error or fraud. Third, the genuine order is correct in all aspects and remains correct, but the bank does not carry it out or the execution is delayed due to, for example, a failure or interruption of the data processing system. The latter, called technical malfunction or system failure, possibly, can be divided into two categories; those which are beyond the control of the bank, and those which are within its control. The realisation of these risks can occasionally give rise to considerable damages: loss of all or part of the principal amount, loss of interest and even loss of a contract due to the imposition of penalty clauses because the order has not been performed correctly[1].

1   See Xavier Thunis, 'Recent Trends Affecting the Banks Liability during Electronic Fund Transfer Operations', [1991] 8 JIBL 297, 299.

12.95   Clause 2.3 of the BNM Guidelines regarding product transparency requires that the terms and conditions for Internet banking services shall include the duties of the banking institutions and customers, contractual agreements for liability arising from unauthorised or fraudulent transactions, mode of notification of changes in the terms and conditions, and information relating to lodgement of complaints, investigation and resolution procedures.

12.96   Clause 2.4 of the Guidelines provides:

'The contractual arrangement for liability should provide for *sharing* of risks between the banking institutions and the customers. Customers *should not be liable* for loss not attributable to or not contributed by them.'

12.97   In a broader context, it can be argued that the BNM requires banks, depending upon the circumstances, to have a fair rule regarding liability in their terms and conditions. On the other hand, the word 'sharing' leads to a specific question. Under what circumstances should the bank and customer share the liability? The answer could be when both the bank and customer contribute to the losses due to fraudulent transactions. The second part of clause 2.4 reinforces this argument. It is almost impossible to think of any other circumstances where a bank and its customer would have to share the risk and liability.

12.98   The terms and conditions of the majority of banks offering Internet banking do not provide for fair rules. They are lopsided. There is no fair apportionment of liability between banks and their customers. Many of the banks attempt to escape liability in whatever circumstances loss or damage may arise. This is done through the inclusion of exclusion of liability clauses in the terms and conditions. Some impose the liability on customers. Others demand indemnity from their customers. The terms and conditions of Maybank2u.com, for example, provide that:

'The Maybank Group and/or its partners shall in no event be liable for any loss and damages *howsoever* arising whether in contract, tort, negligence, strict liability or other contract basis, including without limitation, direct or indirect, special, incidental, consequential or punitive damages, or loss of profits or savings arising in connection with your access or use or the inability to access or use this website, reliance on the information contained in the website, any technical, hardware and software failure of any kind, the interruption, error, omission, delay in operation, computer viruses, or otherwise.'

Note, '*Maybank Group and/or its partners*', words that not only try to exempt the bank from liability but also to extend it to its partners. The terms and conditions, however, also contain a clause that limits the application of this exclusion liability clause. It states 'this exclusion clause shall take effect to the fullest extent permitted by the law'. The impact of this expression is dependent upon the status of the exemption clause, which is discussed later in this chapter.

12.99 The lawyer/lawyers who prepared the terms and conditions of bankislam-.biz adopted almost word for word the Maybank2u.com provisions. The main difference is that the bankislam.biz exclusion of liability clause has an additional phrase, 'whether or not BIMB (Bank) has been advised of the possibility of such damages or loss'. This means that the knowledge of the bank on the possibility that the customer may suffer damage or loss is immaterial.

12.100 Clause 15.2 of the OCBC adopted the same approach, exempting the bank from liability 'howsoever caused':

'OCBC shall not be responsible or liable for any loss, damage or embarrassment incurred or suffered by the Customer in relation to or in respect of any instructions, relating to transactions and/or services which are affected or performed or processed through the OCBC Internet Banking service howsoever caused including but not limited to the Customer's non-compliance with the OCBC Internet banking service instructions and OCBC's liability to provide services as a result of malfunction partial or total failure of any data system, security system, computer tele-transmission or telecommunications system or other circumstances beyond the control of OCBC or any bank, financial institution or any person or any organization involved in the above mentioned systems.'

12.101 The AmBank Group and PBB, to some extent, adopt a fair practice and approach. As far as systems failure is concerned, the banks wish not to be held liable if it is beyond their control. For example, Clause 4.1(v) of the terms and conditions of the AmBank Group states:

'Under no circumstances and under no legal theory, tort, contract, or otherwise, shall AmBank Group be liable to you or any person for any direct or indirect, special, incidental, or consequential damages of any character, including and without any limitation, loss of goodwill, loss of use, profits, work stoppage, computer failure or malfunction, or any and all commercial damages or losses that arise in connection with this website for any system, server or connection failure, *error*, omission, interruption, delay in operation or transmission, or computer virus, malicious codes, Trojan horses or corruption or delay in performance or non-performance of any obligation of AmBank Group herein *due to any cause beyond the control of AmBank Group* including but not limited to the breakdown, strikes or other industrial action or communications or power failure.'

12.102 Arguably, the word 'error' may include error on the part of the bank in making a payment to an unauthorised person. In simple words, it may cover fraudulent transactions. But again, the bank can only escape liability if the fraudulent transaction has happened in such a way that it is beyond the control of the bank to avoid or prevent it.

12.103 It is acceptable to exempt or to limit the bank's liability if failure is involved which is beyond the control of the bank. It is however, unacceptable and unfair for the banks to exclude or restrict their liability for system failure or breakdown within their control. The breakdowns may occur because of the negligence of an employee of the bank or through the bank being negligent in its choice of system or third party maintenance contractor.

12.104 The exclusion of liability clause of the BCBB Internet banking services, channel-e, is the most comprehensive one. Clause 16 attempts to exclude the bank from liability from any loss whatsoever howsoever arising in tort, contract or indemnity. It contains a long list, 19 headings or circumstances, in which the bank cannot be held liable. Among other things, first, any malfunction or breakdown or failure of computer or system operated and/or maintained by the bank. Second, the corruption, destruction, alteration or loss of, or error in, the customer instructions. Third, any loss, theft or unauthorised use of the customer PIN or User ID. Fourth, any loss, which is caused by third parties, and fifth, any unauthorised access and/or use of Channel-e and the banking services by any person. Clearly, this is an attempt to exclude the bank from liability for losses due to systems failure, losses suffered by the customer due to the bank's failure to carry out the customers' instruction, and losses due to fraud by third parties. Again, there is no fair allocation and share of liability between the bank and its customers.

12.105 Interestingly, the terms and conditions of two of the banks examined mentioned their liability. The RHB admits liability in certain limited circumstances. Clause 16.1 of its terms and conditions provides:

> 'We shall only be liable for your direct losses and damages caused solely by our gross negligence and/or wilful default. In no event will we be liable for any other losses or damages, whether direct or indirect, exemplary, consequential, incidental, punitive, special losses or damages, or loss of income, profits or goodwill (including those of any third parties, and even if advised of the same) howsoever arising, and all such damages are expressly excluded.'

12.106 Unlike RHB, ironically, the BCBB's admission of liability relates to the procedure that has been adopted by the bank in handling the customers' complaint. Clause 13 of Channel-e's terms and conditions sets out the procedure for the bank to manage complaints by the customers. It applies to the cases of error on the part of the bank in carrying out the customers' instructions in money transfer. Clause 16.5 admits liability if the BCBB fails to observe this procedure. The failure, however, must be caused by the fraudulent or gross negligent conduct of the BCBB's officers, and it must have prejudiced the outcome of the complaint or resulted in a delay in its resolution. Must the customer prove all those elements? Or is it an internal matter for the management of the bank to decide? The BCBB states that the bank will be liable up to the full amount of the particular transaction, which is the subject of the complaint. Fairness requires the bank to adopt the latter approach. But this would mean putting the trust solely on the bank.

12.107   Another common feature of the terms and conditions of the banks offering Internet banking in Malaysia is that the requirement for customers to indemnify the bank in respect of all liabilities, losses, charges and expenses by reason of or in relation to the use or misuse of Internet banking services or websites of the banks. The terms and conditions of all the banks examined impose this condition on their customers. This means that customers are expected to indemnify the banks for any action by third parties against the banks.

Variation of terms and conditions

12.108   Clause 2.2 of the BNM Guidelines requires the banking institutions to provide notice to customers before they can vary their terms and conditions. It states:

> 'Banking institutions should provide advance notice to customers of variation of terms and conditions of the Internet banking services in relation to imposing or increasing charges, increasing the customer's liability for losses or any material changes'.

The Guidelines are silent on how advance the notice should be. It seems that notice is only required in cases of variation that relate to the imposing or increasing of charges, increasing the customer's liability, and material changes. The Guidelines do not provide any guidance on what amount to material changes.

12.109   The AmBank Group, in clause 10, states that 'AmBank Group reserves the right to amend the terms herein at its sole discretion at any time *without notice*'. While Maybank2u.com has adopted a position which will allow it to vary, perhaps, depending upon the nature of the terms and conditions, with and without notice to consumers. The terms and conditions of access provide: 'the information, material, functions and content provided in the pages of the website may be changed from time to time with or without notice at Maybank Group's absolute discretion'.

12.110   Other banks such as the PBB, bankislam.biz, RHB, OCBC and BCBB state that they will notify the customers before making any modification to their terms and conditions. The OCBC specifically specify '30 days prior notice'. The BCBB's notice is only 14 days prior to modification. The RHB and BCBB state that in certain circumstances, the banks may vary the terms and conditions without notice. The RHB explicitly specify the circumstances: in cases of urgency, in order to protect the security of the Internet banking services, and other circumstances beyond the control of the bank. In those situations, if the bank varies the terms and conditions, the bank will inform the customers of the changes as soon as practicable thereafter, and/or the reasons for such changes. The BCBB simply states where the changes or amendments are necessitated by an immediate need to restore or maintain the security of a transaction. Many banks consider that the continued access or use of the website subsequent to any changes will be deemed as the acceptance of the changes by the customers.

Unfair contractual terms

12.111 Unfair contractual terms basically occur in two ways: first, in the use of standard form of contract, and second, in the insertion of exemption clauses. The Contracts Act 1950 contains no provision dealing with exemption clauses. The Consumer Protection Act 1999 (CPA), in s 71, provides solution for this unfair practice. It reads:

> 'The liability of a person under this Part to a person who has suffered damage caused wholly or partly by a defect in a product, or to a dependent of such a person shall not be limited or excluded by any contract term, notice or other provision.'

12.112 The use of the words, *a defect in a product*, suggests that this section only applies to cases that involve defects in goods. Furthermore, s 2(2)(g) expressly provides that the Act does not apply 'to any trade transactions effected by electronic means unless otherwise prescribed by the Minister'. The Minister is yet to make any such prescription. Consequently there exists the absurd situation that a consumer contract entered into by mail would be covered by the Act, but not an electronic contract. Therefore, the current legal position as to the exemption clause in Internet banking and other electronic transactions would mean having to seek redress from case law.

12.113 The courts have evolved certain canons of construction in construing the meaning of the exemption clauses. These normally work in favour of the recipient of the document. The reason for this is that the party putting forward the document is normally able to impose onerous or unfair terms exempting himself wholly or partially from his just liability under the contract. The courts will apply the contra proferentem rule. This rule means that the court will construe forcibly the words of a written document against the party putting forward the document. However, this rule is only applied if there is any doubt or ambiguity in the meaning and scope of the exclusion clause used[1]. The phrases like 'will not be liable for any damage however caused', or 'arising from any cause whatsoever', will normally be construed to cover liability for negligence. The Malaysian courts seem to adopt the view that no matter how wide a clause is, it cannot exclude liability if there is negligence.

1   *Sharikat Lee Heng Sdn Bhd v Port Swettenham Authority* [1971] 2 MLJ 27, FC.

12.114 In *Sekawan Guards Sdn Bhd v Thong Guan Sdn Bhd*[1], the appellant security company was held liable for the theft which occurred at the premises of the respondent due to the negligence of the employee of the security company, although there was a clause in the contract excluding the liability of the appellant. In *Chin Hooi Nan v Comprehensive Auto Restoration Service Sdn Bhd & Anor*[2], due to the respondents' negligence, the appellant's car was damaged when being driven by the employee of the respondents. The respondents tried to avoid liability based on an exemption clause written on the back of the receipt given to the plaintiff. Siti Norma Yaakob J in holding the respondents liable said:

> 'The law on this [exemption clause] is quite settled in that an exemption clause however wide and general does not exonerate the respondents from the burden of proving that the damages caused to the car were not due to their negligence and misconduct. They must show that they had exercised due diligence and care in the handling of the car.'

1   [1995] 1 MLJ 811.
2   *Chin Hooi Nan v Comprehensive Auto Restoration Service Sdn Bhd & Anor* [1995] 2 MLJ 100.

12.115   It is possible to argue that clauses, which totally exclude banks from liability under 'whatever circumstances' are against, or contrary to public policy. Section 24(e) of the Contracts Act 1950 provides that the consideration or object of an agreement is lawful, unless the court regards it as immoral, or opposed to public policy. What constitutes public policy? There is no definition in the Act itself or in any other legislation. English common law defines public policy as[1]:

> 'that principle of the law which holds that no subject can lawfully do that which has a tendency to be injurious to the public, or against the public good, which may be termed, as it sometimes has been, the policy of law, or public policy in relation to the administration of the law.'

1   *Egerton v Brownlow* (Earl) [1843–60] All ER 970).

12.116   In *Koid Hong Keat v Rhina Bhar*[1], Wan Adnan J. held that what is and what is not injurious to public welfare in Malaysia must be decided in the Malaysian context. In *Polygram Records Sdn Bhd v The Search & Anor*[2] the court held that:

> 'In Malaysia ... there is some support for the view that public policy may, in some exceptional cases, demand that certain contracts which are grossly unfair to one of the parties to a contract ought to be set aside on the grounds of inequality of bargaining power under section 24(e) of the Act.'

Note, *grossly unfair*, words that best describe the terms and conditions of many of the banks providing Internet banking in Malaysia. Let us wait and see how the courts in Malaysia will decide if these terms and conditions are contested in the future.

1   [1989] 3 MLJ 238.
2   [1994] 3 MLJ 127.

Concluding remarks

12.117   Privacy of customer information has taken on an important role in banking today, as customers have grown increasingly sensitive to the treatment of their personal information. This concern becomes even more significant given the increasing use of the Internet by banks to deliver their services to the public. Consumers' fears concerning their personal information could quickly turn to distrust of Internet banking[1]. According to PricewaterhouseCoopers, possible consequences of a privacy failure include: damage to brand, reputation, consumer retention and consumer-focused business strategies; loss of revenue and new business; possible regulatory enforcement actions; potential litigation from consumers, advocates and business partners; civil and criminal penalties for wrongful disclosure of protected health information and interruption of cross-border data flows with applicable penalties in international jurisdictions.

1 John L.Douglas, 'Cyberbanking: Legal and Regulatory Considerations for Banking Organisations' North Carolina Banking Institute (April 2000) p 31.

12.118 As data users, banks and financial institutions are obliged to comply with a number of broadly stated rules formulated in all nine data protection principles of the PDPA. They are also obliged to comply with specific rules of the BNM Guidelines. The good commercial practice is for the banks to develop, publish and implement privacy policies in accordance with these rules.

12.119 The apportionment of liability in Internet banking is extremely crucial. Losses or liability have to be apportioned on an equitable and fair basis, by reference to the extent to which the acts or omissions of the parties have contributed to the loss. Apportionment of losses should take into account factors such as the steps taken by the customer to protect the security of his/her password, the extent to which the system provided by the bank protects the customer against unauthorised transactions on his/her account, and the relative weight of evidence adduced by the parties in support of their respective contentions that the transaction was, or was not, authorised.

12.120 At a minimum, banks should be liable to the customer for any direct, or clearly consequential, loss due to the failure of system within the control of the bank. The English Jack Committee Report noted[1]:

'It will be seen that it is normal practice for banks to disclaim liability for loss whatsoever suffered as a consequence of failure of equipment … [I]n today's conditions, their standard terms and conditions must be construed as somewhat *unfair* on customers. It needs to be recalled that it is the banks that introduce new technology: It is unreasonable that the customer, who had no part in that decision, should be penalised for its consequences, *except in special circumstances.*'

1 Banking Services: Law and Practice, Report by the Law Review Committee (1989) p 90.

12.121 As required by the BNM, customers should not be liable for loss not attributable to or not contributed by them. This, however, is not translated into practice. It is not too harsh to say that banking is not the customer's business, but the bank's. The Jack Committee suggested that the new solutions to problems of law and practice in the banking services field should give priority to four objectives. The first and foremost is to achieve fairness and transparency in the bank-customer relationship[1].

1 Banking Services: Law and Practice, Report by the Law Review Committee (1989) p 24.

12.122 According to the Committee, customers and banks go closely together. If some banks from time to time impose one-sided terms and conditions on their customers, and if some customers from time to time have unjustified expectations of their banks, this may have something to do with the uncertainty both face as to what their respective duties and obligations really are. Hence, there is a need to make those duties and obligations transparent. The customer is normally the weaker partner in the relationship, may well be more at risk; but fairness is not one-sided[1].

1 Banking Services: Law and Practice, Report by the Law Review Committee (1989).

12.123 The Senior Manager of the Legal Department of the BNM, stated that Internet banking in Malaysia is regulated adequately and no new laws are called for. She argued, 'No new regulation will be necessary at the present time unless financial safety and integrity of financial systems or customer protection is compromised'[1]. Obviously, here, consumer protection is compromised. The Financial Sector Master Plan has outlined the strategies to achieve an adequate and effective consumer protection infrastructure. The strategies, among others, include, first, a comprehensive and structured consumer education programme. Second, increased transparency by the financial institutions on the products and services being offered. Third, legal redress for consumers to deal with grievances arising from the purchase of financial products and services. It goes without saying that 'transparency by the financial institutions' obligates them to strictly observe the rules of the business. In the words of the Governor, 'new business rules will only be viable if the appropriate laws necessary to give confidence to the users are formulated and implemented'[2].

1 Dr Lee Foong Mee, 'E-Finance: Minimal Regulation of Internet Banking', a paper presented at the Second MSC International Cyberlaws Conference (5–6 July 2001) Kuala Lumpur, Malaysia.
2 Dr Zeti Akhtar Aziz, 'Banking and Information and Communications Technology Development – Legal Aspects, address by the Governor of the BNM to the Banking and Financial Law School, Kuala Lumpur (24 April 2001).

12.124 The BNM admitted that an active consumerism is healthy in creating a dynamic and responsive banking system. It assurance and commitments to the consumers are[1]:

'Consumers shall be given the opportunity to play an effective role in determining the quality of banking products and services they are getting. This shall be done through improvement in transparency of product offerings as well as the financial performance of banking institutions to generate better-informed consumers. The regulatory framework would be enhanced to provide necessary infrastructure for better consumer protection, while at the same time, consumer education will be focused towards promoting greater awareness on consumers' rights with regard to banking products and services.'

1   Bank Negara Malaysia, Financial Sector Master Plan, (2001) p 11–12.

12.125   Once again, it has to be remembered that a bank has to comply with all the requirements of the Guidelines before approval is given by the BNM to offer Internet banking services. The BNM would have to ensure that all the documentation is in compliance with the Guidelines before granting the approval. The BNM has approved the terms and conditions and privacy policy statements, which are inconsistent with the international fair information practices, PDPA, and its own Guidelines.

APPENDIX I

Electronic Funds Transfer – Code of Conduct

As revised by the Australian Securities & Investments Commission's EFT Working Group

Issued 1 April 2001

Amended 18 March 2002

CONTENTS
Part A

Rules and procedures to govern the relationship between users and account institutions in electronic funds transfers involving electronic access to accounts

Part B

Rules for consumer stored value facilities and stored value transactions

Part C

Privacy, electronic communication, administration and review

Schedule to Code

The EFT CODE

Part A: Rules and procedures to govern the relationship between users and account institutions in electronic funds transfers involving electronic access to accounts

1. Scope and interpretation

1.1 (a) Part A of this Code applies to EFT transactions. EFT transactions are funds transfers initiated by giving an instruction, through electronic equipment and using an access method, to an account institution (directly or indirectly) to debit or credit an EFT account maintained by the account institution. Sub clauses 1.3 and 1.4 limit the scope of application of Part A.[1]

(b)   Part A of the Code governs the rights and duties of account institutions and users (including account holders). It does not directly govern the rights and duties of third parties, such as issuers of access methods who are not account institutions or third parties in an EFT network such as merchants. Account institutions cannot avoid their obligations to users under the Code on the grounds that a third party has caused the failure to meet these obligations.

1.2 A funds transfer is the transfer of value to or from an EFT account (regardless of whether the EFT account has a debit or credit balance before or after the transfer) including between two EFT accounts or between an EFT account and another type of account. Without limitation, the transfer of value may be effected by one or more of the following:

●   adjusting one or more account balances;

●   transferring currency or a physical payment instrument;

●   transferring electronic representations of value (e.g. digital coins or payment instruments); or

●   adjusting amounts of stored value whether recorded on a card or other media (e.g. loading and unloading stored value).[2]

Transaction-type limitation

1.3 Part A of this Code does not apply to:

(a)   that part of a funds transfer which is the debiting of and transfer of value from; or

(b)   that part of a funds transfer which is the receipt of value and the crediting of that value to; an account that is designed primarily for use by a business and established primarily for business purposes.

Exclusion of some funds transfers involving biller accounts

1.4 (a) Except for clause 7, Part A of this Code does not apply to an account institution in respect of the receiving of value in a funds transfer for the credit of a biller account maintained by the account institution.

(b)   Part A of this Code does not apply to an EFT transaction which is a user-initiated funds transfer from a customer's biller account to the account institution to pay the account institution for goods or services (other than financial services) provided by the account institution to that customer (e.g. a debit to the customer's biller account and a credit to an internal account of the account institution).[3]

Interpretation

1.5 In Part A of this Code 'access method':

(a)   means a method authorised by an account institution for use by a user and accepted by the account institution as authority for it to act on an instruction given through electronic equipment to debit or credit an EFT account; and

(b)   comprises the use of one or more components including (but not limited to) devices, identifiers, codes or a combination of these; and

(c)   does not include a method requiring the user's manual signature where the comparison of the appearance of that manual signature with a written specimen signature is the principal intended means of authenticating a user's authority to give the instruction (whether or not that means is used in a particular transaction).[4]

'Account access service' is a service for the purposes of which either or both of the following apply:

(a)   the user must provide one or more codes to a service provider to enable the service provider or another person to access accounts at an account institution on behalf of the user (for example, an account aggregator service); or

(b)   the user must record or store one or more codes in a manner required by the service provider to facilitate the user, the service provider or another person acting on behalf of the user to access EFT accounts at an account institution using that code or codes (for example, the service provider provides the user with a software wallet to store codes and the wallet is used to access EFT accounts by the user or the service provider).

'Account institution' means an institution which:

• subscribes to this Code; and

• maintains EFT accounts for account-holders.[5]

'Biller account' is an EFT account maintained by an account institution solely to record amounts owed or paid by its customer in respect of the provision of goods or services to its customer by the account institution.[6]

'Code' means information:

• the content of which is known to the user and is intended to be known only to the user or only to the user and the account institution;

• which the account institution requires the user to keep secret; and

• which the user must provide (in any manner) to or through a device or electronic equipment in order to access an EFT account.[7]

'Device' means a physical device used with electronic equipment to access an EFT account, for example a card, token or biometric reader.

'EFT account' means an account:

(a)   maintained by an account institution which belongs to an identifiable account holder who is a customer of the account institution; and

(b)   which the account institution permits a user to initiate a funds transfer from or to using an access method through electronic equipment (notwithstanding that there may be a delay between the use of the access method and the debiting or crediting of the account).

In the case of a stored value facility (as defined in Part B), neither the value control record in the facility nor any record held by a stored value operator of the stored value available to be transferred from that stored value facility is an EFT account.[8]

'Electronic equipment' includes electronic terminal, computer, television and telephone.

'Financial services' includes the lending of money, the provision of credit and a financial service as defined in s.12BA of the *Australian Securities and Investments Commission Act* 1989.

'Identifier' means information:

•   the content of which is known to the user but not only to the user and which the user is not required to keep secret; and

•   which the user must provide (in any manner) to or through a device or electronic equipment in order to access an EFT account.[9]

'Institution equipment' means electronic equipment controlled or provided by or on behalf of an account institution to facilitate EFT transactions.

'Institution system' means an electronic system, communications system or software controlled or provided by or on behalf of an account institution to facilitate EFT transactions.

'User' means a person authorised by an account institution (and, if the user is not the account holder, also authorised by the account holder) to use an access method to give instructions to the account institution to debit or credit an EFT account and includes an account holder.[10]

2. Availability and disclosure of the terms and conditions applicable to EFT transactions

2.1 Account institutions will prepare for their users clear and unambiguous Terms and Conditions applicable to EFT transactions, which reflect the requirements of this Code. The Terms and Conditions are to include a warranty that the requirements of this Code will be complied with. The Terms and Conditions will not provide for or be effective to create liabilities and responsibilities of users, which exceed those set out in this Code.

2.2 Account institutions will provide a copy of the Terms and Conditions:

(a)   to the account holder prior to or at the time of initial use of the access method; and

(b)   at any other time when requested to do so by a user.

The availability of Terms and Conditions is to be publicised by account institutions.

2.3 Account institutions will ensure that, before an access method is used for the first time after issue, the user to whom it is issued has been provided with information on:

(a)   any charges for the issue or use of an access method, separate from activity or other charges applying to the account generally;

(b)   the nature of any restrictions imposed by the account institution on the use of the access method (including any daily transaction limit and other periodic transaction limits which apply to the access method, an account or electronic equipment) and an indication that merchants or other institutions may impose additional restrictions;

(c)   a description of the types of transactions that may be made, and of the accounts that may be accessed, with the access method;

(d)   a description of any credit facility, which may be accessed by the user through electronic equipment using the access method;

(e)   the procedure for reporting the loss, theft or unauthorised use of a device or breach of security of a code (such as a telephone number or other means of reporting outside of normal business hours); and

(f)   the means to activate complaint investigation and resolution processes (including the procedure for querying entries on a periodic statement).

3. Changing the terms and conditions of use

3.1 Account institutions wishing to vary or modify the EFT Terms and Conditions to:

(a)   impose or increase charges relating solely to the use of an access method, or the issue of an additional or replacement access method;

(b)   increase an account holder's liability for losses relating to EFT transactions (subject to the liability limits established elsewhere in this Code); or

(c)   impose, remove or adjust a daily transaction limit or other periodic transaction limit applying to the use of an access method, an account or electronic equipment;

will provide written notification to the account holder, and allow a period of notice of at least 20 days (or, where applicable legislation requires a longer notice period, that longer period) before the change takes effect.

3.2 (a) Account institutions will give notice of other changes at the following time:

   (i)   in time to comply with any applicable legislative requirements for a particular period of notice in advance of the date the change takes effect;[11] or

   (ii) where there is no such legislative requirement, in advance of the date the change takes effect.

(b)   Account institutions will provide notice of other changes in the manner required by applicable legislation, or if there are no such requirements, in a manner which is likely to come to the attention of as many account holders as possible.

3.3 Advance notice need not be given when changes are necessitated by an immediate need to restore or maintain the security of the system or individual accounts.

3.4 Where important, or a sufficient number of cumulative changes so warrant, account institutions will issue a single document providing a consolidation of variations made to the Terms and Conditions.

3.5 When account institutions advise account holders of the removal of, or an increase in, a daily transaction limit or other periodic transaction limit, they should, at the same time, advise account holders that the removal of or an increase in that transaction limit may increase account holder liability in the case of unauthorised transactions. This advice is to be clear and prominent.

4. Records of EFT transactions and notice of surcharges

A RECEIPTS

4.1 (a) Except where paragraph (b) applies, at the time of an EFT transaction and unless a user specifically elects otherwise, the account institution will ensure a receipt is issued containing all of the following information:

   (i) the amount of the transaction;

   (ii) the date and time (if practicable) of the transaction;

   (iii) the type of transaction e.g., a 'deposit', 'withdrawal', 'transfer', (symbols may be used only if they are explained on the receipt and easily understood abbreviations may be used);

   (iv) an indication of the account(s) being debited or credited;

(v) data that enable the account institution to identify the customer and the transaction;

(vi) where possible, the type and general location of any institution equipment used to make the transaction or a number or symbol that enables that institution equipment to be identified;

(vii) in the case of a funds transfer to a merchant in payment for goods or services, the name of the merchant to whom payment was made;

(viii) where possible, and where it is not likely to compromise the privacy or security of the user or the account holder, the balance remaining in the account which is debited in the funds transfer (or, in the case of a deposit, the account which is credited).[12]

(b)   If an EFT transaction is conducted by voice communications (including an automated voice response system by telephone), the account institution will ensure that the following information is provided to the user by voice communication at the time of the EFT transaction:

(i) a receipt number;

(ii) the amount of the transaction;

(iii) the type of transaction e.g. a 'deposit', 'withdrawal', 'transfer';

(iv) an indication of the account(s) being debited or credited;

(v) in the case of a funds transfer to a merchant in payment for goods or services, the name of the merchant to whom the payment was made;

(vi) where possible, and where it is not likely to compromise the privacy or security of the user or the account holder, the balance remaining in the account which is debited in the funds transfer (or, in the case of a deposit, the account which is credited). Account institutions may choose to provide users with the option to specify at the time of each transaction that a receipt is not required.[13]

(c)   A charge may not be imposed on a user or an account holder for the issuing of a receipt under sub-clauses (a) and (b).

(d)   In an EFT transaction where the user does not use institution equipment or an institution system and does not communicate with the account institution or a person acting on its behalf, the account institution is only obliged to use its best endeavours to meet its obligations under paragraphs (a) and (b).[14]

B PERIODIC STATEMENTS

4.2(a) Except for those passbook accounts covered by sub-clause (b), for an account to or from which EFT transactions can be made, the account institution will provide a record of account activity at least every six months. Account holders are also to be offered the option of receiving more frequent periodic statements. That option is to be brought to the attention of the account holder at the time the access method is first issued. As well, statements are to be available at the request of the account holder.

(b)   Passbook accounts are exempted for sub-clause (a) where there is no charge for having the passbook updated manually or checking account balances and activity electronically.

[*Historical note:* EFT Code amended 18 March 2002 by replacing para 4.2. The para formerly read:

> '4.2 For an account to or from which EFT transactions can be made, the account institution will provide a record of account activity at least every six months. Account holders are also to be offered the option of receiving more frequent periodic statements. That option is to be brought to the attention of the account holder at the time the access method is first issued. As well, statements are to be available at the request of the account holder.']

4.3 Except for statements issued outside the usual statement cycle the statement is to show:

(a)   in respect of each EFT transaction occurring since the previous statement:
    (i) the amount of the transaction;
    (ii) the date the transaction was debited or credited to the account;
    (iii) the type of transaction;
    (iv) the receipt number, or other means, which will enable the account entry to be reconciled with a transaction receipt;

(b)   any charges relating solely to the use of an access method (identified as a separate item); and

(c)   the address, telephone number or other contact details to be used for inquiries concerning the account or to report any errors in the statement; but a statement issued outside the usual statement cycle is to show as much of the above information as possible.

4.4 Account institutions will suggest to account holders that all entries on statements be checked and any apparent error or possible unauthorised transaction be promptly reported to the account institution. This suggestion will be contained on the account statement. Institutions will not seek to restrict or deny account holders their rights to make claims or to attempt to impose time limits on users to detect errors or unauthorised transactions.

C Security Advice

4.5 Account institutions must include on or with account statements at least annually a clear, prominent and self-contained statement summarising access method security guidelines which are consistent with clause 5 of this Code and which complies with paragraph 5.8(b).

D NOTICE OF SURCHARGES FOR USING 'FOREIGN' ELECTRONIC EQUIPMENT

4.6 An account institution shall include in its agreements with any person who makes electronic equipment available to a user so that the user may perform an EFT transaction, a requirement that the person disclose to the user (at a time which enables the user to cancel the EFT transaction without cost to the user) the amount of any fee (such as a surcharge) charged by the person for the use of its electronic equipment which will be directly passed on to the user or account holder.[15]

5. Liability for unauthorised transactions

A DEFINITION OF UNAUTHORISED TRANSACTION

5.1 This clause deals with liability for transactions which are not authorised by the user. It does not apply to any transaction carried out by the user or by anyone performing a transaction with the user's knowledge and consent.

B NO ACCOUNT HOLDER LIABILITY IN RESPECT OF FRAUDULENT OR NEGLIGENT CONDUCT OF ACCOUNT INSTITUTIONS' EMPLOYEES OR AGENTS; FORGED, FAULTY, EXPIRED OR CANCELLED ACCESS METHOD; LOSSES OCCURRING PRIOR TO RECEIPT OF ACCESS METHOD; OR INCORRECT DOUBLE DEBIT TRANSACTIONS

5.2 The account holder has no liability for:

(a)   losses that are caused by the fraudulent or negligent conduct of employees or agents of the account institution or companies involved in networking arrangements or of merchants or of their agents or employees;

(b)   losses relating to any component of an access method that are forged, faulty, expired, or cancelled;

(c)   losses that arise from transactions which required the use of any device or code forming part of the user's access method and that occurred before the user has received any such device or code (including a reissued device or code). In any dispute about receipt of a device or code it is to be presumed that the item was not received by the user, unless the account institution can prove otherwise. The account institution can establish that the user did receive the device or code by obtaining an acknowledgment of receipt from the user whenever a new device or code is issued. If the device or code was sent to the user by mail or email, the account institution is not to rely only on proof of delivery to the user's correct address as proof that the device or code was received by that person. Nor will the account institution have any term in the Terms and Conditions which deems a device or code sent to the user at that person's correct address (including an email address) to have been received by the user within a certain time after sending; or

(d)   losses that are caused by the same transaction being incorrectly debited more than once to the same account.

C *No Account Holder Liability in Respect of Unauthorised Transactions Occurring After Notification*

5.3 The account holder has no liability for losses resulting from unauthorised transactions occurring after notification to the account institution that any device forming part of the access method has been misused, lost or stolen or that the security of codes forming part of the access method has been breached.

D *No Account Holder Liability Where It Is Clear That The User Has Not Contributed To The Loss*

5.4 The account holder has no liability for losses resulting from unauthorised transactions where it is clear that the user has not contributed to such losses.

E *Circumstances Where The Account Holder Is Liable*

5.5 Where sub-clauses 5.2, 5.3 and 5.4 do not apply, the account holder is liable for losses resulting from unauthorised transactions only as provided in paragraphs (a), (b) and (c).

(a)   Where the account institution can prove on the balance of probability that the user contributed to the losses through the user's fraud or the user's contravention of the requirements in sub-clause 5.6, the account holder is liable for the actual losses which occur before the account institution is notified that a device forming part of the access method has been misused, lost or stolen or that the security of the codes forming part of the access method has been breached, but is not liable for any of the following amounts:
   (i) that portion of the losses incurred on any one day which exceed the applicable daily transaction limit(s);
   (ii) that portion of the losses incurred in a period which exceeds any other periodic transaction limit(s) applicable to that period;
   (iii) that portion of the total losses incurred on any account which exceeds the balance of that account (including any prearranged credit);
   (iv) all losses incurred on any accounts which the account institution and the account holder had not agreed could be accessed using the access method.
   Where an access method includes more than one code and the account institution proves that the user contravened the requirements of subclause 5.6 by voluntarily disclosing or by keeping a record of one or more codes but not all the codes in the access method, the account holder is liable under this

315

paragraph only if the account institution also proves on the balance of probability that the user's contravention of sub-clause 5.6 was the dominant contributing cause of the losses.[16]

(b) Where the account institution can prove on the balance of probability that a user has contributed to losses resulting from unauthorised transactions by the user unreasonably delaying notification after becoming aware of the misuse, loss or theft of a device forming part of the access method, or that the security of all the codes forming part of the access method has been breached; the account holder is liable for the actual losses which occur between when the user became aware (or should reasonably have become aware in the case of a lost or stolen device) and when the account institution was actually notified, but is not liable for any of the following amounts:

(i) that portion of the losses incurred on any one day which exceed the applicable daily transaction limit(s);

(ii) that portion of the losses incurred in a period which exceeds any other periodic transaction limit(s) applicable to that period;

(iii) that portion of the total losses incurred on any account which exceeds the balance of that account(s);

(iv) all losses incurred on any accounts which the account institution and the account holder had not agreed could be accessed using the access method.

(c) Where a code was required to perform the unauthorised transactions and neither paragraph (a) nor (b) applies, the account holder is liable for the least of: $150 (or such lower figure as may be determined by the account institution); or

(i) the balance of those account(s) (including any pre-arranged credit) from which value was transferred in the unauthorised transactions and which the account institution and the account holder have agreed may be accessed using the access method; or

(ii) the actual loss at the time the account institution is notified (where relevant) that the device has been misused, lost or stolen or that the security of the codes has been breached (excluding that portion of the losses incurred on any one day which exceed any applicable daily transaction or other periodic transaction limit(s)).

In determining whether an account institution has proved on the balance of probability that a user has contributed to losses under paragraph (a), all reasonable evidence must be considered, including all reasonable explanations for the transaction occurring. The fact that the account has been accessed with the correct access method, while significant, will not of itself constitute proof on the balance of probability that the user has contributed to losses through the user's fraud or through the user contravening the requirements in sub-clause 5.6.

In determining whether a user has unreasonably delayed notification under paragraph 5.5(b), the effect on the user of any charges imposed by the account institution relating to the notification or the replacement of the access method must be taken into account.

5.6 Where an access method utilises a code or codes, a user contravenes the requirements of this sub-clause if:

(a) the user voluntarily discloses one or more of the codes to anyone, including a family member or friend; or

(b) where the access method also utilises a device, the user indicates one or more of the codes on the outside of the device, or keeps a record of one or more of the codes (without making any reasonable attempt to protect the security of the code records) on the one article, or on several articles, carried with the device or liable to loss or theft simultaneously with the device; or

(c) where the access method comprises a code or codes without a device, the user keeps a record of all the codes (without making any reasonable attempt to protect the security of the code records) on the one article, or on several articles so that they are liable to loss or theft simultaneously;

(d) where, after the adoption of this revised Code by the account institution, the account institution permits the user to select or change a code and, immediately before the user's selection or change of the code, specifically instructs the user not to select a numeric code which represents the user's birth date or an alphabetical code which is a recognisable part of the user's name and warns the user of the consequences of such a selection and the user selects such a numeric or alphabetical code; or

(e) the user acts with extreme carelessness in failing to protect the security of all the codes.[17].

Where 5.6(d) applies, the onus will be on the account institution to prove on the balance of probabilities that it gave the specific instruction and warning to the user at the time specified and in a manner designed to focus the user's attention specifically on the instruction and consequences of breaching it. The user means the actual user, taking into account the capacity of the user to understand the warning.[18]

5.7 (a) Where an account institution expressly authorises particular conduct by a user (either generally or subject to conditions), the engaging in that conduct by the user (within any applicable conditions) is not a contravention of the requirements of sub clause 5.6.

(b) Where an account institution expressly or impliedly promotes, endorses or authorises the use of an account access service by a user (including by hosting an account access service at the account institution's electronic address), no disclosure, recording or storage of a code by a user that is required or recommended for the purposes of using that account access service is a contravention of the requirements of sub clause 5.6.[19]

5.8 (a) For the purposes of this clause, a reasonable attempt to protect the security of a code record includes either or both of:

      (i) making any reasonable attempt to disguise the code(s) within the record; or

     (ii) taking reasonable steps to prevent unauthorised access to the code record.[20]

(b)   An account institution in its Terms and Conditions and other communications to its users may provide guidelines for its users on ensuring the security of an access method which are consistent with clause 5 but it must:

      (i) clearly differentiate those guidelines from the circumstances in which an account holder is liable for losses resulting from unauthorized transactions as set out in this clause; and

     (ii) include a statement that an account holder's liability for such losses will be determined under the EFT Code of Conduct rather than the guidelines.

F NOTIFICATION OF THE LOSS, THEFT OR UNAUTHORISED USE OF DEVICES OR CODES

5.9 Account institutions will provide an effective and convenient means by which users can notify a lost or stolen device or unauthorised use of a device or breach of security of a code; facilities such as telephone hot lines are to be available to users at all times, with notice by telephone being an effective notice for limitation of the user's liability. Where such facilities are not available during particular periods any losses occurring during these periods that were due to non-notification are deemed to be the liability of the account institution providing notification is made to the account institution within a reasonable time of the facility again becoming available.

5.10 Account institutions will implement procedures for acknowledging receipt of notifications, including telephone notifications, by users of the loss, theft, or unauthorised use of a device or breach of security of a code. Such acknowledgments need not be in writing although they must provide a means by which users can verify that they have made a notification and when such notification was made.

G UNAUTHORISED CREDIT CARD AND CHARGE CARD ACCOUNT TRANSACTIONS

5.11 Where an account holder complains that there is an unauthorised transaction on a credit card account or a charge card account, the account institution shall not hold the account holder liable for losses under clause 5 for an amount greater than the liability the account holder would have to the account institution if the account institution exercised any relevant rights it had under the rules of the credit card or charge card scheme at the time the complaint was made against other parties to that scheme.[21]

H DISCRETION TO REDUCE ACCOUNT HOLDER'S LIABILITY WHERE NO REASONABLE DAILY OR PERIODIC TRANSACTION LIMITS

5.12 (a) This clause applies where a transaction is alleged to be unauthorised and the account institution has not applied a reasonable daily or other periodic transaction limit in respect of that transaction. The reasonableness of a transaction limit is to be determined having regard to prevailing industry practice.

(b) Where this clause applies, the account institution or an external dispute resolution body may reduce any liability that the account holder has for the unauthorised transaction under sub clause 5.5 by such amount as it considers fair and reasonable having regard to:

   (i) whether the security and reliability of the means used by the account institution to verify that the relevant transaction was authorised by the user adequately protected the account holder from losses in the absence of reasonable daily or other periodic transaction limits protection; and

   (ii) if the unauthorised transaction was a funds transfer that involved drawing on a line of credit accessible by the access method (including drawing on repayments made to a loan account), whether at the time of making the line of credit accessible by the access method, the account institution had taken reasonable steps to warn the account holder of the risk of the access method being used to make unauthorised transactions on that line of credit.[22]

6. Liability in cases of system or equipment malfunction

6.1 Account institutions will be responsible to their users for loss caused by the failure of an institution system or institution equipment to complete a transaction accepted by an institution system or institution equipment in accordance with the user's instructions.

6.2 The account institution is not to deny, implicitly or explicitly, a right to the user to make claims for consequential damage which may arise as a result of a malfunction of an institution system or institution equipment however caused, except, where the user should have been aware that the system or equipment was unavailable for use or malfunctioning, the account institution's responsibilities may be limited to the correction of any errors in the account, and the refund of any charges or fees imposed on the account holder as a result.

7. Deposits to accounts by funds transfers

A DISCREPANCIES BETWEEN RECORDED DEPOSITS AND AMOUNTS RECEIVED

7.1 Where, in relation to an EFT transaction which is a deposit of funds to an account, there is a discrepancy between the amount recorded by the electronic equipment or access method as having been deposited and the amount recorded by the account institution as having been received, the account holder will be notified of the difference as soon as possible and will be advised of the actual amount which has been credited to the nominated account.

B SECURITY OF DEPOSITS AT INSTITUTION EQUIPMENT

7.2 The security of deposits received at institution equipment is the responsibility of the account institution receiving the deposit from the time the transaction at the institution equipment is completed (subject to verification of amount(s) deposited).

8. Networking arrangements

8.1 For the purposes of clause 8, parties to the shared EFT system include retailers, merchants, communications service providers, and other organisations offering EFT facilities to users, as well as merchant acquirers and account institutions. Merchant acquirers are the institutions which provide EFT transaction facilities for merchants.

8.2 Account institutions may not avoid any obligations owed to their users by reason only of the fact that they are party to a shared EFT system and that another party to the system has actually caused the failure to meet the obligations.

8.3 An account institution shall not require its users to raise complaints or disputes in relation to the processing of EFT transactions with any other party to the shared EFT system, or to have those complaints or disputes investigated by any other party to the shared EFT system.

8.4 Where a merchant acquirer is advised by another party to the shared EFT system, or forms the view, that a transaction has been debited or credited incorrectly to a particular account, the merchant acquirer will notify the account institution concerned of the situation.
The account institution will then, following any investigation it may undertake pursuant to the advice received from the merchant acquirer, make any correction to a user's account it considers appropriate in the circumstances, and any such correction will be included in the user's account statement subsequently issued in the normal course. The account institution will also notify the account holder as soon as practicable after reversing an incorrect credit.
The account institution will provide to the account holder, upon inquiry, any further details required by the account holder concerning the transaction correction appearing on the account holder's statement.

9. Audit-trails

9.1 Account institutions will ensure that their EFT transaction systems generate sufficient records to enable transactions to be traced, checked and where an error has occurred, to be identified and corrected.

10. Complaint investigation and resolution procedures

10.1 Account institutions will establish internal complaint handling procedures which comply with Australian Standard AS4269–1995 or any other industry dispute resolution standard or guideline which ASIC declares to apply to this clause.

10.2 The account institution shall advise users in their Terms and Conditions, upon request and in their general documentation of the procedures for lodging a complaint.

10.3 When a complaint is lodged and is not immediately settled to the satisfaction of both user and account institution the account institution will advise the user, in writing, of the procedures for investigating and handling the complaint.

10.4 (a) The account institution's decision in relation to a complaint is to be made on the basis of all relevant established facts and not on the basis of inferences unsupported by evidence.

(b) Where a user raises a complaint concerning the authorisation of a transaction, the account institution will make reasonable efforts to obtain from the user at least the information outlined in the attached schedule where such information is relevant and available.

(c) Where a user raises a complaint concerning the authorisation of a transaction or a system or equipment malfunction, the institution must investigate whether there was any system or equipment malfunction at the time of the transaction.

10.5 Within 21 days of receipt of a complaint, the account institution will:

(a) complete the investigation and advise the user, in writing, of the outcome of the investigation; or

(b) advise the user, in writing, of the need for more time to complete its investigation.
Unless there are exceptional circumstances, the account institution should complete its investigation within 45 days of receipt of the complaint.[23]

10.6 If an account institution is unable to resolve a complaint within 45 days, it must:

(a) inform the user of the reasons for the delay;

(b)   provide the user with monthly updates on progress with the complaint; and

(c)   specify a date when a decision can be reasonably expected; unless the account institution is waiting for a response from the user and the user has been advised that the account institution requires such a response.

10.7 If an account institution decides to resolve a complaint concerning a credit card account or a charge card account by exercising its rights under the rules of the credit card or charge card scheme:

(a)   the time limits under the rules of the scheme apply in lieu of the time limits in sub-clause 10.5;

(b)   sub-clause 10.6 applies to the complaint with the following modifications:
   (i) '60 days' replaces '45 days'; and
   (ii) 'updates once every two months' replaces 'monthly updates'; and

(c)   the account institution shall:
   (i) inform the user, in writing, of those time limits and when a decision can be reasonably expected; and
   (ii) shall suspend the account holder's obligation to pay any amount which is the subject of the complaint and any credit and other charges related to that amount until the complaint is resolved and inform the account holder of that suspension.

10.8 When an account institution is a member of an external dispute resolution scheme, and the scheme's rules provide that a matter may be referred to it if a decision is not made within a specified time period, then the account institution must inform the user that a complaint may be lodged with the scheme no more than 5 business days after the expiry of the relevant time period.

10.9 On completing its investigation of a complaint, the account institution will promptly inform the user of:

(a)   the outcome of the investigation;

(b)   the reasons for the outcome including references to relevant clauses of the Code;

(c)   except where the complaint has been resolved completely in favour of the user, the further action the user can take in respect of the Code, including the contact details of any external dispute resolution body which the institution belongs to or, if it does not belong to such a body, the contact details for the Consumer Affairs Agency and Small Claims Courts/Tribunals in the consumer's jurisdiction. Such advice is to be in writing except where the complaint is settled immediately the account institution receives the complaint to the satisfaction of both the user and account institution.

10.10 Where as a result of the investigation of a complaint, an account institution decides that the account holder's account has been incorrectly credited or debited, having regard to the provisions of this Code, the account institution will, where appropriate, forthwith adjust the account holder's account (including appropriate adjustments for interest and/or charges) and notify the account holder in writing of the amount with which their account has been debited or credited as a result.

10.11 Where on completion of an investigation the account institution decides that the account holder is liable under clauses 5 or 6 of this Code for at least part of the amount of the transaction subject to complaint:

(a)   the account institution is to make available to the account holder copies of any documents or other evidence relevant to the outcome of its investigation including information from any logs or audit trails relating to the transaction; and

(b)   the account institution must advise the account holder in writing whether there was any system or equipment malfunction at the time of the transaction.

10.12 Where:

(a)   the account institution, its employees or its agents fail to observe the applicable complaint investigation and resolution procedures set out in this clause, or fail to determine the allocation of liability in accordance with clauses 5 and 6, or fail to communicate the reasons for that determination by reference to relevant aspects of clauses 5 and 6; and

(b)   the failure contributed to an institution decision on the complaint (including an initial decision) against the account holder, or the failure delayed the resolution of the complaint (including by contributing to the account holder referring the complaint to external dispute resolution);

the account institution or an external dispute resolution body may determine that the account institution is liable for part or all of the amount of the transaction in dispute as compensation for the effects of that decision or delay on the account holder or the user, even if the account institution or external dispute resolution body ultimately determine that the institution was not liable under clauses 5 and 6.[24]

10.13 Where the account institution:

(a)   decides to resolve a complaint concerning an unauthorised transaction under sub-clause 5.2, 5.3, 5.4 or paragraph 5.5(c); and

(b)   within 7 business days of receipt of the complaint, adjusts the account holder's accounts pursuant to sub-clause 10.10 to give effect to that decision and provides the user and account holder with the information required by subclauses 10.9 and 10.10;

the account institution is not required to comply with sub-clauses 10.3, 10.5, or 10.11 in respect of the complaint concerning the unauthorised transaction.[25]

10.14 The account institution is to provide for the recording of complaints and their resolution so that aggregate data on the type, frequency and resolution of such complaints can be made available as required in Part C of this Code and so that account institutions can identify and address systematic problems.

Part B: Rules for consumer stored value facilities and stored value transactions

11. Scope and interpretation

11.1 Part B of this Code applies to the use by a person of a stored value facility but does not apply to any use of a stored value facility designed primarily for use by a business and acquired primarily for business purposes. If an aspect of a use of a stored value facility is an EFT transaction to which Part A of this Code applies, Part B of this Code does not apply to that aspect of the use of the stored value facility.[26]

11.2 In this Part:

'Authorised deposit-taking institution' has the same meaning as in the *Banking Act 1959* (Cth).

'Issuer' means an entity, which, in the course of its business, provides a stored value facility to a user.

'Payment facilitator' means an entity, which is contractually bound to a user to facilitate the payments the user initiates by using a stored value facility.[27]

'Stored value' means a representation of value that:

(a)   is intended to be used to make a payment (for example digital cash or units of value recorded in a computer chip on a card); and

(b)   may or may not be denominated by reference to units of a currency.[28]

'Stored value facility' means a facility (for example software) which:

(a)   is designed to control:

    (i) the storage of stored value; and

    (ii) the release of that stored value from the facility in the course of making a payment using that stored value;

(b)   is intended to be in the possession and control of a user; and

(c)   contains a value control record.[29]

'Stored value operator' means, in respect of a stored value facility, an entity which subscribes to this Code and which is an issuer or a payment facilitator or both an issuer and a payment facilitator in respect of that stored value facility.[30]

'System participant' means a party to a stored value system and includes issuers, payment facilitators, holders of value received in exchange for stored value, originators of stored value, distributors of stored value, transaction processors, communications service providers and merchants who receive stored value as payment.

'User' means an individual intended by a stored value operator to use a stored value facility (whether or not the identity of the individual is known to the stored value operator) and, in the case of anonymous and transferable stored value facilities, includes the holder of the stored value facility from time to time.[31]

'Value control record' in a stored value facility means an adjustable record of the amount of stored value available to be released from the stored value facility that has the following features:

(a)   the determination of whether there is sufficient stored value available for each payment to be initiated using the stored value facility is made solely by reference to the amount in the value control record and not by reference to any other record of the amount of available stored value (for example a separate value record held by a stored value operator); and

(b)   the amount in the value control record is reduced by the amount of stored value released from the facility.[32]

11.3 In this Part, references to an 'exchange' of stored value for a payment of money or for a credit to an account:

(a)   are not intended to characterise or limit the legal nature of that exchange or the relationship between the parties involved; and

(b)   includes exchange by way of purchase and sale or repayment of a debt or other types of exchange.

11.4 A stored value operator who is obliged to, or elects to, pay money to a user under a provision in Part B has the choice of paying it:

(a)   in the form of Australian currency; or

(b)   by crediting an account at an authorised deposit-taking institution nominated by the user; or

(c)   in any other manner agreed with the user.

12. Availability and disclosure of information and terms and conditions applicable to stored value facilities

12.1 Stored value operators will prepare for their users clear and unambiguous Terms and Conditions for the use of stored value facilities which reflect the requirements of this Code. In respect of the subject matters dealt with in this Code, the Terms and Conditions will not provide for greater liabilities or lesser rights for users than those set out in this Code. The Terms and Conditions are to include a warranty that the requirements of this Code will be complied with.

12.2 Stored value operators will provide a copy of the Terms and Conditions to the user:

(a)   at the time of first providing a stored value facility to a user or, if that is not practical in the circumstances, provide a summary of the main rights and liabilities of users under the Terms and Conditions and a notice of where the user may obtain a copy of the Terms and Conditions; and

(b)   at any other time when requested to do so by a user.
The availability of Terms and Conditions is to be publicised by stored value operators.

12.3 Stored value operators will ensure that, before a stored value facility is used for the first time after issue, the user to whom it is issued has been provided with information on at least the following matters or, if that is not feasible, a summary of the information and a notice of where the user may obtain the full information:

(a)   any charges (imposed or controlled by the stored value operator) for the issue or use of a stored value facility, or the issue, exchange, transfer, loading or unloading of stored value.[33]

     Charges for the issue, exchange, transfer, loading or unloading of stored value do not include charges for funding the stored value (e.g. credit charges for obtaining stored value on credit);

(b)   the period or date (if any and if determinable at the time of issue) after which the stored value facility or the stored value controlled by the facility will not be usable to make a payment;

(c)   the user's rights and the procedure to be followed by the user in relation to exchanging the stored value for money or for replacement stored value;

(d)   whether there is a procedure (and, if so, a description of the procedure) for reporting a malfunction or error in the operation of a stored value facility or the loss or theft of a stored value facility or of stored value controlled by the stored value facility;

(e)   whether there are any circumstances (and, if so, a description of the circumstances) in which the stored value operator may pay to the user some or all of the amount of lost or stolen stored value; and

326

(f)   where the user can obtain more information and the Terms and Conditions for the stored value facility.[34]

13. Changing the terms and conditions of use

13.1 Subject to sub-clause 13.4, stored value operators wishing to vary or modify the Terms and Conditions for the use of stored value facilities will provide notification of the change to users in advance.

13.2 (a) Where the stored value operator knows the identity and contact details of a user and the change relates to the matters set out in sub-clause 13.3, the stored value operator will provide the information directly to the user.

(b)   In all other cases, the stored value operator will publicise the changes in a manner which is likely to come to the attention of as many users as possible and which has previously been advised to users.[35]

13.3 Where the change will:

(a)   impose or increase charges (imposed or controlled by the stored value operator) relating solely to the use of a stored value facility, or the issue of an additional or replacement stored value facility, or the issue, exchange, transfer, loading and unloading of stored value;

(b)   adjust the load or value storage limits applying to the use of a stored value facility;

(c)   affect the user's ability to exchange stored value, notify the loss or theft of stored value or be paid the amount of lost or stolen stored value; or

(d)   reduce the period (if any) during which the stored value facility or stored value controlled by the facility will be useable to make a payment; the stored value operator will allow a period of notice of at least 20 days (or, where applicable legislation requires a longer notice period, that longer period) before the change takes effect except where the user has specifically agreed to a change described in paragraphs (b) or (c).

13.4 Advance notice need not be given when changes are necessitated by an immediate need to manage, restore or maintain the integrity or the security of the system or individual accounts or stored value facilities.

14. Record of available balance

14.1 Stored value operators must ensure that an undamaged stored value facility (either by itself or together with other equipment reasonably available to users) enables a user to ascertain the amount of stored value controlled by the stored value facility, which is available for use.

15. Rights to exchange stored value

RIGHT TO EXCHANGE STORED VALUE FOR MONEY OR REPLACEMENT STORED VALUE

15.1 The user of a stored value facility may require the stored value operator to accept stored value controlled by the facility and in exchange (at the option of the user):

(a)   if the stored value is denominated by reference to a currency, pay the user the equivalent amount of money; or

(b)   credit the amount of that stored value towards providing replacement stored value which is usable for the same purposes.

The stored value operator may charge a reasonable fee for such an exchange but not where sub-clause 15.2 applies.[36]

RIGHT OF EXCHANGE APPLIES WHERE STORED VALUE OR FACILITY IS UNUSABLE

15.2 Where the user's stored value facility or the stored value controlled by the facility is no longer able to be used to make a payment:

(a)   the right in sub-clause 15.1 applies provided the amount of stored value controlled by the stored value facility can be ascertained by the stored value operator using its own equipment; and

(b)   subject to paragraph 15.3(b), the Terms and Conditions may provide that the right must be exercised within a specified period of at least 12 months after the date the stored value or stored value facility is no longer able to be used.[37]

LIMITS ON THE RIGHT OF EXCHANGE

15.3 (a) The stored value operator may refuse to exchange the stored value under sub-clause 15.1 if the stored value operator can prove that:
   (i) the stored value has not been created by a system participant authorized to create stored value;
   (ii) a copy of the stored value has previously been exchanged for money; or
   (iii) the user presenting the stored value for exchange is not doing so in good faith.

(b)   The Terms and Conditions may provide for the manner of exercising the right under sub-clause 15.1 and, in particular, may provide that where a stored value scheme is suspended or terminated for security reasons, the right in sub-clause 15.1 must be exercised within a reasonable time (not less than 14 days) after users are advised of the suspension or termination of the scheme.[38]

328

16. Refund of lost or stolen stored value

16.1 Where:

(a)   a stored value operator, together with relevant system participants, has or can create a reliable record of the amount of stored value controlled by a stored value facility from time to time; and

(b)   the stored value operator and any relevant system participants can prevent any further transfers of stored value from the facility; the stored value operator must:

(c)   provide a means for a user to notify the stored value operator (or other entity specified by the stored value operator) at any time of the loss or theft of the stored value facility; and

(d)   where a user gives notice under paragraph (c), pay the user the amount of stored value which the stored value operator could have prevented from being transferred from the facility.[39]

17. System or equipment malfunction

17.1 The stored value operator is liable to the user of a stored value facility for any losses (including any amount of lost stored value) arising from a failure to execute or the defective execution of the user's transactions, where the failure to execute or the defective execution is attributable to a malfunction of the facility or of a device, terminal or other equipment controlled or provided by or on behalf of the stored value operator, provided the malfunction was not caused by the user knowingly or in breach of the Terms and Conditions of use of the facility.

18. Stored value operator's obligations

18.1 A stored value operator:

(a)   may not avoid its responsibility to meet any obligation owed to users by reason only of the fact that another system participant has caused or contributed to the failure to meet the obligation; and

(b)   shall not require users to raise complaints or disputes regarding the use of a stored facility with, or have these complaints or disputes investigated by, any other system participant.

19. Complaint investigation and dispute resolution

19.1 Clause 10 of this Code (other than sub-clauses 10.10, 10.11, 10.12 and 10.13) applies to stored value operators under Part B of the Code as if they were account institutions under Part A of the Code.

Part C: Privacy, electronic communication, administration and review

20. Interpretation and Multiple Disclosure Obligations

20.1 In this Code:

'Code subscriber' means an account institution as defined in Part A or a stored value operator as defined in Part B.

'electronic communication' means a message transmitted and received electronically in a manner and a format that:

(a)   allows the message information to be presented to the recipient in a manner and format (e.g. visual display or sound recording) that is clear and readily understandable; and

(b)   allows the recipient of the message to retain the message information for subsequent reference (e.g. by printing the message information or storing the message information for later display or printing or listening).

20.2 In this Code, unless the contrary intention appears:

(a)   the singular includes the plural and vice versa; and

(b)   a reference to an access method includes a reference to each of the individual components that are part of the access method (including devices, identifiers and codes); and

(c)   inclusive definitions of a term and examples used to illustrate or amplify the meaning of a term do not limit the meaning of the term.

20.3 Explanatory notes to provisions in this Code do not form part of the Code but may be used to interpret the provisions of the Code.

20.4 Where legislation and this Code both require a Code subscriber to provide notice of changes to Terms and Conditions of use at different times:

(a)   the Code subscriber shall provide that notice at the earliest time it is required under the legislation or this Code; and

(b)   the provision of that notice under the legislation at or before the time required by this Code, will satisfy the Code's requirements for notice.[40]

21. Privacy

21.1 From 21 December 2001 Code subscribers will comply with the National Privacy Principles in the *Privacy Act* 1988 (Cth) or with Codes to which the Code subscriber has also subscribed which are approved and operative under that legislation.[41]

21.2 The following *guidelines* are provided to assist in interpreting the National Privacy Principles and any approved Code referred to in sub-clause 21.1 and in applying them to EFT transactions under Part A:

(a) *where surveillance devices (including visual, sound or data recording) may be used by or on behalf of an account institution to monitor EFT transactions, account institutions should notify users, before the commencement of each transaction or of each session of transactions, that the transaction may be recorded by surveillance devices and the nature of the surveillance;*

(b) *account institutions shall take reasonable steps to ensure that, except where it is being operated by an employee or agent of the account institution concerned, no institution equipment or institution system is capable of providing any information concerning an account unless the correct access method for that account has been used;*

(c) *transaction receipts should not disclose information which would reveal the full account number, name or address of the account holder; and*

(d) *if EFT transactions can be conducted through an account institution's electronic address (e.g. a web site), the account institution should ensure that clear privacy policies are made available at or through that electronic address and can be provided to a user by electronic communication if the user so requests.*
In this sub-clause, terms have the same meaning as in Part A of this Code.

21.3 In deciding whether a Code subscriber has complied with the relevant principles under sub-clause 21.1, the terms of the principles (and not the terms of any applicable guidelines in sub-clause 21.2) are determinative.

22. Electronic communications

22.1 Unless prohibited by legislation, a user (as defined in Part A or Part B) may agree that any information which this Code requires the Code subscriber to provide (by writing or other means) may be provided:

(a) by electronic communication to the user's device, electronic equipment or electronic address nominated by the user; or

(b) by being made available at the Code subscriber's electronic address for retrieval by electronic communication to the user on the condition that:
   (i) the Code subscriber promptly notifies the user by electronic communi- cation under paragraph (a) that the information is available for retrieval at the electronic address and the nature of the information; and
   (ii) the Code subscriber provides the user with the ability to readily retrieve the information by electronic communication (e.g. by providing an electronic link to the relevant information at the Code subscriber's electronic address or the URL of the Code subscriber's website).[42]
The user's agreement to the provision of information under paragraph (a) or (b) or both must be by a specific positive election after receiving an explanation of the

implications of making such an election. The user may by notice to the Code subscriber vary the user's nominated device, electronic equipment or electronic address or terminate the agreement to the provision of information under paragraph (a) or (b) or both and the Code subscriber must inform the user of those rights.[43]

22.2 (a) Except in respect of a user and Code subscriber who have a current agreement that satisfies 22.1(b), and subject to paragraphs (b) and (c), making information available at a Code subscriber's electronic address (e.g. a web site) does not satisfy any requirement of this Code that the information be provided to a user.

(b) Where a user has viewed information available at a Code subscriber's electronic address (e.g. a web site), and has:
   (i) been given the opportunity to retain that information for subsequent reference (e.g. by saving or printing it); and
   (ii) specifically agrees that the user has viewed the information and has been given the opportunity to retain that information and that the user will not be otherwise provided with a copy of the information by the Code subscriber (without a separate request by the user under sub-clause 22.3);
   the Code subscriber is to be treated as having provided that information to the user at the time the user specifically agreed.

(c) Where an EFT transaction is initiated by a user through an electronic address, the account institution may satisfy its obligation to provide a receipt under subclause 4.1 by making the receipt available to the user at the same electronic address immediately on completion of the transaction in the manner and format described in the definition of 'electronic communication' in sub-clause 20.1.[44]

22.3 Where a Code subscriber has provided, or is treated as having provided, information (other than a receipt under clause 4.1) to a user by electronic communication under sub-clauses 22.1 or 22.2, the Code subscriber shall provide a paper copy of that information to the user if the user so requests within 6 months of the receipt of the electronic communication.

23. Commencement and administration

23.1 (a) Subject to (b), the Code shall become binding on Code subscribers on 1 April 2002.

(b) Clause 4.6 shall become binding on Code subscribers on 1 April 2003.

(c) Code subscribers can choose to be bound by this Code at an earlier date than that set down in (a) or (b).

23.2 Code subscribers shall notify ASIC of the fact that they have subscribed to the Code by using the form available from ASIC's website www.asic.gov.au (choose

'Policy and Practitioners'). Completed forms should be sent to Consumer Protection Directorate, ASIC, GPO Box 4866, Sydney NSW 1042.[45]

23.3 (a) A Code subscriber, or prospective Code subscriber, may separately or jointly with another Code subscriber or prospective Code subscriber, apply to ASIC for a modification of the application of the provisions of Part B of this Code in relation to particular products, services or activities of that entity.

(b) ASIC may consult with any third party that might be materially or adversely affected by a decision on the application and with consumer representatives.

(c) If ASIC wants to consult a third party it must obtain the consent of the Code subscriber or prospective Code subscriber before releasing any confidential information that they have provided to ASIC.

(d) ASIC may require any party with which it consults to sign a confidentiality agreement as a condition of being consulted.

(e) In considering whether or not to grant the modification ASIC will give consideration to any relevant matters, including:
   (i) whether or not the modification would significantly undermine the consumer protection objectives of the Code;
   (ii) whether relevant Code objectives can be achieved in some other way;
   (iii) whether failure to grant the modification would cause unreasonable expense to the institution or make a product unviable;
   (iv) whether the modification is needed to prevent the Code interfering with technological and product innovation;
   (v) the need to avoid confusion in relevant markets; and
   (vi) the need to ensure competitive neutrality in relevant matters.

(f) If ASIC grants the modification and publishes a notice setting out the modification on its Website, at www.asic.gov.au, the relevant provisions of the Code apply as modified to that entity for the period specified in the notice.

23.4 After consultation with interested parties, ASIC may publish an order modifying:

(a) the application of one or more of the disclosure requirements in clauses 2, 3, 12 and 13 of this Code in relation to some or all products of some or all Code subscribers in order to avoid Code disclosure obligations operating inconsistently with, or duplicating, disclosure obligations in legislation; and

(b) clause 4.6 to ensure consistency with future legislative or industry practices; and

(c) the standards for industry dispute resolution that apply under sub clause 10.1

23.5 Code subscribers, or their representative associations, will report to the Commonwealth Government annually on compliance with this Code as outlined in sub-clauses 23.6 and 23.7.

23.6 Code subscribers and/or their associations will report in accordance with the reporting guidelines for the industry sector, on compliance with this Code.

23.7 Code subscribers will establish administrative arrangements to ensure their staff receive adequate training on the requirements of this Code. Code subscribers and/or their associations will also report on initiatives in training staff in understanding and implementing the Code.

24. Review

24.1 ASIC, in consultation with Code subscribers and their respective associations, relevant State and Territory government agencies and consumer representatives and relevant independent industry dispute resolution schemes:

(a)   will undertake periodic reviews of the requirements of the Code, including the administrative arrangements set out in clause 23 and the first review of the Code as revised in 2001 will commence not later than 2 years after the date determined under paragraph 23.1(a);

(b)   may issue guidelines interpreting the provisions of the Code.

SCHEDULE TO CODE

Information to be obtained where available and relevant from users making a complaint concerning the authorisation of an EFT transaction as required under clause 10.4.

1.   account type and number, type of access method used

2.   name and address of user

3.   other users authorised to operate on the relevant account(s)

4.   whether device signed

5.   whether device lost or stolen or security of codes(s) breached
   - date and time of loss, theft or security breach
   - time of report to account institution,
   - time, date, method of reporting reported to police or other authority

6.   code details
   - was record of code made

      - how recorded
      - where kept
   - was record of code lost or stolen

      - date of loss, time
   - has code been disclosed to anyone

7.   How loss occurred (e.g. housebreaking, stolen purse/wallet)

8.   Where loss of device occurred, e.g. office, home

9.   Details of transaction to be investigated
     description, date, time, amount
     type and location of electronic equipment used

10. Details of any
     ● circumstances surrounding the loss or theft or security breach of the device or codes, or the reporting of such loss or theft or security breach; or
     ● steps taken to ensure the security of the device or codes; which the user considers relevant to his/her liability in respect of the transaction

11. Details of last valid transaction

End notes

[1] An instruction may be given directly to an account institution (e.g. through the institution's own electronic terminal or Interactive Voice Recognition (IVR) system or electronic address) or indirectly (e.g. the instruction is given through an electronic terminal or IVR system or electronic address belonging to a third party, such as a merchant or another account institution, and then on-sent for ultimate delivery to the account institution which maintains the account).

Where the instruction from the person to the account institution is given indirectly through one or more intermediaries, it is an EFT transaction if the account institution relies for its authority to debit or credit an EFT account on the use (by the person or by an intermediary) of an access method authorised by the institution to be used directly by a user but not if the account institution relies on a different form of authority used by an intermediary (e.g.. a direct debit authority held by the intermediary): see the definition of 'access method'. E.g. If the account institution issues a password to a user who gives it to an intermediary (such as an account aggregator) and the intermediary uses that password to give an instruction to the account institution and the account institution relies on the use of that password as authority to debit an EFT account, it is an EFT transaction. But if the intermediary (e.g. a merchant) transmits a user's payment instruction to an account institution which relies for its authority to debit an EFT account on a different form of authority not authorised for direct use by a user (e.g. the merchant's direct debit authority given by the user), it is not an EFT transaction.

[2] The definition of 'funds transfer' is broad but the Code does not apply to a funds transfer unless it is initiated by giving an instruction, through electronic equipment and using an access method, to an account institution to debit or credit an EFT account.

A 'funds transfer' does include:

● a transaction which is a user-initiated transfer of value by the account institution to a third party (e.g. in payment for goods or services supplied by the third party to the user) and a debit by the account institution to the customer's EFT account to reimburse the account institution for the amount of value transferred (e.g. a credit card payment to the third party). The debit to the customer's EFT account is the relevant funds transfer for the purposes of Part A. It is irrelevant whether the customer's EFT account has a credit or debit balance before the debit was made;

- a credit card cash advance/withdrawal if initiated through electronic equipment using an access method because value is transferred from the cardholder's EFT account by debiting that account.

A 'funds transfer' does not include:

- balance inquiries;

- a transfer of value from a customer's biller account to the biller account institution to pay the account institution for goods or services (other than financial services) provided *by the account institution* to the customer: see paragraph 1.4(b);

- a transfer of stored value unless this also effects the transfer of value to or from an EFT account at an institution (e.g. exchanging stored value for a debit or credit to an EFT account). Thus Part A does not cover transfer of stored value between two stored value facilities as defined in Part B (e.g. between two stored value cards) because a stored value facility (as defined) is not an EFT account (see definition of 'EFT account').

A physical payment instrument delivered as a transfer of value could include a traveller's cheque or bank cheque.

[3] Many companies (e.g. electricity suppliers and department stores) maintain customer accounts to record the amounts owing and paid by the customer for goods or services provided by the company. These accounts are defined as 'biller accounts' in sub-clause 1.5 if the customer can initiate a funds transfer from or to the accounts using an access method through electronic equipment.

Receipt of funds for credit of biller accounts not regulated by Part A except clause 7

Where the customer makes a funds transfer (e.g. by BPay from a bank account) to the company for credit to the customer's biller account (e.g. to pay an electricity bill or pre-pay for anticipated future purchases), Part A may apply to the bank in debiting the bank account but under paragraph 1.4 (a), Part A will not apply to the receipt by the company of the funds transfer for credit to the biller account except for clause 7. Clause 7 deals with the security of deposits received through the company's electronic equipment and with discrepancies between amounts recorded as having been deposited through electronic equipment and amounts recorded as received.

Transfer of Funds from a Biller Account to Pay the Biller Usually Not Covered by Part A

In some cases a company may be paid for goods or services it supplies to a customer by the customer initiating a debit to the customer's biller account and transferring funds to the company (e.g. where the customer has prepaid an ISP account and the customer initiates a debit to that account, using an access method, as the customer uses the service). Paragraph 1.4(b) makes it clear that these funds transfers are not covered by Part A. (The only exception is where there is a customer-initiated funds transfer from the customer's biller account to pay for financial services supplied by the company to the customer. This exception has been included to maintain competitive neutrality with financial institutions.)

Transfer of Funds from Customer Accounts to Pay Third Parties May Be Covered by Part A

Some companies permit their customers to use a customer account as a means of making payments **to third parties** e.g. a customer charges the price of a CD or financial information (supplied by a third party) to the customer's telephone account. The telephone company pays the third party supplier and debits the customer's telephone account and the customer reimburses the telephone company by paying the amount (with any fees) to the telephone company to be credited to the customer's telephone account. This use of a customer account to pay third parties is effectively the same as a credit card or charge card account. (A customer account which can be used to make payments to third parties is not a 'biller account' as defined.) If the customer account is an EFT account (e.g. the customer can initiate a funds transfer from the customer account using an access method through electronic equipment), the use of the customer account to pay third parties is covered by Part A. Sub-clause 1.4 does not alter this coverage.

---

[4] 'Access method' includes but is not limited to physical 'devices', non-secret 'identifiers' (such as account numbers, card numbers, expiry dates) and secret 'codes' (such as a PIN or password which is known only to the user or only to the user and the account institution). It includes a biometric of the user such as a fingerprint, or retinal pattern or voice pattern, whether or not the biometric is an 'identifier' as defined.

• It does not include a method where the intended means of user authentication is based on requiring a user's manual signature and comparing the appearance of that signature with a written specimen signature (e.g. cheques, signed withdrawal slips, signed credit card vouchers) on the grounds that the common law already covers liability allocation for manual signatures. Note that the comparison need not have occurred in any particular transaction (e.g. Signature is not actually compared on many cheques or credit card vouchers but manual signature is the intended means of authentication). Other signature authentication methods not based on comparison of appearance with a written specimen will come within the definition (e.g. signature dynamics where the signer is authenticated by comparing the pressure, speed and stroke order of the signature against a previously obtained electronic record of this data).

- The inclusion of non-secret 'identifiers' means that the use of an account number or card number at electronic equipment without a device or secret code, now comes within the scope of the EFT Code (e.g. use of a credit card number through a telephone or personal computer to make a purchase).

- The user is not liable for unauthorised transactions based on the use of an identifier without a code or a device (see sub-clauses 5.5 and 5.6). The user is liable for unauthorised transactions based on the use of a device (or a device and an identifier) without a code only where the user unreasonably delays in notifying loss or theft of the device (see paragraph 5.5(b)).

- The access method or some of its components need not have been issued by the financial institution e.g. a PKI private key on a smart card issued by a third party.

- An access method such as a code or identifier could be provided by voice communication through electronic equipment.

[5] An account institution need not be a traditional financial institution. The term includes companies which maintain customer accounts and bodies which pay third parties on the instruction of users and debit users' accounts to cover the amount of those payments (provided the accounts are 'EFT accounts').

[6] Examples of a biller account may be an electricity company's or a department store's customer account. A regular deposit account at a financial institution is not a biller account under this definition.

[7] A code:

- does not include codes or cryptographic keys the content of which is not known to the user e.g. a PKI private key on a smart card or computer hard drive because it is too long to be memorised;

- does include a code used to access a device e.g. a PIN used to unlock a card or token even if the code is not used separately to access the electronic equipment.

[8] The definition excludes accounts not belonging to a customer (e.g. suspense or internal accounts). It also clarifies that in stored value systems where the stored value facility contains a value control record, neither the value control record nor other value records are EFT accounts for the purposes of Part A. However, products branded as stored value products which do not have value control records in the product are not covered by this exclusion and may in fact be remote account access products covered by Part A.

[9] An identifier may be, for example, an account number, card number, card expiry date.

[10] There are additional interpretation provisions applicable to the whole Code in clause 20.

338

[11] Sub-clause 20.4 deals with overlapping legislative disclosure requirement.

[12] For example, privacy and security concerns may preclude providing balance information at EFTPOS terminals but not at ATMs. Account institutions should avoid adding non-required information to receipts (such as credit card expiry dates) which increase the risk of unauthorised transactions.

[13] Clause 22 permits electronic provision of receipts.

[14] E.g. The user initiates a credit card payment over the Internet at a merchant's web site. The account institution may not be able to ensure a receipt is provided under paragraph 4.1(a) but must use its best endeavours (e.g. through the merchant's acquiring institution or the card association) to see that the merchant provides a receipt.

[15] This provision only applies to those agreements which would ordinarily be entered into.

[16] The dominant contributing cause of the losses is the cause that is more than 50% responsible for the losses when assessed together with all other contributing causes. A daily transaction limit may apply to the use of an access method, an account or particular electronic equipment or a combination of these. Paragraphs 2.3(b) and 3.1(c) contain relevant notice requirements.

[17] 'Extreme carelessness' means a degree of carelessness with the security of the codes which greatly exceeds what would normally be considered careless behaviour. For example, storing the user's username and password for Internet banking in a diary or personal organizer or computer (not locked with a PIN) under the heading 'Internet banking codes'.
Paragraph (e) does not apply to the selection of codes – paragraph (d) covers this. An access method may also include identifiers but the security of identifiers is irrelevant to liability under clause 5.5.

[18] Institutions may also technically restrict available self-selection choices by users in whatever way they wish.

[19] E.g. an account institution may decide to let its users provide their codes to the institution's own or an associated company's account aggregator service or store the codes in an electronic wallet on the user's personal computer. If the institution promotes or endorses that service or authorises its users to use that service, such conduct by the user is not a contravention of 5.6. If the institution does not promote, endorse or authorise the use of the service, the user's use of the service may breach sub-clause 5.6.
(Note that, while account aggregation services raise a number of issues which could possibly be addressed in the EFT Code, the revised Code does not attempt to deal in any detail with this issue as the services only began emerging towards the end of the 2000 review process and a rushed response was not considered to

be appropriate. It may be that the Code will be amended at a later date to deal with account aggregation issues or these issues could be dealt with elsewhere. The matters addressed in 5.7 were included to address one narrow aspect of the PIN security which was thought to need immediate attention.)

[20] Reasonable steps to prevent unauthorised access may involve hiding or disguising the code record among other records or in places where a code record would not be expected to be found, by keeping a record of the code in a securely locked container or preventing unauthorised access to an electronically stored record of the code.

[21] Account institutions may be able to resolve unauthorised transaction disputes on credit card or charge card accounts by exercising rights (such as the right to charge back a transaction) against other parties to credit card or charge card schemes. This clause does not require account institutions to exercise any such rights. However they cannot hold account holders liable under clause 5 for a greater amount than would apply if they had exercised those rights. The relevant rights under the rules are those that exist at the time the complaint was made. A delayed complaint may mean the rights have expired by the time of the complaint.

[22] Account institutions may impose other periodic transaction limits as they wish e.g. by reference to access method, account or institution equipment used. Other periodic transaction limits apply in addition to the daily transaction limit.

[23] Exceptional circumstances may include delays caused by foreign account institutions or foreign merchants being involved in resolving the complaint.

[24] The purpose of this clause is to provide an incentive to institutions to implement good investigation and decision-making procedures in accordance with the Code and to compensate account holders for the effects of prejudicial decisions or delays.
Because this clause is about procedural compliance, the institution may be made liable under this sub-clause even if the institution ultimately is not found liable on the substance of the complaint under clauses 5 and 6. Liability under this sub-clause might arise for example where an account institution did not obtain from the user the information listed in the Schedule to the Code, did not analyse the liability of the user in terms of clause 5 and informed the user that she or he was liable simply because the correct code was used to access the account. If those failures led to the user seeking senior management review or external review of the decision, then an award of some portion of the amount in dispute against the institution may be justified for the inconvenience and expense caused to the account holder and the user by the institution's failure to properly investigate, analyse and explain its decision on the complaint. An award may be justified for inconvenience and expense even if the institution's decision is upheld on other properly reasoned grounds after full investigation. The amount of the award would be a matter for the senior management or external review body having regard to all the circumstances.

[25] Sub-clause 10.13 is designed to reduce compliance obligations and transaction costs and the risk of liability under clause 10.12 for account institutions which decide quickly to allocate no liability to the account holder or use the no-fault apportionment route in clause 5.5(c).

[26] E.g. the amount of stored value recorded in the value control record of a stored value facility may be increased (or 'loaded') in exchange for a debit to an EFT account. The debiting of and transfer of value from the EFT account may be an EFT transaction – if so, it is regulated by Part A, not Part B. The operation of the stored value facility, including the adjustment of the value control record, is regulated by Part B.

[27] A payment facilitator may facilitate a payment for example by facilitating the reduction of a liability it has to the payer in the amount of the payment and

(a)   facilitating the increase of a liability it has to the payee in the amount of the payment; or

(b)   procuring another entity to increase a liability that entity has to the payee in the amount of the payment.

[28] Different stored value systems may use different representations of value e.g. a balance record of units of value which is decremented or incremented in a payment; or digital tokens assigned a fixed nominal value.
Stored value may be denominated by reference to units of a currency but a stored value unit need not equate to one currency unit. A stored value unit may represent 22¢ or $5.60 or six stored value units may represent $1.00. Stored value need not be denominated by reference to units of a currency e.g. beenz, MyPoints. Stored value may be issued in exchange for money or as a gift or on credit.

[29] A 'release' of stored value from a facility constitutes part but not the whole of a transfer of stored value from the facility to another person in the course of paying the other person. A stored value facility must control the release of value but need not control the completion of the transfer to another person.
A 'release' of stored value includes (without limitation):

●   decrementing the balance of stored value on the facility; or

●   sending digital tokens of fixed nominal value such as digital coins from the facility.

A transfer of stored value includes a release of stored value from a facility and the receipt of stored value by a payee's facility or terminal. Without limitation, the receipt may occur by incrementing a balance on the payee's facility or the receiving and storage of digital tokens by the payee's facility.
A stored value facility includes, for example, software for controlling storage and release of stored value whether that software is supplied to a user for installation on the user's computer (e.g. purse software to manage digital coins) or is supplied to a user already installed on a computer or device (e.g. software that operates the stored purse function on a smart card containing a microprocessor chip).

The stored value facility may also control the receipt of value to the facility (e.g. a reload or receipt of a payment).

[30] Stored value systems may have:

- a single entity who is both the issuer and payment facilitator – that entity is the stored value operator if it subscribes to the Code e.g. a bank that issues digital cash stored value facilities and is the payment facilitator.

- one or more issuers and one or more payment facilitators – those entities can determine which one or more of them should subscribe to the Code and become a stored value operator or stored value operators.

Each issuer and payment facilitator who subscribes to the Code is subject to all the obligations under the Code. Each such entity should ensure it has in place rights against other system participants (including other Code subscribers) which it needs to meet its obligations under the Code (e.g. a right to call on the holder of the funds received in exchange for stored value to meet exchange for money obligations under clause 15) – see clause 18.

[31] For example, a stored value operator may intend that a stored value facility be used:

- only by the identified individual to whom it is issued;

- by another individual authorised by the individual to whom it is issued;

- by any individual within a group or class (e.g. public transport users, students at a university); or

- by any member of the public.

[32] The type of record in a value control record will vary according to the stored value system, e.g. it may be a single balance record or may be the sum of the nominal values of the digital tokens controlled by the stored value facility. The key feature in the definition is paragraph (a). A stored value operator may maintain a shadow account mirroring the value record on a stored value card or software product such as digital coin purse.

If transfers of value initiated by the card or software product are authorised by reference to the value record on the card or software product rather than any shadow balance, the card or software product is a stored value facility (assuming it meets the rest of the definition) regulated by Part B and neither the value control record nor the shadow account is an EFT account for the purposes of Part A (see definition of 'EFT account' in Part A). Part A will only be relevant to a stored value facility where it transfers value to or receives value from an EFT account.

But if transfers of value initiated by the card or software product are authorised by reference to a shadow account or other value record instead of a value control record, then the card or software product is not a stored value facility but more akin to an access device used to access an account record maintained by an institution. The intention is that such cards and software products will be regulated by Part A as access methods used to initiate funds transfers from the shadow account or other value account if that is an EFT account under Part A.

The value control record is the sole determinant of whether there is sufficient stored value available to make a payment. However, reference may be made to a stored value operator's records for other authorisations, e.g. whether the card has been reported as lost or stolen and hence disabled.

[33] A Code subscriber may also be required to disclose some of this information under cl. 2.3 in Part A (e.g. charges for loading or unloading to an account) to a 'user' as defined in Part A. If that person is also a 'user' as defined in Part B, only one disclosure of the same information is required.

[34] Information provided under sub-clause 12.2 prior to first use of a facility which covers items in sub-clause 12.3 need not be re-supplied under 12.3.

All information can be provided by electronic communication in accordance with Part C.

[35] All information can be provided by electronic communication in accordance with Part C.

[36] Any fee must be disclosed under sub-clause 12.3. If the stored value is not denominated by reference to a currency (e.g. loyalty points), there is no obligation to exchange the stored value for money but the obligation to credit the stored value towards replacement stored value still applies.

[37] A stored value facility or stored value may be unusable to make a payment for many reasons e.g. the facility is damaged or malfunctioning, the facility or the value has expired or the amount of stored value remaining is below the minimum needed for a transaction.

[38] Sub-clause 15.1 gives users the right to require the stored value operator to exchange stored value either for credit towards replacement stored value or for the equivalent amount of money. If the amount of the credit is below the minimum issue amount of stored value, the user will have to 'top it up' to the minimum issue amount by using other credits or paying money. The stored value operator can charge a reasonable fee for providing replacement stored value or money in exchange unless sub-clause 15.2 applies. Money may be paid (at the option of the stored value operator) in the form of currency or as a credit to an account at an ADI nominated by the user or in another manner agreed with the user (sub-cl. 11.4).

[39] Under clause 12.3 the stored value operator must inform users whether any action can be taken to prevent unauthorised use of lost or stolen stored value and whether any refund will be made. The ability to provide a refund will turn on technical capabilities including prevention of unauthorised use and having an independent record of the balance on the facility at any time.

[40] Legislation such as the proposed *Financial Services Reform Bill* 2000 may require notice of changes to be provided at a different time than the Code requires the same information to be provided. Sub-clause 20.4 makes clear that Code subscribers should comply with the earliest disclosure obligation (e.g. the Financial Services Reform Bill's) and thus satisfy the timing of all disclosure obligations.

[41] The National Privacy Principles may be found at www.privacy.gov.au.

[42] Information can be readily available from an electronic address for the purposes of sub-paragraph 22.1(b)(ii) even if the user is required to input a code (as defined in Part A) to retrieve the information.

[43] The agreement referred to in sub clause 22.1 may be formed by electronic communications. A user's electronic address could be e.g. an email address or a facsimile number.

[44] Paragraph 4.1(c) imposes only a best endeavours obligation on the institution where the user's communication is with a third party (e.g. an online merchant) and does not use institution equipment.

[45] Subscribers to the existing Code will need to re-subscribe to the new Code. The new Code will apply to a Code subscriber in lieu of the old Code on the date the Code subscriber subscribes to the new Code. The old provisions of the Code cease to operate from 1 April 2002.

APPENDIX 2

Minimum Guidelines on the Provision of Internet Banking Services by Licensed Banking Institutions

Foreword

While the Internet provides important benefits to banking institutions and their customers, it also exposes banking institutions to new and different risks, and these risks must be balanced against the benefits.

A banking institution intending to introduce Internet banking should have evaluated the costs and benefits of providing banking products and services on the Internet and the results of this cost-benefit analysis should clearly be positive. The banking institution should be ready to manage the risks Internet banking brings. The magnitude of risks assumed should be consistent with the banking institution's overall risk tolerance and must not exceed the banking institution's ability to manage and control their overall risks.

Banking institutions should be mindful that Internet banking customers have different expectations than traditional bank customers regarding availability and convenience of services. It is imperative for banking institutions intending to offer banking products and services over the Internet to ensure that they are capable of delivering timely, reliable and accurate services to meet their customers' expectations.

This guideline sets out **minimum** guidelines that licensed banking institutions in Malaysia should observe in providing Internet banking. Banking institutions are free to adopt more stringent measures and are expected to keep abreast not only with technological developments but also the needs of their customers.

Procedures

All licensed banking institutions in Malaysia are allowed to establish Informational websites as defined in the attached guidelines. Banking institutions intending to launch Informational websites do not require the specific approval of Bank Negara Malaysia but should notify Bank Negara Malaysia of the website address at least **two weeks** prior to implementation. However, the banking institutions concerned should ensure that the relevant requirements of the guideline are adhered to, in particular the need to implement appropriate controls to prevent unauthorised alterations to the institutions' servers or websites, requirements on advertisement and website links, and product transparency.

Licensed banking institutions are required to obtain the approval of Bank Negara Malaysia prior to the launching of a Communicative or Transactional website. In this regard, subject to the approval of Bank Negara Malaysia:

i.   domestic banking institutions are allowed to establish Communicative or Transactional websites with effect from **1 June 2000**;

ii.   locally incorporated foreign banks may establish Communicative websites with effect from **1 January 2001;** and

iii. locally incorporated foreign banks may establish Transactional websites with effect from **1 January 2002**.

Banking institutions should submit applications to launch Communicative or Transactional websites to:

Pengarah
Jabatan Pengawalan Bank
Bank Negara Malaysia
Jalan Dato' Onn
50480 Kuala Lumpur
Malaysia

All the documents and information listed below should reach Bank Negara Malaysia **at least two weeks** prior to the proposed launching of Communicative or Transactional websites:

i.   confirmation by the Chairman of the banking institution, on behalf of the Board (Chief Executive Officer in the case of foreign banks) that the banking institution is ready to provide Internet banking (as attached);

ii.   business plans and cost-benefit analysis on Internet banking (at least for two years);

iii. Internet security arrangements and policy;

iv.   risk management practices;

v.   terms and conditions for Internet Banking services;

vi.   client Charter on Internet banking;

vii   privacy Policy Statement; and

viii. any outsourcing or website link arrangements, or strategic alliances or partnerships with third parties that have been finalised.

A banking institution which has obtained approval to launch Communicative or Transactional websites would be required to link its website to Bank Negara Malaysia's for purposes of allowing the public to verify that the website belongs to a banking institution licensed under the Banking and Financial Institutions Act 1989 (BAFIA) or Islamic Banking Act 1983. The banking institution should also provide a link to Bank Negara Malaysia's web page which contains the list of banking institutions approved to provide Internet banking services.

In this regard, a banking institution which has obtained approval to launch Communicative or Transactional websites should submit the following information to Bank Negara Malaysia within a week after obtaining Bank Negara Malaysia's approval or a week prior to the launch of the website, whichever is the later:

i.   a letter providing its website address, confirming the validity of its site and authorising the inclusion of its site in Bank Negara Malaysia's web pages; and

ii.   a soft copy of the banking institution's logo to be included in Bank Negara Malaysia's site.

Contents

Chapter 1: Types of Internet Banking and Risks

1. Definition of Internet banking

1.1 Internet banking refers to banking products and services offered by banking institutions on the Internet through access devices including personal computers, and other intelligent devices.

1.2 The guidelines do not include EDI-related, share order routing and credit card transactions which may be subject to other sets of rules.

2. Types of Internet banking site

INFORMATIONAL SITE

2.1 The website is intended to distribute general information about the banking institution and to advertise its products and services, but provide no interactive capability. Banking institutions may also establish a hypertext link from its website to third parties or advertise products and services of third parties.

2.2 The risk is relatively low, as the information on the website is not linked to the banking institution's internal computer systems that stores information database of the banks. However, the information on the server or website may be vulnerable to alteration.

2.3 Banking institutions providing informational sites should implement appropriate controls to prevent unauthorised alterations to the banking institutions' servers or websites.

COMMUNICATIVE SITE

2.4 The website allows some interaction between the banking institution's systems and the customer. Customers may send information and make enquiries about their accounts. The communication may take the form of e-mail, online forms, account inquiries or static file updates (e.g. name and address changes).

2.5 These sites may represent a higher level of risk than informational sites as they may provide a path to the banking institutions' internal networks via e-mail and attachments.

2.6 Banking institutions should put in place the appropriate controls to prevent, monitor, and alert management of any unauthorised attempt to access the banking institution's internal networks and computer systems apart from implementing virus protection measures.

TRANSACTIONAL SITE

2.7 The website allows customers to execute transactions in addition to the capabilities described above.

2.8 The website represents the greatest risk to banking institutions as it provides a link to the bank's internal network and the computer systems holding the account information and other information assets of the bank. These sites require the strongest level of protection, including encrypted transmission of highly sensitive data.

3. Internet banking risks

3.1 Internet banking risks can adversely impact the banking institutions' earnings and capital, therefore banking institutions offering Internet banking services are required to implement proper and effective policies, procedures and controls to effectively protect information and ensure its integrity, availability and confidentiality. In guiding the banking institutions to identify, quantify and manage risks, it is beneficial for banking institutions to categorise the risks associated with Internet banking into the following sets of risk:

STRATEGIC RISK

3.2 Strategic risk arises from adverse business decisions, improper implementation of decisions or lack of responsiveness to industry changes.

3.3 Banking institutions should pay particular attention to this risk. The risk of banking institutions making incorrect choices or decisions when investing in Internet banking could lead to substantial wastage of banking institutions' resources. Banking institutions would constantly face the need to decide on making investments in new technology.

3.4 Thus, senior management of banking institutions should ensure that the Internet banking products are consistent with the banking institutions' overall strategic plans and the risks and ramifications of offering such products over the Internet is within the banking institution's risk tolerance. Banking institutions should adequately plan for, manage, and monitor the performance of their Internet banking services.

TRANSACTION RISK

3.5 Transaction risk arises from deficiencies in system design, implementation, or ineffective monitoring resulting in fraud, error and the inability to deliver banking products and services.

3.6 Effective security and monitoring are critical in controlling transaction risk. Security controls preserve system performance and mitigate the risk of exposure to unauthorised access and intrusions. Banking institutions must have in place preventive and detective controls to prevent their Internet banking systems from exploitation both internally and externally.

3.7 Senior management should ensure the availability of adequate operating policies and procedures, auditing standards, effective risk monitoring processes including contingency and business resumption plans.

Compliance Risk

3.8 Compliance risk arises from violations of, or non-conformance with, laws, rules, regulations, prescribed practices, or ethical standards. Compliance risk can lead to a diminished reputation, limited business opportunities and the lack of contract enforceability.

3.9 Senior management should ensure that the system for Internet banking is designed and operated in a manner that complies with all relevant laws and guidelines. Senior management should also monitor developments and changes in consumer and banking laws, and regulations and take adequate measures to comply with them.

3.10 Banking institutions are advised to state clearly in the Terms and Conditions for Internet Banking Services and their websites that the governing law is the Malaysian law.

Reputation Risk

3.11 Reputation risks arise when systems or products do not work as expected and cause widespread negative public reaction. Internet banking systems that are poorly executed would present this risk. A banking institution's reputation may also be affected if the Internet banking system is unreliable or inefficient or the products and services offered are not adequately presented in a fair and accurate manner.

3.12 Adverse public opinion may create a lasting, negative public image on the banking institution's overall operations and which may impair the banking institution's ability to establish new relationships or services and continue serving existing customers and business relationships.

3.13 Reputation risk can expose a banking institution to litigation, financial loss, or damage to its reputation.

3.14 Banking institutions should undertake immediate and effective remedies to address operational failures or unauthorised intrusions and ensure that timely responses are taken to address adverse customer and media reaction.

3.15 Banking institutions should also educate their customers on what they can reasonably expect from a product or service and the special risks and benefits that they will obtain or incur when using the system.

TRADITIONAL BANKING RISK

3.16 Banking institutions offering Internet banking are faced with the same types of traditional banking risk such as credit risk, interest rate risk, liquidity risk, price risk and foreign exchange risk. The Internet, however, may heighten some of these risks.

3.17 Banking institutions should develop appropriate systems to manage the various types of traditional banking risks.

Chapter 2: Active Oversight by Board of Directors and Senior Management

1. Good corporate Governance

1.1 The framework for corporate governance should emphasise on effective strategic direction and oversight by the board of directors and the implementation by management of a sound internal system of controls, policies and procedures, and limits for managing material risks.

1.2 The board of directors should oversee the conduct of the Internet banking business and ensure that it is not carried on in such a way as to create a substantial risk of serious loss to depositors.

1.3 The information flow to the board of directors should ensure that they receive adequate financial information accurately and timely and information are provided to shareholders and others to allow them to monitor the directors' actions and to hold them accountable for their performance.

1.4 Good corporate governance would effectively manages all material risks confronting a banking institution, whether those risks come from within or outside the institutions, to ensure that the institution is operating in a safe and sound manner.

2. The role and responsibilities of the Board of Directors

2.1 The board of directors should approve the Internet banking strategy of the banking institution to ensure that it is consistent with the banking institution's strategic and business plans.

2.2 The board of directors should set the level of Internet banking risk and review, approve, and monitor Internet banking technology-related projects that may have a significant impact on the banking institution's risk profile.

2.3 It is the responsibility of the board of directors to undertake various measures to ensure that the Internet banking systems are operated in a safe and sound manner including the availability of contingency and business resumption plans.

2.4 The board of directors should review and approve the information security policies.

2.5 The board of directors has the ultimate responsibility for ensuring that an adequate system of internal controls is established and maintained.

2.6 The board of directors should ensure that senior management takes the steps necessary to identify, monitor and control Internet banking risks and monitoring the effectiveness of the internal control system.

2.7 The board of directors should demonstrate an active oversight of the management of Internet banking risk of the banking institution by receiving periodic briefings that identify the material risks in terms that are meaningful to them.

3. Role of Senior Management

3.1 Senior management should ensure that the Internet banking products are consistent with the banking institution's overall strategic plans and the risks and ramifications of offering such products over the Internet is within the banking institution's risk tolerance.

3.2 Senior management should take the steps necessary to identify, monitor and control Internet banking risks and monitoring the effectiveness of the internal control system.

3.3 Senior management should ensure that the Internet banking system is designed and operated in a manner that complies with all relevant laws and monitor developments and changes in consumer and banking laws, regulations, and interpretative rulings and take adequate measures to comply with them.

3.4 Senior management should set appropriate internal control policies and continually monitor the overall effectiveness of the banking institution's internal controls. There should be a proper system to track and report internal control weaknesses for prompt corrective measures.

3.5 Senior management should ensure the availability of adequate operating policies and procedures, auditing standards, effective risk monitoring processes, contingency and business resumption plans.

3.6 Senior management should ensure that adequate and comprehensive reports are provided to the board of directors for decision making.

3.7 Senior management should ensure that adequate expertise and resources are available to operate and maintain their Internet banking systems.

3.8 Senior management should establish effective channels of communication to ensure that the employees are fully aware of policies and procedures affecting their duties and responsibilities including the clear delineation of lines of authority and responsibilities for managing Internet banking risks.

Chapter 3: Risk Management Practices

1. Risk management process

1.1 Regardless of the level of sophistication, risks are inherent in all electronic processes. Banking institutions should develop a risk management framework that is comprehensive enough to deal with known risks and flexible enough to accommodate changes.

1.2 The risk management process should be subject to appropriate oversight by the board of directors and senior management.

1.3 Traditional risk management programmes will need to be adapted to address new aspects of an electronic environment. The sophistication of the risk management process should be appropriate for the banking institution's level of risk exposure.

RISK PLANNING PROCESS

1.4 Effective planning in implementing Internet banking system helps a banking institution maintain a level of risk that is manageable and within its risk tolerance, and is compatible with banking institution's strategic goals and business tactics.

1.5 When contemplating and implementing uses of technology, senior management should engage in a rigorous analytic process to identify and quantify risks, to the extent possible, and establish risk controls to manage risk exposures.

1.6 The board of directors should review, approve, and monitor Internet banking technology-related projects that may have a significant impact on the banking institution's risk profile.

IMPLEMENTATION OF THE TECHNOLOGY

1.7 Proper implementation of the Internet banking system requires the senior management to establish controls, policies and procedures, training, testing, contingency planning, and proper oversight of any outsourcing.

1.8 It is the responsibility of the senior management to select the right mix of Internet banking technologies and products for the banking institution, and ensure that they are properly installed.

1.9 The senior management should have a general understanding of the risks associated with Internet banking and should supplement their technical knowledge, as needed, with expertise provided by business managers, technology staff, and outside experts.

MEASURING AND MONITORING RISK

1.10 Senior management should use an integrated approach in risk management to identify, measure, monitor and control risks, as with other risks, to avoid excessive risk-taking that may threaten the safety and soundness of the institution arising from the offering of products and services on the Internet.

1.11 The board of directors should receive timely and reliable reports on technologies employed, risks assumed and how those risks are managed. Internet banking systems should be reviewed periodically to ensure that they meet performance standards.

2. Internet banking security programme

2.1 Board of directors should ensure that appropriate policies and procedures are in place to manage Internet banking-related risks.

2.2 The risk management controls for Internet banking should be incorporated into banking institution's overall security programme. The security programme should set forth policies, procedures and controls to safeguard the banking institution's information, define individual responsibilities, and describe enforcement and disciplinary actions for non-compliance.

2.3 The necessary structure and accountability to manage risks, and create awareness throughout the organisation that security is important cultural value should be incorporated into the security programme. Banking institutions should ensure that adequate training are provided to the relevant staff to keep them updated of the new security risks and methods of mitigating such risks.

2.4 Senior management should conduct periodic security risk assessments to identify internal and external threats that may undermine data integrity, interfere with service, or result in the destruction of information.

2.5 Banking institutions should establish specific reporting requirements for security breaches.

2.6 Senior management should ensure that the security measures instituted are current and properly implemented and comprehensive security policies and procedures are rigorously enforced.

2.7 The security policy of a banking institution should establish clear expectations and a commitment to an ongoing programme.

2.8 Banking institutions should adopt a security awareness programme to give users a clear understanding of the procedures and controls necessary for a secure environment. This security awareness programme should reinforce the banking institution's security policy and programme and may include, for example, instructions regarding password protection, Internet security procedures, user responsibilities, and employee disciplinary actions.

3. Contingency and business resumption plans

3.1 Contingency and business resumption plans that have been approved by the board of directors should be in place before banking institutions launch their banking products and services.

3.2 The plans should include data recovery, alternate data-processing capabilities, emergency staffing and a public relations and outreach strategy to respond promptly to customer and media reaction to system failure or unauthorised intrusions.

3.3 Banking institutions should evaluate and determine the importance of the business applications and processes and establish prioritised order of business resumption designed to recover the most critical functions and systems first.

3.4 Banking institutions should also establish procedures that should be taken in the event that their competitors experience operational failure that relies on similar technology.

3.5 The back-up systems should be fully maintained and tested on a regular basis to minimise the risk of system failures and unauthorised intrusions and it is expected that security and internal controls at the back-up location should be as sophisticated as those at the primary processing site.

3.6 Any intrusion, attempted intrusion, or suspicious activity should be immediately reported to the identified key personnel for prompt corrective measures, followed by a report to Bank Negara Malaysia for significant cases.

4. Objective review and audit requirements

4.1 Senior management should undertake an objective review of Internet banking systems to identify and quantify risk, and detect possible weaknesses in the banking institution's risk management system.

4.2 Senior management may rely on internal audit, external audit, or other qualified processional sources to conduct this review.

4.3 The objective review should assess the Internet banking system design, assess the adequacy of internal controls, and ensure that appropriate policies, procedures and standards are developed and practiced.

4.4 The review should be done at least once in **six months** as it provides an important control mechanism for detecting deficiencies and managing Internal banking related risks.

5. Outsourcing

5.1 Banking institutions are allowed to outsource their Internet banking systems to **resident** service providers and software vendors provided:

i.   the process to be outsource do not take away the decision making function of the banking institutions and do not threaten strategic flexibility and process control of the banking institutions;

ii.   the outsourcing arrangement would not impair their image, integrity and credibility of the banking institutions; and

iii.   there is cost savings in outsourcing such functions.

5.2 Banking institutions should ensure that they would be able to manage the risks associated with these new relationships and appropriate oversight programme is in place to monitor the outsourcing vendor's controls, condition and performance.

5.3 Despite outsourcing the Internet banking system, bank management remains responsible for the performance and actions of its outsourcing vendors.

5.4 Without adequate controls, the use of outsourcing vendors to design or support the Internet banking systems could increase banking institutions' exposure to risk.

5.5 Banking institutions would need to be especially cognisant of privacy concerns as outsourcing arrangements present a greater potential for banking institutions to lose control over consumer information. Banking institutions that lose control of consumers' information are subject to liability and reputation risk.

5.6 Thus, when contracting for Internet banking services, banking institutions are required to comply with the following conditions:

i. The banking institution has performed sufficient due diligence to satisfy itself of the outsourcing vendor's expertise, experience and financial strength to fulfil the obligations;

ii. The approval of the Board of Directors to outsource the Internet banking system to the service provider or software vendor has been obtained and documented;

iii. The ownership and control of bank records should remain with the banking institution and the outsourcing vendor should provide the banking institution with a written undertaking on its compliance with the secrecy provision pursuant to Section 97 of the BAFIA;

iv. The banking institution should enter into a service agreement with the outsourcing vendor with a clause on professional ethics and conduct in performing their duties. It should be clearly stipulated in the service agreement that the banking institution reserves the right to terminate the services of the outsourcing vendor if it fails to comply with the conditions imposed. The service agreement should also clearly define the roles, responsibilities and accountability for each party;

v. The banking institution has done a risk assessment of such arrangements including ensuring the availability of back-up arrangements such as the availability of alternative service providers;

vi. The banking institution has the ability to exercise the necessary control to properly manage the Internet banking products or services;

vii. The banking institution should put in place proper reporting and monitoring mechanisms to ensure that the integrity and quality of work conducted by the outsourcing vendor is maintained. Regular testing and review of the work done by the outsourcing vendor must be conducted. The outsourcing vendor must also provide regular reports to the management of banking institutions pertaining to the progress of the work conducted;

viii. The external and internal auditors of the banking institution should have the ability to review the books of the outsourcing vendor and perform audits or to obtain from the outsourcing vendor independent internal control audits. Any weaknesses highlighted during the audit must be well-documented and promptly rectified especially where such weaknesses may affect the integrity of the internal controls of the banking institution; and

ix. The details of the outsourcing arrangement should be forwarded to Bank Negara Malaysia **at least two weeks** before entering into an agreement with the service provider.

5.7 Banking institutions wishing to outsource to **non-resident** outsourcing service providers (i.e. located outside Malaysia) should obtain prior approval from Bank Negara Malaysia.

6. Advertising and website links

6.1 Banking institutions may advertise products and services of others on their websites or establish hypertext links to third party websites provided no fees are imposed for such advertisements by the third parties.

6.2 However, banking institutions may earn service fees for facilitating the payment of the sale and purchase of goods and services of third parties through the banking institutions' Internet banking systems.

6.3 Banking institutions do not require the prior approval of Bank Negara Malaysia for advertisements or web linking arrangements which are specifically allowed in this guideline. Banking institutions should, however, keep Bank Negara Malaysia informed of such advertisement arrangements. The details of the arrangements should reach Bank Negara Malaysia at least one week prior to implementation.

ADVERTISEMENTS BY OTHERS ON WEBSITES OF BANKING INSTITUTIONS

6.4 Banking institutions may advertise products and services of:

i.   institutions in their Group on their websites provided these institutions are **licensed in Malaysia**; and

ii.   third parties (other than foreign institutions providing financial services and products) on their websites.

6.5 Banking institutions should not have any arrangements for products and services of financial institutions not licensed in Malaysia to be advertised on their websites.

ADVERTISEMENTS BY BANKING INSTITUTIONS ON THIRD PARTY WEBSITES

6.6 While Bank Negara Malaysia has no restrictions on the advertisement and posting of financial product information of banking institutions on third party websites including financial institutions operating outside Malaysia, banking institutions should ensure that they have the necessary controls in place to manage risks associated with such arrangement.

6.7 The advertisements should be monitored for completeness, accuracy and timeliness.

6.8 Banking institutions are advised to have a list of websites authorised to advertise their products and services to alert the consumers that information contained in third party websites other than those listed may be incomplete, inaccurate or outdated.

6.9 Banking institutions are encouraged to adopt additional procedures to safeguard customers' and their own interests.

WEBSITE LINKS

6.10 When a banking institution provides linking to third party websites to enable customers to access other third party services or products, the banking institution should analyse the risks presented by these arrangements.

6.11 In managing Compliance Risk, a banking institution providing hypertext links to third parties on its websites should include a clear message to inform the consumers that they would be leaving the banking institutions' website and that the privacy policy of the banking institution would cease prior to the consumers executing the link.

6.12 Banking institutions should advise consumers to read the privacy policy statements of these companies and use disclaimers to indicate that:

i.   a link to another website is not an endorsement of that website; and

ii.   the banking institutions make no warranties as to the information contained on those sites.

6.13 Where the link draws information from a third party's website into the banking institution's website, it is important that the banking institution clearly state the source in order not to mislead or deceive users.

6.14 As part of an overall content management policy, banking institutions should manage their linking practices and enter into linking agreements where appropriate. The linking agreement should include the use and control of user data generated by the links and privacy and data protection obligations.

6.15 Banking institutions providing hypertext links to third parties on their websites or providing advertisement facilities to third parties should also have clear disclaimer statements informing consumers that they are not responsible for the products and services offered by third parties.

7. Strategic alliances or partnerships

7.1 Banking institutions may form strategic alliances with partners in relation to the provision of Internet products and services. (Alliance in the form of an equity-based relationship where a separate entity is established to provide Internet banking services would be addressed in a separate guideline).

7.2 Banking institutions should ensure that the alliances or partnerships do not result in any conflict of interest.

7.3 The details of alliance arrangements should be forwarded to Bank Negara Malaysia **at least two weeks** before entering into an agreement with partners.

8. Staff and expertise requirements

8.1 Banking institutions should have a plan to ensure the sufficient allocation of resources that have the expertise and skills to run and support the Internet banking system and address any related security concerns.

8.2 Senior management should identify special staffing and the training needs for personnel involved in system development, operation, and customer support.

8.3 The training needs of staff should be assessed periodically in light of technological and personnel changes that may occur.

8.4 Where internal expertise is unavailable, management should obtain appropriate external technical support to help plan, operate, and monitor the Internet banking system.

8.5 Training programmes should also include outreach to customers to ensure that a banking institution's customers understand how to use or access the Internet banking system and that they are able to do so in an appropriate and sound manner.

8.6 Staffing plans should also address how systems will be supported if a critical person leaves or if the usage of the system exceeds expectations.

Chapter 4: Security Requirements

SECURITY ARRANGEMENTS

The security requirements of Internet banking system vary depending on the degree of risk presented by the level of services offered and the value of assets at risk. The spending on security should be appropriate to the magnitude and nature of the risks. It is the responsibility of the board and senior management to evaluate the costs and benefits of alternative security measures and decide on the best allocation of the banking institution's resources.

The Internet security arrangements should achieve the following objectives:

(a) **Data Privacy and Confidentiality**
Banking institutions should undertake proper security precautions to ensure that data transfers are not monitored or read by unauthorised parties and data storage systems are well protected.

(b) **Data Integrity**

Banking institutions should take the necessary steps to ensure that data is not altered or modified during transmission. Data integrity could also be compromised within the data storage system if proper controls are not maintained. As such, it is imperative for the banking institutions to prevent unauthorised access to the banking institution's central computer system and database.

(c)   Authentication

Banking institutions should have in place authentication controls to establish the identities of all parties to a communication or transaction to verify that a particular communication, transaction, or access request is legitimate.

(d)   Non-repudiation

To ensure the enforceability of transactions conducted through the Internet, **reasonable** steps must be taken to prohibit parties from disputing the validity of, or refusing to acknowledge, legitimate communications or trans-actions. Banking institutions may wish to use digital certificates issued in accordance with the Digital Signature Act 1997 to address the issue of non-repudiation for high value or important transactions, or transactions at the request of the customers.

(e)   Access Control/System Design

Banking institutions should build distributed systems (customer management) and have strong security measures to prevent unauthorised access attempts which could lead to the destruction, altering, or theft of data or funds, compromised data confidentiality, denial of service (system failures), a damaged public image, and resulting legal implications. Banking institutions should take steps to check the servers regularly for obvious weaknesses.

In this regard, banking institutions should develop security controls that govern network and data access user authentication, and transaction verification apart from implementing virus protection measures.

a.   Network and Data Access Controls

Access controls allow verification and enforcement of a user's authorised right to access a bank network, applications, and data. Access controls should restrict unauthorised individuals from entering critical facilities, retrieving confidential information, or allowing access to bank software applications and operating systems.

b.   User Authentication

Banking institutions should authenticate the identity of Internet banking customers when customers access personal account information or engage in on-line transactions for products or services. Reliable and accurate authentication processes should be selected based on the potential threats and vulnerabilities that the Internet banking system poses, the banking institutions' risk tolerance, and the banking institutions' ability to manage those risks. Banking institutions should provide sufficient authentication for Internet banking customers who access personal account information or engage in online transactions for products or services. The authentication processes should be reviewed and periodically tested for effectiveness through penetration testing and other monitoring methods. Senior management should periodically consider new or developing industry standards which may affect the banking institution's existing use of authentication devices and processes. Banking institutions should use a combination of access, authentication and other security controls to create a secure and confidential Internet banking environment. These generally include passwords, firewalls, and encryption:

i.   Passwords

Banking institutions should assign passwords or PINs to users to control access to Internet banking system and ensure the integrity of passwords by providing instruction on their proper use and protection.

ii.   Firewalls

Banking institutions should use firewalls to protect the bank's internal network and to protect all connection points between the internal network and the Internet. The firewalls should be positioned based on the desired level of security as dictated by the banking institution's risk assessment and data classification efforts. Banking institutions should conduct periodic review and testing of firewalls as part of the banking institution's security monitoring efforts. There should be clearly defined roles and responsibilities for maintaining and monitoring firewalls. If firewalls are designed and implemented by service providers and software vendors, the banking institution should periodically assure that vendors have internally or externally tested firewalls and that they operate properly.

iii.   Encryption

The levels and types of encryption adopted should be based on the sensitivity of data or information being transmitted. There should be clearly defined conditions where encryption is mandatory or optional. Encryption should be used when transmitting sensitive or critical data, such as confidential customer information, over the Internet. In deciding on the use and strength of encryption, senior management should evaluate the data sensitivity and vulnerability to threat or compromise. There should be standards to define data classification categories, and the appropriate security level required to maintain system integrity. The encryption keys should be protected under the banking institution's control and proper education should be given to the consumers regarding the importance of keeping private keys secret. Banking institutions should require customers to report to the banking institutions if a private key is compromised.

c.   **Transaction Verification**

Internet banking agreements should define the procedures for valid and authentic electronic communications between the banking institution and its customers. The agreements should specify that the parties intend to be bound by communications that comply with these procedures. Audit trails of parties who initiate transactions should be maintained to enable a banking institution to verify specific transactions and provide proof of transactions to avoid claims of repudiation by bank customers.

d.   Virus Protection

Senior management should establish a bank-wide detection and prevention programme to reduce the likelihood of computer viruses. This should include end-user policies, training and awareness programs, virus detection tools, and enforcement procedures.

Senior management should place a strong emphasis on using monitoring tools to identify vulnerabilities and, in a real-time mode, detect possible intrusions from external and internal parties. In this regard, banking institutions are required to conduct penetration testing and administer manual or automated instruction detection processes:

(a)   Penetration Testing

Banking institutions should use penetrating testing to identify, isolate, and confirm possible flaws in the design and implementation of passwords, firewalls, encryption, and other security controls. In simulating the probable actions of unauthorised and authorised users, banking institutions are able to evaluate the effectiveness of security controls. The testing should be conducted by an objective, qualified, internal or external source prior to the introduction of Internet banking and at last once a year or whenever substantial changes are made to the Internet banking security systems.

(b)   Intrusion Detection

In addressing external attacks, it is imperative for banking institutions to install strong intrusion detection devices to monitor network traffic on a real-time basis. Such a system must be capable of detecting and recording attempts to break into the banking institution's computer system, with established procedures for handling such attempts. The intrusion detection system must itself be resistant to outside attacks and is capable of identifying and reporting deviations from normal processing. Adequate audit trails mechanism should be in place to prevent internal fraud, and provide a means to detect unauthorised intrusion or transactions.

Banking institutions should ensure that they have a combination of regular monitoring of network activity, a well-configured firewall, and regular reminders of their security policies. The requirement for the staff to report security breaches promptly to appropriate management and Bank Negara Malaysia should be stated in the banking institution's security policy.

Chapter 5: Consumer Protection and Privacy Issues

1. Consumer education

1.1 Banking institutions should consider having a web page to educate consumers on Internet banking.

1.2 Banking institutions should take a pro-active approach to educating consumers about their rights and responsibilities and how to protect their own privacy on the Internet.

1.3 Prior to the offering of Internet banking products and services to their customers, banking institutions are required to ensure that they have complied with the following:

i.   The customers have agreed to the terms and conditions for Internet banking services;

ii.   The customers have been informed of the risks involved in the use of the Internet banking products and services;

iii.   The customers know their rights and responsibilities and are fully aware that they are responsible for their own actions;

iv.   The customers have been informed that they may specify maximum limits for funds transfer to limit their risks;

v.   The customers have been advised to read the privacy policy statements of the banking institution and third parties (refer to 6.12 'Website Links' in Chapter 3: Risk Management Practices) prior to providing any personal information to the banking institution or third parties; and

vi.   The customers have been educated on their role to maintain security of their banking information by not sharing their IDs and passwords with anyone, by changing their passwords regularly, and by remembering to sign off.

2. Product transparency

2.1 Banking institutions are required to ensure that the products and services offered on the Internet are fairly and accurately disclosed. The features of the products and services, terms and conditions including any fees, charges, penalties and relevant interest rates should be made transparent to the consumers in plain language as far as possible. Any agreements or contracts should be made available in a form which the customer can download, print and retain.

2.2 Banking institutions should provide advance notice to customers of variation of terms and conditions of the Internet banking services in relation to imposing or increasing charges, increasing the customer's liability for losses or any other material changes.

2.3 The terms and conditions for Internet banking services shall include the duties of the banking institution and customers, contractual arrangements for liability arising from unauthorised or fraudulent transactions, mode of notification of changes in terms and conditions, and information relating to the lodgement of complaints, investigation and resolution procedures.

2.4 The contractual arrangements for liability should provide for sharing of risks between the banking institution and the customers. Customers should not be liable for loss not attributable to or not contributed by them.

2.5 Banking institutions should only enroll customers into a new product or service which involves a cost to the customers if it has been requested by the customers.

2.6 If a banking institution is found to have engaged in a conduct that is misleading or deceptive, or have made a false or misleading representation with regards to its products and services, Bank Negara Malaysia would not hesitate to alert the public to that effect in whatever form, including Bank Negara Malaysia's website.

3. Client charter on Internet banking

3.1 It is a requirement for every banking institution offering banking products and services over the Internet to have a Client Charter on Internet Banking.

3.2 The client charter should at the minimum state the banking institution's commitment towards ensuring safe operations, privacy of customer information, reliable and quality services, transparency of products and services, and prompt response for enquiries and complaints.

3.3 The Client Charter must be prominently displayed in the banking institution's website.

4. Privacy policy

4.1 Bank Negara Malaysia considers the privacy of consumer personal information to be an important element of public trust and confidence in the Malaysian banking system.

4.2 It is fundamental for banking institutions to promote customers' trust in the institutions and reassure customers that they recognised and respect the privacy expectations of their customers.

4.3 Banking institutions are expected to maintain awareness of emerging consumer online privacy concerns and take the necessary steps to address them.

4.4 Banking institutions should adopt responsible privacy policies and information practices, disclose those policies and practices to increase consumer knowledge and understanding, and take other prompt, effective actions necessary to provide consumers with privacy protections in the online environment.

PRIVACY POLICY STATEMENT

4.5 The privacy policy statements of the banking institutions should be clearly stated and readily understandable by consumers.

4.6 The referencing points or icons for the privacy policy statement should be highly visible at specific locations on the banking institutions' websites where they may be most meaningful to the consumers.

4.7 Banking institutions should at the minimum prompt customers to refer to the banking institutions' privacy policy statements prior to or at the time that individually identifiable information is collected.

4.8 The privacy policy statement must:

i.   Identify the types of information the banking institution collects about customers or consumers and how the information is used;

ii.   Provide a brief description on the kind of security procedures that are in place or clearly state that sufficient safeguards have been put in place to protect the loss, misuse or alteration of information under the banking institution's control including limiting employee access to information and handles information about customers who have ended their customer relationship with the banking institution;

iii.   Identify with whom the banking institution shares this information, including agents, affiliates and non-affiliated third parties and how the banking institution ensure that the confidentiality of information is maintained;

iv.   Explain the choices available to customers regarding collection, use and distribution of the information including the consumers' right to opt-out of disclosure that are not mandatory;

v.   Explain how banking institutions maintain the accuracy of information and how customers or consumers can correct any inaccuracies in the information; and

vi.   Explain how banking institutions handle consumer questions or complaints about the handling of personal information.

CUSTOMER SUPPORT SERVICES AND ENFORCEMENT ISSUES

4.9 Banking institutions are encouraged to supplement their privacy principles with a series of questions and answers about the handling of customer information.

4.10 Banking institutions should provide an e-mail link on their websites for privacy-related questions or complaints.

4.11 Banking institutions should also consider providing customers with written copies of the privacy policies in addition to using their websites as the medium for communicating their privacy policies to customers.

4.12 The privacy policies and information practices can only be effective when accompanied by employee education, adequate internal controls, and meaningful enforcement and redress.

4.13 Banking institutions should take measures to enhance their employees' understanding of compliance with such policies. The staff should be trained about their responsibilities under the banking institution's privacy policies and information practices.

4.14 Banking institutions may also incorporate the banking institutions' privacy policies into the banking institutions' code of ethics, and require the employees to certify their own compliance (annually or periodically) with the ethics code.

4.15 Banking institutions should establish procedures to address internal breaches to deter employee violations of the privacy policies.

4.16 In addition, banking institutions should ensure that online privacy policies and information practices are consistent with the banking institution's offline, or physical environment, information-collection activities.

4.17 Banking institutions should review their internal controls to ensure that these controls prevent the improper disclosure of personal information to third parties. Internal controls should incorporate a monitoring and review mechanism that will test compliance with established privacy policies and information practices.

4.18 Finally, banking institutions should also consider disclosing a procedure by which consumers may inquire about their personal information or inform the institution about the potential misuse of personal information in the online environment.

Chapter 6: Compliance with Other Requirements

1. Exchange control requirements

1.1 Banking institutions should establish procedures to ensure that the necessary exchange control approvals from the Controller of Foreign Exchange have been obtained by the relevant parties involved prior to effecting the transactions, as well as to ensure that all statistical reporting requirements are complied with.

2. 'Know your customer policy'

2.1 In line with 'Know Your Customer Policy', banking institutions are required to have face to face interaction with customers prior to the opening of accounts or extension of credit.

2.2 Banking institutions should also establish appropriate measures to identify consumers who are reached over third party websites. The customer verification procedures should mirror those implemented for face to face verification.

2.3 Banking institutions should implement monitoring and reporting mechanisms to identify potential money laundering activities.

3. BNM inspection

3.1 The web servers, books and records should be maintained in Malaysia for Bank Negara Malaysia's inspection.

Jabatan Pengawalan Bank
Bank Negara Malaysia

Attachment

Attestation by the Chairman on behalf of the Board of Directors that the banking institution is ready to provide Internet banking services

Name of banking institution:

I confirm that:

❑ Internet banking is consistent with the banking institution's strategic and business plans;

❑ The results of the cost-benefit analysis of Internet banking is positive and the banking institution is ready to assume the Internet banking risks;

❑ The board of directors and senior management understand and are ready to assume the role and responsibilities stated in the guideline;

❑ Risk management process is subject to appropriate oversight by board of directors and senior management;

❑ Appropriate security measures and Internet banking security policy are in place;

❑ Performance monitoring of Internet banking products, services, delivery channel and processes has been established;

☐ Internet banking is included in the contingency and business resumption plans; and

☐ There are adequate resources to support the offering of Internet banking business.

Signed by:

Dated:

Name of Chairman:

Index

[all references are to paragraph number]

Unsolicited services
distance marketing, and, **7**.42
USA
account aggregation, and
allocation of liability, **3**.41–**3**.48
computer crime, **3**.35–**3**.36
data protection, **3**.51–**3**.53
legal and regulatory issues, **3**.4
regulation, **3**.75–**3**.77
data protection, and, **6**
Fair Credit Reporting Act 1970,
6.4–**6**.7
Financial Services Modernization
Act 1999, **6**.10–**6**.20
introduction, **6**.3
Right to Financial Privacy
Act 1978, **6**.8–**6**.9
e-money, and, **4**.25–**4**.33
privacy, and
generally, **5**.99–**5**.108
right to privacy, **5**.11
prudential regulation, and, **2**.39–**2**.50
User-driven aggregation
account aggregation, and, **3**.13
Value of personal data
privacy, and, **5**.14–**5**.21

Variation of terms and conditions
Australia, and, **11**.64–**11**.65
Malaysia, and, **12**.108–**12**.110
View-only functions
approaches to Internet banking, and,
1.14
Virtual banks
current status, **1**.15–**1**.25
generally, **1**.11
Visa Cash
e-money, and, **4**.11–**4**.14
Wallis Financial Sector Inquiry
Australia, and, **11**.5
Web harvesting
account aggregation, and, **3**.11
Website design
conduct of business rules, and, **8**.49
Websites
privacy, and, **5**.15–**5**.17
White labelling
approaches to Internet banking, and,
1.8–**1**.9